The Wright *Flyer III* of 1905, the world's first practical powered aeroplane, seen flying above the Huffman Prairie on October 4th 1905

SCIENCE MUSEUM

Aviation

An Historical Survey
from its Origins to the end of World War II

By
CHARLES HARVARD GIBBS-SMITH
**Honorary Companion
of the Royal Aeronautical Society**

LONDON
HER MAJESTY'S STATIONERY OFFICE

© *Crown copyright 1985*
First published 1970
Second edition 1985

This work is based on the author's Science Museum publication entitled *The Aeroplane: an historical Survey*, which was published in 1960. It was awarded a Diplôme de Medaille by the Aéro-Club de France in 1962

SILHOUETTE ILLUSTRATIONS

The silhouette of a stork on the title page is taken from Otto Lilienthal's *Der Vogelflug als Grundlage der Fliege-kunst* (1889); other bird silhouettes: pigeon (page xv), kite (page 219), swift (page 231), bat (page 237), swallow (page 255), gull (page 271) are from the same source

ISBN 0 11 290421 1

Printed in the UK for HMSO   Dd736267 2/85 10170 (2575)

To the Memory of
Wilbur and Orville Wright

Ce sont donc incontestablement les frères Wright seuls qui ont résolu dans son entier le problème du vol mécanique humain.... Ceci par leurs expériences de 1903 à 1905. Hommes de génie, instruits, raisonnant juste, grands travailleurs, expérimentateurs hors ligne, désintéressés, les frères Wilbur et Orville Wright ont, plus que tout autre, mérité le succès qu'ils ont obtenu: ils ont changé la face du Monde.*

CHARLES DOLLFUS
Formerly Curator of the Musée de l'Air, Paris

* It is therefore incontestably the Wright brothers alone who resolved, in its entirety, the problem of human mechanical flight. . . . This resulted from their tests from 1903 to 1905. Men of genius—erudite, exact in their reasoning, hard workers, outstanding experimenters, and unselfish—the brothers Wilbur and Orville Wright have, more than anyone else, deserved the success which they achieved. They changed the face of the globe.

Contents

Introduction . . . . *page vii*

Preface to Second Edition . . . . *ix*

Prologue . . . . *xi*

1. Dreams, Myths and Devices 1

2. From Classical Antiquity to the End of the Sixteenth Century . 4

3. The Seventeenth Century 10

4. The Eighteenth Century 14

5. Cayley, and the First Half of the Nineteenth Century . . 21

6. The 1850's and 1860's 31

7. The 1870's 43

8. The 1880's 52

9. The Powered Prelude to Practical Flying: 1890–1903 . . 58

10. The Gliding Prelude to Practical Powered Flying: 1890–1903 . 72

11. The Wright Brothers and the Invention of the Practical Aeroplane:
     1899–1905 94

12. The Beginnings of Practical Aviation in Europe: 1902–08 . . 105

13. The Aeroplane as an accepted Vehicle: 1909 . . . 139

14. Practical Powered Flying: 1910–14 152

15. The First World War: 1914–18 172

16. Between the wars: the First Period: 1919–29 . . . 181

17. Between the Wars: the Second Period: 1930–39 . . . 195

18. The Second World War: 1939–45 206

Quotations on Flying 221

Table of Powered Flights 233

Chronology 239

Glossary 257

Bibliography 273

Conversion Tables, etc 283

Addenda 289

Index 295

Introduction

This work originally appeared in 1960 as *The Aeroplane: an historical Survey*. It has now been re-written in the light of subsequent research, and brought to a close at the end of World War II, a time which saw the practical start of the jet age. As before, the intention has been to record the origin, birth and final establishment of the aeroplane in our civilisation, where it came to inaugurate—as Sir George Cayley had truly foretold—"a new era in society".

Of the scope and treatment adopted, I would first say that I have again devoted what might be felt an over-preponderance of space to the origins and early days of the aeroplane; that is to say, up to World War I. But I still feel that it is the early development of ideas, then the slow technological climb from Cayley to the Wright brothers, and the final achievement of the practical powered flying-machine—followed by the oddly slow progress it made in Europe during the period 1902–09—that should be firmly established in their general features, in order properly to lay the foundations of the aviation history to come. The later periods are, in any case, well covered by others.

Regarding, almost with nostalgia, the earlier state of aeronautical history—with its amorphous personal recollections, the tentative recording of events, and its often semi-fictitious chronicles—it is nevertheless gratifying to see how the subject has now become established as an important branch of technological history, with large numbers of books appearing on every aspect of the subject. These works often cover parts of the field in the greatest detail; whole books, for example, have been written about the aircraft manufactured by one firm, or one type of machine (such as the bomber) used by a single country; and there are even books dealing with individual makes of aeroplane, along with articles in periodicals which delve ever deeper into the minutiae of construction, development and performance. But my purpose has been quite different: it has been to describe the historical origins upon which the vast industry of modern aircraft manufacture has been raised. I therefore deal with later flying more briefly, in order to keep the whole subject in historical perspective. Regarding my fuller treatment of the early periods of ideas, endeavours and achievements, I would say that I have attempted, broadly speaking, to deal with them mainly from the evolutionary standpoint, concentrating upon the main formative influences.

Expressing thanks to all those who have aided me would involve, for the second time, a very long list of names; I have already paid tribute to many of them in the original version of the book. But I would again express my sincere thanks to the Director of the Science Museum, Sir David Follett, and to his colleagues Miss Margaret Weston, Mr. Brian Lacey, and Commander Walter Tuck, for all their encouragement and many kindnesses. Then I would like to express deep gratitude to my friends at the Royal Aircraft Establishment at Farnborough, especially Dr. Percy B. Walker, C.B.E., formerly Head of the Structures Department; Dr. Dietrich Küchemann, C.B.E., F.R.S., Head of the Aerodynamics Department, and John Bagley,

A.F.R.Ae.S, of the same department. To my colleague Mrs. Beryl Edginton I owe an ever increasing debt for her many labours in connection with my books, not the least of which is the laborious task of checking and reading the proofs. Finally in Her Majesty's Stationery Office itself, there are many old and new friends to thank for their extreme good nature and ever-willing co-operation with someone who must certainly rank as one of their most demanding and most enraging authors; but particular mention should be made of Mr. David Napthine, Deputy Head of the Layout Section, who has so admirably designed this book, both in its original form, and as it appears today.

Not being happy with the somewhat "spotty" appearance of the text illustrations in the previous work, I decided greatly to increase their number, and place them in "page groups" throughout the historical narrative. Most of the drawings which illustrate aircraft prior to about 1910 are taken from original documents. Mr. Napthine and I then felt that it would preserve a certain essential harmony of appearance if we could continue this "idiom of line" throughout the history. I had—in the original work—been allowed to use a number of the highly talented drawings made by Mr. Douglas Rolfe in the U.S.A.; but I now required nearly double the number that I had originally used. It is therefore with especial gratitude that I here record the generous permission to use this large number of the Rolfe drawings, accorded me by The Condé Nast Publications Inc., of New York City, publishers of *Air Progress* magazine.

Every historian, no matter what his subject, must seek aid and advice from a variety of authorities within the field he explores. But every historian must also, and inevitably, make mistakes, as well as overlooking misprints. As before, I would finally appeal to readers to kindly inform me of any mistakes they find. Where it is a question of my facts being thought incorrect, I must ask to be provided with reliable documentary evidence of any alterations which they feel should be made.

Preface to Second Edition

Since the stocks of the first edition of this book were exhausted there has been a continuing demand for copies, and the Science Museum decided that it should be reprinted.

For some time before his death in December 1981, Charles Gibbs-Smith had started preparing for a fully revised second edition. Unfortunately his own notes were too fragmentary, and the burden of completing his work too onerous, to permit of this complete revision; so the decision was taken in conjunction with the production staff of HMSO that revisions would be kept to a minimum. A significant number of minor corrections have been made, particularly in Sections 2,3 and 10 with the help of Professor Clive Hart and of Philip Jarrett.

Beyond that, the main change has been the deletion of numerous references to the projected Volume II—tentatively entitled *Early Aviation History: Studies and Problems*—which was intended by Charles Gibbs-Smith as a compendium on miscellaneous topics which had attracted his attention. In the event, the most important parts of this work were subsumed into his study of the influence of the Wright Brothers on the European pioneers, which was published as *The Rebirth of European Aviation 1902–1908* in 1974; and other items were published separately. However, there remained a series of studies on a topic of particular concern to Charles Gibbs-Smith: various claims advanced in recent years for powered flight before the Wright Brothers. I have thought it right to add a brief summary of this work, on pages 289–292.

I know that Charles would have wished any second edition of his book to contain acknowledgement of the help received from a number of people: Tom Crouch, Tony Elsworthy, Clive Hart, Gene Husting and Philip Jarrett would certainly have been among that number.

JOHN A BAGLEY
Curator, National Aeronautical Collection
Science Museum, London.
January 1984

Prologue

The practical realisation of voyaging through air and space has been a truly international achievement, in which some ten or more great nations have taken most honourable part, each making vital contributions to the development of the balloon, the airship, and the aeroplane. Disputes, claims and counter-claims should find no place in this great company.

The birth-place of civilisation would naturally have provided the breeding-ground for many of the world's basic inventions: thus the ancient Chinese made three fundamental contributions in the field of aeronautics and propulsion when they invented the kite (c. 1,000 B.C.), gunpowder (9th century A.D.), and the rocket (c. 1100 A.D.). The kite was the archetypal aeroplane wing, as well as the world's first aerial vehicle; for man-lifting kites were certainly in use in China within a few centuries of the invention of the kite, their first application being in the service of military observation. All three of these inventions found their way along the trade routes of the ancient world, and appeared in Europe during the Middle Ages.

The ancestry of the airscrew is obscure, but although the Chinese may have evolved it, the European airscrew did not originate in China, but appeared first in the uniquely European form of post (or tower) windmill, and was in widespread use by the 13th century. The passive role of the windmill's sails became an active propulsive airscrew by the 14th century, in the form of what were at first thought of as windmill toys, but were in fact pure helicopters of the string-pull type.

So, by the end of the 14th century, we had in Europe the two inventions which were to form the core, so to speak, of the powered aeroplane—the rigid inclined wing of the kite, and the active propulsive airscrew—not to be combined in one structure for some five centuries, but active in separation, and ready to come together when the historical processes had reached their appropriate stages of evolution.

As might be expected, the luxuriant explosion of art, science and letters which we call the Italian Renaissance brought forth the first man of great attainments to describe the flight of birds, to speculate on aviation and to design ornithopter flying machines (Leonardo da Vinci, 1485–1510).

Meanwhile, by way of some saints and many sinners, the idea of air-mindedness was to be nourished by brave and foolhardy men who fitted themselves with wings, and jumped to death or mutilation from high places.

Visions of military destruction from the air soon followed, and were first focussed and set down by a priest of Baroque Portugal (de Lana, 1670); and it was another Portuguese priest who took the first tentative steps towards gliders and hot-air balloons in model form (Gusmão, 1709).

As the eighteenth century was celebrated as the Age of Reason, and as France was the land of Diderot and Voltaire, it was properly in character for the French to accomplish the enclosure of a "cloud in a bag", and for the first time to travel through the air in great gas balloons sustained by hot air or hydrogen (the Montgolfier brothers, *and Charles, 1783). Soon after, came the practical parachute and the first human drop from the air (Garnerin, 1797).*

As the Industrial Revolution was initiated in Britain during the same century, it was appropriate that the applied science of aerodynamics, and the first formulation of the practical flying machine—as well as the prefiguring of the aeroplanes to come—should be accomplished in the land of Isaac Newton and James Watt (Cayley, 1799–1809; Henson, 1843; Wenham, 1866).

In the meantime, France and Britain had both envisaged the elongated, powered and dirigible balloon (Meusnier, 1785; Cayley, 1809–16). Then, after a long interval, France took the lead, and brought to fulfilment the first tentative airship (Giffard, 1852), and the first near-practical airship (Renard and Krebs, 1884).

It was almost inevitable that France, with her lasting interest in aerial affairs, would also come to exploit the aeroplane products of the British "race of shopkeepers", and to establish for some years an aeronautical ascendancy of experimentation, exploitation and panache (Du Temple, c. 1857; Le Bris, 1857–68; Pénaud, 1871; Tatin, 1879). It was also inevitable that the tradition of British speculative physics should again re-assert itself by producing the first aeroplane model with superposed wings (Stringfellow, 1868), and by proving the superior lifting qualities—with the aerodynamic raison d'être—of double-surface cambered wings (Phillips, 1884, 1891).

Brave efforts to build and fly full-sized powered and piloted aeroplanes in France, Russia and Britain met with minimal success, only to the degree that, by various means, these machines were launched from the ground and into the air; but none of them could sustain themselves, and so could not fly (Du Temple, c. 1874; Mozhaiski, 1884; Ader, 1890; Maxim, 1894).

The all-important engines—which were later to make practical flying possible—grew from a French invention, the gas engine (Lenoir, 1860); and then took root and flourished in the atmosphere of well-patronised practicality then prevalent in the states of the German princelings, which thus saw the invention of the four-stroke petrol engine (Otto, 1876); its brilliant application to automobilisme was also brought about by Germany (Benz, 1885; Daimler, 1886).

It was the unified and emergent Germany, with her thoroughness and pertinacity, which produced the first man to mount magnificently into the air, to ride the wind on gliders, and directly to inspire the next generation of pioneers to master the craft of mechanical flight (Lilienthal, 1891–96).

Finally, the vigorous upsurge of pioneering energy, enterprise and practical experimentation, traditionally associated with the New World, made it appropriate that the ultimate triumph of achieving the practical powered aeroplane should take place in the United States of America (the Wright brothers, 1899–1908).

To bring about this practical flying-machine, a number of parallel streams of endeavour and invention had to be born, to develop, and to coalesce, before the Wright brothers could apply their creative faculties to achieve a satisfactory mechanism. These streams were: (1) the science of aerodynamics; (2) the technology of structures and aeroplane configuration; (3) fuel technology; (4) engine technology; (5) airscrew design; (6) flight-control.

Thus the age-old dream that human beings would fly through the air by mechanical means was ultimately brought about by citizens of the great nations of the modern world, all working towards a common end, and for the common good of humanity; for the spur of war played little part in it.

The airship finally came to fruition in the first years of the twentieth century through the efforts of a Brazilian, a German and a group of Frenchmen (Santos-Dumont, 1899 and on; von Zeppelin, 1900 and on; the designers and builders of the Lebaudy, 1902 and on).

The first type of powered aircraft in the Western world was the helicopter toy, powered by the pull of string wound on its rotor spindle; this first appeared in the 14th century, in Flanders. Ever since then, a continuous history of these models can be traced in Europe, with two in particular (Launoy and Bienvenu, 1784; Cayley, 1796) being much publicised, and leading direct to the development of the modern helicopter, the first of which just to take off freely and vertically under its own power, with a man on board, was Cornu's in France (1907). It was in Germany that the first successful helicopter was flown (Focke-Achgelis, 1936), aided by the influence of the helicopter's "half-way house", the Cierva Autogiro (1923). Then an ex-patriate Russian, working in the United States, introduced the helicopter as a practical vehicle to the world (Sikorsky, 1942), since when it has taken its place as one of the most important types of flying machine in both peace and war.

The reaction propulsion of aircraft—by jets of one kind or another—was first envisaged in France (Montgolfier, 1783); the first jet aeroplane was designed in France, but not built (De Louvrié, 1865); the first rocket-propelled and piloted aeroplane was the product of Germany (Von Opel et al., 1928) which was prophetic rather than practical. Then the whole vast realm of jet propulsion, by turbo-jet engines, was pioneered by Germany and Britain in the first two successful flights with such engines designed by von Ohain (1939), and Whittle (1941), the latter—because of Germany's defeat in World War II—being left to lead the world, and directly to inspire the United States.

Space travel, in the person of the artillery rocket, was born in China about 1100 A.D.; it was first mightily employed against an adversary by Tipu Sultan's army in India (1798–99), which immediately led to the successful re-invention and exploitation of the European war rocket by Britain (Congreve, c. 1805; Hale, 1867). Powerfully stimulated en route by French science-fiction (Jules Verne, 1863 and on), the rocket remained in both the armouries and the imagination of the world—but for the most part ineffectually—until an American pioneered the use of the liquid-fuel rocket, which was the direct ancestor of modern space-flight (Goddard, 1926 and on). This work was then enthusiastically taken up in Germany, whose scientists (in 1944) launched a successful long-range rocket bomb which was the immediate parent of all the space vehicles of today. It was Russia—with her interest in space flight reaching back to Ziolkowsky in the nineteenth century—who achieved the first space-ship to orbit our Earth and carry its pilot (Gagarin, 1961), and who sent the first woman into space (1963). Finally, the dream of centuries came true when American astronauts first set foot on the Moon (Armstrong and Aldrin, 1969).

The conquest of space, following the conquest of the air, has been accomplished by the greatest of the world powers; not, perhaps as a League of Nations, or as the United Nations, but as member states working in amicable rivalry one with another, each of them intent on aims and objects far beyond the confines of parochial nationalism; but here it was war that set the pace.

"Per ardua ad astra"—"through hardship to the stars"—is a fitting motto to sum up the aspirations of brave and far-sighted men from the earliest days of civilisation to the present day—and beyond.

The History

Fig. 1. The earliest-known illustration in history of a powered aircraft: *c.* 1325. It is a string-pull helicopter model, shown in a Flemish manuscript in the Royal Library at Copenhagen (No. 3384.8). This type of 'toy'—called by the French a "moulinet à noix" (see page 6 and Plate 1)—can be clearly plotted through the succeeding centuries; from it evolved the contra-rotating model of Launoy and Bienvenue (1784), which was copied by Cayley (1796) and published by him (1809), through which it became the direct ancestor of every helicopter flying today

1. *Dreams, Myths and Devices*

THE idea of human flight has engaged the waking and sleeping thoughts of men from the time when they developed visual imagination and began to regard the birds with envy. With the envy came the ambition to emulate. For flying has never appeared to its devotees as a mere method of transportation, faster or more convenient than travel by land or sea; nor was it finally achieved by any pressure of economic need. Aviation has drawn its strength from an appeal to the emotions; an appeal to the longing for escape, or to the desire for exhilaration and power. Some have simply seen it as a symbol of aspiration. Desire for rapid locomotion came later.

"O that I had wings like a dove," wrote the Psalmist, "for then I would fly away and be at rest." And a modern writer speaks of when "he closes his hands over the controls, and little by little in his bare palms he receives the gift of this power".

In time there came prophecy to accompany desire, prophecy of achievement in both war and peace: in 1670 de Lana wrote of his proposed 'aerial ship': "Where is the man who can fail to see that no city would be proof against surprise ... houses, fortresses, and cities could thus be destroyed, with the certainty that the aerial ship could come to no harm, as the missiles could be hurled from a great height." And Tennyson "dipt into the future, far as human eye could see, Saw the Vision of the world, and all the wonder that would be; Saw the heavens fill with commerce, argosies of magic sails, Pilots of the purple twilight, dropping down with costly bales".

Realising that the prophecies were nearing fulfilment, the early pioneers were beset by more rational doubts concerning the uses that mankind might make of flying. And so both faith and hope—more technically informed— were added to prophecy, in a striving to temper the winds of Fate. In 1894 Octave Chanute was to write:

> "So may it be; let us hope that the advent of a successful flying machine, now only dimly foreseen and nevertheless thought to be possible, will bring nothing but good into the world; that it shall abridge distance, make all parts of the globe accessible, bring men into closer relation with each other, advance civilisation, and hasten the promised era in which there shall be nothing but peace and good-will among all men."

Even though the dream of mechanical flight had haunted its slaves over millennia, it could not be realised until modern technology had evolved a powerful and reliable prime mover of small relative weight; and until there emerged a science of aerodynamics and structures, and a technique of pilotage. As it turned out, the foundations of aerodynamics (laid in 1799–1809) preceded the prime mover by a century, and had to mark time while a host of misguided and eccentric characters ran riot over the field of aviation in the 19th century, while a few wise men strove to keep it on the right lines of development. But we should now go back for a moment to the origins of flying, and also consider some remarkable aeronautical devices which man came to invent in the early epochs of his history.

Nature has not always suggested the basic tools of civilisation—*vide* the wheel, for example—but here can be no doubt that it has been the bird which has provided the chief inspiration for men to fly. Only later came the less dynamic inspiration of the clouds, whose passive flotation was to appeal to the less adventurous spirits. Hence there arose the basic division of human flight into aviation (heavier-than-air flight) with its aviators, and aerostation (lighter-than-air flight) with its aeronauts. But even the latter, after the invention of the balloon in 1783, became irked at being at the mercy of the winds, and went on to develop the 'navigable balloon', or airship. It is also interesting to note that the teeming squadrons of the insect world have never played a significant part in inspiring men to fly, probably owing to their being too small to allow of any effective *rapport* with human beings. Nature, of course, numbers other airmen among her creatures, the most accomplished of whom is the bat, followed by such far less talented exponents as the flying fish and flying squirrels, both of which are, however, only gliders: but none of these was important in aviation until the bat came to influence a handful of workers in the 19th century.

Earth—and heaven—has been peopled by aerial creatures of the imagination since the earliest days of recorded time: and the makers of myth, religion and legend often invoked the power of flight to transport their heroes, gods and holy men through the sky. Sometimes the voyages were made in cars or chariots, with or without the help of birds and other beasts; sometimes the passengers were provided with wings; and occasionally the sacred aeronauts were simply invested with the power of levitation. All such celestial activity encouraged the will to fly; and from the earliest times there was no lack of prophets who arose to forestall the conquest of the air, as well as the blessings and calamities that would attend it. Thus Egypt came to have her winged deities; Assyria her winged bulls; and Arabia her flying carpet, of mysterious origin. The Far East had not only many levitated beings and bird-gods, but flying chariots, some equipped with paddle-wheels. Classical Greece and Rome produced such familiar figures as the winged god Mercury, the winged horse Pegasus, and the flying chariot of Triptolemus. Then came the angels and *putti* of Christianity, the former—through countless thousands of pictures—providing a constant stimulus to airmindedness throughout the centuries, for cleric and layman alike.

Worth their weight in gold for the creation and maintenance of airmindedness, were also the aerial legends that grew up in Europe. And the modern airman's legend par excellence is, of course, that of Daedalus and his son Icarus, which was possibly based on an early attempt at flight: Daedalus, who had constructed the Cretan labyrinth for King Minos, later incurred the King's wrath: so Daedalus made wings for them both to escape from Crete, where they were imprisoned; but he warned Icarus not to fly near the sun: Icarus disobeyed, and the sun melted the wax which glued together his wings, causing him to crash to his death in the sea (Fig. 2*a*):

Daedalus made a safe landing in Sicily. Almost as picturesque was the legendary journey of Alexander the Great to view the heavens by means of gryphons harnessed to his chariot, the beasts being persuaded to fly upward by meat fixed out of reach above them (Fig. 2*b*). There is also our own national story which tells how the legendary King Bladud of England—founder of Bath and father of King Lear—overtaxed his powers of necromancy by trying to fly over London with artificial wings, and was killed in the attempt (*c.* 852 B.C.).

Remaining over from the early days of civilisation, and still in use in various parts of the world, are a number of what might be called 'aeronautical devices'. First came the arrow and the boomerang, whose ages are incalculable: the arrow is, of course, only an aeronautical device by virtue of the stabilising effect of the feather(s), which are aerofoils. But the boomerang is virtually a power-launched rotating glider, and a highly remarkable aircraft at that, which returns to the man who launches it, if it misses its target: the aerodynamics of the boomerang are of considerable complexity, and it taxes the mind to imagine how such a device could have been developed by comparatively primitive tribes.

The kite—which is really a tethered glider—is a device of great antiquity in the East, being known in China for probably a thousand years B.C., and becoming known in Europe certainly by the 13th century[1]: it is the true ancestor of the aeroplane, and has played an important part in the history of flying. The kite was first to take part in aeroplane flight when it formed the wings of Cayley's first model glider in 1804.

How the European type of post (or tower) windmill—with its horizontal spindle and vertical sails—came into being, is still a mystery. The earliest known illustration of one is in the Windmill Psalter in the British Museum, and is dated *c.* 1290 (fig. 4); but, so far, it has no ancestors, although it must have come into use much earlier, and appears to be indigenous to Europe. For the Middle Eastern windmills, along the trade-routes to China, seem always to have had vertical spindles and horizontally-set sails, half of which were boxed in so that the wind would strike only the blades on one side. This 'paddle' system would accord with the fact that paddle-wheel propulsion—and hence passive paddle-wheel rotation—were well known in China at an early date; and the principle, along with many other ideas and inventions, travelled westwards over the trade-routes. But there is no trace of the transit, or arrival in Europe, of the upright type of mill, with its horizontal spindle. This familiar form of European windmill is the passive ancestor of the active aircraft airscrew; and it is interesting to note that certainly by the early 14th century, the passive 'airscrew' of the windmill had already become an active airscrew in the form of the string-pull toy helicopter. It was these toys—rather than the full-size windmills from which they were derived—which were the immediate ancestors of the modern aircraft airscrew—the first airborne use of which was on Blanchard's balloon of 1784—and of the modern helicopter.

[1] As the ancient Chinese are known to have used man-lifting kites, the kite is—strictly speaking—the first man-carrying aircraft of history, but without the ability to travel from place to place.

3

2. *From Classical Antiquity to the End of the Sixteenth Century*

ALTHOUGH classical mythology produced some intriguing figures equipped for flying, such as the winged horse Pegasus, as well as the airman's classic legend of Daedalus and Icarus, the civilisations of ancient Greece and Rome seem to have been singularly uninterested in aeronautical matters. Only the figure of Archytas of Tarentum emerges mistily about 400 B.C.: he is said to have made a wooden dove, which may have been propelled, when hung from a whirling arm, by a jet of steam.

There follows an astonishing interregnum of nearly one and a half thousand years, during which time, if there were recorded events of men with wings, they do not survive, except for vague statements of an apocryphal nature.

Then emerge the historical figures of 'Abbas b. Firnas, an Arab savant who covered himself with feathers and attempted a flight in Spain, around 875; and of Eilmer,[1] a Benedictine monk who jumped off the tower of Malmesbury Abbey about 1010. He had equipped himself with wings, and is reported to have flown about 200 metres before crashing and breaking both legs: he is said to have regretted not fitting a tail surface. Then in 1162 the so-called 'Saracen of Constantinople' became famous by jumping to his death from a tower: he wore a voluminous cloak with stiffening battens forming sail-like wings. In all probability, there were many of these brave but foolhardy 'tower-jumpers' who lived and died, and whose names have slowly faded out of history: they at least had the courage of their conviction that men must one day fly (Fig. 3).

Aeronautical speculation—both on lighter- and heavier-than-air flying—was indulged in by a Franciscan monk, Roger Bacon (1214–92), whose work *De mirabili potestate artis et naturae* (written *c.* 1250, but first printed in Paris in 1542) contains references to hollow globes of copper filled with 'aetherial air', which would float in the atmosphere; and a flying machine in which a man would sit and propel himself by turning a mechanism of some kind: but such vague speculations must have been made by many a learned monk over the centuries but not written down; or having been committed to paper, were destroyed or lost to view, as indeed Roger Bacon's were lost for some centuries.

Then, at the end of the 13th century there suddenly appears, as already stated, the familiar form of the windmill with a horizontal spindle, which seems to spring into Europe fully developed, without origins or antecedents

---

[1] Owing to a mis-reading of the manuscript, Eilmer appears in earlier histories as Oliver of Malmesbury. Similarly, 'Abbas b. Firnas appears as Armen Firman in earlier books.

4

Fig. 2a. The classic airman's myth of Daedalus and Icarus, showing Icarus crashing; from a woodcut of 1493

Fig. 2b. Alexander the Great drawn through the air by gryphons; from a woodcut of 1506

Fig. 3. Modern illustration of one of the 'tower-jumpers' of early history

Fig. 4. (a) Earliest illustration of a European windmill: c. 1290
(b) European windmill: c. 1410

5

(Fig. 4), but it must have been in use long before this illustration was made.

In 1326–27, there was produced a remarkable illuminated manuscript by Walter de Milemete (*De nobilitatibus, sapientiis et prudentiis regum*), now in the library of Christ Church, Oxford, which contains an unfinished drawing of what might fairly be called the first true aircraft in the Western world (Fig. 5); it is a kite being flown over a beleaguered city, with a finned bomb hanging from it. The kite is the first known illustration of a type which grew increasingly familiar in Europe during the 14th and 15th centuries. It has a large, rigid, plane-surface head made of parchment, and a long, flexible cloth tail. Detailed instructions about how to build and fly one are found in a manuscript in Vienna, dated about 1430. Whether such kites were ever built large enough to carry a bomb in battle is perhaps doubtful but, if so, three knights (as shown in the illustration) could well have been needed to control them.

The earliest printed illustration of a kite of the familiar diamond type (imported from the East Indies) appears in a Dutch book of 1618 (Pl. I).

The first illustration of a helicopter toy appeared in the first quarter of the 14th century—say *c.* 1320–30 in a Flemish psalter now at Copenhagen (see Fig. 1 on page xvi), with its four-bladed rotor derived from windmill sails: this type of little model, of which the most sophisticated of the early examples is that at Le Mans (Pl. I) came to be called by the French, "moulinet à noix" ('noix' referring to the pulley-wheel of a spindle): it is the earliest form of the active airscrew, and the direct ancestor of every helicopter flying today. The simpler toy, with an 'airscrew' solely rotated by the wind, was called a "moulinet à vent" (see Fig. 6), and possibly dates back as early as the helicopter toy. Both were probably invented in the 12th century, soon after the introduction of the classic tower type of windmill in Europe. Apart from the kite and the doll, these toys must have the longest continuous history of any plaything in history.

Then, about 1420, we find in the well-known manuscript of the engineer Giovanni da Fontana, in the Staatsbibliothek at Munich (Cod. iconogr. 242) an illustration of the first rocket 'aeroplane'; it is a model bird with outstretched wings, and the efflux emerging from the tail (Fig. 7): hereafter winged rockets appear at intervals. The early history of the rocket is still somewhat unclear, although it is generally believed that it originated in China and reached Europe via the Mongols and Arabs. (See Chapter 2 of *History of Rocketry and Space Travel*, W von Braun and Frederick I Ordway, 1966.)

It is impossible to judge what it was that Regiomontanus (Johann Müller) made between about 1460–75; but it was described alternatively as an artificial eagle or as an "iron fly"; it was probably a small model of some kind, and might easily have been a glider-model built by trial and error. There were probably a number of such models made through the years which remain unrecorded.

In 1496, an old cantor of Nuremberg broke an arm in trying to fly.

In 1498—after some previous attempts—the Italian mathematician, G. B. Danti, who had attached wings to his arms, was seriously injured when he made a tower-jump at Perugia. A few years later, in 1507, the Italian

Fig. 5. First illustration in the Western world of an aircraft (a kite), and a bomb: 1326–27

Fig. 7. First illustration in history (by Fontana) of a rocket-propelled 'aeroplane' (i.e. a model bird): *c.* 1420

Fig. 6. Early representation of a simple airscrew toy (*moulinet à vent*): *c.* 1485

Fig. 8. First design for a parachute, by Leonardo da Vinci: *c.* 1485

Fig. 9. Design for a sail-derived parachute by Veranzio: *c.* 1595

7

'emigrant' John Damian, Abbot of Tungland, tried to fly with wings from the walls of Stirling Castle in Scotland; the record states that he "fell to the ground and brak his thee bane", at which we would count him lucky.

Now—in the midst of the Italian Renaissance—there had just arisen the greatest all-round genius of history, to whom flying was a major obsession.

Leonardo da Vinci (1452–1519) provides an absorbing chapter in aeronautical history. He was the first man of high scientific attainments to investigate the problems of flight, and although a few of his aeronautical notes and drawings may have been lost, the bulk seem to have survived and it is fairly clear where his ambitions and achievements lay. Most of his work dealt with flapping-wing aircraft (ornithopters), based on bird and bat flight; and his concern with the human imitation of birds amounted to "the most obsessing, most tyrannical of his dreams", in the words of one biographer. As a result of his emotional, rather than rational, approach to flying he did not on the whole subject it to the disciplined scrutiny he applied to other of his scientific activities. Perhaps it was the symbolic urge to escape and to conquer the air which led him to cling so tenaciously to the ornithopter idea, and neglect the idea of the fixed wing glider in all but a few of his later drawings. His obsession with the ornithopter was peculiarly fruitless owing to two factors: (*a*) his belief that the wings of such an aircraft "have to row downwards and backwards . . . write of swimming in the water (he says) and you will have the flight of the bird through the air"; and (*b*) that human muscles could properly power a machine. A bird cannot beat its wings backwards. The tradition that Leonardo launched a full-size ornithopter is without foundation, because any flight test based on downward and backward wing movements would have immediately wrecked the machine, with serious results for its pilot. As for human muscle as a power plant, Leonardo—if he had not been subject to his overpowering ornithopter obsession—could easily have arrived at the conclusion that a man's muscles could never have propelled even the lightest of his suggested machines, let alone the huge and cumbersome contraptions his fancy ultimately drove him to; only today, with the ultra-light materials now available, has it become possible to make the briefest of man-powered flights. Leonardo designed various prone-position types of ornithopter and a standing-position type, most of them to be powered by combined arm and leg movements via machinery of fascinating but misplaced ingenuity. But there were times when his acute mind seems to have tired of its emotional tyrant, and he has left sketches of two aircraft types which show a completely different approach. One is an ornithopter powered by a bow-string mechanism (to be rewound by the pilot when in flight); the other has the outer wing-panels flapping down at a greater angle than the inner—a device which under modern conditions, and with the knowledge of how a bird is propelled, might be successful. Leonardo also designed some prophetic aeronautical instruments and devices,[1] including a flap-valve system of wing construction for ornithopters, a head-harness working an elevator (which anticipated

---

[1] Tradition also credits Leonardo with the invention of the hot-air balloon, but this is not true. See my *Leonardo da Vinci's Aeronautics*.

Lilienthal's body harness), a retractable undercarriage, and various finned projectiles. Until the discovery of medieval helicopter models, the helicopter was thought to have been the invention of Leonardo, whose machine was a helical screw operated probably by clockwork (Pl. I). But he did invent the parachute—in the form of a pyramidal tent—with a pole from the apex to the jointure of the shroud-lines (Fig. 8). Both Leonardo's helicopter and parachute were recorded as almost thumbnail sketches, and unfortunately he did not return to them. There was then a device, of which Leonardo may have been the inventor, for turning a roasting spit, which consisted of a properly bladed propeller on a shaft, rotated by hot air rising from the fire. If he had envisaged the blades being turned by a prime-mover and displacing air, instead of the air turning the blades, he would have pioneered the proper airscrew. Leonardo also made studies of the air and its forces, which included investigations concerning the centres of gravity and pressure; and he understood the principles of streamlining, but only seems to have applied them to bodies moving in water. Curiously enough, it was after the main force of his ideas on the ornithopter were spent that he wrote his remarkable book on bird flight, *Sul Volo degli Uccelli* (1505), without, however, solving the problem of bird propulsion. Finally, late in life, he made some thumbnail sketches of a man clinging to a flat board which is seen in gliding descent like a falling leaf, a concept which might have led to vital changes in his outlook and to a mature concept of the glider. It is such glimpses of his mind working unhampered on the problems of flight that cause posterity to regret that he did not concentrate on the fixed-wing glider, a type of aircraft of which he might well have been the pioneer (Pl. I).

Leonardo's remarkable work in aeronautics deserved to play a major role in the centuries of experimentation that followed; but owing to the culpable stupidity of his executor Francesco Melzi, it had no direct influence on the history of flying, and was not even known to the world until the last quarter of the 19th century, more than a hundred years after the rediscovery of the parachute and the helicopter, and when aerodynamics was already an advanced study. If his researches had been published sooner—as he wished them to be—his achievements and mistakes would have spurred on others to experiment, correct, and develop, and his genius would have provided a powerful inspiration throughout the centuries.

With the death of Leonardo in 1519 there follows nearly a century's pause in serious aeronautical thinking.

In 1536 an Italian clock-maker, Bolori, was killed when attempting to fly from the Cathedral of Troyes in France.

About the year 1595 there was published in Venice a work entitled *Machinae novae* by Fausto Veranzio, in which he described and illustrated a 'homo volans', which provided the first published illustration of a parachute in history (Fig. 9): unlike Leonardo's device, Veranzio's was clearly derived from a ship's sail, and it is interesting to note that the most obvious ancestors of the parachute—the sunshade or umbrella—took no part in either of the first two parachute designs to appear in the west, although they were directly to inspire the first viable parachutes which were to appear in the 18th century.

9

3. *The Seventeenth Century*

BEFORE describing the chief contributors to aeronautics during this century, there is a small but important item to note in 1618, when there occurs the first illustration—in a Dutch engraving—of what we have come to think of as a standard type of diamond-shaped kite, complete with tail (Pl. I.).[1]

This enlightened century produced some interesting figures in the world of 'flying'. In 1638 two books were published in England, both works on the moon, by Francis Godwin, Bishop of Hereford (1562–1633), and by another bishop, John Wilkins, Bishop of Chester (1614–72), a founder member of the Royal Society. Godwin's book, published posthumously in 1638, was *Man in the Moone*, and told the story of the hero Gonsales who trained wild swans—tied to a framework—to transport him to the moon. Wilkins' work, *Discovery of a New World*, first published anonymously in 1638, was a speculation on the moon being inhabited. This was followed in 1640 by his *Discourse concerning Flying*, and in 1648 by *Mathematical Magick*: the former dealt with aerostation and the latter with various means of flying, i.e. with the spirits of angels, with the help of fowls, with wings fastened to the body, and with a flying chariot. These were the speculations of a shrewd man, but were not significant in history.

One of the few records of an actual model aircraft being built, concerns Tito Livio Burattini (born in Agordo, 1617), who settled in Poland about 1644. In 1647 he is said to have made working models of a flying-machine, with four pairs of wings in tandem (the two middle pairs for lifting, the bow pair for propulsion, and the stern pair for propulsion and lift) with a tail-unit for control: this is said to have been worked by springs, and to have raised a cat. Burattini is said also to have made a full-size version of this machine in 1648, but the account is probably untrue.

The most interesting figure in the 17th century, aeronautically speaking, was the great English scientist Robert Hooke (1635–1703) who, independently of Borelli, came to the conclusion that human muscles are not strong enough to provide the power for flying, and that an engine was essential. He appears to have made an ornithopter model operated by some spring device in 1655 which, as he said "rais'd and sustain'd itself in the Air": this form of words probably, at the time, referred to travel through the air, and not helicopter flight. He then appears to have worked out designs for a man-carrier. This is by far the most tantalising of 'cases', and one wonders if some sketch—as yet unrecognised—may not survive among his papers.

[1] The first to be found in Britain is in Bate's *Mysteryes of Nature and Art* (1635), shown in Fig. 10. The fully-developed winged wind-sock type of dragon-kite is shown in Fig. 11, which was published as late as 1665.

Fig. 10. European plane-surface kite, from Bate's
Mysteryes of Nature and Art: 1634

Fig. 11. European winged
dragon-form kite: 1665

Fig. 12. Design for an aerial ship,
by De Lana: 1670

Fig. 13. Fanciful representation
of Besnier attempting to fly at
Sablé: 1678

The German mechanic Johann Hautsch of Nuremburg, who is known mainly for his manumotive road carriage and his contribution to fire-fighting machinery, is also credited with building a flying carriage about 1660, but no details of this device are known. In 1673, one Charles Bernouin, a surgeon from Grenoble, is said to have flown from a tower at Regensburg in Germany using sail-like wings and rocket assistance, but to have then broken his neck flying at Frankfurt-on-Main.

Reports of attempted flights by tower-jumpers occur quite regularly during the century. Among the less successful were the Italian painter Guiddotti who fell through a roof at Lucca around 1600, and the anonymous Russian peasant who was severely beaten for failing to fly in 1680. On the other hand, Ahmed Hezârfen is celebrated in Turkey for a claimed flight of several kilometres to a successful landing in the market-place at Scutari around the mid-century.

A small item of light relief occurs during this period in the Marquess of Worcester's *Century of Inventions* (1663) where, under invention number 77, one reads: "How to make a man fly; which I have tried with a little Boy of ten years old in a Barn, from one end to the other, on a Haymow".

Among the most constantly reproduced pictures in aviation history is that of the French locksmith Besnier (Fig. 13), who attempted to fly at Sablé in 1678 with an apparatus working on a similar principle to that of the waterbird's webbed feet. He is said to have made many careful experiments, and finally soared over a house and landed safely; this probably means he descended from the roof of the house. The apparatus he used must clearly have been more sophisticated and many times larger than that shown, which is a concept similar to that of the flap-valve. It would just be possible for a man to make a floundering glide without coming to grief, if the 'machine' parachuted him down, which would seem to be the explanation of those survivals and maimings with which fortune favoured a few.

In this connection it should be recorded that Francis Willughby, who died in 1672, unwittingly helped to perpetuate the idea of the man-powered ornithopter when, in his posthumously published *Ornithologiae libri tres* (1676), he said that it was a man's legs which were comparable in strength to a bird's wings, and not his arms; therefore the human makers of wings must harness leg-power to them.

The man who did most to discourage the 'tower-jumpers', and other experimenters with man-powered wings, was Giovanni Alphonso Borelli (1606–79), professor of mathematics at Messina, and later at Pisa. His *De motu animalium* was published posthumously at Rome in 1680, and became a major milestone in history; for in this work, Borelli proved that the musculature for a man—as compared with a bird—was inadequate for lifting himself and his apparatus, and flying. Today, with the ultra-light materials available, and the advanced knowledge of aerodynamics, man-powered flight is just physically possible; but up to a few years ago, it certainly was not; and Borelli's cold water on such schemes was badly needed. "It is impossible", he wrote, "that men should be able to fly craftily, by their own strength."

In 1657–59, a Jesuit named Gaspar Schott published his *Magia universalis naturae et artis*, in which he went over the ground of speculation on aerostation, but did not contribute anything to ideas on aviation. Much more important was another book concerned with aerostation by the Jesuit Father Francesco de Lana de Terzi published in Brescia in 1670. This work—*Prodromo overo saggio* (etc)—contained de Lana's design for, and description of, his aerial ship; this consisted of a vessel supported by four copper spheres which were to be emptied of all air, and hence rise: but de Lana did not appreciate that these spheres would be collapsed by atmospheric pressure (Fig. 12). His descriptions of aerial bombing, and airborne invasion, by his ship, are among the classic anticipations of modern warfare.

In 1650 there had appeared the first edition of Cyrano de Bergerac's *Histoire comique, ou Voyage dans la Lune*, with the first English translation appearing in 1659: Cyrano is of interest in that his fantasy methods of travel to the moon were ingeniously conceived. One of these methods was to strap round himself bottles of dew, which the sun would soak up, and take him up too: another was an inadvertent voyage in his aerial car after soldiers had fixed fireworks—presumably rockets—to it, and sent it up into space.

4. *The Eighteenth Century*

IN the year 1709 there occurred a somewhat mysterious event. One of the best known of aeronautical engravings shows an apparently ridiculous contraption called the *Passarola* (Great Bird), which until recently has been treated as pure fantasy. But the evidence now suggests that some well-meaning artist drew from hearsay an actual aircraft—a small model glider in the form of a bird. It was made by a Brazilian, Father Laurenço de Gusmão (1686–1724) and launched at Lisbon, perhaps achieving a tentative flight (Fig. 14). He seems first to have constructed an inevitably earthbound full-size aircraft, and then made the model to rescue his reputation: its most interesting feature was an upper hood, or 'parachute' cover, a device to give more lift, which rested on a frame when the machine was not flying, and would immediately have the wind catch it from the underneath when flight commenced. A similar device was to be employed by Trouvé in 1870. Gusmão also seems certain to have achieved a primitive model hot-air balloon.

In northern Europe, the Swedish mystic Emmanuel Swedenborg somewhat surprisingly suggested an aeroplane design in 1714 (it was published in *Daedalus Hyperboreas* in 1716), which consisted of a car fixed below a huge wing-canopy, which could be reefed like a sail, and propelled by flappers made on the duck's webbed-foot principle, and worked by "a spiral spring". There was to be a pendulum device projecting below the craft to give it automatic stability, and a sort of beetle-like shield above the wings, for no very good reason. Coming from a man of such eminence, this idea is interesting, but is—except for the pendulum stability—without much merit historically.

Despite the teachings of Borelli, the 'tower-jumpers' still flourished, and perhaps the most famous of them all was the Marquis de Bacqueville, who attempted, about 1742, to fly the River Seine in Paris, with wings fixed to his arms and legs: he seems to have taken off from a riverside house and to have floundered down on to a washerwoman's barge, breaking his legs (Pl. I). The 'paddles' shown in the illustration are clearly some simplification, and are on far too small a scale, of the equipment used for this foolhardy but brave attempt at flight. The belief that a certain John Childs tried to fly in England, and then from a tower at Boston (U.S.A.) in 1757, is now known to be untrue, and was based on a misinterpretation of early records.

The kite first came into its own as a vehicle for scientific research—a role it was thereafter to fulfil for more than a hundred and fifty years—in the year 1749 when the Professor of Astronomy at Glasgow University, Alexander Wilson, measured the temperature of clouds at about 3,000 feet by means of a thermometer attached to a train of four or five paper kites; Wilson also

Fig. 14*a*. The well-known and much-ridiculed
illustration of Gusmão's *Passarola*: 1709

Fig. 14*b*. Reconstruction by the present writer
of how the *Passarola* probably appeared

Fig. 15. Flying Gawry, from
Paltock's *Peter Wilkins*: 1751

Fig. 16 Design for a fixed-wing aeroplane, with
flap-valve rocker for propulsion, by Bauer: 1764

seems to have antedated both Franklin and Jacques de Romas in the utilisation of kites for the study of atmospheric electricity. It was in 1752 that Benjamin Franklin made his celebrated experiment with a kite in a thunderstorm, in which he was nearly killed by the current.

The model helicopter—in use certainly since the 14th century as a toy—has recently been claimed by the Russian authorities to have been revived in 1754 with a twin contra-rotating rotor model operated by clockwork, made by the well-known scientist Michael Vasilyevitch Lomonosov, which is said to have flown successfully: but we have no documents. In 1768 the French mathematician, A. J. P. Paucton, in his *Théorie de la Vis Archimède*, suggested a man-carrying and man-powered helicopter with two helical screws (ptérophores), one to sustain it and the other to propel it: it was never built. But, oddly enough, this must rank as the first specific suggestion for horizontal aerial propulsion by an airscrew.

There was discovered in 1921 in the Staatsarchiv of Thuringia, at Greiz, a collection of remarkable diagrams, giving the detailed design for an aeroplane, by Melchior Bauer, and drawn in 1764: it was to consist of a four-wheeled car for the pilot, fixed by struts to a large braced and dihedrally set low aspect-ratio wing above it, and manually propelled from the car by means of a rocking system of flappers hinged on to a single large frame extending on both sides of the machine; this was to be rocked, so that when the port side of the frame was rising (with its flaps down), the starboard side was descending, with its flaps up, thus producing a rearward thrust (Fig. 16). It is not impossible that Bauer had read, or heard of, the account of Swedenborg's machine.

In 1772, a Canon Desforges, of Étampes, built and tested—inevitably without success—a wickerwork 'voiture volante', which was equipped with manually operated wings both for sustentation and propulsion, and topped by a huge canopy of fabric to help support it in the air. He had himself launched from the Tour Guinette at Etampes, and luckily suffered only minor injuries.

There was one outstanding pioneer of the pre-balloon era in the person of Karl Friedrich Meerwein, architect to the Prince of Baden, who in 1781 experimented with what one may call a glider-ornithopter (Fig. 17), which he described in his pamphlet *L'Art de voler à la Manière des Oiseaux* (1784). Meerwein calculated that 126 square feet of wing-surface would support him, and he apparently made one or two short glides—probably combined with flapping—which, in the absence of any tail or other auxiliary surfaces, would have been only tentative in the extreme, but highly creditable. Meerwein lay prone beneath the wings of his machine, and could bring about some up-and-down movements of the wings by means of a mechanism which was only briefly specified.

Jean-Pierre Blanchard was to become of great importance in aerostation, but his first appearance in 1781 was as builder of an amphibious 'vaisseau volant', which looked like a huge tented house-boat, and was equipped with large manually operated flappers on rods, and a huge rear rudder: needless to say, it stayed firmly on the ground in 1782 (and later) when it was tested. In the same year Blanchard made a creditable full-size manually operated

PLATE I

a String-pull helicopter model, the second earliest known: *c.* 1460

b Standing-type ornithopter, designed by Leonardo da Vinci: *c.* 1485–1500

c Prone-type ornithopter, designed by Leonardo da Vinci: *c.* 1485–1500

d Helicopter, designed by Leonardo da Vinci: *c.* 1485–1500

e The earliest known illustration of the conventional kite: 1618

f Attempt by the Marquis de Bacqueville to fly the Seine: *c.* 1742

3+A.

PLATE II

a First human parachute descent from the air, by Garnerin: 1797

b The re-invention of the artillery rocket, by Congreve: 1805–07

c The first airscrew-driven aeroplane design, by Henson, which had far-reaching influence in history: 1842–43

d Reproduction of Stringfellow's near-successful powered monoplane model: 1848 helicopter, which although ingenious, also remained earthbound.

The works of aerial fiction and satire which appeared in the 18th century were widely read, and they too played their part in encouraging air-mindedness. Joseph Addison wrote of flying in the *Guardian* (1713), Swift in *Gulliver's Travels* (1726), Samuel Brunt in *A Voyage to Cacklogallinia* (1727), R. O. Cambridge in *Scribleriad* (1751), Robert Paltock in *The Life and Adventures of Peter Wilkins* (1751), Ralph Morris in *The Adventures of John Daniel* (1751), Doctor Johnson in *The Rambler* (1752) and *Rasselas* (1759), La Follie in *Le Philosophe sans Prétention* (1775), Hildebrand Bowman in *Travels* (1778), and Restif de la Bretonne in *La Découverte Australe* (1781). These and many others dealt with a variety of flying men, women, and machines, providing excellent reading and sometimes shrewd prophecy. Of particular interest was Restif's work, whose illustrations show winged men with what seem like parachutes above their heads, which are in fact auxiliary wings, which could be opened and closed at will; and the winged males and females (Glums and Gawries) whose expert flying is described by Paltock (Fig. 15).

The invention of the practical balloon in 1783 was to have a profound effect on aviation, both as direct incentive and rival method of aerial navigation, and as a testing ground for various aeronautical devices such as the propeller and the parachute. Balloon flying also led to the consideration and application of aero-engines to transform the 'sphericals' of different kinds into dirigibles; and to the building up of a wide-ranging personnel accustomed to travelling through the air.

In 1766, Henry Cavendish isolated hydrogen for the first time; described it as an element; and produced it in a sizeable quantity. He was followed by Joseph Black and Tiberius Cavallo (in England) who respectively suggested and carried out experiments to show the lifting power of hydrogen, the latter with hydrogen-filled soap-bubbles. Then, working along totally different lines, the brothers Étienne and Joseph Montgolfier, paper-makers of Annonay, near Lyons, hit on the lifting power of hot air, without knowing why it lifted, and—after private experiments—made the first public demonstration with a small hot-air balloon of 11-metre diameter in the market place at Annonay on June 5th 1783. When news of this ascent reached Paris, it was decided there to improve on the Montgolfiers' efforts—the Parisian scientists also did not know what had raised the Montgolfier balloon—and the result was that J. A. C. Charles decided to use hydrogen for his balloon. First off for an aerial journey with men on board, however, was a Montgolfiere on November 21st 1783, at Paris (Fig. 18); then soon after, also at Paris, the first man-carrying hydrogen balloon set off on December 1st 1783; and ballooning was thus launched into the world. And so, after centuries of imaginative striving and speculation by the flappers, it was the floaters who first took to the air by courtesy of a "cloud enclosed in a bag". Man at last could be airborne at will.

In 1784, within a year of the first balloon ascents, the airscrew was revived for the helicopter model, and also first applied to forward propulsion. The model demonstrated on April 28th, in Paris by Launoy and Bienvenu consisted of two two-blade fabric rotors contra-rotating on the ends of a short pole, worked by a wound bow-drill mechanism (Fig. 19): it was this

Fig. 17. Meerwein's glider-cum-ornithopter: 1781

Fig. 18. Montgolfier hot-air
balloon, shown tethered: 1783

Fig. 19. Contra-rotating
model helicopter by Launoy
and Bienvenu (modern
reconstruction): 1784

Fig. 20. First use of an airscrew (it actually
had six blades) on a full-size aircraft, by
Blanchard, on his balloon: 1784

model which—through Cayley's copy of it in 1796—led direct to all subsequent helicopter development. Meanwhile, following the attempt by Vallet to propel a river-boat with an airscrew in 1784, the indefatigable Blanchard had fitted a small six-bladed airscrew to the car of the balloon in which he took up the Royal Academy's Doctor John Sheldon on October 16th 1784 from Chelsea (London): he called it a 'moulinet', or little windmill, and rotated it ineffectually by hand; but nevertheless, this was the first application of the airscrew to a full-size man-carrying aircraft (Fig. 20). Next year (1785) saw General Meusnier's prophetic design for an airship, to be manually driven by three huge airscrews, but never built.

Last among the pioneers of heavier-than-air flight at this time were such men as A.-J. Renaux, who designed[1] an ornithopter in 1784; Gérard, who in the same year designed a similarly futile 'flapper', but realised that an engine would be essential (he is wrongly credited with the proposal to apply rocket propulsion); and a certain Monsieur Ariès who was reported to have flown—meaning glided—at Embrun, also in 1784. It is not impossible that Ariès and others, equipped with rigid wings, or stiff-ribbed cloaks, succeeded in making some short floundering 'parachute' glides. The 'tower-jumpers' and visionaries, no matter how misguided they may now seem, all played their part in sustaining the tradition, and furthering the cause, of flight.[2]

It was Jean-Pierre Blanchard (1753–1809) who pioneered the use of the parachute from balloons when he started, in 1785, the questionable practice of sending down animals on small parachutes to entertain the crowds. But it was Jacques Garnerin (1770–1825) who on October 22nd 1797, made the first human descent: using a large ribbed parasol-like canopy, he ascended at Paris under a balloon, and released himself over what is today the Parc Monceau at a height of about 3,000 feet. The parachute, which was taken up closed, opened out as designed, and the descent was a great success (Pl. II). Dollfus describes this act of deliberate experimentation as "un des grands actes d'héroisme de l'histoire humaine"; and it was praised in similar terms by Wilbur Wright. "Cette modeste coupole d'étoffe" has since saved more than 200,000 human lives. Parachute drops thereafter became a standard showman's act throughout the 19th century, the parachute often being taken up by hot-air balloons, a cheap operation in which the balloon was quickly recovered when its air had cooled.

It is interesting to note that the idea of jet propulsion—reaction propulsion—entered aeronautics within a week or two of the first balloon ascents in 1783; aptly enough, the first suggestion came from Joseph Montgolfier himself, in a 'mémoire' delivered to the Academy of Lyon in October 1783, in which he said: "We have sought power in the same fire which serves to keep the vessel aloft. The first which presented itself to our imagination is the power of reaction (la puissance de réaction), which can be

---

[1] The words 'designed', 'suggested' or 'proposed', without mention of a model or full-sized machine being built, imply that only drawings and/or descriptions were produced.

[2] An engraving of 1784, which shows men descending from a balloon, each wearing a 'habit aerostatique'—a kind of parachute cloak—along with manual paddles, is credited to Thibault de Saint-André; but this 'event' did not take place.

applied without any mechanism, and without expense:" he went on: "it consists solely in one or more opening in the vessel on the side opposite to that in which one wishes to be conveyed." This is the first technical statement in history on the subject of the jet propulsion of aircraft.

The first balloon with this Montgolfier system of propulsion—which, of course, would be totally ineffective owing to the lack of pressure—was the huge Montgolfier balloon built by Father Miolan and M. Janinet in 1784, which was destroyed by the unruly crowd on July 11th 1784, when it failed to ascend from the Luxembourg Gardens at Paris.

There were a number of other suggestions for 'jet' propelling balloons—by rockets, compressed air, etc.—made during the years before the outbreak of the French Revolution in 1789 as well as an increasing number thereafter.

No further events of importance took place before France was engulfed in her Revolution of 1789. What may be called the 'pre-history' of aviation had now ended. With the more peaceful Industrial Revolution in Britain rapidly bringing forth new ideas, new techniques, and new men, it might have been supposed that a new spirit would infuse the whole tradition of flying experiments; but with the exception of one great man—Sir George Cayley, who was to stand almost alone for half a century—this was not so.

Due perhaps to the universal unrest of that time, with major wars being fought the world over, the only novel innovation in aeronautics, apart from the parachute, was to be found in the first use of balloons for military observation by the French army at Maubeuge in 1794. It is also of interest to note that in some fantasy projects of the Napoleonic era, of which engravings survive, not only are balloons shown as troop transports for the invasion of England, but kites are seen being flown by the English, each manned by a soldier with a gun—a curious prevision of Fighter Command.

Before closing this section, one other device must be mentioned as being in full-scale use in the Orient, ready—as it were—to invade Europe and so lead in direct evolution towards the conquest of space. The war rocket had been introduced into India from China, and at the end of the century was a major weapon in the hands of Tipu Sultan's troops who were fighting Wellington's army in Mysore. Although the pyrotechnic rocket had been in constant use throughout Europe for generations, and war rockets had been used sporadically on the Continent, it was reports of Tipu's military rockets which caused Sir William Congreve to start his experiments and about 1805 to produce the first modern rocket missile (Pl. II).

Although in no way concerned with flying, there was of course much basic scientific research carried out in the 18th century which was later to prove important to aviation. One sphere, of particular applicability, comprised the studies in aerodynamics in the service of ballistics and windmills made by various investigators.

5. *Cayley, and the First Half of the Nineteenth Century*

"THE true inventor of the aeroplane and one of the most powerful geniuses in the history of aviation" are the words used by a modern French authority, Charles Dollfus, to describe Sir George Cayley (1773–1857), a scholarly Yorkshire baronet who until recently was comparatively unknown to historians of applied science. This curious state of affairs has now been righted by the researches of the late J. E. Hodgson, of Dollfus, of Captain J. L. Pritchard, and of the present writer, who have secured universal agreement in regarding Cayley as the basic originator of the modern aeroplane.

Cayley, who lived and did most of his research work at Brompton Hall, near Scarborough, first had his aeronautical imagination fired by the invention of the balloon in 1783—when he was ten—and his active concern with flying lasted until he died in 1857. In the year 1796 he made a helicopter model on the lines of that invented by Launoy and Bienvenu—without knowing its origin—a device he later modified and improved, and which received wide publicity from the time Cayley published it in 1809; it led directly to the whole of subsequent helicopter development (Fig. 21). Within a few years, with no previous workers to guide him or suggest the lines of approach, he arrived at a correct and mature conception of the modern aeroplane, and so laid the secure foundations upon which all subsequent developments in aviation have been built. He had, of course, paid careful attention to the work of Robins and Smeaton with whirling arms (18th C.) who pioneered the study of air resistance in relation to ballistics and windmills; but none of these investigators ever conceived the application of their researches to aircraft. It was typical of Cayley's genius that, with the central idea of flight in mind, he sought data in whatever fields he saw were relevant, and applied them to his own problems: thus in 1804 he turned to the whirling arm—first used by Robins in 1746—and obtained valuable results which he applied to aircraft wings. Cayley first formulated the basic problem of mechanical flight in these words: "to make a surface support a given weight by the application of power to the resistance of air". On a silver disc (Fig. 22) now preserved in the Science Museum, and dated 1799, is an engraved diagram showing the forces of lift, drag and thrust. The disc also bears, on the other side, an initialled sketch of a fixed-wing glider, with the wing shown in sharp perspective, and the fuselage below in which the pilot is seen sitting: the machine is fitted with a tail-unit comprising vertical and horizontal control surfaces, and a pair of manually operated flappers in lieu of an airscrew. We have here, in the last year of the

Fig. 21. Cayley's version of
the 1784 Launoy and Bienvenu
helicopter model: 1796

Fig. 22. Silver disc engraved
by Cayley with sketch for his
fixed-wing aeroplane: 1799

Fig. 23. Cayley's drawing of his fixed-wing design, the
first modern configuration aeroplane of history: 1799

Fig. 24. Cayley's sketch of his first experimental
model glider, with its kite-wing: 1804

18th century, the aeroplane of today in embryo: it marks the start of a new epoch and the true beginnings of practical aviation. In the same year Cayley made a general arrangement drawing of his machine (Fig. 23).

In 1804, after this remarkable man had realised the true aerodynamic significance of the kite, he made the first proper and successful aeroplane of history. It was a five foot long model glider with a kite-form main plane set on a pole at a 6 degree angle of incidence, a tail-unit attached by a universal joint—to act as a combined rudder and elevator control—and a movable weight to adjust the centre of gravity (Fig. 24). In 1809 he constructed a full-sized glider with a wing area of 200 square feet which was flown successfully, unmanned, as well as being tested carrying a boy for a few yards at a time.

It was in 1809–10 that Cayley published his triple paper "On Aerial Navigation", in *Nicholson's Journal*, a paper which laid the foundations of aerodynamics and flight-control, upon which the whole vast science of flying is founded. He was precipitated into publishing this epoch-making work by hearing—and believing—in 1809 that Jacob Degen had flown unaided by muscle-power, which, of course, he had not.

In 1843 Cayley published a design for a highly ingenious convertiplane, which seems to be directly inspired by the drawings of a young man named Robert Taylor, Cayley never acknowledging his debt to Taylor—the only dishonest act of his long life: incidentally, Cayley turned Taylor's monoplane convertiplane into a biplane, and thus created the first biplane design in history, and the first twin-airscrew design.

After constructing further models, he returned in later life to achieve full-size triplane gliders; the first, in 1849 (Pl. III) was flown free in ballast, and also tentatively flown (including being towed) with a boy aboard; the second in 1853, when his reluctant coachman was sent across a small valley at Brompton in the first gliding flight of history; both of these machines had fixed (but adjustable) tail-units, inherent longitudinal and lateral stability, and a separate pilot-operated elevator-cum-rudder. In 1852, Cayley had published in the *Mechanics Magazine*, for all to see, the design—with a brilliant description of how to fly it—of a fixed-wing glider (Fig. 27); but no one took any notice of it, and it was not even mentioned at any of the meetings of the Aeronautical Society, which was founded in 1866.

In the course of his long life Cayley revealed a mind similar to Leonardo da Vinci's, and in many ways as remarkable. The more we discover about Cayley, the more fully may we endorse the opinion that he was the true inventor of the aeroplane, and the founder of the science of aerodynamics. More specifically, he was the first man in history:

(*a*) to divorce the system of thrust from that of lift, and so inaugurate the concept of the modern fixed-wing powered aeroplane;

(*b*) to use a whirling arm for aeronautical research;

(*c*) to use model gliders for aerodynamic research;

(*d*) to design, build, and successfully make to fly, proper aeroplanes (unpowered) in the form of both model and full-size man-carrying machines supported by fixed wings, stabilised by an adjustable tail-unit and wing-dihedral, and controlled by a combined elevator and rudder;

(*e*)   to formulate and to publish the basic aerodynamics of the fixed-wing aeroplane, including longitudinal and lateral stability (by means of both the dihedral angle and pendulum construction), and to apply this to both model and full-size man-carrying aeroplanes;

(*f*)   to suggest, build and make to fly man-carrying multiplane (triplane) gliders;

(*g*)   to realise the presence of a region of low pressure on the upper surface of a wing, and its lifting power;

(*h*)   to surmise that a cambered aerofoil gives greater lift than a flat one;

(*i*)   to investigate the movement of the centre of pressure;

(*j*)   to formulate, and demonstrate in practice, flight-control by means of elevator and rudder;

(*k*)   to suggest, build, and incorporate in a full-size aeroplane, a separate and adjustable tailplane-cum-fin, and pilot-operated elevator-cum-rudder;

(*l*)   to design, build, and apply a light cycle-type undercarriage;

(*m*)   to investigate aeronautical streamlining; design a solid of least resistance; and use instruments to test streamlining;

(*n*)   to properly understand and describe the basic technique of bird flight;

(*o*)   to suggest an internal combustion engine for aircraft propulsion;

(*p*)   to design a developed form of convertiplane: this was, apart from his 1796 helicopter model, the only significant invention he derived from another inventor (i.e. Robert Taylor).

In addition, although he did not invent the aircraft airscrew, Cayley was fully conversant with its principles, and incorporated it in his ideas for propelling both aeroplanes and airships, as well as considering ornithoptering 'winglets' analogous to the propelling wing-tips of a bird.

Cayley also paid great attention to the dirigible airship: he realised that the practical difficulties of constructing powered aeroplanes would postpone success for many years and be preceded by the airship. "I think", he wrote in 1846, "that balloon aerial navigation [airships] can be done readily, and will probably in the order of things come into use before mechanical flight can be rendered sufficiently safe and efficient for ordinary use." He was right: the first airship, designed by Giffard, flew tentatively in 1852.

Not only did Cayley achieve towering merit in aeronautics, his favourite sphere; but, fortunately for posterity, he was careful to publish his brilliant theories and conclusions, and so led directly to all subsequent research and development in aviation. His articles were translated into French, and thus fertilised the French inventors of the 1850's and 1860's. It was William Henson who conferred on him in 1846 the simple and definitive title of "the Father of Aerial Navigation".

As if all this were not enough, Cayley researched and invented indefatigably in many other fields, mechanical and social, such as land reclamation, unemployment relief, artificial limbs, theatre architecture, railways, life-boats, finned projectiles, optics, and electricity. He also contributed to applied science two other major 'firsts' of lasting importance by inventing the expansion air engine (colloquially called the hot-air engine) about 1805; and the caterpillar tractor in 1825, which has equipped agriculture and warfare with one of their most important means of locomotion. His social work was further made notable by his founding of the original Regent Street Polytechnic in 1838, thus greatly furthering technological education.

To round off the picture of this Georgian giant, it is interesting to record that Cayley was a poet in some of his spare moments, a Whig in politics (and even served for a short time as M.P. for Scarborough), a devout Unitarian by religion, and a devoted husband and father. It is interesting to note that he was the great-great-great grandfather of the present Duchess of Kent (formerly Miss Katharine Worsley);.

"Aerial navigation", wrote Cayley in 1809, "will form a most prominent feature in the progress of civilisation." He would not have been disappointed.

Although Cayley published his first researches into heavier-than-air flight in 1809–10, he could not persuade the scientific world to take the idea of mechanical flight seriously—neither then nor at any time during his long life. But within two decades of his death his true greatness was recognised, and his 1809–10 paper was republished in England and France (1876 and 1877). In 1809 he had written of "the art of flying, or aerial navigation as I have chosen to term it for the sake of giving a little more dignity to a subject bordering upon the ludicrous in public estimation". This neglect and contempt prevented any vigorous follow-up of his basic researches, and retarded the development of aerodynamics for a generation, leaving only Cayley himself to press on, accompanied—with the exception of Henson and Stringfellow—by a series of eccentrics, showmen, and near-charlatans.

*　　*　　*　　*　　*

Other Inventors: 1800–1850

Before describing the work of Henson and Stringfellow we must turn back to the 'curiosities' of the first half of the century. The 'flappers', although a dying race, still persisted both in theory and practice, and we find in 1801 the French General Resnier de Goué—at the age of seventy-two—testing an ornithopter based on a design he had made as long ago as 1788, with which he made a flapping dive from the picturesque ramparts of Angoulême into the River Charente, without injury. He later made another attempt, over land, and broke a leg. He was a fine and courageous old man.

Quite the most notorious experimenter of the time—who seems to have had an excellent publicity sense—was the Swiss clockmaker Jacob Degen (1756–1846) who lived in Vienna. Between 1807 and 1817, he built and tested his ornithopter, which was an ingenious machine of 130 square feet wing area with the wings made on the flap-valve principle of opening on the upstroke and closing on the downstroke. At first he tested it hung against a counter-weight, but then—particularly in 1809—he attached a hydrogen balloon to it which, whilst he exerted his full strength on the ornithopter, gave him a 90 lb. lift, with the result that he and his apparatus (which weighed about 160 lb.) were enabled to be raised off the ground in what became in this century the sport of balloon-jumping (Fig. 25). He managed to gain a wide reputation for having flown unaided, the balloon not being

Fig. 25. Degen's ornithopter suspended from a balloon,
which supported most of the weight: 1809

Fig. 26. Design for a fixed-wing tandem monoplane,
with amidships flapper propulsion, by Walker: 1831

mentioned, and seldom thereafter illustrated: it was a report to this effect that directly precipitated Cayley's epoch-making paper of 1809–10. In October of 1812 Degen was injured by the crowd in Paris after failing to satisfy them, and he was—somewhat unfairly—described as a "miserable charlatan". Degen was, in fact, a serious and devoted experimenter, however mistaken his ideas; and in one field, the helicopter, he was well to the fore, and in 1816 made a small clockwork-driven model with contra-rotating rotors.

In 1811, using a copy of Degen's machine, but minus the balloon, Albrecht Berblinger (the Tailor of Ulm) flapped miserably off the Adlerbastei at Ulm and into the River Danube, from which he was rescued without having seriously injured himself.

In 1810, an English portrait painter, Thomas Walker, had published *A Treatise on the Art of Flying by Mechanical Means*, a specious work which tried to revive interest in ornithopters; it illustrated his own design for one, in which the pilot used arms and legs to flap the wings, and of which he stated a successful model had been made. But Walker was to have a strong influence on posterity; for in 1831 he published a new edition of his book in which he illustrated a novel idea, that of a tandem fixed-wing monoplane with propulsive flappers amidships (Fig. 26). This probably influenced D. S. Brown toward the same configuration in 1874 and, through him, Langley[1] and Blériot. Walker also looked forward to the day when aircraft would be used for exploration and the carrying of mail.

The ornithopter tradition died hard, as said above, and in 1818 the French Count Adolphe de Lambertye designed—but did not build—a Blanchardesque monster with beating wings, but added a touch of prophetic ingenuity in suggesting a helical-screw helicopter to ply between his aerial vessel and the ground. F. D. Artingstall, fired by the progress of contemporary railway locomotives, varied the ornithopter theme by the first attempt to make a full-size two-wing ornithopter powered by steam: when suspended from the ceiling (in 1829 or 1830), it flapped itself violently to pieces, and then the boiler exploded. With a second machine, with four wings beating alternately, the boiler also exploded, and that was an end of his experiments.

A novel 'aeronautical' vehicle, which at least worked in a wayward fashion, was made and tested by George Pocock, and was called a 'char-volant', or kite-drawn carriage; it consisted of a kite flown from a horseless carriage, and allowed to draw the latter along, provided there was not too much 'difference of opinion' between the wind direction and the steering-gear of the carriage[2]: the 'char-volant' made a successful journey on the road between Bristol and Marlborough in 1827. Pocock's preoccupation with kites had previously led to his precarious achievement of man-carrying kites which, about 1825, took up amongst others, Pocock's daughter Martha, a passenger who was to become the mother of W. G. Grace, the cricketer.

Among the popularisers of the helicopter were the Italian Vittorio Sarti, who designed but did not build, a contra-rotating device in 1828; and an

---

[1] In 1815, Cayley had designed and sketched the first tandem aeroplane, a monoplane with outer flapping wing-panels, but he did not publish it.　　[2] First tested in 1822.

English carpenter, David Mayer, who went as far as constructing a large man-powered helicopter in the same year, which naturally remained grounded, but whose lack of performance was euphemistically described by its inventor as "very flattering, though not perfectly successful". But the most remarkable development in the helicopter field took place when, in 1842, W. H. Phillips completed and flew successfully a helicopter model driven by steam jets from the rotor tips—like Hero's aeolipile—the jets being the result of the combusion of charcoal, nitre, and gypsum: it flew up fast and crossed two fields. Phillips showed a replica of this model at the 1868 Exhibition held by the Aeronautical Society at the Crystal Palace. Next year (1843) saw an English engineer named Bourne construct and fly successfully some small model helicopters comprising feathers stuck in corks, *à la* Cayley, but driven by watch-springs. In 1845, an inventor named Cossus described, but did not build, a full-size steam-driven helicopter composed of a large central rotor (for lift), flanked by two small ones whose angles could be varied in order to propel and steer the machine.

One of the most outstanding and influential aeroplanes in history was never built, and the model made from it could not fly. This was the *Aerial Steam Carriage*, designed in 1842–43 by William Samuel Henson (1812–88) and first published in April 1843, after its patent was granted (see Pl. II). Owing to W. S. Henson having an astute publicity agent named Frederick Marriott, romantic imaginative engravings, which closely followed the superb patent drawings, were published the world over; and, due to the excellence of the design, continued to be published throughout the century, and beyond. It was the first design in history for a fixed-wing airscrew-propelled aeroplane of modern configuration, which incorporated the following:

§ Wire-braced monoplane configuration, with rectilinear main wings, fuselage, and tail-unit comprising elevator and rudder;

§ Engine, in fuselage, driving two pusher airscrews;

§ Tricycle undercarriage;

§ Double-surfaced cambered wings, built up with spars and shaped ribs, which was to become standard practice from 1908 onwards.

Henson intended the machine to have a span of 150 feet, a wing area of 4,500 square feet, and a steam engine of 25–30 horse-power, and it was to be launched down a ramp to save power. However, it was not these details which immediately impressed themselves on his contemporaries, and won world-wide publication in 1843 through such journals as *The Illustrated London News* and *L'Illustration* in France, and by means of many prints and souvenirs; but that here, for the first time, was a logical, consistent embodiment of what one may call the 'aeroplane idea', for all to see and copy. The *Aerial Steam Carriage* never lost its popularity and influence throughout the century, and was reproduced in countless articles and books the world over.

Henson, who was in the lace trade at Chard in Somerset, had based the *Ariel* (as it was also called) on the teachings of Cayley, whom he acknowledged as "the Father of Aerial Navigation"; he had somewhat grandiose dreams of its future as the inaugurator of an international airline—scenes from which fantasy-future appear in some of the published prints—and tried to form an Aerial Transit Company, with his friend John Stringfellow (1799–1883), also an engineer in the lace trade. All this activity took place before even a model was completed, let alone a full-size machine.

The model, with a span of 20 feet and wing area of 62·9 square feet was fitted with an excellent little steam engine built primarily on Henson's designs, but improved by Stringfellow: the machine was tested at Bala Down, near Chard, from 1845 to 1847. But after descending the ramp, it could not sustain itself. Henson thereupon abandoned his model, married, and emigrated to the U.S.A. in 1848.

Stringfellow, however, carried on and built another model in which he fitted a new engine of an improved Henson design which he had built: this little machine was a variation on the Henson theme, and had curved wings of 10·5 feet span and 12 square feet area, with flexible trailing edges—a feature copied from the bird, which was wrongly believed to act as a gust damper and make for stability—along with a Henson tail; it was launched from an overhead wire in a shed at Chard in 1848, and at Cremorne Gardens (Pl. II). Much controversy has taken place over whether it ever flew in the sense that it overcame the momentum of its launch, and maintained a horizontal or rising flight path. Captain J. L. Pritchard (see Bibliography) has shown that there is no contemporary evidence that it ever flew, and good reason to believe that it did not; and even the cautious Octave Chanute said that this "machine cannot fairly be said to have 'demonstrated the practicability of making a steam engine fly' ", the quotation within the quotation being by Brearey, Secretary of the Aeronautical Society. In view of this, perhaps one could say that this Stringfellow model showed some evidence of being able to fly; but it does mean that the first authenticated model flight must now be credited to Du Temple in *c*. 1857–58. For some years Stringfellow seems to have abandoned aeronautics; but he took it up again in the mid-1860's with far-reaching results (see next section).

There are two special events in the field of parachutes to record during the first half of the century. Garnerin made the first parachute descent in England over London—his fifth jump—and properly started British parachute history, on September 21st 1802. Cayley, having considered Garnerin's device, suggested in 1809 an inverted (dihedral) parachute to overcome the wild oscillations suffered by Garnerin, owing to the lack of porosity in the canopy.[1] This suggestion of Cayley's was almost certainly the cause of an elderly water-colour painter, Robert Cocking (1777–1837), deciding to make and test a Cayley-type parachute in 1837: unbelievably, he did not first test it with a dead weight, and on July 24th of that year ascended in his device, suspended beneath a balloon piloted by Charles Green: at a height of some 5,000 feet, Cocking released himself; but the parachute broke up in the air and crashed near Lee Green, in Kent, Cocking dying of

[1] With the early parachutes, it was soon considered that a hole in the crown tended to bring about a stable descent: it was not realised that the main stabilising factor is the porosity of the fabric.

his injuries. As a result of this accident, the American balloonist John Wise experimented at Philadelphia, with dropping a dog on a Garnerin type of parachute, and a cat on a Cocking type: the cat made a steady comfortable descent, whereas the dog oscillated violently, but the Cocking type was not to be used thereafter.

As a tail-piece to this section one ought to mention a splendidly eccentric suggestion put forward by Georg Rebenstein, of Nuremberg, which consisted of a cubiform hot-air balloon which could be collapsed like a concertina in mid-air, and then used as a glider to descend to earth (1835). There was also Doctor W. Miller's frivolous—but beautifully engraved—design for a man-powered ornithopter in 1843; and further fruitless designs for ornithopters by Duchesnay (1845), von Drieberg (1845), Marc Seguin (1846) and others.

Significant dates in other fields (*1800–49*)

1801   First practical steamboat in operation (the paddle steamer *Charlotte Dundas* in Britain).
1805   Battle of Trafalgar.
1807   First commercial success of the steam paddle-boat (Fulton's *Charlotte Dundas*).
1807   First commercially successful steamboat (Robert Fulton's *Claremont* on the Hudson River, U.S.A.).
1812   First commercially successful steam-boat in Europe (the paddle-steamer *Comet* on the Clyde).
1815   Battle of Waterloo, and final eclipse of Napoleon.
1822   First iron steamship built (in England for France).
1825   Stockton—Darlington railway opened.
1829   Stephenson's *Rocket* service.
1830   Liverpool and Manchester railway opened.
1831   British Association founded.
1833   Emancipation of slaves in the British Empire.
1835   Colt revolver introduced.
1836   British Patent Office established.
1837   Accession of Queen Victoria.
1838   First successful screw steam ship (the *Archimedes*, in Britain).
1838   Brunel's ship *Great Western* inaugurates regular trans-Atlantic service.
1838   Cayley founds the Regent Street Polytechnic Institution.
1840   Penny post introduced in Britain.
1840's Railway networks spread throughout Britain and the Continent.
1840's First successes with the electric telegraph.
1840's Daguerreotype and Calotype photography come into limited use (both were patented in 1839), and start the age of photography.
1842   The *Illustrated London News* first published.
1848   Revolutions in Paris, Venice, Parma, Milan, Sicily, Vienna and Berlin.

6. The 1850's and 1860's

The 1850's

HEAVIER-THAN-AIR aeronautics at mid-century, and for nearly two decades thereafter, was still shunned by the established and conventional world of science. But a number of technically minded individuals, engineers and other professional men, were beginning to concern themselves with the problems of mechanical flight; and by the mid-sixties these pioneers were to make their work and interests felt by a larger professional audience and at last begin to attract attention in the higher ranks of science.

At the beginning of this period, with Cayley's fundamental groundwork already laid, and the spectacular publicity attending Henson's *Aerial Steam Carriage* strongly affecting the more adventurous minds, the aeronautical initiative—for reasons difficult to diagnose—passes almost wholly to France. But it should again be noted here that Cayley's remarkable design for a controllable glider was published in 1852 (Fig. 27), yet passed unnoticed. After an ornithopter-cum-helicopter suggestion from Aubaud (1851), we find the first consistent French design for a powered aeroplane put forward by Michel Loup in 1853: it consisted of a rigid bird-form monoplane with two propellers, one let into each wing, and a tricycle undercarriage (Fig. 28). About 1853 Cayley designed, but did not publish, a model with propulsive flappers to be driven by rubber cords stretched round a spool; and in 1858 Pierre Jullien made an airscrew-driven model with the same type of 'motor' which flew some 40 feet. Bréant then continued the fruitless ornithopter tradition by suggesting a machine in which the pilot pulled down the wings, and elastic raised them (1854). In 1856, Viscount Carlingford had suggested a monoplane somewhat similar to Loup's with a single tractor propeller in the nose; he built a full-size (non-powered) version of his so-called 'aerial chariot' which he seems to have flown as a kite, or attempted to launch unmanned as a glider, in Ireland.

First tested in 1853, and then in 1854, was a parachute-type glider built by Louis Charles Letur (Pl. III) which was the first pilot-operated heavier-than-air machine to be tested in the air: it was composed of a canopy wing (which could be pulled down at various points), beneath which sat the pilot operating two large flappers. After some safe descents from a balloon in France and England, Letur was killed in his machine when it was accidentally dragged over trees near Tottenham (London) when trying to land after he had discovered a defect when in the air: he was still attached to the balloon: this crash was on June 27th 1854, and Letur died of his injuries on July 5th.

Then appears an adventurous French sea-captain Jean-Marie Le Bris

Fɪɢ. 1

Fɪɢ. 2

Fig. 27. Cayley's published design for a fixed-wing glider, to be launched from a balloon, with inherent longitudinal and lateral (roll) stability, and cruciform tail-unit for flight-control: 1852

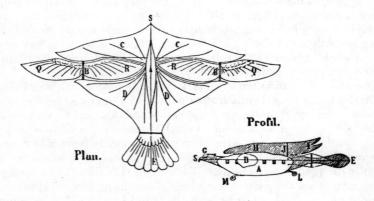

Fig. 28. First consistent French design for a powered aeroplane, by Loup: 1853

PLATE III

a Cayley's 'boy-carrier' triplane: 1849

b Letur's parachute-type glider: 1853

c Lenoir's gas-engine: 1860

d La Landelle's fantasy helicopter: 1863

e Ponton d'Amécourt's steam-driven model helicopter: 1863

f The first design for a jet-propelled aeroplane, by de Louvrié: 1865

a First delta-wing aeroplane design, by Butler and Edwards: 1867

b Stringfellow's model triplane, which led to all future designs with superposed wings: 1868

c The second Le Bris glider, seen on its launching cart (reversed): 1868

d Lilienthal tests his ornithopter against a weight: 1869

Fig. 29. Du Temple's patent drawings for his tractor monoplane with swept-forward wings: 1857

(1808–72), pursuing a courageous aerial career between about 1856 and 1868. He built a full-size glider based on the albatross—a bird he had studied on his voyage to South America—at Trefeuntee in France; and he had this machine placed on a cart, driven along a road and released on the way (1857). In this manner, he made one short glide, but crashed at the second attempt, breaking his leg: the wing area of the machine was said to have been 215 square feet, and the span 23 feet. Later, in 1868, he tested a second machine near Brest, which he seems wisely to have launched on most occasions with ballast on board, but no pilot. It finally crashed and was destroyed; but Le Bris stands as one of the earliest pioneers in practical flying. Evidence about the construction of his gliders is scanty, although a photograph exists of the second machine. They seem to have consisted of a boat-shaped car with wings whose angle of incidence is said to have been adjustable, and a movable tail, the structure and movements being based on the albatross (Pl. IV).

With another French seaman, the naval officer Félix Du Temple (1823–1890),[1] one of the first of the new generation of experimenters mentioned above, comes upon the aeronautical scene. Du Temple produced a maturely realised monoplane design after experimenting in the early fifties with an ingenious model which was engined first by clockwork and then by steam: it first took off under its own power, sustained itself and landed safely (*c.* 1857–58). This model—with the 'demotion' of Stringfellow—now ranks as the first successful powered aeroplane to sustain itself in the air. The design (Fig. 29) that followed this achievement led Du Temple to another important 'first', the first full-size—albeit unsuccessful— would-be powered aeroplane ever constructed. The design was patented in 1857, and the machine built soon afterwards. It was a machine with swept-forward wings set at a dihedral angle, a tailplane and rudder, a tractor airscrew to be driven by hot air or steam, and retractable undercarriage. Dollfus has established that much later (*c.* 1874) it became the first powered man-carrying aeroplane to leave the ground—just—after a down-ramp take off (Fig. 42). Lack of suitable engines was for long to remain the chronic hindrance to full-scale experiments.

Interesting relief to the main experiments in aeronautics had come in 1852 with the first feasible powered airship, made and flown by Henri Giffard, which was driven at 5 m.p.h. by a steam engine; also in 1852 when James Nye proposed propelling airships with rockets; and in 1859 when an Irish priest, E. J. Cordner, designed, built and even tested a multiple man-carrying kite for ship to shore rescue work.

The work of the Frenchman Louis Mouillard, who lived in Algeria and Egypt, and who built his first glider in 1856, is noted on page 52.

Significant dates in other fields (1850's)

1850's   First free municipal libraries in Britain.

---

[1] There were two brothers involved—Félix and Louis—and the full family name was Du Temple de La Croix: it was Félix who played by far the greater part.

1851   Singer introduces the first practical sewing machine.
1851   The Great Exhibition is held in Hyde Park, London.
1854   Otis, in the U.S.A., introduces the first safety lift for buildings.
1854–56 Crimean War.
1855   Newspaper tax in Britain is repealed, with consequent increase in number of
        papers issued.
1856   Bessemer process brings in cheap steel.

*   *   *   *   *

The 1860's

The year 1860 marks an important, though indirect, milestone in the history of aviation, for it was then that the French engineer, Lenoir, invented the gas engine (Pl. III): this was to lead, in the 1870's, to the Otto and Daimler petrol engines, and at last to a light but powerful enough motor to propel a heavier-than-air aircraft.

During the decade, there was still a crop of ornithopterists who were "an unconscionable time a-dying", and who may claim a little attention. Smythies in 1860 proposed a complex machine of fixed and flapping surfaces, the latter operated by a steam engine: he included the interesting notion of a shifting pilot's seat to alter the centre of gravity of the machine, a device resorted to for a short period by Blériot in 1907.

In 1863, an Alsatian industrialist, J. J. Bourcart built an ornithopter (Fig. 30) with two pairs of feathering wings, with which he claimed promising results; but it came to nothing, as was inevitable. But it was also Bourcart who, at some time in the 1860's, made a most creditable effort to encourage aviation when he offered a prize of 5,000 francs for an airborne duration of 20 minutes, and another of 2,000 francs for a duration of 5 minutes at a minimum height of 3 metres.

Then, in 1864, Struvé and Telescheff suggested a man-powered ornithopter with five pairs of wings, in the belief that they would thus overcome the problems of stability. Also in 1864 Claudel patented a curious machine which consisted of a combination of fixed wings and longitudinally rotating surfaces which were to twist into propellers. In 1867 the great German pioneer Otto Lilienthal was first feeling his way in aviation, and in this year his experimental six-wing ornithopter was tested suspended against a counter-weight. Like Cayley, he was never quite to escape from the idea of ornithopter propulsion, even after his epoch-making gliding experiments with fixed-wing gliders, from 1891 to 1896 (see Pl. IV). In 1868, J. M. Kaufmann, a Glasgow engineer, attracted considerable attention with his model shown at the Crystal Palace exhibition of that year (Fig. 35) in which a steam engine—with locomotive funnel on the boiler—was to activate two long flappers, and quadruplane wings were to provide lift; the flapping wings were to beat downwards and backwards, and forwards for the upstroke: the model flapped itself to pieces, and the experiments were at an end. Still in 1868, Charles Spencer made a pair of fixed wings of 110 square feet area, attached to which were two outer flappers (with a total area of 15 square feet) which, by man-power, were to propel the machine, which was

35

also equipped with a tail: Spencer seems to have achieved some minor success with this contraption, but did not follow it up. In the same year Spencer patented a delta-wing machine—which he clearly copied from Butler and Edwards the year before (see below)—with both fixed wings and flappers up forward.

One of the more curious developments in aeronautical history took place in France during the early 1860's: this was a sudden rise in enthusiasm for helicopters in France, which manifested itself not only by a number of helicopter designs and models, but by the foundation of an active society to promote them. The helicopter seemed at that time to offer an uncomplicated way of flying, with screws to sustain the machine, and another to propel it. But the enthusiasts soon found their prime-movers were inadequate, and so they did not have to face the aerodynamic difficulties which fixed screw blades would lead to. There is an ingenious contra-rotating helicopter design of 1861 to record, by the Vicomte Ponton d'Amécourt; he built this in 1863, in model form, powered by a steam engine; but it was not successful (Pl. III). But his little clockwork-driven models of the same year flew well, and one of them was made to descend by parachute when the engine ran down. The human dynamo who brought the enthusiasts together was one of the great French 'Victorians', the romantic and justly celebrated aeronaut-photographer who called himself simply Nadar; in reality he was Félix Tournachon. In 1863 he founded a society for the promotion of specifically heavier-than-air flying, the Société d'Encouragement pour la Navigation Aérienne au Moyens d' Appareils plus lourds que l'Air: this was soon abbreviated to simply the Société d'Aviation, after La Landelle had coined the word "aviation" in 1862. In 1864, Nadar founded the journal *L'Aeronaute: Moniteur de la Société générale de Navigation aérienne*. Although only five issues were produced, the journal was revived in 1868 by Abel Hureau de Villeneuve with the modified title *L'Aeronaute: Bulletin mensuel de la Navigation aérienne*. It then ran until 1912, providing the first continuous record of developments in the theory and practice of aviation. Nadar gathered round him a group of talented men, of whom the best known was Gabriel de La Landelle, who became well known for his much-reproduced fantasy helicopter project of 1863 (Pl. III), and Ponton d'Amécourt, who has already been noted. La Landelle also created the word 'aviateur' in 1863.

One of the outstanding men of the 1860's was the French Count Ferdinand Charles Honoré Phillipe d'Esterno (1806–83), who in 1864 published his *Du Vol des Oiseaux*; this book was of great importance, as it was the first to draw attention to the soaring—as opposed to the gliding—flight of birds. D'Esterno might also be said to have 'discovered' soaring, and wrote "in soaring flight, a man can handle an apparatus carrying 10 tons, just as well as one carrying only his own weight". In his analysis of bird flight, one seeks in vain for any notion of mature lateral control, but finds only the shifting of the centre of gravity laterally for control: his description of the multiple movements of a bird's wings included a torsion of its wings, but only as steering air-brakes, and not concerned with control in roll. Incidentally, d'Esterno's passages on the sliding seat for the pilot, to alter the

Fig. 30 Bourcart's man-powered ornithopter device: 1863

Fig. 31. D'Esterno's design for a glider: 1864

Fig. 32. Wenham's multi-wing glider of 1858–59, published in 1866

Fig. 33. Design for a delta biplane with airscrew rotated by tip-jets, by Butler and Edwards: 1867

Fig. 34. Design for a jet-propelled delta-wing monoplane, by de Telescheff: 1867

37

machine's centre of gravity, may well have influenced Lilienthal in his choice of the hang-glider type of machine, in which the pilot hangs in the machine by his arms and swings his hips and legs in any direction he desires. D'Esterno designed and patented in 1864 what must be recorded as the first machine for soaring (Fig. 31), which was never built, but which included wings whose angle of incidence and dihedral could be changed; which could be swung forwards or backwards in the horizontal plane, and which had large flexible rear portions to act as gust dampers, and a spreading tail fixed to the car by a universal joint, which could swivel and fold up. D'Esterno was the first, and one of the most influential, apostles of man's imitation of the soaring bird, which can, he said, "sail indefinitely upon the wind without further flapping his wings". It is also probable that he influenced Ader.

In 1863–68 the French inventor Joseph Pline, produced a series of interesting model fixed-wing gliders which incorporated the principle of combining a number of longitudinal barrel-like aerofoils—similar to the barrel-vaults of 12th century churches—to make up the main wings: although ingenious, the idea led nowhere. In 1865, L. P. Mouillard, who was to become the second apostle of soaring flight, made the first of his tentative glides. In 1869 there is a strange freak to record, which is said to have been constructed by Frederick Marriott, Henson's publicity agent in his Aerial Transit Co., project of 1842–43: it was a steam-propelled airship-cum-aeroplane, with a wing built out on either side of the envelope for more than halfway along from the nose of the dirigible, and a Cayley-type tail-unit at the tail of the envelope: it was said to have been tested over Shell Mound Lake (California) in 1869. This idea is not quite so absurd as some writers have made it, as airships have often been operated in a heavier-than-air condition, developing dynamic lift from the aerodynamic forces on the body and control-surfaces.

The jet propulsion of aeroplanes, properly speaking, dates from 1865, when there appeared the world's first mature design for a jet-propelled aeroplane, by the French engineer Charles de Louvrié. His machine, the *Aéronave* (Pl. III) was originally designed in 1863 and was then (in 1865) redesigned, but not built, to be propelled by the burning of "hydrocarbon, or better, vaporised petroleum oil" ejected through two rear jet pipes. There soon followed in 1867 the remarkable and prophetic patent of J. W. Butler and E. Edwards: this was a multiple patent, whose chief interest lies in the delta-wing monoplane configuration—possibly suggested by the schoolboy's dart—which was presented as jet-propelled by steam, compressed air, or inflammable gas and air (Pl. IV): the inventors also proposed a biplane delta machine, propelled by a pusher propeller rotated by angled jet pipes at the blade ends (Fig. 33). The single delta version was widely publicised. Another remarkable French jet design followed hard on the heels of the *Aéronave* and of the Butler and Edwards delta designs: still in 1867 a Russian officer, Nicholas de Telescheff, also took out a French patent for a delta jet monoplane design (Fig. 34) with a cylinder where a combustible liquid was to be vaporised, compressed, mixed with air, and ignited to produce the jet efflux.

One of the most important dates in flying history is the year 1866, when there was founded in London the Aeronautical Society (now Royal) of Great Britain. Although not the first society devoted to flying[1] it was by far the most important and influential. Under the Presidency of the Duke of Argyll it soon attracted those men of science and vision who realised that mechanical flight was ultimately possible, and who were determined to study and solve its problems. From now on, the main development of aviation was to lie in the hands of scientifically or technologically trained men. The subject of flying, to which the world had already been acclimatised through ballooning, now took on a new meaning and a new seriousness; and although man-carrying aeroplane flight would continue to be looked upon for many years as visionary, it now became accepted as a proper subject of investigation. Members of the new Society, with their contemporaries on the Continent, now commenced the regular publication in technical journals of their researches and suggestions, and this constant dissemination of knowledge was to become of mounting importance for those engaged in the study of aeronautics.

At the first meeting of the Aeronautical Society on June 27th 1866, a classic paper entitled *Aerial Locomotion* was read by Francis Herbert Wenham (1824–1908), a marine engineer, and was immediately recognised as another milestone in aviation. Following up Cayley's advocacy of the cambered wing, Wenham pointed out that all bird's wings were cambered and of thicker section at the leading edge: he established that such a wing, at a small angle of incidence, derived most of its lift from the front portion; hence that a long narrow wing (i.e. of high aspect ratio) would be the best type of wing for lifting; and, again following Cayley, that such wings superposed would provide the maximum lift with a manageable structure. Tests were made (*c*. 1858–59) successfully with a model, also tentatively with two full-size five-plane gliders (in which he lay prone), which demonstrated the correctness of his wing-shape theories and marked the practical beginnings of the modern rigid-surface wing, and of the multiplane aircraft (Fig. 32). Wenham conducted a prolonged study of cambered wings and aspect ratio, and—with John Browning—had the distinction of building the first wind tunnel, in which later tests were made (1871). His influence on the history of the aeroplane was profound: this influence was twofold—through the prominent position he came to take in the newly formed Aeronautical Society, and by the publication of his paper on *Aerial Locomotion*, in the Society's first annual report (for 1866). Wenham also came later to conduct a fruitful correspondence with Octave Chanute, from 1892 to 1908.

In June 1868 the young Aeronautical Society put on at the Crystal Palace the first aeronautical exhibition to be held in history; it was a curious and not very significant jumble of specimens in the fields of aerostation and aviation, along with fifteen ingenious model engines driven by steam, gun-cotton, gas and oil. But the display was important in its indication of the growing status of ideas and experiments in flying, and of particular interest in its inclusion of a model steam-powered triplane contributed by John Stringfellow, who

[1] The first was the Société Aérostatique et Météorologique de France, founded in Paris in 1852 which, in 1873, was merged with Nadar's society, and then became the Société Française de Navigation Aérienne, which flourished until 1930.

had temporarily emerged from obscurity (see Pl. IV). He had evidently been spurred to this effort by reading Wenham's paper, but Cayley must also have been clearly in mind, as the old gentleman had specifically recommended the triplane structure in an article criticising Henson's *Aerial Steam Carriage* in 1843. The new model, clearly showing its Cayley-Henson ancestry, was somewhat poorly designed and, when tested, proved a failure; but despite its poor performance, it caught the imagination both of contemporary and later inventors. As with Henson's *Ariel*, illustrations of it began appearing the world over, and continued to appear; and there is no doubt that it was the leading influence in persuading Chanute—and through him the Wrights—to adopt a superposed plane configuration. Thus this unsuccessful triplane provided the main 'influence bridge' between Cayley and the modern biplane.[1] Stringfellow also exhibited another of his little steam engines, and was awarded a £100 prize for it. There is no doubt that Stringfellow was an able engineer, but equally no doubt that he was not very gifted aeronautically. Few other items at the exhibition are now of interest, except the replica of the Phillips helicopter model of 1842, and a fixed-wing glider with ornithopter flappers made by Charles Spencer, which was to remain uncompleted.

The year 1868 also saw the first specific proposal for control of an aircraft in roll, in M. P. W Boulton's British patent No. 392. The patent is primarily concerned with schemes for jet propulsion, using steam or other gases, but among its numerous proposals are moveable surfaces or vanes projecting from the sides of the body of an aircraft. The vanes can be rotated differentially to generate aerodynamic forces to roll the aircraft about its longitudinal axis. Boulton envisaged that the vanes would be operated automatically by a pendulum device to counter any accidental rolling motion of the aircraft, but he also mentioned the possibility of manual control by the pilot. To this extent, he can be said to have foreshadowed the use of ailerons for roll control; but he does not seem to have attempted to put any of his ideas into practice, and there is little evidence that he had any significant influence on later inventors.

Two years later, Richard Harte's British patent No. 1469 of 1870 proposed a monoplane with hinged flaps on the trailing edges of the wings, which look even more like modern ailerons (see Fig. 36). Harte described these control surfaces acting in three ways: (a) deflected together to act as elevators; (b) deflected oppositely through a small angle to counteract propeller torque; (c) deflected differentially to turn the aircraft. In the latter mode, the effect is to increase the drag of one wing more than the other, and thus to turn the aircraft on to a new heading. To describe this function, I use the term "steering air-brakes" suggested by my Farnborough advisors. Such devices have been re-invented several times, and occasionally used on aircraft; although geometrically similar to conventional ailerons, they function quite differently. Downward deflection of an aileron increases the lift on the wing to which it is attached, causing the aircraft to roll about its

---

[1] It has already been noted that history's first biplane design was Cayley's convertiplane of 1843.

longitudinal axis, thus inclining the lift force to turn the aircraft on to a new heading.

A word must be said here about one of the greatest of 'aeropropagandists', Jules Verne (1828–1905). With his novel *Five weeks in a Balloon* (1863) and then for more than thirty years, he produced a wealth of aeronautical romance, speculation, fantasy and prophecy, which undoubtedly played a large part in firing the imagination, and acclimatising the minds, of Victorian youth throughout the world. The performance of his fantasy helicopter vessel *Albatros* (1886) foreshadowed that of present-day helicopters. But Verne is now known to have played an even more vital role in history, not in aeronautics, but in rocketry and space travel. For the American Dr. Robert Goddard—from whom all modern rocketry directly derives—has recorded that it was the reading of Verne's *From the Earth to the Moon . . . and a Trip round It* (English ed. 1873), which alone inspired him to take up the subject of rockets.

Significant dates in other fields (*1860's*)

1860	Over 1,000 newspapers are now published in Britain.
1860's	First great spread of photography throughout the world (with the collodion wet-plate process, invented in 1851).
1860's	Open-hearth process (1867) further cheapens steel manufacture.
1860's	The cycle industry starts in France, then in Coventry, England.
1862	Second International Exhibition held in London.
1866	Britain and U.S.A. now permanently linked by telegraph.
1867	Nobel invents dynamite, but its epoch-making role in civil engineering was to come later.
1869	Suez Canal is opened.

Fig. 35. Kaufmann's steam-powered model quadruplane, with flapper propulsion: 1868

Fig. 36. Harte's design for ailerons to counteract airscrew torque: 1870

Fig. 37. Trouvé's model ornithopter, driven by blank revolver cartridges: 1870

Fig. 38. Pénaud's own plan-view sketch of his stable model 'Plano-phore' (with tail airscrew): 1871

Fig. 39. Tandem-wing model glider with rear elevator, by Brown: 1873–74

7. The 1870's

THE decade of the 1870's was highly productive aeronautically, most of the inventions being French; this was possibly not unconnected with the Prussian invasion of France (July 1870) and the extreme nationalistic feelings and strivings, after the war ended in February 1871. But there was, too, a great expansion of technology throughout Europe, and aeronautics was to benefit from the advances made in many of its branches. In aviation, the ideas came thick and fast; they were good, bad, and indifferent, although even the worst had some touch of ingenuity about them.

The decade was dominated by one great man, Alphonse Pénaud (1850–80), "doux et modeste, esprit d'une lucidité et d'un bon sens extraordinaires, précurseur en tout ce qu'il a abordé", as Dollfus says. He is one of the aeronautical gaints—ranking with Cayley and the Wrights—a sad and brilliant figure who finally committed suicide after losing courage, hope and health; his was a tragedy brought about by mischievous, and probably jealous, criticism and denigration. After a hip disease prevented him following his father (who was an admiral) into the navy, Pénaud devoted himself entirely to aeronautics. In 1870 he introduced a "motor" of twisted rubber to power models, which incidentally was to do more than anything else to foster air-mindedness amongst the youth of the world.[1] In that year he made the first of his successful model helicopters, and standardised one of the types of contra-rotating helicopter model which still lives on as a toy. The next year (1871) saw his 'planophore', which marked a major milestone in aviation history and provided the modern aeroplane with one of its most important ancestors: as with the Henson and Stringfellow designs, it was constant publication which kept Pénaud's 'planophore' before the later inventors, and built it into the minds of posterity. This model was a stable monoplane of 18 inches span, and wing area of 76 square inches, with its tapering wings bent up at their tips to provide dihedral, and a small diamond-shaped tailplane, also with dihedral tips; it was propelled by a two-bladed pusher propeller at the tail, driven by twisted rubber, with a diameter of 8 inches. This historic machine was the first inherently stable aeroplane to be seen in public: lateral stability was provided by the dihedral wing-tips, and longitudinal by setting the tailplane at a negative angle of 8 degrees to the chord-line of the main wings: the centre of gravity was placed just in front of the centre of pressure (Pl. V and Fig. 38). This model was demonstrated in the Tuileries Gardens in Paris on August 18th 1871, before the Société de Navigation Aérienne, and flew 131 feet in 11 seconds. Pénaud

---

[1] As noted before, he was not the first to introduce rubber; but he was the first to bring it to public attention, and all rubber-driven models derive from Pénaud.

thus repeated Cayley's work on stability without at first knowing of it, and further established the character of the modern aeroplane, with mainplanes in front and a stabilising tail-unit. (Later, it was Pénaud who revived interet in Cayley, whom he greatly admired, and re-established him in the minds of inventors.) Pénaud worked out both the theory and practice of stability, and went on to make and publish many fruitful suggestions and inventions in both aviation and aerostation, as well as the method of instantaneous photography which Marey used soon after for his bird photographs, and which led to the stroboscopic technique. In 1874 Pénaud also made a successful and popular little ornithopter model. But the crowning achievement of his short career was his design—with the assistance of his mechanic Paul Gauchot—for a full-size amphibious tractor two-seat monoplane, which was patented in 1876, but never built (Fig. 44). It incorporated all his ideas for the practical aeroplane of the future: twin tractor propellers, counter-rotating; elliptical wings with curved surfaces, set at a slight dihedral angle and at a 2 degree angle of incidence; twin rear elevators; vertical fixed fin, to which the rear rudder was attached; a glass-domed cockpit; a prophetic single control column to operate the elevators and rudder; a retractable undercarriage with rubber or compressed-air shock absorbers; tail-skid; and other ingenious features, including flight instruments such as a compass, a level, a barometer (as altimeter), etc. The movable trailing edges which were also provided were not ailerons, as is so often said, but steering air-brakes to act as an auxiliary rudder (see page 40). The estimated weight was to be 2,640 lb. and the speed 60 m.p.h. It was, as Dollfus says, "un magistral brevet d'aviation". Pénaud's work became widely known, and was one of the main formative influences in aviation history: he did, indeed, leave behind him an achievement "marked entirely by genius (entièrement marquée du génie)".

From now until the end of the century, the idea of the inherently stable aeroplane—the machine which resists any forces which tend to disturb its equilibrium, and which automatically returns to equilibrium in flight if disturbed—becomes a pre-occupation with the European experimenters, equal to their efforts to secure an engine of satisfactory power–weight ratio. Inherent stability is, of course, a relative term covering an infinite variety of degrees of stability—in pitch, yaw and roll—and it was not until Farnborough's *B.E.2C* of 1913 that satisfactory all-round inherent stability was first attained in a flying machine. As the only feasible flying machines were for long to remain models, it was obvious they they would not fly successfully unless they were inherently stable. Thus inherent stability became an *idée fixe* with the French inventors, which tended to blind them to the fact that the more stability which was built into an aeroplane, the more difficult would it be to control and manoeuvre, once a human pilot was on board to fly it. This idiom of inherent stability—especially longitudinal—so necessary for model flying, was mistakenly but understandably overdone when it was carried over to full-size aircraft: it hindered and held back the European pioneers until the Wright brothers at last recognised it as a stumbling block, and designed a specially unstable aeroplane, whose equilibrium in the air had to be maintained continuously by the pilot's skill; and which, as a result, was as sensitive and responsive as a horse to its rider. After these extremes, and after the achievement of the stable *B.E.2c*, proper compromises were progressively worked out to fit the varying needs required.

In the fixed-wing field, after Pénaud, there are various other inventors to consider, some of importance. In 1873 Charles Renard tested a superposed wing model glider—with ten wings—based on Wenham's idea, with an ingenious device for maintaining directional stability by a pendulum operating two winglets which acted as steering air-brakes.

Next, about 1874, comes the world's first powered take-off by a piloted full-size aeroplane, designed and built by Félix Du Temple, but it was down an inclined ramp; which was not a powered flight, but a highly creditable performance: the pilot was a young sailor, and the machine is believed to have been powered by a form of hot-air engine, which was later exchanged for a steam engine: but the machine was apparently not tested with it. The approximate configuration, with tractor propeller, swept-forward wings, tailplane and rudder beneath, is shown here (Fig. 42).

From 1874, there survives the elegant little 'aeroplane kite' made by Otto Lilienthal in his preliminary studies towards gliding (Fig. 40). And a certain Monsieur Biot claims inclusion as a courageous amateur who built himself a glider (1879), and succeeded in becoming slightly airborne on a number of occasions: his machine, in the Paris Musée de l'Air, is the earliest surviving full-scale heavier-than-air aircraft in the world, which is an odd distinction.

Victor Tatin (1843–1913) was later to become one of the most respected of aviation's 'elder statesmen', whose writings in *L'Aérophile* and elsewhere came to be regarded as highly authoritative during the rebirth of European aviation in 1902–08. In 1876 he had begun by making rubber-driven ornithopter models; but in 1879 turned finally to the fixed-wing model flying machine, and his fame mostly depends on his one model of that year, a twin tractor propellered monoplane on three wheels, with a spreading tail and a barrel-like fuselage which held the compressed air by which the little motor was worked (Pl. V): it had a span of 1·9 metres (6·2 ft.). The machine was flown tethered to a central pole, and flew for over 15 metres at an 8–10 degree angle of incidence. Tatin was especially a 'model' man, and, even when he was in the thick of the Wright controversies of 1903–06, paid almost no attention to flight-control. This little model of 1879 did not represent any significant advance, but it was widely publicised and was a good advertisement for the modern-type monoplane configuration.

It is rather surprising to find—in the 1870's—the sudden rise of the tandem monoplane idea, which had been dormant since Walker's design of 1831. We first have a vague tandem design by Prigent in 1871, which was an ornithopter intended to imitate the two pairs of wings of the dragonfly. Then, in the same year, there is a visionary and even less plausible design by Danjard, who wanted the best of all possible worlds: he proposed a machine with a triangular sail fixed on to the front pair of his tandem fixed wings, and a pentagonal sail fixed to the trailing edge of the rear pair: between the wings were two propulsive flappers; and, for good measure, there was a pusher propeller out back, above the rear sail.

But the most important of the tandems was the rectilinear model made

45

and tested by D. S. Brown in 1873–74 (Fig. 39): Brown was a member of the Aeronautical Society, and conducted tests in longitudinal stability with a number of tandem-wing monoplane models.[1] It is just possible—but unlikely—that he knew about Danjard's design, but he almost certainly would have known of Walker's design of 1831: as Brown's illustrated report of his model tests appeared in the Society's Annual Report for 1874, and it is known that Langley both read these reports and visited England before adopting the tandem configuration for his own machines, it is more than probable that it was Brown who influenced Langley, especially in view of the similarity in layout.

In 1874, Thomas Moy in England completed, and in 1875 tested, a large model steam-driven tandem-wing monoplane, called the *Aerial Steamer*, in tethered flight around the fountain at the Crystal Palace (Fig. 43): Moy, an engineer and patent agent, had come to aviation from ballooning, and since 1865 had devoted himself to the study of aeroplanes. The front wing had an area of 50 square feet and the rear one 64 square feet, a total lifting surface of 114 square feet. The 3-h.p. steam engine drove two large fan-type propellers of 6 feet diameter between the wings; and in June 1875 the machine lifted 6 inches off the track during a test, the first time a steam-driven model aeroplane had raised itself off the ground. Its total weight was some 120 lb. There was, however, little of originality about Moy's *Aerial Steamer*, and—especially regarding its configuration—it did not influence anybody thereafter. The machine was later wrecked by a storm; Moy rebuilt it in what he hoped was an improved form; but there is no news of it. But in 1879 he demonstrated to the Aeronautical Society, of which he was a member, a sophisticated little rubber-driven tandem-wing model with two tractor propellers, and the front wing very much larger than the rear one.

In the year 1877 there are the first models[2]—tandem monoplanes with two rubber-driven pusher propellers—to be made by W. Kress, who was to build a full-size flying-boat in 1901.

The 'flappers' came strangely though fruitlessly into prominence during the 1870's, but mostly in the role of model-makers. Returning to 1870, there was an ingenious freak made by Gustave Trouvé (Fig. 37), which was probably the first ornithopter ever to fly: it was flapped by twelve blank revolver cartridges automatically fired into a Bourdon tube, which beat down the wings, the spring action of the tube bringing them up again for the next 'shot': it could fly in this way, after a mid-air launch, for over 60 metres (say 200 feet). It was above this model that an auxiliary lifting canopy (or hood) was fixed, as was mentioned in connection with Gusmão. Trouvé, after contemplating and mercifully abandoning a larger version of his ornithopter, took to investigating fixed-wing flight, and between 1881 and 1886 carried out research into propellers: but his work was not important.

In 1871 Jobert, after experimenting with various sources of power for his

---

[1] It has been a little confusing for historians to find that Brown logically called his tandem monoplane type of model an 'aero-bi-plane'.

[2] One of these models was the second (Du Temple's was the first) to take off the ground under its own power.

Fig. 40. Lilienthal's 'aeroplane' kite: 1874

Fig. 41. De Groof's semi-ornithopter on which he was killed: 1874

Fig. 42. Approximate appearance of the first powered aeroplane to take off, but down a ramp, by Du Temple: *c.* 1874

Fig. 43. Large steam-powered tandem-wing model, by Moy: 1875

47

models, applied rubber in tension for his first two-wing ornithopter; and then next year (1872) twisted rubber to power his four-wing model ornithopter. Also in 1872, the indefatigable Hureau de Villeneuve—who in all made some 300 ornithopter models—built his most successful 'bird', with two beating wings powered by twisted rubber.

It was Profesor J. Bell Pettigrew, in his *Animal Locomotion* (published in 1873) who was one of the few investigators since Cayley to realise that the tips of birds' wings act like airscrews. One cannot tell how many men took to making ornithopter models after learning this, except for the device specifically suggested by Dandrieux (see below). Most of the model ornithopters were made on the principle of having a rigid leading edge, which beat up and down, with a flexible part aft: it therefore produced both lift and thrust components.

By a curious coincidence, another book on birds and animals was also published in Paris in 1873: this was E. J. Marey's *La Machine Animale*, of which a translation, under the title *Animal Mechanism*, was published in London the following year. Marey was to lay the foundations of cinematography, and this book included rapid-sequence photographs of flying birds; it was a book which was to be closely studied by the Wright brothers. Marey's work was already known to English readers through a translation of his lectures published in the Annual Reports of the Aeronautical Society (1871 and 1872); he later extended his interests to photographing the flow of air over variously shaped bodies, by means of smoke in a wind tunnel, thus introducing a method of aerodynamic research which was to prove of great value to later experimenters.

In 1874 a full-size semi-ornithopter, with some parachute-like features, appeared on the scene: it was built and tested by a Belgian shoemaker, Vincent de Groof, who had for some years been unable to persuade the Continental authorities to allow him to experiment in public. The machine had two wings, and a 20-foot 'tail', to be flapped by arms and legs. So he came to London, and ascended beneath a balloon from Cremorne Gardens on June 29th 1874; but he made no free descent. On July 9th of the same year, he went up again, and cut himself loose from the balloon at quite a low altitude; but the 220 square feet of his surfaces was far too much for him to hold down: the wings and tail streamed up, and de Groof plunged to his death (Fig. 41). This was the third fatality in history of a heavier-than-air machine, after Cocking (1837) and Letur (1854).

In 1874 Pénaud built a rubber-driven model ornithopter; he was followed in 1875 by Tatin, using the same method. And, in 1877, de Louvrié proposed what he called *Anthropornis*, an ornithopter with its wings to be flapped by a steam or petroleum motor, with a spring device to rise them. Then there was Dandrieux suggesting an outlandish man-operated ornithopter to imitate the airscrew action of a bird's wings, as described by Pettigrew. And F. W. Brearey—Secretary of the Aeronautical Society—making, and flying in 1879 with limited success, a 'wave action aeroplane' model, or better, an 'undulator'; in this rubber-driven model, two tapering pieces of fabric were fixed, one to either side of a pole (with tailplane attached), with rigid spars attached to their leading edges: when these bars

Fig. 44. Patent drawings for a tractor monoplane amphibian, by Pénaud and Gauchot: 1876

beat up and down, an undulating movement was communicated to the fabric, like a skate fish, and the model was propelled forward.

The helicopterists were also active in the 1870's. In 1871 Pomés and De la Pauze suggested a helicopter with a huge adjustable-pitch rotor to be driven by gunpowder. Renoir in 1872 experimented fruitlessly with a screw of 15 feet diameter which he rotated by pedals. And Achenbach, in 1874, designed an outsize helicopter driven by steam, with added propellers for propulsion.[1] In 1877 Emmanuel Dieuaide experimented with a large contra-rotating model, driven by steam, the boiler being on the ground and the steam taken to the machine through a hose. Also in 1877, Melikoff designed a helicopter model shaped like a helical spearhead, which would screw itself up, and parachute down; but his suggested motor and fuel were remarkable, in that he planned for it to "be rotated by a gas turbine, consisting of eight curved chambers, into each of which charges of the vapour of ether mixed with air were to be successively exploded by an electric spark, and the charge allowed to expand in doing work" (Pl. V). Still in 1877, we find the second—after Phillips—successful steam-driven helicopter model built by the Italian engineer, Enrico Forlanini, later to become well known as an airship designer (Pl. V): Forlanini's machine weighed (loaded) only 7·7 lb., because he hit on the idea of heating up the boiler until the requisite pressure was obtained, then attaching it to the machine and opening the throttle: there were two large contra-rotating two-bladed rotors, the upper one worked by the engine, the lower one fixed to the engine and framework: the machine would rise to some 42 feet, and stay in the air for 20 seconds. In 1878 a French engineer, P. Castel, built an elaborate compressed-air-driven helicopter model weighing 49 lb., which had eight rotors arranged in two sets of four and counter-rotating: the compressed-air reservoir was kept on the ground and connected to a hose: but the machine was smashed against a wall, and wrecked, before any successful tests had been made; it was then abandoned. Finally, in 1878 and 1879, Dandrieux made and flew successfully a series of little 'butterfly' helicopter toys worked by rubber; most of these consisted of one or more rotors, with a butterfly-like wing below, or in the middle, or on top: these machines would screw up into the air and glide down (Fig. 45).

Following Renard's 'decaplane' of 1872–73 an obscure Briton named Linfield made a somewhat similar model to the Renard machine and tested it on a railway truck drawn by a locomotive.

In view of the decisive role in aviation soon to be played by the United States, it should be said here that she was as yet too far from the main stream of endeavour to properly participate. But sporadic inventions had been, and were now being, made there; ornithopter patents were granted to W. F. Quimby (1869), A. P. Keith (1870), F. X. Lamboley (1876), M. H. Murrell (1877), and I. M. Wheeler (1887). And helicopter designs were put forward by L. C. Crowell (1862), J. Wootton (1866), J. B. Ward (1876) and others.

Last to be mentioned in this decade is an engine which one day was to

---

[1] This patented design was also the first in history to include a small vertical rotor to counteract the rotation of the fuselage.

make aviation possible, the first four-stroke cycle petrol engine, invented in 1876 by the German engineer N. A. Otto; it was the world's first practical internal-combustion engine to use liquid fuel, and it marked a great stride forward in engine technology.

The importance to aviation of fuel technology cannot be over-emphasised, but it is seldom mentioned. Although petroleum has been known for thousands of years, from the Egyptians onwards, the beginning of the modern petroleum industry, after a tentative start in Britain, is generally considered to be the drilling of the oil well at Titusville (Pennsylvania), U.S.A. in 1859, to produce much-needed kerosene for lamps. What today is called petrol (or gasoline) was subsequently a by-product of distillation, and not at first readily marketable.

Significant dates in other fields (1870's)

1870–71 Franco–Prussian War, and use of photo-microfilms for transmission of letters, etc. by pigeon.
1870's The practical electric motor and dynamo are introduced.
1870's Principal cities of the world are now linked by telegraph.
1871 German Empire is established under the influence of Prussia.
1876 Otto invents the four-stroke cycle gas engine.
1876 Bell invents the practical telephone.

8. The 1880's

THE 1880's might appear to provide a lull after the vivid and varied activity of the previous decade. It seemed as if a saturation of effort had been achieved amongst inventors—except for Phillips—and that no vital step was taken, or forward drive made. But this decade now shows up as a period when the lesser men were indeed abandoning problems they found too daunting; whereas for the larger figures, conscious that the epoch of speculation and model-making was almost played out, it was a time of widespread germination. The latter, some of them less gifted than others, began acquiring a more mature vision of what lay ahead, and started to think and plan with the whole picture of human flight in view rather than isolated lines of research. These men were aware of a new climate in scientific thought, and were now passing from romantic speculation to a mood of confidence and determination.

To usher in the decade, E. Dieuaide of Paris published in 1880 one of the important 'propaganda' items of the century, in the form of a large wallchart entitled *Tableau d'Aviation* which illustrated, with a brief note on each, over fifty heavier-than-air designs from Leonardo da Vinci to date: it was very popular—as was a companion chart of aerostation—and showed the would-be pioneers a large variety of configurations, many of which were constantly republished thereafter.

In 1881 there was published in Paris yet another work on bird flight, *L'Empire de l'Air* by L. P. Mouillard (1834–97), which was—after d'Esterno—the second major source of inspiration to subsequent pioneers on the subject of soaring and gliding flight: it was later read by Chanute and the Wrights, in a partial English translation, which appeared as a publication of the Smithsonian Institution in 1893, under the title *The Empire of the Air*. Mouillard, isolated in Cairo, continued to make practical gliding experiments in machines of his own design and construction, none of which were successful. In 1897 he took out a patent for his last glider type (1896), in which it was alleged on his behalf that he had introduced control in roll by means of ailerons: this was untrue, as all he suggested were steering air-brakes, as Pénaud and others had thought of, which had nothing in common with aileron action (see page 40). Mouillard had been building ineffectual gliders since 1856.

There are, for the first time in this century, significant items to record in Russia. First, in 1881, a suggestion was put forward for a rocket aeroplane, with a swivelling jet for both vertical and horizontal propulsion: this came from N. I. Kibalchitch, when he was in prison and awaiting execution as one of the assassins of Czar Alexander II. Then, still in Russia, there was the much advertised alleged flight by a Captain of the Imperial Russian Navy,

Alexander F. Mozhaiski, who had designed an aeroplane based on Henson which was patented in 1881. The actual aeroplane seems to have been completed in 1883, and tested in 1884 (not 1882, as often said), at Krasnoye Selo, near St. Petersburg, with an anonymous passive pilot (Fig. 46). The machine was a steam-powered monoplane—the engine was English[1]—with cruciform tail-unit, driven by one large tractor propeller, and two small pusher propellers let into the trailing edges of the wings: it took off down a 'ski-jump' ramp, and was said to have been airborne under this impetus for some 20–30 metres (say 65–100 feet): there was no question of a sustained controlled flight. This has been claimed as the first powered flight, which of course it was not; nor was it even the first assisted powered take-off, which stands to the credit of Du Temple, about 1874. But it can claim to be the second assisted powered take-off in history. Mozhaiski seems to have abandoned further testing of his machine.

In 1883, a Frenchman M. A. Goupil designed and constructed a tractor monoplane—minus the engine and propeller—with a bird-shaped fuselage, and deeply cambered bird-shaped wings: he had already designed an engine for this machine, but not built it. He tested the airframe tethered, and obtained very interesting results; in a 13-m.p.h. breeze it lifted itself and two men, a total weight of 400 lb. This project was not proceeded with, but he pubished in 1884 his book, *La Locomotion Aérienne*, in which he set down his theories—including the belief that the stability of a bird was dependent upon the curve of its stomach—and the finished design for his new monoplane, which was never built. Its most interesting feature were the two elevons set on the fuselage just ahead of, and well below the wings (Pl. V); the chief function of these surfaces was to co-operate with the horizontal movable tail to act as elevators; but they were also to be for control in roll, as ailerons: this was the third time an inventor had had a simple idea of control in roll by ailerons; but, without simultaneous rudder action, which was not in Goupil's mind, they would probably have been ineffective if the machine had ever been built and tested. Goupil and his design played a small part in the Wright patent controversy, when Zahm unsuccessfully attempted to show that Goupil had anticipated part of the Wright's control system.

Also in 1883, the first serious but not significant American pioneer, John J. Montgomery, built his first monoplane glider which was destroyed just after its first take-off. In 1885 he built a second machine, with spring-hinged gust-dampers, which was unsuccessful; and in 1886, he built his third, with bird-form wings which could be made to rotate about their span-wise axis; but this too was a failure. Montgomery was then to wait until 1905, before starting on the construction of tandem-wing gliders *à la* Langley.

In 1884 there occurred an event of the utmost importance in aviation, when there first appeared on the scene one of the great men of flying history, Horatio F. Phillips (1845–1926); for in this year he was granted his first patent for what became the true foundation of modern aerofoil design, i.e. his two-surface wing sections (Fig. 47). He had been considering and

---

[1] This engine was published in *Engineering* for May 6th 1881, where it was entitled, "Compound engine for aeronautical purposes, constructed by Messrs. Ahrbecker, Son, and Hamkens, Engineers, London".

experimenting with aerofoils, and was concentrating on designing different aerofoil sections and testing them at various angles of attack. He built a wind tunnel in which the airflow was induced by steam injection—the first practical wind tunnel since that made for the Aeronautical Society—and which anticipated the injector drives on supersonic wind tunnels today. Phillips conducted experiments in which curved wings of "every conceivable form and combination of forms were tried", and took out his first, and most influential, patent in 1884; and his second in 1891. Phillips called his creations "blades for deflecting air", which were double-surfaced aerofoils of differing thickness and camber; he proved his belief that if a thick cambered wing is used, and if it is curved more on the upper surface than on the lower, then the greater part of the lift generated is due to a reduced pressure (suction) above, and the lesser to the positive pressure underneath. He made a number of varying wing sections to demonstrate these forces, and was later to build two large models and two full-size powered machines to show them in actual practice. The presence of an area of low pressure above a cambered wing had been surmised by Cayley; Phillips now properly established the facts, and published them widely; and thereby exerted a powerful influence on aviation thereafter (see also page 68 and Fig. 51).

It was in the year 1885 that the small world of aeronautics first heard the name of Lawrence Hargrave (1850–1915); but the news came from New South Wales, Australia, and it was the fact of his working so far from the main stream of aviation endeavour, that prevented this remarkable inventor from rising to the heights of men like Lilienthal, Pilcher, and the Wrights; for he was of their calibre. Hargrave's main contributions will be described in the next section but one, but it was in 1882 that he first dedicated himself to aviation, and 1885 when he read his first paper on aeronautics to the Royal Society of New South Wales, of which he had been a member since 1877, and to which he was to contribute no less than twenty-three papers on subjects which ran from his trochoidal theory of propulsion to the active design and building of aeroplanes. By 1884 he had experimented with some fifty rubber-driven models, and had firmly established his belief in propulsion by flappers. His flappers imitated the action of the primary feathers of a bird, in that each was supported rigidly by a spar on the leading edge, and was unsupported aft: when the spar beat downwards, the flapper surface "heeled" upwards (as Cayley described it), thus producing a thrust component forwards. Hargrave—somewhat unnecessarily—termed this movement trochoidal: it was, in fact, a simple twisting of the surfaces. One of the most successful of his models is shown here (Pl. VI): all his model propulsion until 1888 was by stretched rubber. In 1889 Hargrave built the first rotary engine to be applied to aeronautics, a three-cylinder unit driven by compressed air. His model aeroplanes up to the turn of the decade consisted of elongated dihedrally-set flat surfaces of an aspect ratio far less than unity, designed to trochoid inversely to the flappers.

The idea of the "appareil mixte"—aerostation-cum-aviation—was represented in the 1880's by a number of machines never built, particularly by the Frenchman Olivier, who suggested in 1884 an elongated dirigible with a flat horizontal tail and large dihedrally set wings attached to the top of the

Fig. 45. Rubber-powered helicopter toy in the form of a butterfly, by Dandrieux: 1878–79

Fig. 46. General arrangement drawings of Mozhaiski's steam-powered monoplane, which was tested near St. Petersburg: c. 1884

Fig. 47 Phillips' patent drawings of double-surface aerofoil sections: 1884

envelope. And by a Mr. John Beuggar, who patented in 1888 a navigable balloon built in "the shape of a biconvex lens", and equipped with two propellers in the car slung beneath: "the lifting power of the balloon alone is not sufficient to cause an ascent, so that it is only when the propellers force the machine ahead, causing the balloon to act as an aëroplane, that flight can be accomplished."

In 1886 a Monsieur de Sanderval in France experimented with a tail-less glider tethered by a cable.

A little-known machine was completed, also in 1886 by F. J. Stringfellow—John Stringfellow's son—but apparently not tested successfully: this was a powered model biplane, the first in history, which remained unknown to the other pioneers, and did not influence aviation development.

The great aviation master of the later 19th century, Otto Lilienthal, had been maturing his ideas about human flight during this decade; and in 1889 he published one of the classics of aviation history, *Der Vogelflug als Grundlage der Fliegekunst* (Bird Flight as the Basis of Aviation), in which he discussed the flight of birds and—of pivotal importance in aviation history—gave tables of air pressures on curved surfaces at different angles of attack. The epoch-making gliding work of Lilienthal will be described in the section after next.

The flappers still persisted with their dreams, paper conceptions, and machines: there was John K. Smythies in 1882 with his steam-driven ornithopter; Pompeien Piraud in the same year in France who actually built his bat-formed ornithopter, intended to be attached beneath a balloon appropriately named *L'Espérance*: William Cornelius in England in 1884, with his design for a manually-operated ornithopter, with a foot-operated tail; and the Frenchman Pichancourt with his little rubber-driven ornithopter models in 1889. Coming almost within the realm of the flappers was another Frenchman named Hérard, who had built about 1888 a huge machine consisting of five frames of narrow slats which rotated on a horizontal axle, and remained firmly on the ground. In 1888, a curious 'first' in aviation may be noted, when the first photographs were automatically taken from a kite, a device invented in France by Arthur Battut, and operated in this year at Labruguière (Tarn).

The last year of the decade (1889) also saw the beginnings of practical experiments and research in aviation by Sir Hiram Maxim, S. P. Langley, and—above all—Octave Chanute, all of whose activities were to mature in the 1890's, and will be discussed in the appropriate sections to come. Maxim apart, this represents the true inauguration of aviation in the United States, which will soon gain the final ascendency.

Among important matters other than aviation, which should be noted during this decade, are the following: the invention (1884) by Charles Parsons of the steam turbine, which was one of the greatest achievements in the history of technology, and was also to lead indirectly to the practical jet propulsion of aeroplanes in the late 1930's and 1940's. Then comes the first near-practical airship, *La France*, built by Charles Renard and A. C. Krebs in 1884, and propelled by one huge bow propeller driven by a Gramme electric motor delivering 9 h.p.: she made some six flights in 1884 and 1885, the best of which was a 23-minute circular flight of 5 miles on August 9th 1884, during which a maximum speed of 14·5 m.p.h. was attained. Next year (1885), there occurred a much more important event for aviation, when the first practical petrol engines were built independently by Benz and Daimler: the high-speed Daimler engine was by far the most important. Also in that year the first practical motor car built by Benz took to the road (Pl. V): it was automobilisme that alone was to develop the petrol engine, and bring it to a state of sufficiently satisfactory lightness and power as to permit of its application to aviation.

The automobile industry was later to become of vital concern to aviation, both for the engines it provided, and for the engineers who were to be on hand in great numbers by the time aeroplanes had become practical. The internal combustion engine goes back to its origin in the Lenoir gas engine of 1860, which operated on coal gas. Next, in 1876, Otto introduced the four-stroke cycle petrol engine. Although Gottlieb Daimler had in 1884 invented the light, high-speed petrol engine (he first fitted one to a bicycle in 1885) in which year Carl Benz (who had also been developing his petrol engine) built the first successful motor car: the Benz car was not a tricycle, as sometimes claimed, but a robust three-wheel vehicle to seat two. In 1886, Daimler produced his first motor car, which was a four-wheeler.

Significant dates in other fields (1880's)

1880's	Dynamite now in general use in civil engineering.
1880's	National telephone networks are being developed.
1880's	Typewriters now in general office use.
1880's	Dry plate photography (which could record moving objects) now in general use, after its invention in 1871.
1881	House of Commons and Savoy Theatre are lit by electricity.
1882–88	Marey invents the cinematograph.
1884	Parsons invents the steam turbine.
1884	Maxim gun invented.
1885–86	Benz and Daimler independently introduce the first practical petrol engines and motor cars, the first being the Benz (1885).
1885	Rover safety bicycle is introduced, which leads to universal spread of cycling.
1886	Commercial production of aluminium by modern methods introduced.
1886	Linotype printing first used (in the U.S.A.).
1888	Dunlop introduces the pneumatic tyre.
1888	Eastman introduces his first Kodak camera, using celluloid roll-film.
1889	Eiffel Tower built in Paris.

9. *The Powered Prelude to Practical Flying: 1890–1903*

In the last decade before men were to fly in powered aeroplanes, three streams of endeavour were being gradually brought to fulfilment; the study of aerodynamics, including propellers—the "forces acting on bodies moving in air"—pilotage, and engine construction. Slowest came the engine, whose chief problem so far as flying was concerned remained its too great weight for the power produced, whether worked by steam, electricity, gas, oil or petrol. This lack of a suitable engine was keenly felt by all the experimenters, as the wiser of them realised their knowledge of aerodynamics and control depended for further advance on the lessons to be learnt in the air, especially with full-size aircraft manned by a pilot.

Looking back for a moment at the men who have been appearing on the aviation scene since the 1850's to date, they have mostly been of two types; (*a*) the academic inventors whose creations—sometimes ingenious, but more often wayward or visionary—were realised only on paper, and (*b*) the model-makers, who were content to experiment only in miniature. Only here and there have there been the descendants of the 'tower-jumpers' of old, who have tried to fly, such as Letur, Le Bris, and de Groof.

Now, as the dream of centuries comes near fulfilment, there are to be a growing number of new men—more skilled and sophisticated—who are determined to take to the air: but among such pioneers, who are to be willing to risk life and limb in full-size experiments, two vitally significant streams will appear, whose whole concepts of aviation are distinct from one another; (1) the stream of what may be called 'chauffeurs', and (2) the stream of true 'airmen'. The chauffeur attitude to aviation regards the flying machine as a winged automobile, to be driven into the air by brute force of engine and propeller, so to say, and sedately steered about the sky as if it were a land—or even marine—vehicle which had simply been transferred from a layer of earth to a layer of air.

The true 'airman's' attitude was evident in the pilot's desire to identify himself with his machine—"je veux faire corps avec la machine", as Françoise Sagan puts it—or ride it like an expert horseman. The 'chauffeurs' came to devote themselves mainly to the pursuit of thrust and lift, and thereby proved singularly unfruitful: they invariably tried to take off in powered machines before they had any true idea of flight-control. Whereas the 'airmen' thought primarily in terms of control in the air, and quickly realised that the unpowered glider was the vehicle of choice, in which a man might emulate the technique of gliding birds, and learn to ride the air successfully before having himself precipitated into the atmosphere in a powered flying-machine without knowing what would happen, or what he should do, when once airborne. This distinction between chauffeurs and airmen was to prove pivotal in the final conquest of the air.

From now onwards, one can only afford to discuss the more important figures in aviation. Well-meaning and often talented eccentrics had played their part in sustaining interest and helping to create a suitable climate for development; there was to be no lack of them, even into our own century, but they no longer deserve either space or much credit, although the reader is asked to imagine them perpetually in the background. Also in the background must be left most of the dogged sceptics and disbelievers—some of them able scientists who should have known better—who continued to preach the impossibility of mechanical flight, even after it had been accomplished.

In this section will be discussed the men who concentrated mostly on the powered aeroplane, men who believed that mechanical flight was feasible, and who were determined to bring it about. Oddly enough, each of the three important figures suffered from one serious lack, one serious disability. The lack was the lack of a suitable engine, which led two of them away from the petrol engine (which they should have pursued) and back to the steam engine. The disability in each case was their inability to view the problem of mechanical flight as a whole, a a collective problem involving lift, thrust, and—above all—control. They had neither the mentality nor the vision of true airmen, a psychological disability which led them to put the aviation cart before the horse, to neglect the basic problems of control, and to take the chauffeur's point of view. As mentioned above, this distinction is fundamental, as will be seen from the events to come: it is the distinction which was to allow the gliding pioneers to lead the way direct to powered flying, and rob the dogged and ingenious 'power pioneers' of success.

Clément Ader

The first major 'powered' figure of the 1890's was the distinguished French electrical engineer Clément Ader (1841–1925) who became interested in aviation, and might—if he had been less of a chauffeur than an airman—have played a powerful part in aviation history. He made a study of bird and bat flight, had in 1873 experimented with the lift of a 'glider' anchored to the ground by four ropes—he never made a gliding flight—and in 1882 started the construction of his first powered aeroplane, the *Éole*, which was completed in 1890. He developed a very fine type of powerful but light steam engine, which was his major achievement; but it often appears that his conception of the aeroplane was as romantic and unrealistic as the conception of his engines was practical. The *Éole* was a bat-formed monoplane with great canopied wings of 15 metres span, and a single steam engine of 18–20 h.p. driving one tractor propeller (Fig. 48). In the grounds of a château at Armainvilliers, near Gretz (S. et M.) on October 9th 1890, the *Éole* made a take-off from level ground under its own power, piloted by Ader, which covered about 50 metres (say 165 feet). This achievement was highly creditable, and was the first piloted powered aeroplane to raise itself from the ground without assistance; but it was rightly accepted by Ader—and by historians ever since—as only 'tentative', and in no sense a sustained or controlled flight. Also in 1890, Ader took out a patent for the *Éole*: a study of this, of the *Avion III* (which survives), and of Gabriel Voisin's account of an interview with him, shows clearly that Ader had only the most rudimentary conception of flight-control and of stability, thinking of the former at best in terms of varying the propulsive power to climb or descend, with the addition of a rudder, and (later) differential airscrew speeds for steering. There was no elevator. He tried to reproduce mechanically as many of the movements of a bat's wings as possible, except for their propulsive flapping, to allow of complicated adjustments in flight which he at first considered necessary for aerodynamic reasons. To make matters worse, Ader put the seat for the pilot at the back, behind the boiler, which necessitated his leaning far out to left or right to see where he was going. In view of Ader being known to have in his house a file of the journal *l'Aéronaute*, and various works on aeronautics, containing all the relevant data about past and contemporary aeroplane designs, it is difficult to understand how he came to design such an aircraft, and even harder to comprehend why he did not abandon such a type of machine when he came to build his next aircraft.

In 1892 Ader was commissioned by the French War Ministry to build a new aeroplane; and, in spite of his later remarks to the contrary, received a generous subsidy to that end. He abandoned *Avion II* before completion— he gave the word 'avion' for aeroplane to the French language—and set about building *Avion III*. Instead of adopting a monoplane of contemporary configuration and controls, and pursuing the rapidly developing petrol engine, Ader kept to his great canopied single-surface bat-wings, of 17 metres span, and fitted two of his finely made 20-h.p. steam engines driving two tractor propellers whose discs, however, overlapped: the total weight with pilot, was about 400 k.g. (say 880 lb.). Also in spite of the wealth of knowledge available, Ader still did not fit an elevator, and relied as before on increase or decrease of power; he still sat at the back, and again behind the boiler installation. Although he still paid next to no attention to flight-control, he drastically reduced the variety of wing movements, and the wings could only now be moved in one manner, i.e. they could be swung backwards or forwards in the horizontal plane to shift the centre of pressure; but they could only be altered by many turns of a handle and screw: there was a small rudder, which was linked to the rear (steering) wheel in order to keep the machine on the track: he also incorporated a differential speed device for the two airscrews to aid in steering. It was, indeed, an almost chimerical machine to see the light as late as 1897, considering the numerous and advanced designs which had become available by that time in France and Britain, and which Ader knew well of (Pl. VI). To make matters worse, he chose to test the machine on a circular track, which made any proper trial most difficult; whichever way the wind was blowing he had to suffer it from all sides as he went round in a circle: this was, indeed, asking for trouble.

Avion III was tested only twice, on October 12th and 14th 1897, on this specially prepared circular track at the military ground at Satory, near Versailles. On October 12th the machine was simply run once round the track and remained on its wheels all the time. On October 14th, after a short run along the track, the *Avion*—while still on its wheels—was blown off the track on to the rough ground, slewed round, and came to a stop: Ader had wisely stopped the engines as soon as he felt himself being carried away. The details of both tests were conscientiously recorded in the official report written at the time by General Mensier, who witnessed both tests. Unfortunately, this report was not published until November 1910, and no one outside the War Ministry knew the true story of the tests until that date.

Meanwhile, in 1906, annoyed by an ill-considered statement by Ernest Archdeacon that Santos-Dumont was the first to fly, and that he (Ader) had not flown in 1890, Ader suddenly—in November 1906—claimed for the first time (*a*) that he made another test with *Éole* in 1891, in which he had flown for 100 metres; (*b*) that on October 12th 1897, he had made a number of hops; and (*c*) that on October 14th he had made an "uninterrupted flight of 300 metres" (say 985 feet): all these claims are demonstrably mendacious. Owing to the refusal of the French War Ministry to publish Mensier's official report, these claims by Ader succeeded in gaining wide credence, not only at the time, but ever since: they have unfortunately been accepted by many writers, despite the publication of Mensier's report in 1910.

Charles Dollfus—who had the official task of examining Ader's papers after his death—has declared categorically that "Ader n'a pas volé un seul instant à Satory au cours des expériences des 12 et 14 Octobre 1897 (Ader did not fly for a single instant at Satory during the tests of October 12th and 14th 1897)."[1]

Ader's machines seem to us like some romantic prehistoric creatures which have survived into another age; with his great canopied single-surface wings, his steam engines, and his extraordinary lack of proper flight-controls or stabilising surfaces, he was a bold, but even then outmoded, pioneer in 1890; but in 1897, he was a veritable anachronism. He influenced nobody and nothing in aviation history, as he was always too far from the productive lines of research and development which were being pursued by the advanced pioneers.

Sir Hiram Maxim

England can almost parallel the story of Ader in the activities of the expatriate American inventor Sir Hiram S. Maxim (1840–1916), who was already well known as the inventor of the Maxim gun. But, unlike Ader, Maxim was never truly concerned with the problem of practical flying; for he set himself only "to build a flying machine that would lift itself from the ground", not a flying machine that would fly. He started in the late 1880's with the testing of aerofoils in a wind tunnel and on a whirling arm, and also experimented with propellers. He also developed a remarkably light steam

---

[1] For a detailed survey of the Ader claims, see the present writer's Science Museum publication entitled *Clément Ader: his Flight-Claims and his Place in History* (1968).

engine. Then, in 1889 and 1891 he took out somewhat vague patents for his proposed vehicle.

In 1893 he built the machine in the grounds of Baldwyns Park, Kent. It was not in any true sense a flying machine, but what one might now call a huge 'lift test rig' (Pl. VI). It was basically a biplane, with the outer wing panels set at a pronounced dihedral angle, and two monoplane elevators, one in front and one behind: the total lifting area was no less than 4,000 square feet. Maxim equipped this machine with two 180 h.p. steam engines, each driving a pusher propeller of 17·8 feet diameter; there was a four-wheel 'undercarriage' of steel wheels which ran along a straight railway track of 1,800 feet; in addition, there were four extra raised wheels on outriggers which, if the machine rose more than about 2 feet, engaged a wooden guard rail on either side directly above them, and restrained the vehicle from rising any higher. The total weight of this monster rig, including its three-man crew, was some 8,000 lb., thus giving a wing-loading of about 2 lb. per square foot.

On the third test run, on July 31st 1894, Maxim had the boiler pressure at 320 lb. per square inch; and after running along the track for 600 feet, the outrigger wheels were all engaged with their upper rails, and the machine was airborne: but, soon after, a rear outrigger axletree broke, and the machine fouled the guard rails, whereupon Maxim shut off steam and brought it to a stop. Although the machine was rebuilt, and further tests and demonstrations were made during 1894–95, that was virtually the end of Maxim's practical work in aviation until 1910 (which see), when he built a machine which never succeeded in leaving the ground.[1] He had spent, on his own admission, £30,000.

It had all been time and money wasted: Maxim's contribution to aviation was virtually nil, and he influenced nobody. Owing to his reputation as an inventor much attention is still often paid to Maxim's aeronautical work; but even the older and generous-minded aeronautical historians, such as J. L. Pritchard and M. J. B. Davy, can find little to say for him: the former speaks of Maxim's "great and expensive and not very useful experiments"; and the latter writes that "the value of his work in regard to mechanical flight seems to lie mainly in his demonstration that the steam engine complete with boiler, etc., could be lightened to weigh from 8 to 9 lb. per h.p. without fuel and water". He was not only chauffeur-minded, but was not in the least interested in the practical problems of flying: he was concerned with lift and thrust, and demonstrated their workings; but that was all, and it was in no way original.

In his book *Natural and Artificial Flight*, published late in 1908, he blandly stated that:

"it is very gratifying to me to know that all the successful flying machines of to-day are built on the lines which I had thought out at that time [i.e. 1893–94], and found to be the best. All have superposed aeroplanes of great length from port to starboard, all

---

[1] Maxim's machine is sometimes seen in photographs, minus its outer wing-panels; most of these are of the machine when it was used to run members of the public up and down the track, for a local charity, later in the year, when these panels were purposely removed.

have fore and aft horizontal rudders,[1] and all are driven with screw propellers. . . . the fact that practically no essential departure has been made from my original lines, indicates to my mind that I had reasoned out the best type of a machine even before I commenced a stroke of the work."

It is hard to imagine anyone uttering more egregious nonsense, and it is sad to think that these remarks were made by a man who was certainly talented.

S. P. Langley

We come now to the first major aeronautical figure in the United States, Samuel Pierpont Langley (1834–1906), and he is in many ways a tragic figure: for he was ultimately beaten down by "contumely and ridicule" for his unsuccessful man-carrying aeroplane of 1903, and died a disappointed and bitter man. Langley was a distinguished mathematician and astronomer, and latterly became Secretary of the Smithsonian Institution, the great National Museum of the U.S.A. He had had an interest in the problems of human flight for many years, but when he finally had time to indulge it, he emerged as a talented but chauffeur-minded investigator. It was almost entirely his chauffeur attitude to aviation which caused the ruination of his later hopes and ambitions.

He had started his serious investigations of flight in 1887, when he constructed a whirling arm "of exceptional size, driven by a steam engine", in order to determine "what amount of mechanical power was requisite to sustain a given weight in the air, and make it advance at a given speed". He came to the conclusion that 1 h.p. could sustain over 200 lb. in the air, at a horizontal speed of somewhat over 60 feet per second. From 1887 onwards, apart from testing stuffed birds on his whirling arm in 1889, Langley made and tested some thirty to forty rubber-driven models which, with variations, reached nearly one hundred types. In this laborious work he was chiefly inspired by Pénaud. In 1892–93 he built his first four steam-driven models, starting oddly enough with *No. o*, then *Nos. 1, 2* and *3*, which were all failures, and which—with scant regard for etymology (see Glossary)—he called *Aerodromes*. His *No. 4* (1893) and *No. 5* (1894), both also steam driven, were also both failures. Langley had endless trouble, particularly with his catapult-launching mechanisms (on a house-boat by Quantico on the Potomac River), also with stability, and with wing-distortion in flight. By the end of 1894, he remarked sadly that "what might be called a real flight had not yet been secured". In 1895, he rebuilt the *No. 5* as a tandem-wing monoplane, to which configuration he now confined himself, and which it is almost certain was suggested by one of the tandem-wing models tested in England by D. S. Brown in 1873–74 (Fig. 39), and illustrated in the Aeronautical Society's Annual Report for 1874. Also in 1895, he completely rebuilt the *No. 4*, which now became *No. 6*. With these two models Langley at

---

[1] Incidentally, no aeroplane of the time—or previously—had both fore and aft elevators: Maxim could not have looked very carefully at the Wright machine (which had no horizontal surfaces aft), nor at the Voisins, which had rigid biplane tailplanes.

last achieved success next year on 6th May 1896 when *No. 5* made a flight of 3,300 feet, the first successful flight of any of the large models he had made; and on November 28th 1896, when the *No. 6* flew well for ¾ mile.

The *No. 5* had a wing area of about 65 square feet, a steam engine of about 1 h.p. driving two propellers amidships, and a cruciform tail-unit: its all-up weight was some 30 lb. (Fig. 49).

Satisfied at last that he had proved the possibility of mechanical flight, and realising that a full-size aircraft would entail much time and expense—although he would have liked to build one—Langley "made the firm resolution not to undertake the construction of a large man-carrying machine".

That Langley did ultimately build a man-carrying *Aerodrome* was due partly to the United States declaring war on Spain in 1898, but mostly to the far-sightedness of President McKinley himself, who was impressed by Langley's models, and appointed a military committee to report on them. The result was that Langley, in December 1898, accepted a bold and enlightened invitation by the War Department to build a man-carrier, with a $50,000 subsidy. The United States thus became the second of the world's governments—following France's commissioning of Ader in 1892—to officially support the building of aeroplanes.

Langley rightly regarded the engine as the main problem, and he commissioned (in 1898) Stephen M. Balzer of New York to build a petrol engine to weigh not more than 100 lb., and the output be not less than 12 h.p.: it was intended that two such engines should be used in the *Aerodrome*. In 1899, Balzer delivered a 5-cylinder air-cooled rotary engine, which derived from his automobile engine of 1894. But this Balzer engine, although its weight was within the prescribed limit, would not produce more than 8 h.p., and that for only a few minutes. The engine side of the *Aerodrome* was in the hands of Langley's assistant Charles Manly, who then tried to purchase a suitable engine from the trade, but without success. Manly, after unsuccessfully modifying Balzer's engine as a radial, took over the whole project, and himself redesigned it to conform with Langley's new demand that a single motor should be produced, to give 24 h.p. The redesigned engine (still five cylinders) was completed in December 1901, and first tested in January 1902, when it gave 52·4 h.p. at 950 r.p.m., with a power/weight ratio of 3·96 lb. per horse-power, a remarkable achievement. The name of Balzer was until recently almost unknown to historians, as it had been dishonourably suppressed by Manly in his official contribution to the Langley *Memoir on Mechanical Flight*; and Manly has therefore always received the entire credit for the engine. But credit should be about equally divided between the two men, as Balzer had a remarkable flair for the petrol engine, and certainly provided the basis of Manly's design. However, the Manly-Balzer engine would probably not have provided enough power for the *Aerodrome* in any case, as Mr. Robert Meyer, of the National Air and Space Museum, Washington, D.C., has shown (see Bibliography).

Langley first built—and completed in 1901—a quarter-size model powered by a small petrol engine, which ultimately gave 3·2 h.p. at 1,800 r.p.m.: this little engine was also supplied by Balzer as a rotary; and after it

PLATE V

a One of the most influential machines of history; Pénaud's stable model monoplane: 1871

b Forlanini's steam-driven model helicopter: 1877

c Melikoff's design for a gas-turbine helicopter screw: 1877

d Tatin's influential compressed-air-driven model: 1879

e Goupil's aeroplane design, with ailerons: 1884

f First practical automobile (Benz): 1885

PLATE VI

a One of Hargrave's compressed-air models: 1891

b Phillips' large multiplane model: 1893

c The box-kite, invented by Hargrave: 1893

d Maxim's steam-driven biplane test-rig: 1894

e Ader's unsuccessful steam-driven *Avion III*: 1897

f Langley's quarter-size petrol-driven model *Aerodrome*: 1901

Fig. 48. The first piloted aeroplane to take off under its own power, but not to fly: Ader's *Éole*: 1890

Fig. 49. Langley's steam-powered model *Aerodrome No. 5*: 1896

PROPELLER

PROPELLER

PENAUD TAIL

ENGINE

RUDDER   KEEL   AVIATOR'S CAR

Fig. 50. General arrangement drawings of Langley's full-size petrol-powered tandem-wing *Aerodrome A*: 1903 proved a failure, was also converted by Manly to a radial. This quarter-size model was also a failure: it could not sustain a horizontal flight-path when it was tested two or three times in June 1901; and only made a successful flight in August of 1903. But it takes a minor place in history as the first petrol-engined aeroplane to fly tentatively (1903) (Pl. VI). In May–June 1901, Langley fitted his quarter-size petrol-driven tandem-wing monoplane with another set of wings, transforming it into the world's first tandem-wing biplane. As with the original monoplane—to which configuration it returned—this temporary expedient was a failure. The official photograph of the biplane is dated June 11th 1901.

The full-size *Aerodrome*—the *Aerodrome 'A'* as it was called—was completed in 1903, and was a tandem-wing monoplane, with the wings set at a pronounced dihedral angle: the total lifting area was 1,040 square feet, and the span 48 feet. The pilot sat in a cockpit between, and below, the trailing edges of the front pair of wings, with the engine and twin propellers just behind him. Aft of the propellers, and set below the connecting boom of the aircraft—and connected with the cockpit by a keel—was a wedge-shaped vertical rudder of 95 square feet; and aft of the second pair of wings was a large cruciform tail-unit set at a negative angle of incidence, which was fitted with spring attachments to the boom-fuselage to act as a gust-damper; this, in addition, was to be used as the elevator, but not rudder. The total weight of the *Aerodrome*, with pilot was about 730 lb. (Fig. 50).

When the machine was ready for testing, Langley indulged in the folly of perpetuating the catapult-launching technique he had used for his models, except now that it was a catapult below—not above—the machine: this mechanism was placed, as before, on the top of a house-boat on the Potomac. An over-water take-off was apparently planned to avoid physical injury to the pilot. It was the brave Manly who volunteered as that pilot. The extent of such monumental folly may be truly gauged if one remembers that Manly had never even tried to fly a glider, let alone a completely untried powered machine, and he was now to be precipitated into the air at some 30 m.p.h., without the slightest idea of what would happen when he got going; he would have a rudder and an elevator, but no experience in the cockpit-working of them, and no idea at all as to how they would affect the flight of the *Aerodrome*. Manly did not know that, when he applied the rudder, the outer wings would start rising as well as turning. What is almost as bad was that, whether the *Aerodrome* came down on land or water, the first part of it which would impact the surface was Manly's frail cockpit, as it hung well below the rest of the machine, including the safety floats provided. It seems incredible to us today that Langley should have been prepared to risk a man's life in this way. Considering the unlimited flat space available nearby, where Manly could have safely tested the *Aerodrome* in longer and longer hops, and gained some idea of what effect the controls would have, it is impossible to understand Langley's thought process. This launching madness represented the final *reductio ad absurdum* of the chauffeur's attitude to aviation.

What happened, in the event, must certainly have been a blessing in disguise for Manly; for on both of its only two tests, on October 7th and

December 8th 1903, the *Aerodrome* crashed straight into the Potomac, with Manly struggling out unhurt after each ducking. On both occasions, the machine had apparently fouled the launching mechanism; but some authorities believe that the second crash was due, at least partly, to the aircraft's structural weakness (Pl. X).

From the official War Department report on the tests (written in 1903) two passages may be quoted:

> "The claim that an engine-driven, man-carrying Aerodrome has been constructed lacks the proof which actual flight alone can give. . . . In the meantime, to avoid any possible misunderstanding, it should be stated that even after a successful test of the present great aerodrome, designed to carry a man, we are still far from the ultimate goal, and it would seem as if years of constant work and study by experts, together with the expenditure of thousands of dollars, would still be necessary before we can hope to produce an apparatus of practical utility on these lines."

It is ironic to consider that in December of that very year 1903, the Wrights made the first flights in history; and in 1905 they were to build a fully practical aeroplane which could easily keep flying for half an hour; and the cost of all this was borne by the modest profits of a bicycle business.

Langley abandoned all further work in aviation, primarily owing to the vicious and totally unjustifiable attacks on him by Congressmen and the Press. But in face of such attacks, the War Department also withdrew its support, regretting that they were "not prepared to make an additional allotment at this time for continuing work". Langley died, heartbroken, on February 27th 1906.

The tragedy of Langley was the tragedy of a man whose basic attitude to the problem of flight was misconceived. His was the approach of a talented scientist who fervently believed that the aeroplane could be successfully achieved, but achieved from 'outside'; it was almost a spectator's attitude. Instead of approaching aviation through the glider, and realising it was flight-control that was the pivotal problem, he believed he could best come to the subject through powered models; and then advance to a full-size powered machine. And he had taken from 1887 to 1903—sixteen years—to fail in his solution of the problem, a failure stemming directly from his chauffeur's attitude of mind. But even allowing for this attitude, it it still impossible to explain his choice of a catapult-launch over water for a completely untried powered machine.

Langley's technical influence in aviation was virtually nil; many of his figures turned out to be wrong, and so did some of his most important theories; and his tandem-wing concept did not have any appreciable effect on his successors. But his influence as a well-known scientist, who was prepared to risk ridicule for his belief that man could, and would, fly in the air in powered aeroplanes, was great; it was to be one of the main factors in the Wrights taking up aviation. Perhaps, because of this, Wilbur Wright should speak his epitaph here: "It is really pathetic", wrote Wilbur to Chanute after Langley's death, "that he should have missed the honour he cared for above all others, merely because he could not launch his machine successfully. If he could only have started it, the chances are that it would have flown sufficiently to have secured to him the name he coveted, even though a complete wreck attended the landing. I cannot help feeling sorry for him. The fact that the great scientist, Professor Langley, believed in flying machines, was one thing that encouraged us to begin studies."

The powered machines—model or full-size—designed or made by Hargrave, Pilcher and Lilienthal, will be discussed in the next section, as their creators' greatest contributions to aviation came through gliders or kites.

Other Inventors

We must now return to Horatio Phillips, and to note first his patent of 1890, in which he suggested a cigar-shaped fuselage topped by a tandem multi-wing structure, each set of wings comprising thirteen superposed 'slats'; and then his later patent of 1891, which developed his 1884 patent by providing the double-surface aerofoil with a bi-convex leading edge (Fig. 51) intended to decrease drag, and preserve the lifting properties of his previous aerofoils; but this type of wing-section was to some extent a retrogresion. In 1893, Phillips decided to add practice to theory by building and testing his first 'Venetian blind' multiplane machine (Pl. VI) which was tested tethered on a circular track at Harrow in May; the span of this large model was 19 feet with a chord of only 1½ inches, the total area being 140 square feet. This test-rig was powered by a steam engine driving a 6·5 foot tractor propeller, and ran around a track of 323 feet circumference: with the front wheels always on the ground it rose some 2–3 feet off the circular track when running at about 40 m.p.h. Later—the exact date is as yet unknown—Phillips built another, and similar, machine with a larger track of 628 feet circumference, and it lifted some 385 lb. After these convincing displays of his high aspect-ratio aerofoils, Phillips abandoned practical testing until 1904 and 1907 (see page 124).

Victor Tatin returned to active aviation in 1890 with the first test of a remarkable steam-driven model aeroplane built in collaboration with Charles Richet. This large machine, with its steam engine enclosed in a nacelle driving two airscrews in tandem, one at either end of the nacelle, had a span of about 21 feet, the wings being given a pronounced dihedral. There was a Henson-type horizontal tail. The first test took place over the sea at La Hève in 1890: it was launched down a ramp and started well, but then the tail became twisted, and the machine crashed into the sea. Rebuilt, it was tested again in 1896 and 1897 over the roadstead at Giens, and made three flights—the best of which covered about 460 feet—before the machine dived into the sea. But events elsewhere were now too advanced for this aeroplane to influence the main stream of aviation, and it must be looked upon as a creditable but isolated achievement.

There was also the 1890 project—realised in unsuccessful model form—of the Frenchman Graffigny, who designed a steam-powered tractor monoplane with three pairs of wings in tandem, and two pairs of propellers, with a tailplane-cum-elevator, but no rudder.

One of the most interesting of the minor pioneers was Gustav Koch of

Fig. 51. Drawing from Phillip's second patent for double-surface aerofoils: 1891

Fig. 52b. Design for a powered monoplane, by Steiger: 1891

Fig. 52a. Design for fuselage section of a powered monoplane, by Steiger: 1891

Fig. 53. Design for a monoplane with airscrews aft, by Steiger: 1892

Fig. 54. Design for a powered monoplane by the Russian space-travel pioneer, Ziolkowski: 1894

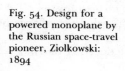

Munich, who unsuccessfully indulged an interest in gliding flight, and also (in 1891) designed a tandem-wing powered machine, also unsuccessful; but he also designed (in the 1890's) a monoplane, whose fuselage was constructed like a Venturi tube, with a turbine inside, using an unspecified fuel.

The important work of F. W. Lanchester in aerodynamics will be noted later (see Section 12): but he must appear here briefly. It was early in 1892 that he first started experiments with model gliders. The first announcement of his circulation theory of sustentation was in a paper entitled *The Soaring of Birds and the Possibilities of Mechanical Flight*, which he read to a meeting of the Birmingham Natural History and Philosophical Society on June 19th 1894. This historic paper was not printed: what is even worse is that Lanchester did not bother to preserve a copy. During 1895 and 1896 he revised and expanded the paper, and it was this revision, containing one of the most vital discoveries in technological history—the circulation theory of sustentation—which was refused for publication by the Physical Society in 1897: this refusal has brought much subsequent ridicule on the Society, but the truth is that Lanchester's language was almost incomprehensible (see page 125).

In 1891 there appeared in Munich a book by a Swiss artist, with a taste for physics and mathematics, named Carl Steiger-Kirchofer (generally known as Carl Steiger), called simply *Vogelflug und Flugmaschine* (Bird Flight and the Flying-Machine). In it Steiger displayed a remarkable grasp of many fundamentals of the aeroplane, and he included designs of what he proposed, which were many years in advance of his time (Fig. 52): unfortunately, as so often with men who did not primarily seek for experience in the air—although Steiger seems to have made a few attempts to glide—his flight-control concepts were primitive: he intended control in yaw to be by such methods as rocking the tailplane about its longitudinal axis (the equivalent to a bird twisting its tail), by differential speeds of two airscrews, and by the use of steering air-brakes. For control in pitch, by shifting the centre of gravity, swinging the wings fore and aft to shift the centre of pressure, and faster rotation of the airscrews. He also provided for oddly modern-looking enclosed cockpits in his 1891 book (Fig. 52a) and in his patent for a flying machine taken out in 1892 (Fig. 53). Steiger, whom I have only recently been able to study, may well repay more attention in the future. Also in 1892, the Austrian Professor Wellner proposed a rotating-paddle machine, in which the paddles rotated on longitudinal axes to support the machine, rather than propel it.

A curious incident in aviation history came in 1893, when the inventor of the turbine, Charles Parsons, had the passing whim to make a model helicopter, which he then turned into an aeroplane, without really being concerned with aviation at all. He used them as a testbed for his small ¼-h.p. steam engine to test the effect of steam-jacketing: with a total area of some 22 square feet, it flew for about 300 feet.[1]

One of the more interesting suggestions of the decade came in a paper of

[1] It is preserved in the Science Museum.

1894 by the great Russian 'father' of space travel, K. E. Ziolkowski, who in that year published his *Der Aeroplan, oder die vogelähnliche Flugmaschine*, in which he suggested a powered monoplane based on the rigid arched wings of the soaring bird, with a tractor propeller, a streamlined fuselage, a cruciform tail-unit, and a four-wheel undercarriage (Fig. 54).

A somewhat surprising would-be aviator has recently been revealed in the person of another Swiss artist, the famous romantic, Arnold Boecklin, who had a minor passion for flying, and who both attempted gliding experiments, and—in 1894—proposed a Henson-derived powered monoplane with braced high aspect-ratio wings, and a tail-unit: but nothing came of Boecklin's enthusiasm, or his design.

Strange as it may seem, the ornithopter was still alive in 1890, and an elaborate full-size machine was built by E. P. Frost in that year; but its steam engine did not produce its estimated power, and the tests came to nothing; no less a man than F. W. Brearey eulogised this hopeless machine, and described it as a "beautiful illustration of the winged machine . . . devised and constructed with perfect imitation and arrangement of every feather in the wing of a crow": the machine weighed about 650 lb., minus pilot.

A special word must be said here about the Aéro-Club de France (founded 1898) and the Aero Club (later Royal) of Great Britain (founded 1901). The French club, apart from initiating a decade of sporting ballooning—as did the British one across the Channel—came to play a unique role in European aviation as the focus for all the aviation pioneers, the disseminator of scientific information, and the inspirer to perpetual effort in the conquest of the air; whereas the British club remained almost exclusively social and sporting.

One of the most important events in the 1890's did not at the time concern aviation, but was later to prove of far-reaching influence in the history of the aeroplane: this was the winning of the legal freedom of the roads for the automobile in Britain in that year 1896, when it became no longer necessary for a man with a flag to precede every motor vehicle on the highway. The result of such mechanical freedom from bondage was a vast expansion in Europe of the automobile industry: this led to a major proliferation of sportsmen and other potential pilots, and—far more important—of mechanics, a large reservoir of whom were thus available when the powered aeroplane came to need them[1] (Pl. VII).

Claims of various kinds have been made by, or for, a number of men during this period, i.e. Gilmore, Herring, Pearse, Watson, and Whitehead: these cases are briefly discussed on page 289 et seq.

---

[1] An indication of the importance and spread of automobilisme, was the founding of the two great national clubs, the Automobile-Club de France, founded in Paris in 1895, and the Automobile Club (later Royal), founded in London in 1897.

10. *The Gliding Prelude to Practical Powered Flying: 1890–1903*

IT was through the glider that men came to fly in powered aeroplanes. The philosophy behind this sequence of events was the simple one of flight-control. A glider is a slow machine—and can even remain stationary in relation to the ground—and it is a comparatively safe task to learn how to fly it, provided one has the necessary talent, and that one perseveres and learns properly how to control it in pitch, roll and yaw. Having mastered the flight-control of gliders, it is then easy to progress to a powered machine, and master the additional problems that it presents.

If the glider-approach to flying is not followed, the risks and dangers are immense; and it was foolhardiness or ignorance which prompted those early pioneers who attempted to build powered aeroplanes to start with. To think of being cast into the air—as Langley was willing to cast Manly—in a powered flying machine without the pilot having had a moment in the air previously, is to partake of a nightmare. Even if the tests are made by a progressively longer series of hops, the dangers are still great; as the matter of 'hopping', as such, does not meet the bill of full commitment to the air, which is what the pilot must ultimately contend with. In fact, the better that the pioneer has solved the aerofoil and engine problems, the more dangerous will the tests be, since the aviator will be more quickly at the mercy of such an alien environment.

This was the reason why the Wrights, with their outstanding talent, were able to solve the basic control problems in the three short 'seasons' of gliding (1900–02); and to take confidently to the air in powered machines in three further seasons (1903–06). Whereas a whole 'team' of European pioneers, from Ferber in 1902 onwards—who also had the complete set of flight-control clues from the Wrights in 1902–03—unwisely abandoned the glider approach to flying and consequently took until November of 1907 before any of them could stay in the air for a single minute; until September of 1908 before they could keep flying for an half an hour at a time; and until 1908–09 before they learnt the Wrights' lessons in flight-control, and could properly manoeuvre aeroplanes in the air.

Otto Lilienthal

The key figure in aviation during the last decade of the century, and one of the greatest men in the history of flying, was the German Otto Lilienthal (1848–96). The past culminated in him, and the future was born in him. He was the first man in the world to launch himself into the air and fly. It was his gliding that led directly to the work of Chanute and the Wrights, whom he resembled in his approach to aviation, in his talents, and in his high qualities of integrity and humility. Lilienthal, says Dollfus simply, "est le père de l'aviation moderne" (Pl. VII).

His decisive influence in bringing aviation to its penultimate phase owed a great deal to photography and the printing industry; for in 1871 Maddox invented the dry-plate negative, whose emulsion was rapid enough at last to arrest movement; and by the 1890's the dry-plate camera had become a fine and sophisticated instrument. Also in the 1890's, the methods of printing photographs in journals and books had resulted in the half-tone block. The outcome of this combination of technologies—along with the photographic skill of the operators—was a superb series of photographs of Lilienthal gliding, which were reproduced photographically the world over, and brought home the true reality of his flying to the pioneers-to-be: Lilienthal was, indeed, the first man to be photographed in an aeroplane. Most important of the publications in which the Lilienthal photographs and text were published were an issue of *McClure's Magazine* of 1894, which was probably the first serious illustrated description of Lilienthal which the Wrights saw, and Means' *Aeronautical Annuals* for 1896 and 1897.

Lilienthal was born in 1848 at Anklam in Pomerania, and was given an excellent technical education at Potsdam and Berlin. From childhood he had been interested in human flight; and, with his brother Gustav, had been enthusiastically engaged in youthful flying 'experiments' with flapping wings. In 1869 (not 1867 as previously thought) the brothers experimented with a six-wing ornithopter suspended against a counterweight (Pl. IV). From 1867 until 1870, Otto studied at the Berlin Technical Academy; he had only just graduated in mechanical engineering when the Franco-Prussian War was upon him, and he volunteered for service and was present at the siege of Paris. He was demobilised in 1871, and went into engineering professionally.

Lilienthal resumed his flying experiments immediately after release from the army, and he was still bent on developing the orthithopter. Curiously enough, he remained devoted to the ornithopter all his life, and only took to fixed-wing gliders as a preparation for powered flight; he also warmly recommended gliding as a worthwhile open-air sport. He later wrote:

> "One can get a proper insight into the practice of flying only by actual flying experiments. . . . The manner in which we have to meet the irregularities of the wind, when soaring in the air, can only be learnt by being in the air itself. . . . The only way which leads us to a quick development in human flight is a systematic and energetic practice in actual flying experiments." (1896)

Thus spoke a true airman, whose whole ambition and effort were devoted to getting up into the air and flying. But although he became fully convinced that he must first learn to fly a fixed-wing glider, he harboured the curious conviction that it was the ornithopter with which man would ultimately triumph. This is reflected in another typical passage of his:

> "Natural bird flight utilises the properties of the air in such a perfect manner, and contains such valuable mechanical features, that any departure from these advantages is equivalent to giving up every practical method of flight." (1889)

73

It must be said unequivocally that it was a blessing for the future of aviation that the fixed-wing gliding prelude to his powered attempts took so long, as it was in this field that his great strength and influence lay. In this he was unlike Pilcher, who was in a hurry to fit an engine, and who spent too little time in gliding to get on "intimate terms with the wind", in Lilienthal's felicitous phrase.

Lilienthal determined that he must study bird-flight much more intimately than it had been studied before; not only the structure and types of bird-wings and their aerodynamics, but the application of the data gained—especially that dealing with wing areas and lift—to the problem of human flight. He was among the first, since Cayley discovered the principles, to realise that bird propulsion is brought about by the airscrew action of the outer primary feathers; and he fully described the technique. The results of his researches were published as a book in 1889, entitled *Der Vogelflug als Grundlage der Fliegekunst* (Bird Flight as the Basis of Aviation), which is one of the classics of aeronautical literature. Although this book was not available in an English translation until 1911, excellent articles in English both by, and about, Lilienthal were available from 1894 onwards, as has been said; but it is worth noting that, in 1901, Chanute lent the Wrights a copy of the *Vogelflug* with a partial translation in typescript, whilst Lilienthal's table of wing areas and lift had already been published in the *Aeronautical Annual* for 1897.

By 1889, Lilienthal had come to the conclusion that he must now learn the air and its moods in fixed-wing gliders; and in that year he built his first fixed-wing machine, which will be called the *No. 1* glider.[1] This was a tailless bird-form glider and was not successful. Nor was the *No. 2* of 1890 successful, although it probably had a tail.

These first experiments were made from a springboard at his home in Berlin-Lichterfelde, and on convenient ground nearby. The first serious tests were made in 1891 at Derwitz, between Werder and Grosskreuz, near the Magdeburg railway. Then in 1892, Lilienthal moved his test location to a gravel pit between Berlin-Steglitz and Südende. Early in 1893 he moved again to a height called the Maihöhe at Steglitz, on which he erected a hangar from whose roof he took off in his gliders, the total height above the level ground below being some 10 metres (say 33 feet). Then still in 1893, he found the ideal places in the Rhinower hills, first between Neustadt a.d. Dosse and Rathenow; and then the slightly higher Gollenberg, near Stölln, not far off. In order also to have a convenient experimental station nearer at hand, Lilienthal had an artificial hill thrown up in the spring of 1894, near a brick-works in Lichterfelde, a suburb of Berlin: this hill was—with a hangar built into the conical top—about 15 metres high (say 50 feet), and had a base diameter of 70 metres (say 230 feet), which allowed flights in any direction to be made, according to the direction of the wind.

All Lilienthal's machines were hang-gliders, in which the pilot hung by his

[1] The numbering system adopted here is taken from the late Gerhard Halle's *Otto Lilienthal und seine Flugzeug-Konstruktionen* (1962), a booklet which Herr Halle kindly wrote at my instigation: it was published by the Deutsches Museum, Munich. All gliders before *No. 13* were monoplanes.

arms; he could therefore swing his torso and legs in any desired direction to shift the position of the centre of gravity, and thus achieve a limited—but combined—control in pitch, roll and yaw.

Lilienthal's first mature and tentatively successful glider was his *No. 3* of 1891; it first had a 10 square metre wing area (say 107·5 square feet), which was soon reduced to 8 square metres, the camber being 1 in 10: this machine had a fixed tailplane in front of the rear fixed fin. His *No. 4* of 1892, of 14·7 square metres and 9·5 metre span, had pinched in, and pointed wing-tips, and a camber of 1 in 12: no details of tests survive. The *No. 5*, also of 1892, had an area of 16 square metres (say 172 square feet), with cambered wings of pronouncedly arched dihedral, and a tailplane placed again in front of the vertical fin: this machine made flights of some 80 metres when launched from a height of 10 metres; but it was only flown in light breezes, owing to its large wing area.

Early in 1893, he built his *No. 6*, of 14 square metres (say 150 square feet) and 6·6 metre span, which had arched and rounded cambered wings, radiating spars, and still with the tailplane in front of the fin: this machine was the first to be provided with folding wings to facilitate transport, and also the first to be fitted with a freely upward-moving tailplane—still in front of the fin—in order to avoid the tail being pushed up if the machine was gusted to a halt, thus risking a nose-dive: all subsequent Lilienthal gliders incorporated this device. The radiating spars allowed him to rig the machine with different cambers, and thus compare their efficiency. It was this moderately successful glider which formed the basis for Lilienthal's patent of 1893 (No. 77916–77). With this machine he made many successful glides (Fig. 55).

In the same year, 1893, Lilienthal built his *No. 7* glider for those days when there were only light breezes; it was similar to the *No. 6*, but with the wing area increased to 17·5 square metres and the span to 8·7 metres. During 1893–94, he built his *No. 8*, of 13.4 square metres, which was probably the first machine of which Lilienthal built a few replicas, one of which he sold to a Herr Seiler.

It was still in 1893 that Lilienthal turned briefly to his ultimate ambition; but it was too early. For he built the first of his two powered machines (*No. 16*), with a wing area of 13·2 square metres which included the bulk of the surface—which was fixed—as well as the ornithoptering imitation of the outer primary feathers with which Lilienthal proposed to propel the machine:these consisted of six 'slats' on either side, which would twist into propeller feathers. The power was to be provided by a 2-h.p. carbonic acid gas motor. But no powered flights were attempted, and the machine was tested in 1894 as a glider (Pl. VII), first without the engine, and then with the engine installed—to test the weight—but not operating. This machine was included in the same patent of 1893 as his *No. 6* glider.

Lilienthal's *No. 9* glider of 1894, which he named *Modell Stölln*, was the first machine he flew at the Stöllner Hills, and was of 14 square metres, with the tailplane still in front of the fin; but, out front, there was now fixed for the first time a horizontal hoop of willow as a shock-absorber, called a 'Prellbügel' (literally a 'rebound-bow'). It was on this glider—an excellent

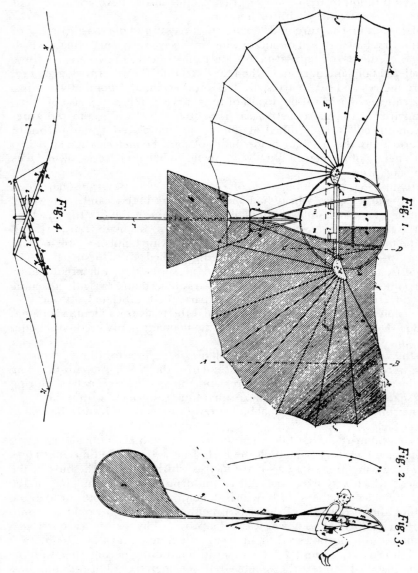

Fig. 55. Lilienthal's patent drawings for his hang-glider, which had already been built as his type *No. 6* (note the up-swinging tailplane): 1893

Fig. 56. Lilienthal's sketch of his model biplane, with side-curtains: 1895

Fig. 57. Hargrave's sketch of his first full-size machine, a tandem-wing glider: 1894

Fig. 58. Hargrave's sketch of his second design for a man-carrying box-kite aeroplane: 1896

Fig. 59. Sketch of Hargrave's third design for a man-carrying aeroplane, a multiplane box-kite type: 1902 machine—that Lilienthal suffered the only serious crash before the one which killed him: it stalled, turned over, and nose-dived into the earth, the Prellbügel burying itself in the ground as it splintered, and saving Lilienthal's life. It was the graphic description of this crash, translated and printed in the *Aeronautical Annual* for 1897, which was the main cause of the Wrights (and their European followers) placing their elevators out front, which they believed would prevent such nose-dives.

The *No. 10* glider of 1894, of which we do not know much, was a machine of only 9 square metres (say 97 square feet), which he called his *Sturmflügel-modell* (storm-wing model) built for flying in strong winds.

It was Lilienthal's *No. 11*, also of 1894, that became his most trusty machine, and indeed he called it his *Normal-Segelapparat* (standard sailing machine); it had a wing area of 13 square metres (say 140 square feet), and was the first of his gliders to have the tailplane "surrounding" the fin, and hinged to the latter's leading edge, thus making a longer lever arm (Pl. VII). Lilienthal built at least eight replicas of this machine, which he sold or presented to other would-be pioneers, but to little effect. He had come to the conclusion that a camber of more than 1 in 12 was inadvisable, and that from 1 in 15 to 1 in 18 was generally most satisfactory, which was the approximate camber of the *No. 11* and those replicas delivered to friends and clients. With this machine he could make successful controlled glides of up to about 350 metres (say 1,150 feet).

In 1895, on his *No. 12*, with a wing area of 20 square metres, a span of 8·8 metres, and a camber of 1 in 20, Lilienthal put into practice his newly patented full-span leading-edge flaps, which hinged downward; he hoped that this device would aid in raising the front of his machine in his ever-dreaded fear of a nose-dive: he also tested, on this machine, wing-tip steering air-brakes. But he wisely abandoned these devices after a few tests.

Lilienthal then, in 1895, took to the biplane: he felt he could better control a machine of shorter span, provided the lifting surface was maintained at the same area, a problem which the biplane solved. After testing various models (Fig. 56), whose stability surprised him, he built three biplanes, two in 1895, and the third over the turn of the year, and tested them all from his artificial hill: their wing areas were respectively 18 square metres, 25 square metres and 20·5 square metres (Pl. VII). He was very pleased with the results, and could trust himself in winds of 24 m.p.h. and over, sometimes soaring stationary, and talking to the photographers: he was at this time contemplating circling flights (see the quotations, page 222); but he never achieved them, as he could not succeed in going high enough to avoid colliding with his take-off hill when he wheeled back.

It is curious to find that only in 1895 did Lilienthal seriously turn his attention to methods of flight-control other than body-swinging. In a letter to his pupil Alois Wolfmüller, dated October 3rd 1895, Lilienthal outlined designs for (*a*) simple wing-warping, (*b*) moving the whole tail-assembly to one side or the other and so turning the fin into a rudder, and (*c*) providing also a steering air-brake at each wing-tip. The seemingly obvious question of an elevator, Lilienthal left to the day before he was killed, when he made a sketch of his up-flapping tailplane fitted so that its lowest position could be raised at will by means of a neck-harness: as the tailplane still moved upwards freely, the device was only intended to lower the glider's tail and raise the nose. Lilienthal might soon have come to making all movements of the tailplane solely dependent on the pilot, to be raised or lowered at will, and hence to become an elevator.

He had started in the Spring of 1895 constructing his second powered machine (the *No. 17*) on the same lines as before, but with an area of 20 square metres, and designed to take a new carbonic acid gas motor, which weighed only 5 kg.: this machine appears to have been completed, but not tested, before Lilienthal was killed next year in August. It would seem that he was now planning to devote himself more and more to powered flight by means of ornithoptering wing-tips; although his last machine (*No. 18*)—which was also commenced in that year 1895—was a return to the monoplane hang-glider type, but with double-surface, thick-section, wings: it is believed that this, too, was completed, but it was not tested.

On Sunday, August 9th 1896, which was a beautiful summer's day, Lilienthal was gliding from the Gollenberg in one of his standard *No. 11* monoplanes, when he was suddenly gusted to a standstill: he threw himself as far forward as possible to get the nose down, but the glider stalled, the starboard wing dropped, and the machine side-slipped into the ground, crumpling the wing but leaving the rest of the structure undamaged. But Lilienthal's spine was broken in the fall: he was taken next day to the Bergmann Clinic in Berlin, but an operation was found to be impossible. He died that day, August 10th 1896. The machine which killed him is often said to have been a biplane: this mistake is due to Pilcher.

Lilienthal used to make the remark, from time to time, that "Opfer müssen gebracht werden" (sacrifices must be made). It forms a tragically appropriate epitaph for this great man, and the words are carved on his gravestone in Lichtefelde cemetery.

If he had lived, Lilienthal—like Pilcher—would almost certainly have accomplished some degree of powered flight before the Wrights. He had had long experience of the air, and made some 2,500 gliding flights; he was arriving at the true concept of flight-control; and he would have arrived sooner or later at the propeller aeroplane. Above all, like Pilcher and the Wrights, he was a true airman, and a person of high talents and complete integrity. It is hard to overestimate the vital force which this outstanding pioneer injected into aviation, as much after his tragic death as before. His influence was universal and profound: extracts from his technical writings were translated and read by all who were convinced that mechanical flight would one day be accomplished, and—as said above—the overall effect of his work was greatly increased when his successful flights were well photographed, and published the world over by means of the then new method of half-tone reproduction, and other techniques, in books and periodicals; these photographs, and the information which accompanied them, also demonstrated forcibly that it was necessary and possible for a man to be launched into the air, and fly, in order to gain essential experience in design and control, before he embarked on powered flights. Lilienthal was the direct inspirer of Pilcher, the Wrights and Ferber, and may fairly be described as the world's first true aviator; that is to say, he was the first man to fly practical heavier-than-air aircraft consistently and successfully.

Lawrence Hargrave

In some respects the work of Lawrence Hargrave (1850–1915) in the 1890's should have been discussed in the previous section on the powered prelude. But although his ambition lay in the direction of powered aviation, and although his work in this field was excellent and original, it was his invention of the box-kite that placed him most firmly in the front rank of history. Hargrave was a remarkable man, of a high talent and integrity, and of great generosity, who refused to patent his inventions, and published his researches for all to see and use, however they liked, "in order that all might benefit from the results of my labour". (For his earlier work, see page 54.)

Hargrave invented the box-kite—in various forms—in 1893 (Pl. VI), but it was the simple version which was to play such an important part in aviation history. The result was an admirably stable ensemble, with great lifting power; on one occasion (1894) he himself was lifted 16 feet off the ground in a 21 m.p.h. wind by a train of four of these kites. He records that his box-kite was a combination of two previous concepts.

But in 1894, when he designed and built his first full-size machine, it was a glider which emerged, which was not of box-kite, but of monoplane tandem-wing configuration, with dihedral, and a wing area of 150 square feet; this was inspired by Lilienthal, and represented the latter's inspiration combined with Hargrave's new concept. This machine (Fig. 57) was caught by a side gust and wrecked in June 1894, either when tethered or flying freely.

But Hargrave returned to the greater stability of the box-kite configuration—where he needed additional lifting surface—for his first powered man-carrier design in 1895 which, with a wing area of 480 square feet, was to be powered by a steam engine; but this machine was not constructed, owing to the poor performance of the engine which was built first. A particular feature of this design was that he intended it should first be tested suspended from a train of box-kites, to ensure the safety of the pilot.

In 1896 Hargrave completed the design for his second powered man-carrier, which was a box-kite biplane, and was to incorporate a steam engine driving four flappers (within the front box-kite cell), and a small forward cruciform control-surface acting as elevator-cum-rudder; with this machine it was intended to make free take-offs from water, and four wing-tip floats were provided for this purpose. But again, the engine was a failure; and the machine never left the drawing board. Although this design was to remain completely unknown to the world, it bears a striking resemblance to the Voisin-Archdeacon float-glider of 1905 (Fig. 58 and Pl. XI), which was indirectly descended from the Hargrave box-kite, their common ancestor.

In 1899, Hargrave decided to visit England, with his family, to make the personal contacts he so badly lacked in Australia; and the most important

PLATE VII

a Lilienthal in his monoplane hang-glider No. 7: 1894

b Standard (No. 11) Lilienthal hang-glider: 1894

c Powered Lilienthal machine (No. 16) being flown as a glider: 1894

d Lilienthal biplane hang-glider (No. 13): 1895

e Lilienthal biplane hang-glider (No. 13): 1895

f Automobiles gain the freedom of the roads in Britain: 1896

PLATE VIII

a Chanute's classic biplane hang-glider: 1896–1904

b Pilcher's hang-glider, the *Hawk*: 1896

c Wright No. 1 glider being flown as a kite: 1900

d Wright No. 2 glider, at the Kill Devil Hills: 1901

e Wright No. 3 glider in its first form, with two fixed rear fins: 1902 event of his stay in this country was the paper on his kites which he delivered to the Aeronautical Society in London, with Percy Pilcher in the Chair, on May 26th 1899. It was on this occasion that he showed his box-kites, the first time they had been seen 'in the flesh', so to speak, in Europe. He also presented some of them to the Society, and these were later borrowed by Pilcher. Incidentally, it is still not clear why information about these box-kites, with their promise of inherent stability, was not acted upon sooner: they were published in the 1893 Chicago Conference Proceedings (1894), in Chanute's classic *Progress in Flying Machines* (1894), and in Means' *Aeronautical Annual* (1896). Gabriel Voisin records that he first heard of them in 1898; yet it was not until 1905 that he incorporated the box-kite in the float-gliders he built for Archdeacon and Blériot.

Hargrave's third and last full-size design came at the beginning of 1902, when he had moved to a new waterfront home at Woollahra Point, on Sydney Harbour. This machine, which was built in a modified form—of tubular tinplate—was interesting (Fig. 59), with multiple main wings, and a smaller multiplane tail-unit, with a steam engine driving a single tractor propeller.[1] The design was subsequently modified to have a single large float placed centrally, with two smaller side floats. But Hargrave's twenty-fifth engine proved to be a failure, at the end of 1903. Then, in 1906—and it is hard indeed to find an explanation for this delay—Hargrave turned again to the petrol engine; it was, however, to power flappers instead of a propeller. But this engine, too, was a failure. In March 1906, Hargrave abandoned his full-time aviation experiments.

The story of Hargrave is one of the most curious in aviation history. His geographical isolation from the only stream of history was previously thought to have been the only stumbling block to his becoming a more influential figure in history: but this is now seen to be only a half-truth. For he not only had an excellent aeronautical library, but he was kept *au courant* with what was going on in America and Europe by correspondence with Chanute, Baden-Powell and others. And there was also his visit to England in 1899. But it is Mr. Hudson Shaw—the leading authority on Hargrave—who has pointed to a vital lack in Hargrave's life; this was the lack of a technically-minded friend within his own environment, with whom he could constantly discuss his work, and through whom he could clarify his own ideas. This diagnosis is surely correct; but I feel that Hargrave also possessed some inherent disabilities—or weaknesses—which were due to the fact that he was basically chauffeur-minded; he was not a true airman in his approach to aviation. The only occasions on which he was ever airborne were a few tests with his 1894 glider, and a few feet off the ground beneath one of his kite-trains. He had, after all, been actively experimenting with model

---

[1] A small point has come to light concerning the drawing of Hargrave's third multiplane design for his third man-carrying aeroplane shown in Fig. 59. This was not actually done by Hargrave himself: it turns out to have been drawn by his friend Sidney Holland, to whom Hargrave sent a rough sketch of his design on September 26th 1901: Hargrave indicated a machine with six main planes forward, and four tailplanes, with three floats, and the pilot lying prone. Holland drew out a tractor machine following these lines, even to the slings for the prone pilot; so the sketch may be taken as a true rendering of what Hargrave had in mind.

aeroplanes since about 1885; and in that year he told the Royal Society of New South Wales that he had already experimented with nearly fifty models.. He was then to continue active experiments, including the construction—surely misguided—of no less than twenty-six motors, until 1906. Thus we have a talented man spending some eleven years in researching and testing, apparently without its ever having crossed his mind that he should have built, and properly mastered the glider and its flight-control, before proceeding to powered flight.[1] If he had gone from the fully controllable glider to the powered aeroplane, he would in all probability have achieved powered flight long before his financial position became strained. Hargrave was certainly one of the great aviation pioneers of history, but he did not possess enough of the peculiar mixture of talents and characteristics necessary to achieve his end. He was indeed a splendid character, but one cannot help feeling that he was an aeronautical genius *manqué*.

Octave Chanute

Another of the outstanding figures in aviation history was the French-born American civil engineer Octave Chanute (1832–1910), who lived in Chicago. His importance was fourfold: (1) he was the first great historian of aviation, who provided the would-be pioneers with an exhaustive description of all that had been done in the past in aviation, and who provided clearly expressed ideas on what had to be done next; (2) he became the chief go-between, and disseminator of aeronautical information, between America and Europe, keeping each Continent informed about the activities of the other, and also making a vitally important visit to Europe in 1903; (3) he finalised the Lilienthal-type hang-glider in biplane form; and (4) he was the much-valued friend and encourager of the Wright brothers. As a result of these activities, he was universally regarded (from about 1896) as the 'grand old man' of aviation, and rightly accorded the respect due to the elder statesman of flying.

Chanute had first become interested in aeronautics about 1855, not—as previously thought—as a result of having met Wenham in England. At intervals in a very busy and successful career, he collected every piece of information available on the history of heavier-than-air flying; and after sifting and assessing a vast amount of material, he wrote a series of articles for *The Railroad and Engineering Journal*, starting in October 1891, and continuing for twenty-seven issues; these were reprinted, with additions, in book-form in 1894, under the title *Progress in Flying Machines*, a volume which soon became—and will always remain—one of the classics of aviation. This work, and Lilienthal's *Vogelflug*, became the two bibles of flying, and were read by every experimenter the world over. Anyone who read and

---

[1] It is interesting to find even Hargrave believing in the idea of steering air-brakes. In a statement to the Royal Society of New South Wales on June 3rd 1885, he said: "In larger machines this (i.e. body-movement) would have to be done by making the area of the tail-surface variable for ascending or descending, and tilting one corner up or down for turning to either side."

digested Chanute's book would have before him the whole picture of aviation up to date, and then be in a position not only to appreciate what had already been accomplished, but what directions should next be taken to achieve human mechanical flight.

Then, in 1896, inspired by the example of Lilienthal, Chanute publicly exhorted inventors to build full-size gliders, and get into the air and experiment for themselves. Although at this time he was sixty-four, and too old to fly himself, Chanute designed a number of man-carrying gliders, and secured the help of a young engineer, A. M. Herring, to help him with their design, and to pilot them. Chanute had but one main ambition, and that was to achieve, as he said, "an apparatus with automatic stability in the wind"; he aimed at "automatic equilibrium exclusively". But owing to some curious misstatements and misunderstandings which have arisen over the years, and gained a regrettably wide currency, he has been wrongly credited with various ideas and achievements which he never attained or even claimed. So, for the record, the following should be set down: (1) Chanute never employed hinged control-surfaces, either rudders or elevators; (2) he aimed at as high a degree of inherent stability as possible; (3) where pilot-control was concerned, he only employed the Lilienthal hang-glider technique of body-swinging control, although Chanute aimed at reducing the necessary movements, and Herring contributed a further technique—to increase the controllability—of the pilot pushing and pulling his whole body backwards or forwards, using smooth horizontal bars under his armpits as 'rails' (Pl. VIII and Fig. 60); (4) Chanute introduced the excellent 'Pratt-truss' method of rigging his multiplanes; (5) Chanute considered applying power to his gliders, but did not proceed with the idea.

Chanute selected a location on the south shore of Lake Michigan, near Miller (Indiana) as the most convenient place for testing his machines. His first two machines, both built and tested in 1896, were a multiplane hang-glider, and a biplane glider.

Chanute's multiplane machine was a hang-glider with pivoting multiplane wings—at first eight pairs, then four pairs—with a separate fixed surface placed above all, a tailplane and a fin. The main wings, restrained by rubber 'springs' from a nose bowsprit, could swivel backwards from the roots (in the horizontal plane) under sudden gusts in order—it was fruitlessly hoped—to shift the centre of pressure. It was first tested in July 1896, and made some 300 short glides, but it was not successful. A second machine of this type was built, and tested again without success by Herring at the Wright's camp at the Kill Devil Hills in October 1902.

Chanute's second machine became the classic biplane hang-glider which helped to determine the Wrights' biplane configuration and rigging, and represented the finalisation of the Lilienthal type of biplane hang-glider: he called it his "two-surface" machine. It was the direct descendant of the Stringfellow triplane model of 1868, and also owed a debt to the Lilienthal biplanes of 1895. This machine of Chanute's was first designed—and first tested on August 29th 1896 for a few glides—as a triplane; then the lower wing was removed, leaving it a biplane of 12·45 square metres (say 134 square feet) wing area (Fig. 60). It had an elongated Cayley-type cruciform tail-unit on a semi-flexible outrigger, the upward elasticity—secured by rubber 'springs'—being introduced by Herring according to a modified Lilienthal practice, in the hope that it would act as a gust-damper. This famous biplane was successfully flown by Herring from August to mid-September 1896, and made flights of up to 109 metres. At least two of these machines were built; one of them was rebuilt for the St. Louis Exposition of 1904, and it was there flown by William Avery to test Chanute's new launching device, which consisted of a cable wound over an electrically operated drum. It was this 1904 machine which a French pioneer, Jacques Balsan, bought in St. Louis, and later presented to the Musée de l'Air in Paris.

Chanute's last machine was a strange oscillating-wing triplane hang-glider, built in 1902, and tested unsuccessfully by Herring in October of that year at the Wrights' camp at the Kill Devil Hills, near Kitty Hawk. The triplane wings were pivoted span-wise, and their angle of incidence could be collectively reduced by sudden air-pressure, as they were restrained by rubber 'springs': it had a Cayley-type cruciform tail-unit.

It was in 1900, at the age of sixty-eight, that Chanute was contacted by the Wrights, and a close friendship developed. Chanute quickly realised their true merit; he spared no pains, through voluminous correspondence and several meetings, in encouraging them in everything they did, in discussing with them their problems, and even offering them financial assistance—which was gracefully declined. But it should be emphasised, in view of certain partisan books and articles, that the only technical debts the Wrights owed Chanute were his excellent Pratt-trussed biplane structure, and the suggestion of catapult launching: in the all-important spheres of aerodynamics and flight-control, they owed him nothing, and Chanute freely admitted this. Their friendship and mutual trust was threatened for some years—as can now be clearly established—by Chanute claiming the Wrights as his pupils, which claim was as absurd as it was untrue. The Wrights were never, in any sense of the word, Chanute's pupils.

To Chanute, as the supreme middle-man of aviation, goes the credit of being the unique channel through which information about—and illustrations of—the two first Wright gliders were first presented to Ferber in 1902; and of the vital third glider to the Continental world of aviation in general, in 1903; thus directly precipitating the revival of aviation—and the birth of practical flying—in Europe. Octave Chanute's immense prestige on both sides of the Atlantic ensured the maximum advertance to what he reported; his influence was always for the good, and always exerted in the absolute conviction that mechanical flight was imminent: nothing pleased him more than when the Wrights finally conquered the air during the years 1903, 1904 and 1905. Let us leave the last word to Wilbur Wright: "In patience and goodness of heart he has rarely been surpassed; few men were more universally respected and loved."

Augustus Moore Herring, who was Chanute's assistant, is remembered today chiefly as the pilot of Chanute's gliders. But he has also a small place in history as the first American to buy a Lilienthal glider from the master himself: hoping to improve it with alterations—in what particulars it is not yet clear—he tested it in 1896 at Chanute's 'station' on Lake Michigan, but it was not successful. Herring later (1898) built a powered biplane, powered by a compressed-air engine. Herring made hops of 50 and 72 feet with this machine at St. Joseph (Michigan) in October 1898. (See note on page 290.)

Percy Pilcher

The most distinguished British pioneer in practical aviation since Cayley was undoubtedly Percy Sinclair Pilcher (1867–99). He and Lilienthal were the only two men in the world whose work—up to the time they were killed—showed that they might well have flown powered aeroplanes before the Wrights, had they lived. He was a man similar to them in antecedents, in approach, in temperament, in outlook, and in his determination to get up in the air and fly: he was a true airman in every respect. His personal characteristics of integrity, modesty and pertinacity were also similar to the Wrights'; he was rightly described by Chanute as "a most lovable character".

After six years in the Royal Navy, he retired in 1885 to take up engineering. After going through the shops in Glasgow, he attended lectures at London University. He worked in a Southampton shipyard, then in 1893 he was appointed Assistant Lecturer in Naval Architecture and Marine Engineering at Glasgow University. In 1896 he joined Maxim as an assistant, and in 1897 became a highly valued member of the Aeronautical Society; he was elected to its Council in the same year. He left Maxim in 1897 and soon after he became a partner in the engineering firm of Wilson and Pilcher.

Aviation had for long interested him, and he was first able properly to indulge his interest at Glasgow during the early months of 1895. Pilcher was a direct product of Lilienthal's inspiration, but his independence of spirit showed itself in his remark that he "had seen photographs of Lilienthal's apparatus, but I purposely made my own [glider] before going over to Berlin to see his, so as to get the greatest advantage from any original ideas I might have".

In the event, he went to Berlin in April 1895, after he had completed his first glider, the *Bat*, but before testing it. Pilcher refused to believe Lilienthal's assurance that a tailplane, as well as a fin, was essential for flight. This view of Pilcher's indicates not only a certain naïvéte of approach at this time, but a quite extraordinary ignorance of the literature of aviation, where he would have found abundant evidence of the necessity of a tailplane. Pilcher started to experiment with the *Bat* at Cardross, on the Clyde: it was a Lilienthal-type hang-glider with the wings given a very pronounced dihedral, and only a vertical fin aft: he found he could not fly with it at all. "I would not believe him," wrote Pilcher of Lilienthal, "but found out that he was quite correct." So he converted his tail-unit into a cruciform structure of fixed fin and tailplane, and thus succeeded in making some promising glides; but he found that his overpronounced dihedral tended to "capsize me sideways, which always meant a breakage in the machine". The *Bat* had a wing area of 150 square feet, a weight (empty) of 45 lb.; with Pilcher on board, it weighed 190 lb. thus giving a wing loading of about 1⅓ lb. per square foot.

Pilcher's second glider, the *Beetle*, was built during the summer of the same year 1895: it was also a hang-glider, but with square-cut wings of 170 square feet area, no dihedral, and a high-set cruciform tail-unit composed of two intersecting discs: but the pilot hung with his head below the wings, giving a low centre of gravity and making the machine difficult to handle; the machine was also heavily built and weighed 80 lb. Pilcher soon abandoned the *Beetle*, and went back to using the *Bat*, now with reduced dihedral. With the glider in this form he obtained the best results so far. On September 12 he hovered 12 feet above the ground for half a minute, and flights under tow were made on other occasions.

His third machine was named the *Gull*, built at Glasgow late in 1895 and "intended for practice only on calm days", and having a wing area of 300 square feet. But he said he had not the patience to wait for such calm days; he twice had the *Gull* broken in stiff breezes, and finally did not bother to repair it.

Late in 1895, Pilcher learned of Lilienthal's new biplane gliders, but he mistrusted them, believing that there was too much surface above the centre of gravity. When he visited the German pioneer for a second time, in June 1896, he flew one of these machines, but still remained sceptical of their stability, especially in squally conditions.

Pilcher's fourth glider, the *Hawk*, was his classic machine (Pl. VIII). It was built in Glasgow during the winter of 1895–96, and first flown in the following summer at Eynsford in Kent—after he had come south to work for Maxim. It was also a hang-glider; but, for the first time, there was a wheeled undercarriage, each wheel being fitted with a "very stiff spiral spring". This, incidentally, was the first sprung undercarriage of history.[1] The slightly arched wings, with a camber of up to 5 inches (situated 2½ feet from the leading edge) had an area of 180 square feet, and a span of 23 feet 4 inches; the tail-unit a triangular tailplane to which a triangular fin was later added, which could hinge up *in toto* from near the trailing edge of the wings, but not down. In all his previous machines, Pilcher had varied Lilienthal's practice of hinging only the tailplane. It would appear from Pilcher's writings that he did not fully appreciate Lilienthal's reasons for this device (see later). The weight of the *Hawk* was 50 lb.; with pilot, 195 lb.; there was thus wing-loading of just over 1 lb. per square foot. The pilot, supported by his shoulder-blades and forearms, had his head, shoulders and most of his chest, above the wings.

Launching gliders was always to present a difficult problem, as winds neither held their direction consistently, nor their strength: so Pilcher, from 1895, employed a towing technique, with a fishing-line passed over a pulley on the top of one hill, with he himself in his glider poised for take-off on the

---

[1] It is sometimes said this was also the first wheeled undercarriage in history. It was, of course, far from being so. Quite apart from the many designs and models with wheels, the following full-size machines had wheeled undercarriages prior to the *Hawk*: Cayley's gliders of 1849 and 1853; Du Temple's powered monoplane of *c.* 1874; Mozhaiski's powered monoplane of 1884; Ader's *Éole* of 1890; and Maxim's huge test-rig of 1894.

top of a neighbouring hill, and then pulled into the air. This form of assisted take-off produced many excellent glides, including his record of some 750 feet, which he achieved on June 20th 1897.

Pilcher had for long—if not from the beginning—intended to build a powered machine; and in 1896 he took out a remarkable patent (No. 9144 of 1896), the illustrations to which have been largely forgotten (Fig. 61). This was the world's first practical design for a powered aeroplane based on glider experience, and capable of being built and flown at least tentatively. Pilcher wrote in 1897:

> "It is my intention this winter to make another machine very similar to this [the Hawk], but having small oil [i.e. petrol] engine situated just in front of me on the machine, with a shaft passing over my head, working a screw propeller of about 4 feet diameter, situated behind me. The machine will be started in exactly the same way as the soaring machines, by running down an incline, and when in the air the screw will be started to revolve, and in this way I hope to be able to maintain horizontal flight. From soaring machine experiments, it appears that an expenditure of about two H.P. per minute is necessary; I shall therefore use an engine of about four H.P., because of the inefficiency of the screw and other losses. The flying speed would be about 30 miles per hour."

Here, in 1897, is a formulation of a practical powered aeroplane undreamt-of anywhere else in the world at this time: it is the colloquial description of his patent of the year before.

There is only one aspect of Pilcher's work that calls for historical criticism, which may best be dealt with here; that is his neglect of flight-control by movable surfaces, and his reliance on the hang-glider configuration with body-control; this even applies to his 1896 patent for a powered machine. He often speaks of a "rudder", but reference to his patent, and to the *Hawk* itself, which is preserved in the Royal Scottish Museum, makes it clear that it was only a fixed fin. The only movable surface he provided for was the upward (only) hinging of his tailplane, at first *à la* Lilienthal; then, in the *Hawk*, of the whole tail-unit: this was to minimise the effect of the tail's possible impact on the ground when landing, to prevent the tail from being pushed up—if the machine was gusted to a halt—and so causing a nose-dive, and to make the machine's reaction quicker when the pilot threw his body backwards to raise the nose. Pilcher may not have realised the second of these reasons, which nearly caused Lilienthal's death in 1894, as in his patent he only gives the first and third as reasons for his hinged tail-unit. This lack of attention to control-surfaces is a very curious feature in a man who looked upon gliders as a means of acquiring flying experience before advancing to powered machines; and in a man trained in marine design, where the control-surfaces on submarines must have been well known to him.

Pilcher, like the Wrights, having sought in vain for a commercial engine of suitable power/weight ratio, decided to build one of his own. He reckoned that the *Hawk*, being of a total all-up weight of some 190 lb. glided at about 20–25 m.p.h., with a pull on the launching tow-line of 20–30 lb. Pilcher therefore estimated that a powered version of the *Hawk*, once it was launched, and with the weight of the engine included, would require an engine of 4 h.p. to sustain it in the air, driving a propeller of 5 feet diameter, with a 4 feet pitch: engine and propeller would weigh 40 lb. and 3½ lb. respectively; i.e. 43½ lb. in all.

Pilcher, along with his other work, spent most of the next year (1898) in constructing this engine at the works (in which he was a partner) in Great Peter Street, Westminster. We know from the inquest that the engine was completed and even bench-tested, by 1899. Also in 1898, he was trying to form a company to promote his flying machines. He wrote to Professor Fitzgerald, in Dublin, at the end of 1898:

> "during the last year [i.e. 1898] I was not able to do anything with the flying work, as we were very busy getting our new business into going order; but the Summer before, when I was able to devote some time to it, the results we obtained were most encouraging, and consequently we are most anxious not to let the experiments drop altogether. In America, experiments are continually being made,[1] and it would be heartrending not to try and keep one's place in the work that is being done."

But 1898 was most notable as the year in which Pilcher's ideas underwent a radical change. This was brought about by an exchange of correspondence with Octave Chanute in the USA. Accounts of the numerous successful and accident-free flights made by the quadruplane and biplane at Indiana in 1896 (see page 83) finally convinced Pilcher that a safe multi-surface glider could be built. After first drafting a design for a quadruplane inspired by the Chanute machines, in 1899 he built a triplane into which he intended to fit his engine, abandoning the powered *Hawk* proposal.

On May 26th 1899 the Australian Lawrence Hargrave gave a talk to the Aeronautical Society in London—at which Pilcher took the chair—in which he demonstrated his box-kites (which he had invented in 1893), and soaring kites, several examples of which he presented to the Society. The soaring kites, resembling tethered gliders, greatly intrigued Pilcher. He later borrowed some of these kites and tested them.

It was then that Fate struck. Pilcher had arranged to give a gliding demonstration for Henniker Heaton, M.P., on September 30th 1899 at Lord Braye's seat, Stanford Hall, near Market Harborough, in Leicestershire, where he was now making his flight trials. In addition to the tried and tested *Hawk*, Pilcher had his newly-completed triplane on show, and some of the Hargrave kites. The weather was miserable, with gusty winds and showers, but it eased a little in the afternoon and Pilcher decided to go ahead with the demonstration of the *Hawk* following trials of the kites.

On its first flight, the *Hawk*, with Pilcher piloting, was successfully launched from level ground: it was towed off by a line which ran over a pulley, and was attached to two horses: all went well, and the machine was rising smoothly, when the tow-line parted, and the *Hawk* glided gently to earth. The same thing happened next time, and then Pilcher decided on a third attempt. When the *Hawk* was at about 30 feet above the ground, a bamboo rod in the tail-assembly suddenly snapped; the tail-unit collapsed; and the *Hawk* dived into the ground. Pilcher was alive when released from

---

[1] This refers to Chanute's gliding experiments.

Fig. 60. Chanute's
biplane hang-glider,
utilising the Pratt
truss system of
rigging: 1896

Fig. 61. Pilcher's
patent drawing for
his first powered
machine: 1896

Fig. 62. Model glider built and
flown by Means, the Editor of
the *Aeronautical Annual*: 1893–94

Fig. 63. The first Wright aircraft
to incorporate their wing-warping
system; the biplane kite: 1899

89

the wreckage; but, after lingering on through the Sunday, he died early in the morning of Monday, October 2nd 1899, without recovering consciousness.[1]

Pilcher was one of the great aviation pioneers of history; and, if he had been spared, he might have attained proper powered, sustained, and controlled flight before the Wright brothers. Like Lilienthal, he approached the problem of flight with a balanced and mature attitude, knowing that theory and practice must constantly interplay and develop together. Chanute lists Pilcher's specific achievements as (1) the demonstration that too much dihedral reduces stability in side winds; (2) that an unduly low centre of gravity makes the machine difficult to control; (3) that safe take-offs can be made by towing; and (4) that a light-wheeled undercarriage is convenient for moving the machine about, and for absorbing shocks in landing. After his death, practical productive work in aviation in Britain became virtually moribund until the arrival of Cody's machine of 1908.

A suitable epitaph for Pilcher—a true airman—might be the following words he himself wrote in 1897:

"The object of experimenting with soaring machines is to enable one to have practice in starting and alighting, and controlling a machine in the air. . . . They are excellent schooling machines, and that is all they are meant to be, until power, in the shape of an engine working a screw propeller, or an engine working wings to drive the machine forward, is added; then a person who is used to sailing down a hill with a simple soaring machine will be able to fly with comparative safety."

Other Inventors

Of less technical stature than Chanute, but of great importance in aviation during the last decade of the century, was another American, James Means (1853–1920).[2] He was an industrialist who was primarily an intellectual, and gave up his business when he amassed enough money for his family to live on, and devoted himself to the promotion of aviation. He had a fine mind, excellent judgment, and high integrity. Although Means productively studied bird-flight, then kites and gliders, and designed model gliders in 1893–94 (Fig. 62), it was in the literary field of information and propaganda that his influence was most strongly felt. For in 1895 he issued the first of the three volumes of his *Aeronautical Annual*, a triple work of far-reaching importance and influence, which appeared in 1895, 1896 and 1897. As Means himself said, later on, he "thought that if he could gather the best of the world's literature on the subject and publish it, it might bring experimenters together, thus preventing waste of effort". This, Means proceeded to do, and to great effect. Like Chanute, he was determined to disseminate as much information about flying as possible, being convinced that mechanical flight would one day be achieved. So he collected and edited

---

[1] By an odd coincidence, it was also in this year 1899 that the first automobile driver (and his passenger) were killed in Britain, at Harrow: the driver was E. R. Sewell.

[2] For a long time Means was a figure of mystery: this has now been excellently remedied with a delightful and sympathetic biography by his son, Dr. James Howard Means, to whom historians owe a sincere debt of gratitude.

the most significant papers he could find on past and current developments, including the work of Lilienthal, Chanute, Langley, Hargrave and others; and also performed a valuable service by reprinting some of the classic papers by Cayley and Wenham, besides giving bibliographies and other useful material. These admirable volumes, which were also published in London, were read and studied by everyone seriously interested in heavier-than-air flight, and provided them with valuable data and encouragement. But it is symptomatic of the general apathy of the public, and the fin-de-siècle doldrums into which aviation had fallen, that Means was depressed enough to place the following dedication at the head of his last volume (1897), just six years before the Wrights flew: "To the memory of those who, intelligently believing in the possibility of mechanical flight, have lived derided, and died in sorrow and obscurity." He was happily to live—to his great satisfaction—to discover how much his *Aeronautical Annuals* had meant to the Wright brothers; and to witness, not only the triumph of the Wrights, but the general triumph of the aeroplane as a practical vehicle. Means was always to pursue his interest in, and concern for, aviation, and himself proved to be an inventor of a high order. In 1909 he patented a smoke-signal device for signalling from aircraft, and (also in 1909) an aircraft launcher: then in 1909 and 1911, he patented a simplified control-column for aeroplanes. But his lasting value lay back in the 1890's, where he helped others to make history.

On January 27th 1894 an interesting event occurred at Pirbright Camp in England when Captain B. F. S. Baden-Powell (brother of the first Chief Scout) made his first ascent sitting suspended from kites; he used monoplane kites, and flew first with one kite, then with a train of them. He should thus be reckoned as the first partially successful user of man-lifting kites outside the Orient, despite Pocock and Cordner: he thus started a minor fashion in military aerial observation techniques, which Cody was later to perfect.

Amongst the aviation pioneers there have been a number for whom extravagant claims have been made—as has already been noted—by persons not wholly disinterested. One of the most notorious—notorious because his very minor talent has been exploited in campaigns to discredit the Wrights—was the so-called 'Professor' John J. Montgomery of Santa Clara College in California, U.S.A. Oddly enough the best account—plain and unvarnished—of his work, appeared in the official court records of an action brought by his heirs against the United States Government (1917–25) which they lost when seeking to invalidate the Wrights', and other, patents. Montgomery first constructed models and unsuccessful full-size gliders during the years 1883–86. He then abandoned his experiments until late in 1903; then, having been impressed by the form of Langley's *Aerodromes*, he designed and built Langley-derived tandem-wing machines, but unpowered, which he intended should be taken up beneath hot-air balloons and released. A balloon parachute-jumper named D. Maloney agreed to pilot one of these balloon-borne gliders, and on March 16th 1905, he made a perilous descent from about 500 feet. On April 29th of 1905, a public display was planned, and Maloney again cast off and "luckily reached the ground without accident". On July 18th of the same year, another glide was made from a balloon and the machine crashed, killing Maloney. A Mr. Wilkie was then persuaded to pilot one of these gliders, and he narrowly escaped with his life on February 22nd 1906. Finally Montgomery himself was killed in 1911 in an 'improved' glider which he had constructed. Montgomery was not lacking in courage, but he lacked essential knowledge and experience and, despite the ingenious idea of launching a glider from a balloon—which had been proposed by Cayley in 1852—achieved little but publicity. He made no real contribution to aviation (Pl. XII).

*   *   *   *   *

Practical aviation in Europe at the turn of the century had reached a regrettable state of moribundity. Lilienthal and Pilcher were dead; Kress had abandoned his work after the crash of his machine in 1901; Jatho was making tests which were to lead nowhere; and only Ferber was enthusiastically but fruitlessly following Lilienthal before he was to be re-orientated by news of the Wright gliders. Airships and balloons were occupying most of the aeronautical stage, and as far as the public was concerned the achievement of mechanical flight was still far off. This view was also shared by many serious but discouraged investigators in England, France and Germany. What was worse, the few men who preserved their vision were often ridiculed, and the sceptics could proudly point to such great scientists as Lord Kelvin to support them. Kelvin even went so far as to commit his views to paper in a now notorious letter (it was written in answer to Major Baden-Powell's invitation to him to join the Aeronautical Society).

> "Dear Baden-Powell, I am afraid I am not in the flight for 'aerial navigation'. I was greatly interested in your work with kites but I have not the smallest molecule of faith in aerial navigation other than ballooning or of expectation of good results from any of the trials we hear of. So you will understand that I would not care to be a member of the Aeronautical Society. Yours truly, Kelvin."

This remarkable letter was dated December 8th 1896; in this year Lilienthal had died, Pilcher was gliding successfully in England, and Langley making powered models in America: just seven years later the Wrights were to fly a powered aeroplane.

Far away in Australia, Lawrence Hargrave laboured at the problem, but he was too far off the beaten track. The initiative in aviation had passed to the United States; but even there only a few men believed in the 'cause' and only one—Langley—was making any satisfactory progress, although Chanute was busy with ideas.

But with the wisdom of hindsight we can now see that this apparently barren field had been richly sown, and was only awaiting the favourable weather conditions to bring up a rich crop. The petrol motor, in the service of both automobiles and motor cycles, had reached a stage when it could be adapted for flying machines; and in 1896 the motor car had finally been given the freedom of the roads in Britain (Pl. VII), and the spread of automobilism thereby became fast and furious: apart from the immense technical advance which followed this emancipation, there was rapidly built up a great reservoir of trained mechanics, men who would be ready to serve powered aviation when it should arrive. There was a great deal of technical information on aerodynamics lying in somewhat obscure books and periodicals, and Chanute's *Progress in Flying Machines* (1894) conveniently summed up the historic and contemporary endeavours for anyone who wished to know how the land lay; and there was also to hand a growing number of competent and enthusiastic mechanics and amateurs dedicated to the pursuit of 'automobilisme', but ready and willing to transfer their allegiance to the aeroplane whenever it should arrive. Finally there was a growingly air-minded public and press, thanks to the long tradition of ballooning and the recent developments in practical airship building, especially in Santos-Dumont. There was, therefore, an admirable overall 'climate' awaiting the birth of the new vehicle.

Then, in the last year of the century, all the necessary talents and circumstances conspired finally to favour two modest but determined cycle makers of Dayton in Ohio, who in that year 1899 became seriously determined to conquer the air; and, within the span of four short years, were to succeed brilliantly.

Significant dates in other fields (*1890's*)

1890's   Electric tramways now in general use throughout the world.

1890's   Telephones now in general use.

1890's   Half-tone reproduction of photos now in universal use (after first commercial development in 1882).

1895   Automobile-Club de France founded.

1895   First cinema theatre opened (by Brothers Lumière in Paris).

1896   Freedom of the roads granted to motor cars in Britain, leading to a vast expansion of the motor industry.

1896   Parsons introduces the marine turbine, and puts on a startling and decisive demonstration with his *Turbinia* at the Spithead Review of 1897.

1897   Practical wireless telegraphy introduced by Marconi (first trans-Channel, 1899; first trans-Atlantic, 1901).

1897   Diesel makes first successful compression-ignition engine (which he had patented in 1892).

1897   Automobile Club (later Royal) founded in London.

11. *The Wright Brothers and the Invention of the Practical Aeroplane: 1899–1905*

WILBUR and Orville Wright were the first men to make powered, sustained, and controlled flights in an aeroplane, and land on ground as high as that from which they took off. They were also the first to make and fly a fully *practical* powered aeroplane, one that could take off and land without damage to itself or its occupant, and could fly straight, turn and circle with ease. Finally they were the first to make and fly a practical passenger-carrying aeroplane. The first of these achievements was brought about on December 17th 1903; the second by the autumn of 1905; and the third in 1908. The Wrights were also first to build and fly properly controllable gliders, and the first to master glider flight. All these successes—and more—are fully documented and established, and are unequivocally accepted by all modern aeronautical historians. Beside these monumental achievements it seems pointless to place any other claims for prior powered flights. Every claim to ante-date the Wright brothers involves events of such minuscule significance when compared with what the Wrights accomplished, that they can never possess more than minor historic interest: what is more, none of the activities which have been the subject of such claims has materially contributed to the advance of aviation.

Wilbur (1867–1912) and Orville (1871–1948) were the sons of a United Brethren Church Bishop, and lived in Dayton, Ohio. They had progressed from the selling of bicycles to their manufacture, and built up a modest business which alone provided the funds for their work in aviation. They had had an interest in flying since boyhood, and had read all they could find on the subject—including Marey's *Animal Mechanism*—but the interest was not crystallised in the mind of Wilbur, who took the initiative in the early days, until 1896: "my own active interest in aeronautical problems", he wrote, "dates to the death of Lilienthal".[1] He was still to take no definite action until 1899, when his study of bird-flight suddenly determined him to take up aviation seriously, and gave him an important starting point for his experiments: "My observations of the flight of buzzards", he wrote, "led me to believe that they regain their lateral balance when partly overturned by a gust of wind, by a torsion of the tips of the wings." It should be made clear that it was Chanute who, in 1903, invented the misleading term 'warping',

---

[1] There is now evidence to show that it was an article on Lilienthal in an issue of *McClure's Magazine* in 1894 (pp. 323–31) which first aroused Wilbur's interest: it was excellently illustrated by dramatic photographs of Lilienthal gliding, and this magazine is known to have been subscribed to by the Wright family. Lilienthal's death in 1896 probably finally focussed Wilbur's active attention.

which—as a kind of shorthand term—was also adopted by the Wrights. The word 'twisting' or better still, 'helical twisting', was what the Wrights themselves had previously used: but Chanute's term became accepted; and the French translated it literally as 'gauchir' and 'gauchissement'. I have used the words 'warp' and 'warping' (etc.) in accordance with what became common—but misleading—usage. This idea of 'wing-warping' for providing control in roll became closely associated in the public mind with the Wrights' flying, and was later to be misunderstood and distorted: it has led to many misapprehensions and fruitless controversies about what the Wrights claimed and performed.

In May of that year (1899) Wilbur wrote to the Smithsonian Institution in Washington, asking for information about books and articles on flying: a list of works was duly sent to him, and one of the most influential of those recommended was Chanute's *Progress in Flying Machines*, published in 1894. Orville was soon to be as enthusiastic as his brother, and from then onwards they read omnivorously and began rapidly to develop the latent qualities which—within a comparatively short time—were to transform two young bicycle makers into outstanding engineers and inventors. After an exhaustive collection of their technical papers was published,[1] it has been possible to trace their astonishing evolution in applied science, and view it in proper relation to their personal qualities and capabilities. This publication should also put an end, once and for all, to the popular belief that the Wrights were little better than ingenious mechanics who had more than their share of good fortune.

The Wrights built their first aircraft in August 1899: it was a biplane kite of 5 foot span, with a fixed horizontal tailplane, designed to test the efficacy of wing warping, but with the added feature of wings which could be shifted forward or backward in relation to one another in order to control the centre of pressure, the tailplane then acting as an elevator (Fig. 63).

In 1900 Wilbur wrote to Chanute, telling him of their work and their idea of warping, and seeking his encouragement and advice on how they could enlarge the scope of their reading and information. This letter was to lead to a long and close friendship, only marred in later years by a little jealousy. Although they constantly discussed their work with Chanute, and welcomed his appraisal and criticism, they received only three contributions from the old man, which they freely acknowledged: the basic idea of a biplane, which Chanute himself had adopted—*via* Cayley and Stringfellow—having first tried a triplane configuration, following Stringfellow's model of 1868; the Pratt-truss method of rigging it[2]; and constant friendly encouragement. They owed him nothing else of technical importance, which Chanute was later to admit: indeed, as a result of their own experiments they later had to revise much of the data and conclusions arrived at by Chanute, Lilienthal and others. But it was to Lilienthal that they owed their chief introduction to aerodynamics, and they always held him in high esteem, discussing his findings and their own in many letters to Chanute over the years.

[1] *The Papers of Wilbur and Orville Wright.* Edited by Marvin W. McFarland, 2 vols., New York, 1953.　　　[2] Other forms of truss could have been used.

In this first period of enthusiasm and determination, the Wrights arrived at certain basic conclusions which were to become of the highest importance to practical flying. In their careful and extensive study of other men's work they came to realise the two radically different concepts of aviation already held—though unconsciously—by the pioneers, despite the fact that the practical aeroplane had not yet been born. These concepts, and attitudes, have already been described in this book; they are the chauffeur's and the airman's. The former, deriving direct from the previous generations of model-makers and experimenters, looked upon an aeroplane as a machine which men designed, constructed and made to work, the inventors regarding themselves as 'outside' the machines they created. As engines became more efficient they set to building full-size aircraft on the same principles—especially the incorporation of a high degree of inherent stability—which the human pilot would have to drive and guide, as a chauffeur would an automobile or a seaman a ship. Typical of this school were Ader, Maxim and Langley, and after them the early aviators of Europe between 1905 and 1909. This somewhat rigid 'outside' attitude kept the chauffeur inventors too intent upon inherent stability, and led them to neglect control and manoeuvrability in the air, or at best to treat these vital matters in a dangerously cavalier fashion.[1]

The airmen school of experimenters, although just as concerned with theory and research as their rivals, saw themselves as essentially 'partakers' in the enterprise of flying, living and working as 'parts' of their aircraft and thus co-operating and identifying themselves with the machines they made. They looked upon the aeroplane—first the glider and then the powered machine—as something to experience, to learn in, and to fly in. Each could say, with Mlle. Françoise Sagan, "Je veux faire corps avec la machine", which I have already quoted, but whose excellence will bear repetition. Typical of this attitude, following long after Cayley and Le Bris, were Lilienthal, Pilcher, Ferber, Chanute and the Wrights. The men of this school at first took up into the air the same concept of inherent stability, inherited from their ancestors: but the very problems facing them as they rode their gliders into the wind, began to make them consider a more dynamic approach to control and stability. Unfortunately the first 'airman' pioneers flew at continual risk of their lives—"a hundred necks have to be broken", wrote Cayley in 1846, "before all the sources of accident can be ascertained and guarded against"—and both Lilienthal and Pilcher were killed before they could get far towards solving the problems of control and stability in the air.

So when the Wrights built their first glider in 1900 (Pl. VIII) it incorporated two ideas which the brothers were to utilise throughout their early work—the intentionally unstable aeroplane which could be kept flying satisfactorily only by the pilot's skill, and the warping of the wings for control in roll. "We therefore resolved", wrote Wilbur, "to try a fundamentally different principle. We would arrange the machine so that it would not tend to right itself." Their technique of wing-warping consisted of a helical

[1] It has been suggested that such 'chauffeurs' as Maxim and Langley were comparatively old men, whereas the 'airmen' were young; but many young men were also 'chauffeurs' and the aged Chanute was a true 'airman'.

PLATE IX

a Wright No. 3 glider, in its second and final form, with a single rear rudder: 1902

b Wright *Flyer I* making the world's first powered, sustained and controlled flight on December 17th 1903 (Orville piloting): this was the first of four flights that day

c Wright *Flyer III*, the world's first practical aeroplane: 1905 (see also Frontispiece)

8+A.

PLATE X

a The Kress tandem-wing powered float-plane on the Tullnerbach reservoir: 1901

b Santos-Dumont's airship No. 6 circles the Eiffel Tower: 1901 (model)

c Jatho's powered semi-biplane: 1903

d Langley's full-size *Aerodrome A* on its launching catapult above the Potomac River: 1903 twisting of the wings, which produced a positive angle of incidence on one side, and a negative angle on the other, thus causing the machine to return to the horizontal, or to bank: they also believed—mistakenly—that they would be able to steer to right or left by warping alone, but no attempts at such steering were made until 1901.

The glider was completed in September of 1900 at Dayton and transported to the lonely sand-dunes of Kitty Hawk,[1] on the coast of North Carolina, a place decided upon after receiving from the Washington Weather Bureau a comparative table of locations having strong and constant winds. This *No. 1* glider was similar to the kite, but had fixed biplane wings of 17 feet span, with warping control, a movable forward elevator—which they called a "horizontal rudder"—and a prone pilot position in order to be more comfortable, make landing safer, and to reduce head resistance: the wing area was 165 square feet. It had no tail surfaces. This tentative machine was flown during October, and provided the Wrights with the first confirmation of their basic ideas. It was mostly flown as a kite (the controls worked from the ground); owing to lack of strong winds, only a few manned pilot-controlled kite-flights were made, and only a few free piloted glides: it showed good response to the elevator and to the wing-warping device (Pl. VIII). The forward positioning of the elevator, on this and on all Wright aircraft until 1910, was dictated by their belief that it provided the safest fore and aft control, especially when the centre of pressure on the wings travelled backwards and caused the machine to nose-dive. This glider also confirmed their disbelief in any automatic stability: they had at first rigged it with a dihedral angle and found it flew badly in gusty winds; so they abandoned dihedral, and temporarily rigged their wings level.

They returned to Dayton well pleased with their short stay at Kitty Hawk. They were now all the more determined to fly; but also to proceed carefully and logically, concentrating particularly on control in the air: "When once a machine is under proper control under all conditions, the motor problem will be quickly solved", wrote Wilbur when building this first glider.

Next year (1901) they constructed their biplane glider *No. 2*, with the wing area increased to 290 square feet, a span of 22 feet, an anhedral 'droop' of 4 inches, and the warping wires worked by a hip-cradle (Pl. VIII). The Wrights had been working on figures for wing area and camber compiled by Lilienthal—which they read in translated articles—and other experimenters, and they decided on a camber of 1 in 12 for the new machine. In July they transported it to the Kill Devil sand hills near Kitty Hawk, and made the first glide on the 27th of the month. The flights continued through the first half of August, and many were witnessed there by Chanute on the first visit which he paid to the camp. The glider was launched by two men—one of the brothers and a 'local'—who grasped the wing-tips and ran the machine the short distance necessary for it to become airborne. They soon found that their wing camber was too deep, and was producing an excessive movement of the centre of pressure as the angle of incidence changed. So they reduced the curvature to 1 in 19, and the performance and control were greatly

---

[1] From 1901 onwards, they flew from the Kill Devil sand hills, 4 miles south of Kitty Hawk, where they set up a hutted camp.

improved. Glides of up to 389 feet were made, and control maintained in winds of up to about 27 m.p.h.

The Wrights returned to Dayton with mixed feelings. They had achieved a certain measure of success, but they realised that their results were far from satisfactory. They now began to suspect the accuracy of Lilienthal's calculations, upon which they had relied until now. The aircraft also showed an alarming tendency—when being warped—for the positively warped wings to swing *back*, and for the whole machine to slew round as it side-slipped, and crash. "Having set out with absolute faith in the existing scientific data", wrote Wilbur, "we were driven to doubt one thing after another, till finally, after two years of experiment, we cast it all aside, and decided to rely entirely upon our own investigations."

It was this dissatisfaction with the whole situation that then led them, between September 1901 and August 1902, to undertake a vigorous and intensive programme of research, including the testing of aerofoil sections in a wind-tunnel and on a bicycle, as well as thoroughly reworking all their aerodynamic problems. In this way they laid the secure foundations for later success, and then set about building their new glider (*No. 3*) with confidence.

It is interesting to note that Wilbur, at Chanute's request, gave a lecture in Chicago (September 18th 1901) on the two short 'seasons' of gliding, in which he not only gave a description of the machines but also of the wing-warping technique. "A devilish good paper", was how Chanute described it, "which will be extensively quoted." It is also interesting to remember that Langley, in 1901, had made his unsuccessful petrol-powered model *Aerodrome* which was to precede the full-size machine tested in 1903.

The new glider (*No. 3*), built of spruce and cloth and "to withstand hard usage", was constructed during August and September of 1902, and first flown on September 20th (Pl. VIII). Between that date and the end of October nearly a thousand glides were made; they met and surmounted their last major control problem; and by the end of the season possessed a fully practical machine which had only to be copied and slightly modified before they were ready to fit an engine. This new biplane glider had a wing area of 305 square feet, a span of 32 feet 1 inch, a camber of 1 in 24 to 1 in 30, the same anhedral 'droop' or 'arch' as the *No. 2*, and the same warping system: but there was added to the rear a double fixed fin to counteract (by its weather-vane action) the swing-back of the wings on the positively warped side, in the case either of regaining lateral balance after being gusted out of the horizontal, or of the pilot initiating a bank. The machine, which was launched by two men, like its predecessor, behaved well in some of the glides; but severe trouble arose with deliberate warped banks or gust-produced (non-warped) banks, when the pilot—in trying to limit the bank or in trying to return to the horizontal—applied positive warp to the dropped wings in order to raise them: instead of coming up, these dropped wings would sink or swing back, and the machine would spin and crash.

The Wrights diagnosed the basic trouble as warp-drag (aileron-drag today) where the positive warp increased the resistance of the wings on one side, and the negative warp decreased it on the other, causing them not only to bank, but to turn about their vertical axis in the opposite direction to that originally anticipated. The addition of the fixed rear fin caused them much more trouble than it cured. For, in the acts of banking noted above, the resulting side-slip caused the fin to act as a lever, and rotate the wings about their vertical axis, thus increasing the speed (and thus the lift and height) of the raised wings, whilst retarding and lowering the dropped wings. When the pilot applied positive warp to the dropped wings, it simply aggravated the situation, and produced a spin, by swinging back the dropped wings through warp-drag, thus increasing their incidence beyond the stalling angle.

This problem was solved by converting the fixed double fin into a single movable rudder, which—with its cables fastened to the warp-cradle—was always turned towards the direction of bank, thus counteracting the warp-drag (Pl. IX). As the rudder was also (but unintentionally) adjusted to more than compensate for the warp-drag, the machine could also be made to perform a smooth banked turn. Experience with this glider also convinced them that all their machines should continue to be made inherently unstable to allow of sensitive and immediate response to the controls.

After this vital step, the Wrights had a practical and highly successful glider, with which they made nearly a thousand perfectly controlled glides often in winds of up to 35 m.p.h.; they set a distance record of 622½ feet, and a duration record of 26 seconds. "The flights of 1902", wrote Orville, "demonstrated the efficiency of our system of control for both longitudinal and lateral stability. They also demonstrated that our tables of air pressure which we made in our wind-tunnel would enable us to calculate in advance the performance of a machine."

Both brothers became experienced and skilful pilots; and with so much flying behind them both, and so many theoretical and practical problems solved, they felt fully justified in their fundamental idea of constructing an unstable machine whose stability and control in the air depended solely upon the pilot's skill. They realised that if such a machine could be suitably engined they would have in their hands not only a machine that would fly, but a practical aeroplane that would be almost as sensitive and manoeuvrable as a bird.

The combination of warp and rudder, rather than the warping idea itself, was the most essential feature of the patent applied for by the Wrights in 1902, and granted in 1906 (Fig. 64). This feature of the Wrights' work is consistently misunderstood—and hence misrepresented—by many writers.

They returned to Dayton justly elated and fully confident of success. But there were still two major problems facing them—the engine and the propeller. The engine was not at first seen as a serious question since they thought one of the numerous automobile engines on sale at that time would be suitable: but on enquiry, they found that none of them were light enough for their power. And so these remarkable men set to, and not only designed their own motor, but built it: it was of 12 h.p., was water-cooled, and weighed (with all accessories, plus water and fuel) about 200 lb. When it came to the question of propellers, the Wrights realised that the problem was indeed formidable, as the small amount of published material was useless to them: so they conducted their own basic research, developed a satisfactory airscrew and so finally surmounted their last major obstacle.

It was in 1902 and 1903 that news and illustrations of the Wrights' gliders became available in France; and, first through Ferber, then through Chanute's lecture in Paris (on April 2nd 1903), the Europeans were directly influenced to revive aviation on the Continent.

The Wrights' first powered machine, the *Flyer*—a name they applied to all their powered machines—was constructed during the summer of 1903; it was transported to the Kill Devil Hills on September 23rd–25th, where the brothers found their camp in bad repair, and the 1902 glider damaged. They repaired the glider to practise on, giving it a new double rear rudder like the one on the new *Flyer*. Then came weeks of careful preparation, practice gliding, and many minor but exasperating set-backs. Mechanical breakages, repairs, replacements, and adjustments of one kind and another delayed having the *Flyer* ready for tests until December 12th, when all was in good order. But unfavourable weather postponed the first test until December 14th. The brothers summoned as witnesses their friends from the nearby Kill Devil Life Saving Station, and carried their machine to the end of the starting rail.

The powered *Flyer*,[1] which stood there ready for its first trial, was a biplane of 40 feet 4 inches span, a wing area of 510 square feet, and camber of about 1 in 20, supported on two long skids; the 12-h.p. engine drove two pusher propellers by means of cycle-chains, one of which was crossed to produce counter-rotation (Pl. IX). In appearance and control it was similar to the *No. 3* glider of 1902, except that both the vertical rear rudder, and the front elevator were now double structures.

On this day, December 14th, it was placed on the 60-foot launching rail which had been laid downhill and into wind. The Wrights tossed a coin to decide who should be the first pilot, and Wilbur won. But the test was a failure: the *Flyer* ran down the rail, rose from the carrying truck, climbed steeply, stalled and ploughed into the sand, causing minor damage to the structure. Wilbur admitted that the failure was due to his error in putting on too much elevator, and thus bringing the nose up too high. The damage was soon repaired and they again waited for a suitable day. Incidentally, even if this first trial had succeeded, it would not have counted as a true flight, as the take-off was downhill and so assisted by gravity.

On Thursday December 17th conditions were again suitable, with a wind of some 20–27 m.p.h., and the take-off rail was laid down on level ground. Local witnesses were again summoned, who now numbered five, and a camera was set up and trained on the end of the take-off track. With Orville at the controls—it was now his turn—the engine of the *Flyer* was run up, and at 10.35 a.m. the holding rope was released and the machine was off.[2] It rose

---

[1] In later years the machine became known by the historically incorrect and inappropriate name of *Kitty Hawk*, a name which has now unfortunately 'stuck' to it.

[2] It has sometimes been stated that the Wrights used an accelerated take-off device for their first flights. This is not so. In 1904, as described later, they invented the weight-and-derrick method of assisted take-off in order to operate from the confined space of the Huffman Prairie near Dayton, and to make them less dependent upon the weather.

from the truck after a run of about 40 feet and made an undulating flight of some 12 seconds, covering 120 feet before it landed. The rise and fall was due to inexperience with the elevator, which was too evenly balanced, and to consequent over-correction; airspeed was about 30 m.p.h. Although of only 12 seconds' duration, this flight was, in Orville's words, "the first in the history of the world in which a machine carrying a man had raised itself by its own power into the air in full flight, had sailed forward without reduction of speed, and had finally landed at a point as high as that from which it started" (Pl. IX). (For telegram, etc., see page 225.)

After a minor repair, three more flights were made that morning, the brothers alternating as pilot: the second flight covered about 175 feet; the third some 200 feet; and the fourth, which lasted 59 seconds, covered 852 feet; but the true distance through the air was just over half a mile, owing to the head wind.[1] On landing after this last flight the elevator was damaged, and it was decided to end the trials. The machine was carried back to the camp and there, a few minutes later, it was overturned by a gust of wind and wrecked. "As winter was already well set in, we should have postponed our trials to a more favourable season, but for the fact that we were determined, before returning home, to know whether the machine possessed sufficient power to fly, sufficient strength to withstand the shocks of landing, and sufficient capacity of control to make flight safe in boisterous winds, as well as in calm air. When these points had been definitely established, we at once packed our goods and returned home, knowing that the age of the flying machine had come at last."

The Wright brothers had tentatively conquered the air four-and-a-half years after they had written to the Smithsonian Institution asking for books on flying. Now, in 1903, Wilbur was thirty-six yearas old, Orville thirty-two. They had made the first powered, sustained and controlled flights, and possessed the first potentially practical flying machine. No aeroplanes other than the Wrights could remain in the air for more than 20 seconds until November of 1906; and it was not until November of 1907 that a full minute's duration was achieved by a European machine. The Wrights' task now was to produce a properly practical machine, which they evolved successfully in 1904 and 1905.

Owing to a curious chain of circumstances the world was only given a garbled description of the flights of December 17th, and they were therefore treated as the wayward efforts of two eccentric brothers. But even more astonishing was the fact that the Wrights flew in public continually in 1904 and 1905 without attracting world-wide attention.

Back in Dayton the brothers began designing their powered *Flyer II* and a new motor. Construction was finished in May, and a new 'aerodrome' established eight miles east of Dayton, near Simms Station: it was a 90-acre field called the Huffman Prairie (or Pasture) lent to the brothers by a Dayton banker, Torrence Huffman. This, the world's first aerodrome for aviation, saw the first tests of *Flyer II* on May 23rd or 26th. The new machine, basically similar to the *No. 1*, had the camber decreased from 1 in 20 to 1 in 25, a

---

[1] This was the Wrights' own estimate.

much more efficient engine of 15–16 h.p., and lower gearing to new propellers. During the summer, autumn and winter, 105 trials and some 80 brief flights were made, the Wrights concentrating on becoming familiar with the controls, the care of the engine, and the use of the assisted take-off device which they first employed on September 7th. The latter consisted of a weight hung from a rope inside a tall derrick: the rope travelled to the top of the derrick, down to the starting end of the launching track, along the track to the take-off end, then back to the starting end, where it was attached to a hinged rod on the lower wing. When the weight was released, the rope—working over pulley wheels—drew the aircraft on its truck fast along the length of the launching track. This assisted take-off device was used by the Wrights—and by all Wright aircraft—until 1910, although a few owners of Wright machines were attaching wheels to the skids in 1909. Although the majority of flights in the 1904 season were short, they were of great importance; were often witnessed by friends, including Chanute; and were photographed. The first circular flight was made by Wilbur on September 20th—after which the manoeuvre became commonplace—and the first flight of over 5 minutes took place on November 9th, when Wilbur made almost four circles of the pasture, a distance of about 2¾ miles.

The flights in 1904 were all made at very low heights, so that in learning both the particular characteristics of the aircraft and the craft of pilotage in general, they had a good chance of survival in a crash. This low-flying policy was also retained for a further reason: there was still one flying problem they could not understand or solve, and that was the *Flyer*'s tendency not to respond to the controls, then stall and go out of control, when making a tight turn. This trouble was not mastered until September of 1905.

As their patent was pending in America and other countries, the Wrights allowed witnesses close up to the machine, but no photographs were allowed to be taken other than their own. Groups of pressmen had visited them by invitation on two days at the start of the season, but weather and mechanical failure had prevented flights on both occasions, and the disillusioned Press had refused to take notice of them thereafter until late in 1905, despite constant reports from the local farmers and others, who through 1904 and 1905 came to take the sight of a flying aeroplane for granted at a time when many authorities were asserting that mechanical flight was impossible.

In 1905 the Wrights designed their *Flyer III* and completed it in June. It proved a thoroughly successful vehicle, and ranks as the first all-round practical aeroplane in history (Frontispiece and Pl. IX). Wing area was slightly reduced, to 503 square feet; the span was 40 feet 6 inches; the camber was put back to 1 in 20; the wings were rigged horizontally flat with no anhedral droop; the biplane elevator was enlarged and placed farther out in front of the wings; the double rear rudder was also enlarged and placed farther back; and the whole machine was mounted higher on its skids and made more robust. New propellers were fitted, but the excellent 1904 engine was retained. This new machine made its first flight at the Huffman Prairie on June 23rd and its trials went on until October 16th. They made over forty flights this season, and were airborne for just over three hours; this time they were out for reliability and endurance. In September, the trouble they were having in tight turns was diagnosed as a tendency of the lowered wings to slow up and stall; and the cure seen to be in putting down the nose to gain speed when turning. On September 26th they flew 11⅛ miles in 18 minutes 9 seconds; on September 29th, 12 miles in 19 minutes 55 seconds; on October 3rd, 15¼ miles in 25 minutes 5 seconds; on October 4th, 20¾ miles in 33 minutes 17 seconds; and on October 5th, 24⅕ miles in 38 minutes 3 seconds, at an average speed of 38 m.p.h., a flight, as with others of this series, which only stopped because the fuel was exhausted. The last flight of the season was made on October 16th. Apart from the achievement of a practical aeroplane, the Wrights had made a final and important change in their flying control system during the latter part of this season. In the course of seeking a cure for the stalling on turns, they had disconnected the warping and rudder wires. This allowed of any desired degree of warp or rudder movement being made, either together or separately; and, amongst other things, made reestablishment of lateral equilibrium in gusts, etc. possible without any turning movement being brought about by the rear rudder. This freeing of the controls, and their proper co-ordination in the air, contributed still further to the mastery of mechanical flying. The final step was to seat the pilot upright, which was done when the 1905 *Flyer* was modified for practice flying in 1908, when upright seating for two was fitted. It was not to be until October 16th 1908 that a European pilot was to equal the Wrights' 1905 performances, when Henri Farman (who was then British) flew for 41 mins. 32 sec.

With the *Flyer III* of 1905 the Wrights had now for all practical purposes "conquered the air": in the words of Charles Dollfus, speaking of the brothers' work, "ils ont changé la face du Monde" (Frontispiece).

As the year 1905 had progressed, and as the Wrights' flights had become ever more impressive, word of their success had been reaching various commercial and military quarters, and even the Press was slowly awakening to what was going on. However, the Wrights, who had decided that they would not reveal their invention to the world without legal protection and some financial reward for their work, grew worried about the preservation of secrecy. As their patent was still pending—it was not to be granted until 1906—they were not anxious to have shrewd spectators come close up to the machine. They had tried to interest the United States Government on three occasions, but, to their anger and astonishment, they were stupidly rebuffed on the grounds that the Board of Ordnance was not interested in aircraft that did not exist! The Board could not understand that the Wrights were offering it a completed practical machine. Thereafter they began looking overseas for recognition, starting first with an offer to the British Government. By the end of 1905 and the start of 1906, informed quarters in France were convinced that the Wrights had had a triumphant and successful season in 1905, and had produced a practical aeroplane: this view was put forward unequivocally in the January (1906) issue of *L'Aérophile*, and caused widespread consternation in Europe, and a confused determination to rival the Wrights' achievements (see pages 116–9). In England, where public, and even technical, opinion was moribund in the extreme, only a few men realised the true significance of what was happening: chief of these was

Colonel J. E. Capper, Superintendent of the Government Balloon Factory (to become later the Royal Aircraft Establishment), who had met the Wrights[1] and privately written to the War Office on January 30th 1905:

> "I wish to invite very special attention to the wonderful advance made in aviation by the brothers Wright. I have every confidence in their uprightness, and in the correctness of their statements . . . It is a fact that they have flown and operated personally a flying machine for a distance of over three miles, at a speed of 35 m.p.h."

Negotiations with the United States government broke down when the U.S. Army completely refused to accept the fact that the Wrights were offering them a finished aeroplane, and not—as the Army thought—asking for financial assistance in building one: this was despite the most explicit statements and explanations by the Wrights. Disillusioned and rightly resentful of the treatment they had received from their own Government, they then (in 1905) decided to offer their *Flyer* to the British Government. Negotiations with Britain dragged on for some years, and foundered chiefly on the Wrights' demand—understandable but short-sighted—that no one should be allowed to view the machine until after the purchase had been completed; such purchase depending on an agreed performance having been carried out by the machine. They did not want the *Flyer* examined, then some excuse made for not purchasing it, despite its ability to perform as stated.

There was also some question of the French purchasing the *Flyer*; but that, too, fell through for the time being.

So they decided to stop all flying, and thus provide no opportunity for commercial or military spying, or other unwelcome visitations; then to continue negotiations with anyone who was interested in the idea of buying the *Flyer*.

And so it came about that for two and a half years, from October 16th 1905 until May 6th 1908, they never once left the ground, nor allowed any stranger to see their aeroplanes. And so the first great phase of the Wright brothers' career came to an end, to be followed in 1908 by a second and no less triumphant one.

It is perhaps appropriate to close this section with Sir Walter Raleigh's words: "It is not extravagant to say that the 17th of December 1903, when the Wright brothers made the first free flight through the air in a power-driven machine, marks the beginning of a new era in the history of the world."

---

[1] Capper was sent by the War Office to report on the aeronautical aspects of the St. Louis Exposition of 1904. When he was in the U.S.A., he went to see Chanute, Langley, and the Wright brothers. He visited the Wrights on October 23rd 1904. He was one of the few people to whom the Wrights showed photographs of their machines in the air. Capper was deeply impressed by the brothers, and was high in their praise long before he wrote the memorandum quoted here from the R.E. Committee; and much of the inspiration for Cody's first powered aeroplane of 1908 came from the Wrights *via* Capper.

12. *The Beginnings of Practical Aviation in Europe, and Elsewhere: 1902–1908*[1]

DURING the opening years of this century in Europe the prospect of achieving a practical powered aeroplane seemed very remote. Aeronautical attention was fixed on the balloon and the dirigible airship, the latter coming rapidly into prominence. In 1900 Count von Zeppelin flew his first giant airship over Lake Constance: in 1901 Santos-Dumont piloted his dirigible *No. 6* round the Eiffel Tower, thereby winning both a prize and the acclaim of Europe (Pl. X). In 1903 the Lebaudy brothers achieved the really practical dirigible when they saw their ship piloted on the first properly controlled aerial voyage in history; on November 12th it flew 38 miles from Moisson to the Champ-de-Mars, inside Paris. With these, and an ever-growing series of flights, the practical airship 'arrived' in the world of transport after its birth with Giffard in 1852.

1902 and 1903

The true revival of aviation, and the birth of practical flying, in Europe was due directly to the Wright brothers, as is clear both from the configurations adopted and from the numerous contemporary statements by the pioneers themselves. The revival was effected through the work of four Frenchmen in 1902–04, and resulted in two parallel streams of development of the biplane; and later in the revival and development of the monoplane.

The Wrights precipitated the European revival in two phases, the one reinforcing the other. First to be influenced was Captain Ferdinand Ferber, of the French artillery, the only European disciple of Lilienthal still seriously pursuing aviation in 1901: he was experimenting with a hang-glider derived from the great German pioneer. He had begun by making and testing gliders in 1899, influenced by Lilienthal, and from that year until the end of 1901 made four machines, starting with kite forms and ending with a Lilienthal type glider; all, however, were pursued without success. Then, about October 1901, he happened to read a magazine article on gliding: this led to a correspondence with Chanute in America and, in January 1902, to Ferber receiving from him a reprint of Wilbur Wright's first Chicago lecture (given on September 18th 1901) describing and illustrating the *Nos. 1* and *2* Wright gliders of 1900 and 1901 and their wing-warping; neither had rear

[1] For greater detail, see C. H. Gibbs-Smith, "*The Rebirth of European Aviation, 1902–1908*", HMSO London 1974.

fin or rudder. This event proved decisive for Ferber and thus for European aviation.

Ferber promptly abandoned the Lilienthal tradition and, as he said of himself, took "solely to the Wright type in 1902", the first of which he tested at Beuil in June 1902 (Pl. XI). This was Europe's first Wright-type glider, but it was crudely constructed and did not even incorporate wing-warping. In *L'Aérophile* for February 1903, this machine was well described and illustrated. It was the first piloted Wright-type glider to be properly 'seen' by the Europeans. The Ferber machines had non-rigid surfaces, the most primitive elevator control, and no warping: later he placed a triangular vertical rudder at each wing-tip. The results, as might be expected, were poor; and Ferber had at that time neither the knowledge nor experience to make much improvement. Thus the form of the Wright aeroplane first came to Europe in 1902 without its substance. Meanwhile Ferber, who was dogged and ambitious, had also built a powered twin-propeller Wright-type glider without an elevator, which he hung and tested on a giant whirling arm at Nice in December 1902: this machine was also a primitive affair, with totally inadequate lifting surfaces and controls, and was a complete failure. But Ferber was later to have a powerful influence on European flying.

There were four other European pioneers who deserve mention during these barren early years. The first, isolated in Austria, was Wilhelm Kress who had been experimenting with rubber-driven models since 1877, and in 1880 published a remarkable design for a powered flying-boat.[1] In 1898–99—curiously paralleling Langley's models—he constructed a full-size man-carrying flying-boat: it was a tandem-wing machine with rear elevator and rudder, powered by an over-heavy 30 h.p. Daimler petrol engine driving two propellers. Kress had to wait until October 1901 to test it: then unfortunately the machine was capsized and wrecked by too sharp a turn while taxying on the Tullnerbach Reservoir, before any flight test could be made. Although ingenious, and the first full-size petrol-driven aeroplane to be built, it did not influence the course of aviation (Pl. X).

In Germany, Karl Jatho briefly emerged to take a small place in the early history of the aeroplane, but he did not influence aviation. Jatho was a civil servant in Hanover, and in 1903 completed what was little more than a large powered kite: it had a 9-h.p. petrol engine and a primitive pusher propeller, but there were neither tail-unit, nor control-surfaces forward of the 'planes', and only rudimentary rudder and elevator devices. On August 18th he made a 'running jump' claimed to be 18 metres; then in November, with the structure modified to biplane form, the machine made another hop of 60 metres (say 200 ft.). These tests took place on the Vahrenwalder Heide, north of Hanover with take-offs, probably down hill; they are not claimed as true flights, even in Germany, where the word "Flugsprung" (leap into the air) has been used for them: he therefore may make the minor claim to be the first German to leave the ground in a powered aeroplane (Pl. X), somewhat like Ader in France.[2]

---

[1] Kress was a Russian, of German origin, who became an Austrian citizen. He was at first inspired by Pénaud.   [2] Ader, however, did take off from level ground.

In England, S. F. Cody (who will appear more importantly later) was following Baden-Powell in experiments with man-lifting kites. Cody patented his man-lifting kite in 1901, and it consisted of a train of kites supporting a cable, up which ran another kite—the actual man-lifter—with a seat hanging beneath, the rise and fall of this big kite being controlled by the pilot altering its angle of attack. The kites had an excellent form, being basically a Hargrave box-kite with wings built out from the top—the large aerofoils being on the front cells and the small on the back. These kites were tested by the British War Office in 1904–05, and officially adopted in 1906.

1903 and 1904

In March 1903 Octave Chanute arrived on a visit to Europe, and on April 2nd gave an illustrated talk in Paris at a 'diner-conférence' of the Aéro-Club de France, describing in detail his own and the Wrights' gliders; but this time it was the sophisticated *No. 3* Wright glider in its final form that received most attention, along with the information—but not raison d'être—of the simultaneous use of warping and rudder. This pivotal lecture was followed by illustrated published reports of it, and fuller articles written by Chanute and others, including (in August) scale drawings of the Wright machine. It was these new revelations of the Wrights' successful gliding—Chanute's own gliders were largely disregarded—and the excellent accompanying photographs and drawings of the Wrights' *No. 3* machine, which precipitated the chief revival of aviation in Europe. This revival had as its mainspring and leader the rich lawyer-sportsman, Ernest Archdeacon, who now (1903) created an Aviation Committee in the Aéro-Club de France to promote heavier-than-air flying; the avowed intent was to beat the Wrights in the race to achieve the powered aeroplane.

The Comte de La Vaulx—who was to found the Fédération Aéronautique Internationale in 1905—wrote later (1911) of Chanute's lecture:

"For most of his [Chanute's] listeners, except Ferber and his friends, it was a revelation, a revelation even a little disagreeable; when we spoke at times in France rather vaguely about the flights of the Wright brothers, we were far from doubting their remarkable progress; but Chanute was now admirably explicit about them and indicated their full significance. The French aviators at last felt that, despite their own enlightened views, they had been resting on the laurels of their elders a little too long, and that it was time for them to get seriously to work if they did not wish to be left behind. These facts particularly impressed themselves on the mind of one man, who was to play a great role in the evolution of French aviation—Ernest Archdeacon. . . . Anxious to keep for his country the glory of seeing born the first man-carrying aeroplane which would raise itself from the ground by its own power . . . Ernest Archdeacon decided to shake our aviators out of their torpor (de secouer le torpeur de nos aviateurs), and put a stop to the indifference of French opinion concerning flying machines."

Although feeling was running high, as contemporary documents make very clear, Archdeacon, Ferber and their friends seemed strangely complacent, and were content to make haste slowly. Archdeacon was a wealthy Paris lawyer, automobilist, balloonist and patron of flying, and it was not until next year (1904) that he had made at Chalais-Meudon "une reproduction de l'appareil Wright", which was flown briefly with only minor success at Berck-sur-Mer (Merlimont) in early April 1904: the pilots were Captain Ferber and a newcomer from Lyons, a young architectural-student-turned-engineer named Gabriel Voisin, who had for some years been interested in heavier-than-air flight. Surprisingly enough, the machine had no wing-warping or other control in roll (Pl. XI).

Inspired by Archdeacon to emulate the Wrights, an able engineer named Robert Esnault-Pelterie also built and tested in May 1904 what he falsely claimed was an exact copy ("absolument semblable") of the 1902 Wright glider, except for details; he found it was unsatisfactory and decided to improve it. He clearly could not make the warping work properly, and—like the other Europeans—did not understand the significance of Chanute's description of the simultaneous use of warping and rudder. Esnault-Pelterie then asserted that warping was structurally dangerous. In October 1904 he tested a rebuilt version, using—for the first time in history—ailerons, or rather primitive elevons, instead of the warping and front elevator (Pl. XXII): this machine, despite its ingenuity, was a crude affair and a failure, and Esnault-Pelterie—like his friends—would not take the trouble to experiment, modify and improve. The deplorable influence of Esnault-Pelterie on French aviation did not take effect until 1905, when his lecture was given, and published later in the year.

But having recorded both the new inspiration and the tradition-inspired modification—as well as the overt imitation of the Wrights by Archdeacon and Esnault-Pelterie—the historian can only view the general situation in Europe with amazement. Contemporary statements show clearly that the impact of Chanute's talk, and his articles, were profound; and that Archdeacon and his friends were at first genuinely determined to press ahead with gliding, and then powered flight. As already mentioned, Chanute described and illustrated his own 1896 glider, but gave greatest prominence to the key machine of the Wrights, their successful modified glider of 1902. The French pioneers of the time made it abundantly clear that it was the gliding successes of the Wrights that directly inspired them to emulation; not one of these men turned even briefly to the Chanute type of hang-glider, although a handful went off on quite different tacks (see below). It was the 1902 modified Wright machine which, by its success, now came to dominate the French mind, and was to directly inspire and precipitate the main stream of French—and European—aviation, despite the lack of understanding of its control system.

Next there is the question of what Chanute said, and what he subsequently published. It has often been assumed that he gave only a sketchy idea of the vital machine, the Wrights' modified *No. 3* glider; this assumption is quite incorrect. Chanute not only published detailed descriptions, scale drawings, and excellent photographs of this machine in flight, along with descriptions of the elevator, warping, and rudder controls; but actually mentioned the simultaneous use of warping and rudder, the key discovery in the Wrights' control system. The only points Chanute did not reveal—because at that time he did not know them—was how this simultaneous application was effected, or its aerodynamic raison d'être. This description by Chanute was part and parcel of his stressing the mastery of flight-control achieved by the Wrights, which was then followed by his statement that they would soon proceed to build a powered machine.

The next consideration is the Aéro-Club de France—which Chanute was addressing, and where the leading French pioneers congregated—which could rightly boast a great profusion of talent, along with ample finance to encourage experimentation. We now face head-on, so to speak, the following extraordinary and still largely unexplained state of affairs.

Chanute had expounded clearly, together with his telling photographs, that the necessity for complete control in the air by the pilot was the message of paramount importance imparted by the Wrights, and that mastery of glider flight was the essential preliminary to powered flight; he described the mechanisms whereby such mastery of flight-control could be obtained, and gave—in his mention of simultaneous use of warping and rudder—a vital clue to the operation of these mechanisms. He also made perfectly clear the necessity for intensive test flying and modifications, before the problems of flight-control could be solved and mastered: *yet the Europeans disregarded or misapprehended every one of these points.* Esnault-Pelterie was the only one who attempted control in roll—the others simply dismissed it—but did not seek to understand what it involved, and did not press on and make it effective until he came to produce his powered machines of 1907–09, when he returned to use the Wrights' warping system, which he had previously dismissed as dangerous. The neglect of control in roll by the French pioneers up to 1908 was a thoroughgoing neglect up to mid-1906; then a misconception of it until Wilbur Wright first flew in France in August 1908. This neglect was among the more inexcusable features of early French aviation. Although the lack of gliding experience accounts for some of the neglect, it is extraordinary that not one of these pioneers envisaged its vital role even before they started gliding, despite the vital clues which had been provided.

None of the Europeans, after Lilienthal and Pilcher, spent more than an aggregate of a few minutes in the air during all of their glides, and indeed none of them were ever to achieve a practical glider. No systematic, persistent and progressive study of the problems of glider control was made, hence no one came near to any kind of proficiency in gliding, let alone mastery; none of them thought out and tested the significance of combined warping and rudder movements. The Wrights, in their determination to master control, made over a thousand gliding flights during their three short seasons 'in the field' (1900–02), to say nothing of the model tests they made at home. The Europeans had available all the necessary facts and clues in Chanute's articles, and—if they had troubled to read them—in the two excellent Wright papers of 1901 and 1902, which were easily accessible.

Yet during the three years since Ferber heard from Chanute (1902–04), the total produce of European endeavours amounted to only some four ineffectual gliders, none of which were ever properly tested and developed.

First to be considered is the general attitude and 'flight philosophy' in Europe at this time (1902–04): this attitude may be summed up by what, earlier on, I have called the 'chauffeur's' attitude to aviation, where the pilot looks upon his machine as a winged automobile to be driven off the ground and steered about the sky, as if it has simply left the flat layer of earth to move in a slightly less flat layer of air. Aerodynamics and control, conceived in such an attitude of mind, was resolved into brute thrust applied to one or more aerofoils, with the maximum of inherent stability and the minimum of control by the pilot, the elevator and the rudder being the only necessary controls. The strange thing about such a flight philosophy is that it should apply only after proper flight-control has been achieved: for until the pilot has experienced, and can anticipate and control the behaviour of his machine in the air, he cannot decide what is necessary (or possible) to leave to built-in qualities or automatic mechanisms.

The Europeans had now virtually repudiated the real 'airman's' attitude, as championed by Lilienthal, and were only willing—some, of course, more than others—to commit themselves to the air with great caution: they did not see themselves as parts of the machines they flew. Their ideal was to drive an aerial automobile rather than to ride a winged horse.

Secondly, they were only half prepared to believe the story of glider mastery which Chanute had reported of the Wrights: "they soon attained almost complete mastery over the inconstancies of the wind," he had said. Esnault-Pelterie, for example, showed obvious satisfaction in claiming that he had built an exact copy of the Wright glider (when he clearly had not) and that it would not behave as the Wrights said theirs did; therefore, he implied, the Wrights were making false claims when describing their gliding achievements. But he did at least give fleeting attention to control in roll.

Thirdly, and allied to the last point, there was present in France a very evident jealousy of what they half felt the Wrights had achieved, and a pronounced chauvinistic ambition to rival and defeat them: "Will the homeland of the Montgolfiers have the shame of allowing the ultimate discovery of aerial science to be realised abroad?" asked Archdeacon in April 1903. "The aeroplane must not be allowed to be perfected in America", cried Ferber: to which the editor of *L'Aérophile* added the significant exhortation, "there is still time, but let us not lose a moment". Victor Tatin, one of the great veteran pioneers, in closing a lecture to the Aéro-Club de France in Paris in February 1904, "protested against the tendency we seem to have in France of slavishly copying (à copier rigoureusement) the gliding machines of the Americans. . . . Shall we some day have to read in history that aviation, born in France, was successful only because of the labours of the Americans, and that only by slavishly (servilement) copying them, did the French thereafter obtain any results?"

Fourthly, there is no doubt that the Europeans, to a man, greatly underestimated the complexities of learning to design, build and fly an aeroplane: they had simplified the whole subject in their minds to such a degree that they felt, now that the Americans were getting up in the air in gliders, they would do the same in no time at all, and then progress easily to the triumph of powered flight.

There was not one pioneer at that time—and they all revealingly spoke, wrote, or tried to build flying machines—who had more than a faint conception of the difficulties involved. Their attitude was well summed up by the editor of *L'Aérophile* (January 1904), when he wrote: "gliding flight, so vigorously launched by Monsieur Archdeacon, will not be long in bearing its own fruit. What do we lack? A few specialists trained in the tricks of the trade."

Fifthly, arising out of the last, was the strange state of mind which seemed collectively to possess the Europeans. This prevented them from arriving at a clear idea of what they were about; from formulating the basic problems to be solved, and from methodically going about the solution of them. This state of mind seems to have been an amalgam of over-confidence, inertia and a certain distrait dilatoriness, coupled—incredibly—with an inability to appreciate the essentials of the subject: I say "incredibly" in view of the fact that we are considering Frenchmen of undoubted talent; not only one or two individuals, but a whole group of them ostensibly dedicated to the pursuit of aviation. This extraordinary state of mind among the members of the French Aéro-Club, and those few outside it, resulted in a persistent but leisurely kind of 'slapdashery', despite the aims and protestations of Archdeacon's Aviation Committee.[1] A particular feature of this attitude was the refusal by all the French pioneers to persist in their efforts, to 'go at' a problem until it was solved, and to make more than a few glides in any of their machines before abandoning them, or radically changing their configuration. It was this attitude, and its outcome, which was later to lead to bitter self-criticism by the officials of the Aéro-Club for "notre inexcusable torpeur". Perhaps there was not a deep enough will to fly.[2]

The first three leading French pioneers, Ferber, Archdeacon and Esnault-Pelterie, all started by copying (as they thought) one or other of the Wright gliders, and went on to modify them: yet, it must be repeated, by the end of 1904 there had only been some four primitive gliders built and tested, and not one of them came anywhere near to being a properly flyable machine (Pl. XI).

There can be little doubt that if the Europeans had possessed the necessary devotion, humility and pertinacity, they could—with all the information and clues Chanute provided—have speedily duplicated the Wrights' gliding achievements, and added far-reaching improvements in stability, by the middle of 1904; successful powered flight on the Continent would have followed rapidly thereafter. With the variety of engineering talent available in Europe, the year 1906 (at the latest) should have witnessed there the full conquest of the air, with adequate inherent stability added to the Wrights' control philosophy. The military and political influence of such a development would have proved of prime importance in the history of Europe, and of the world.

There was one fundamental concept which the European school arrived at and clung to, after failing to understand the construction, operation or

---

[1] A Committee of the Aéro-Club formed by Archdeacon in May 1903, to stimulate the French pioneers.
[2] It was the abandoning of all efforts to master flight-control in gliders that led the Europeans to fight shy of any assisted take-off device; they realised that they would be helpless if they were ever to be precipitated into the air at speed.

significance of the Wright glider. This was the concept of inherent stability, which they came to find had been dominant in their almost forgotten traditions. Inherent stability they could understand and pursue, while control still meant little to them beyond rising from the ground and steering automobile fashion. It is interesting to note that the type of stable, tailed, machine they were slowly groping towards was basically a more practical type of vehicle, with a greater development potential, than the Wright type; but the considerations noted above drastically retarded its growth. It was Ferber who took the next step towards this cherished ideal of stability, at the end of 1904.

Ferber, who had abandoned the front elevator on his glider (having inexplicably failed to make the surfaces rigid), again fitted one and made some tentative glides. He also used an ingenious testing device before launching out in free flight, consisting of an inclined rope between wooden towers with a trolley running down it, from which the machine was hung. Then (1904) he made a vitally important and influential move. He completely rebuilt his glider and created a new type, with both forward elevator and fixed horizontal tailplane, as well as the two triangular wind-tip rudders (Pl. XI). This machine marks the beginnings of the full-size stable aeroplane. With this novel glider Ferber now established a new configuration, a new dogma, which was to dominate European aviation for nearly a decade—the dogma of the longitudinally and laterally stable aeroplane consisting of Wright-type main wings set at a dihedral angle, and forward elevator, with a fixed horizontal rear tailplane: the rudder was later to retreat to the rear and become part of the tail-unit. Ferber, also in this year 1904, made the first tentative flight with a passenger in a heavier-than-air machine, when he took his mechanic Marius Burdin for a short glide at Chalais Meudon.

Ferber's debt to the Wrights was put on record in his own book *L'Aviation* (1909) in which he headed one of his chapters "Ferber in pursuit of the Wrights, from 1902 to 1906." He was also to say (in 1908) of Wilbur Wright, "without this man I would be nothing . . . without him my experiments would not have taken place." And, without Ferber, France's progress would have been even more delayed.

Also worthy of mention is the first machine designed by Leon Levavasseur, who also designed the engine, the first of what were to be the famous line of Antoinette engines, named for Mlle Antoinette Gastambide. This huge bird-form monoplane (not a canard type) had curved dihedral on the wings: it was powered by one Antoinette engine driving two four-bladed airscrews, and ran on rollers down two tracks. It was tested without success in 1903 at Villotran, near Chantilly. This machine has the odd distinction of being the first French aeroplane to be powered by an internal combustion engine.

In 1904, two scientific papers were published which would later be recognised as fundamental contributions to aerodynamic theory. Ludwig Prandtl, of Göttingen University, demonstrated that the effects of viscosity in air flow could be neglected except in a thin "boundary layer" close to the surface of a body. This discovery made it possible to calculate the drag due

PLATE XI

a Ferber on his first Wright-type glider: 1902

b Archdeacon's first Wright-type glider: 1904

c Esnault-Pelterie on his Wright-type glider, fitted with elevons: 1904

d The start of the European biplane configuration, Ferber's tailed Wright-type glider: 1904

e The Voisin-Archdeacon float glider, combining Wright and Hargrave features: 1905

f The beginning of the European monoplane configuration, the Vuia machine of 1906

PLATE XII

a Montgomery's tandem-wing glider, released from a balloon: 1905

b Ellehammer's *No. II* (semi-biplane) in a tethered hop-flight: 1906

c Santos-Dumont's *14-bis*, which made the first hop-flights in Europe: 1906

d Hop-flight being made by the *Voisin-Delagrange I*: 1907

e Blériot's prophetic but unsuccessful tractor monoplane, his machine *No. VII*: 1907

f De Pischof's trend-setting tractor biplane: 1907

g Levavasseur's *Gastambide-Mengin I*: 1908

to skin friction; and it also provided the key to understanding how the flow over a wing changes as the angle of incidence increases.

At the University College of North Wales, G. H. Bryan produced a mathematical theory of aircraft stability and control, which was to be used by E. T. Busk and others at Farnborough from 1912 as a design method to develop a practical stable aircraft. Modern methods of calculating aeroplane stability characteristics are still essentially founded on Bryan's analysis.

In October of 1904 various prizes were announced by the Aéro-Club de France, to stimulate aviation in Europe, among which were the: Coupe Ernest Archdeacon for (*a*) the first powered machine to cover 25 metres, for which the pilot would win a trophy (this was won in 1906 by Santos-Dumont), and (*b*) for the first powered machine to cover 100 metres, for which the pilot would receive a prize of 1,500 francs; and the Grand Prix d'Aviation Deutsch-Archdeacon for the first man to fly 1 kilometre in a circle, the prize for this being 50,000 francs (this was won by Henri Farman on January 13th 1908).

The roster of the significant aircraft produced as a result of the new drive to emulate the Wrights was as follows, only the last-named showing any sign of practicability:

1903 Ferber Wright-type glider; and powered machine;
1903 Ferber Wright-type glider (modified); Levavasseur powered monoplane;
1904 Wright-type gliders by Archdeacon, Esnault-Pelterie, and Ferber.

1905

The Europeans continued their slow and confused progression. The only significant feature of Continental aviation—which in practice still meant French aviation—was in conception, not execution: this was the crystallising of their determination to pursue the inherently stable tailed aeroplane, rather than the inherently unstable machine espoused by the Wrights. In this they were maturing the stability concept laid down by Cayley in 1809, publicised by Henson in 1843, popularised by Pénaud in the 1870's, and perpetuated by most of the model makers and full-size designers in Europe thereafter. In more detail, the European situation that matured in 1905 may be itemised as follows:

(*a*) the complete abandonment by the Europeans of the Wrights' doctrine of inherent instability;
(*b*) the consequent settled pursuit of inherent stability;
(*c*) the consequent abandonment of the pure Wright glider configuration of forward elevator, wings, rear rudder, and no rear horizontal surfaces;
(*d*) the development—following Ferber's inherent stability idea—of the Wright glider-plus-tailplane configuration;
(*e*) the inauguration of the second type of European biplane configuration, i.e. the Wright-glider-cum-Hargrave-box-kite;

113

(f) the final, but still tentative, European attempts to fly gliders; then the abandonment of this basic flight philosophy of Lilienthal and the Wrights (which postulated that mastery of glider flight should precede attempts at powered flight);

(g) the tentative application of power to the first European biplane configuration.

The core of the European situation in 1905 was the final failure of her pioneers to comprehend the Wrights' philosophy and technique of aeroplane flight, which prevented the successful building and flying of Wright-type—or any other type—of gliders, despite the descriptions, photographs, and explanations published in 1903. It represented the strengthening of the 'chauffeur' attitude of winged automobilism, as opposed to the attitude of the true airman. This situation was worsened in 1905 by Robert Esnault-Pelterie lecturing to the Aéro-Club de France in January about his 1904 tests with Wright-type gliders, and the publication of his misleading lecture, with illustrations, in *L'Aérophile* for June 1905. This published lecture did much harm, both short and long term, and was one of the chief factors in the further retarding of aviation in Europe. Its one beneficial result was, by virtue of its large and clear illustrations, to put the visual idea of ailerons firmly in the minds of the pioneers, ready for such time—still far ahead—when they would come to realise the true nature of control in roll. All ailerons used in aviation thereafter can readily be traced back to Esnault-Pelterie's two surfaces as illustrated in that issue of *L'Aérophile* of June 1905. "It seems almost ridiculous", Wilbur Wright was, with justice, to say to Chanute in 1906, "that the French have never made any success at gliding in all these years."

In February an added, but minor, stimulus to aviation took place in Paris when the Aéro-Club de France staged an exhibition and demonstration of model aeroplanes, where many unfamiliar shapes appeared along with familiar echoes of Pénaud, Langley, Chanute and the Wrights. Also early in the year, Archdeacon had his second glider built—with a view to an engine being added later—and it was seen that he had followed Ferber into the stability idiom by adding a fixed tail-unit of tailplane and fins, but retaining the Wright-type front elevator: on March 26th, this machine—luckily pilotless—was towed down a wooden slipway and off into the air by an automobile at Issy,[1] but it soon suffered a breakage in the tail-unit, and crashed.

Ferber, encouraged by the performance of this new stable glider, built a similar but slightly larger glider, in which he installed a 12 h.p. Peugeot motor driving two coaxial tractor propellers between the outriggers of the front elevator. He attempted to fly this machine on May 25th at Chalais-Meudon and, although it could not sustain itself in horizontal flight, it made a creditable shallow 'power-glide'; it was launched from an overhead cable. This aircraft therefore ranks as the first rationally conceived and

[1] This first and most famous European aerodrome for aviation was the military "Champ de Manœuvres" at Issy-les-Moulineaux, a Paris suburb on the Seine, south-west of the city. The aviators had to share it with the army, and were restricted to special times for flying. It is now the Paris heliport. The second Archdeacon glider was the first aeroplane to use Issy.

constructed aeroplane to become airborne in Europe, and the first full-size petrol-powered machine to become properly airborne. Although Ferber was to make two more powered machines, the second of which made flights in 1908,[1] he was not to exert any further considerable influence on aviation: but he deserves great credit for establishing the idea of the stable tractor biplane, which emerged out of a failure to build a proper Wright-type glider, coupled with a strong feeling for the traditional European aircraft consisting of a stable tailed aeroplane, a type which was laid down by Cayley and firmly established by Pénaud in 1871: but the Wright forward elevator was still present. Furthermore, and also very much to Ferber's credit, was his preservation of the true airman's attitude to his machine (see below); and although he wished to incorporate inherent stability, he never conceived of the aeroplane as an airborne land-machine, or a semi-inanimate kite. It was clearly Ferber's example that led de Pischof to carry on the tractor biplane tradition in 1907, and thence to the main European stream of that type.

The most significant aircraft of 1905 were the two float gliders designed and built by Gabriel Voisin in co-operation with Archdeacon and Louis Blériot (Pl. XI). Gabriel, with his brother Charles, later in this year set up the first aircraft factory (at Billancourt) and there produced many of the successful—and unsuccessful—early aeroplanes. The Voisin-Archdeacon float glider became the prototype of the 'classic' European biplane: having absorbed some of the lessons of 1904, the designers decided to adhere to the Wright idiom of biplane wings and forward elevator, but to follow the old European tradition in having a stabilising tail-unit: in this they did not follow Ferber, but turned to Hargrave's box-kite (which had become well-known in Europe) both for the main wings and the tail-unit. This decision had a far-reaching effect on aviation; it was a retrogressive step, a step away from considering the aeroplane as a true flying-machine, which Ferber—along with his wish for inherent stability—recognised was the right attitude of mind. The Voisin machines represented the idea of the aeroplane as a flying land-vehicle, to be steered like an automobile rather than being flown like a bird; or, to look at it in a slightly different way, as a giant kite (with or without an engine) to be dragged through the air with a pilot on board to guide it, rather than a flying machine with the pilot as an integral part of the whole aeroplane. It was largely the Voisin machines which encouraged and perpetuated this mistaken attitude. In the Voisin-Blériot glider a dihedral angle was formed by canting the terminal side-curtains: there was a pronounced camber on all the lifting surfaces, a shorter span, and a single cell tail-unit. It is not known how much this variation was due to the views of their new client, Louis Blériot, an engineer who now came into aviation from the profitable business of manufacturing automobile lamps. Voisin was entirely preoccupied by inherent stability about the three axes, and was unaware of the need for any control in roll: this is why the box-kite appealed to him so strongly, and why he was to preserve as many of its features as possible in his later machines (Pl. XIV).

---

[1] From now on, the word 'flight' will often be used for convenience, but the reader is asked to remember that no European was airborne for a single minute until November 1907, or for two minutes until March 1908.

Both of the Voisin gliders were mounted on floats and towed off the River Seine (between Sèvres and Billancourt) by an Antoinette-powered motor-boat, and piloted by Gabriel Voisin. The Voisin-Archdeacon made two tests, on June 8th when it was airborne for 150 metres, and on June 18th when it 'flew' for 300 metres. This machine was later tested without success on the Lake of Geneva; it was finally sold to a Frenchman named Bellamy, who brought it to England in 1906, and put an engine and propellers in it, but without success. The Voisin-Blériot float glider was tested on June 18th 1905, when it crashed, giving Voisin an unpleasant ducking. The Blériot later underwent extensive and not very profitable modifications, which will be noted later. However, the experience with the Archdeacon glider decided Voisin to standardise this basic configuration of the biplane, and although the powered Voisins were not to be fitted with 'side-curtains' on the main wings until the summer of 1908, this machine was the prototype of the first generation of European biplanes.

It was also in 1905 (on July 18th) that Maloney was killed on a Montgomery tandem glider, released from a hot-air balloon at Santa Clara, California (Pl. XII).

In England an almost unknown, and now authenticated, event took place in 1905 when S. F. Cody built, and flew at Farnborough, a biplane kite-glider with Esnault-Pelterie-type ailerons. Cody was an attractive and flamboyant expatriate American (naturalised here in 1909), an expert cowboy, marksman, theatre showman, and friend—but not relative—of Buffalo Bill Cody. He was one of the valuable 'curiosities' of aviation, with no technical training but great energy, common sense, and considerable originality, who contributed to aviation history more by his courage and enthusiasm than by any real innovation, except in the realm of the kite. Having tired of confining himself to man-lifting kites, he made this large manned machine (Pl. XXII) which was flown as a kite and then released to glide down. Its two below-wing elevons were supplemented (in a revised version) by a rear elevator; but despite its brave showing, it was a primitive affair with non-rigid wing-surfaces and inadequate flight-control—the elevons were too small and placed too far inboard—and did not advance aviation technically.[1]

Despite the vociferous appeals and urges to emulate the Wrights which were being uttered in France all through 1903 and 1904, the Continental pioneers—as seen above—took things in very leisurely fashion; the impetus seems to have died down, and during the whole of 1905 the only aeroplanes tested in Europe were the following, none of which were successful:

§ Archdeacon glider *No. 2* § Voisin-Archdeacon float-glider;
§ Ferber powered biplane; § Voisin-Blériot float-glider;
§ Cody glider-kite.

The Wright brothers had, in 1905, produced their *Flyer III*, the first practical powered aeroplane of history, which could bank, turn, circle and

[1] This glider, with its elevons—the second in history—owed much to the Commanding Officer at Farnborough (Col. J. E. Capper) who subscribed to *l'Aérophile* in which a large illustration of Esnault-Pelterie's elevons on his glider was published in 1905.

make figures of eight, all with ease, and could fly for over half-an-hour at a time. This machine was flown from June 23rd to October 16th 1905, and when the season was ended, with some forty flights accomplished, the Wrights knew that they had well and truly conquered the air. News of this spectacularly successful season of flying reached France in successive accounts during that Autumn, the first to hear of it being Ferber in a letter from the Wrights of October 9th 1905, just before they closed their series of flights: but the French public first read it in a letter from the Wrights published in *L'Auto* on November 30th. It was an admirably lucid and matter-of-fact letter, describing some of their flights, and giving details of such matters as their troubles with lubrication: they referred to their half-hour flights as matters of interest between technicians, and what must have immediately affected Besançon—to whom it was addressed—was the obvious ring of truth in every word. After the news of their 1903 success had died away, with many pioneers in Europe not really believing it (and nothing much happening for nearly two years) this fresh news—with the long flight durations—came as a veritable bomb-shell to the Continent. "One may imagine the stupefaction of most of the French aviators", wrote the Comte de La Vaulx, "when they read the letter." From the vociferous and mixed chorus of belief and disbelief, there emerged the confirmation of Chanute and other witnesses, and of a French journalist sent over to the U.S.A. to investigate. So in January 1906 the Editor of *L'Aérophile*, followed by Victor Tatin (in the same issue), admitted publicly that the Wrights had done what they claimed. Here is the Editor (Georges Besançon):

> "Thus we have the definitive proof that aerial navigation by purely mechanical means, has just made the decisive step. We can only regret that it was not to be *chez nous*."

And here is the venerable and venerated Victor Tatin:

> "The glory of having obtained the first results is therefore for ever lost to France, . . . Unfortunately, for some years, in spite of that all it was possible to have in the way of stimulation from the news reaching us of the partial success and the well-founded hopes of the Americans, we have remained in a regrettable state of expectancy, when we had here 'chez nous' all that was necessary to resolve—better and more rapidly—the problem of which the solution abroad has today aroused us;—but aroused us a little too late, alas."

On October 14th, 1905, there was born in Paris the Fédération Aéronautique Internationale, the prime mover being the Comte Henri de la Vaulx. Its aim may be expressed in the words used at the Olympic Congress in Brussels in June of that year:

> "This Congress, recognising the special importance of aeronautics, expresses the desire that, in every country, there be created an Association for regulating the sport of flying, and that thereafter there be formed a universal aeronautical federation to regulate the various aviation meetings, and advance the science and sport of aeronautics."

This great Federation—known everywhere as the 'F.A.I.'—has brought incalculable benefit to world aviation and aerostation over the years.

1906

Although the Wrights did not fly in the year 1906, it was their unseen presence which pervaded the whole European scene, and underlay every move the Continental pioneers made during the year. This was primarily due to the shattering impact of the news of the Wrights' successful 1905 season.

In the midst of this mood of despondency and self-criticism, we are faced with yet one more inexplicable problem: for in the January issue of *L'Aérophile* there was published the basic text of the Wright patent (with illustrations), which had been applied for by the brothers in 1903, and was now granted. The version in *L'Aérophile* was not complete, but it took care to include the Wrights' lucid description both of the means of lateral control—by warping-cum-rudder—and, for the very first time, its aerodynamic raison d'être: in other words, here, in January of 1906 was published for all to see, the chief 'secret' of the Wrights, and the principal key to their mastery of flight-control. Yet no one in Europe took the slightest notice! I can find no informed discussion, let alone appreciation, of the Wrights' flight philosophy in the European writings of the time. We can only surmise that the Continental pioneers were so set in their 'chauffeur' attitude of mind, that the passages in the Wright patent describing warp-drag, and its counteraction by the rudder, meant nothing to them: they were simply not thinking along the lines of dynamic flight-control at all, and had had so little experience with their gliders that they had never experienced warp or aileron-drag (Fig. 64).

To make this whole situation even more extraordinary, we find Archdeacon—in his manifesto of August this year (see below)—saying that the second and greater difficulty about aeroplane flight, after the problem of the light engine which he said had now been solved, was "that of equilibrium and the actual control of the machine", which was "unfortunately far from being solved". One wonders just what he and his friends thought the Wrights were talking about in their patent specification. It is almost inconceivable to us today that such obtuseness should have prevailed among these men, with all the talent and resources they had at their disposal.

Modern readers may wonder why so much surprise is expressed at this European attitude, and the consequent delays. Apart from the same surprise—and indeed exasperation—being shown by the pioneers themselves, one need only consult the periodicals of the day to realise the prodigious amount of time and effort being put into fruitless aviation projects. The technical basis of proper aeroplane flight and control was readily available to all; but a general paralysing malaise seems to have overspread the European pioneers which, as said above, was basically associated with the 'chauffeur' attitude. It was this attitude which kept them preoccupied with the machine on the ground, rather than control in the air, and resulted in so much wasted effort. There was also, strange to say, no single pioneer who would adopt a given configuration, as the Wrights had done, and then—regardless of whether it was the best one—pursue it methodically and relentlessly to the stages of workability and success.

The manifesto by Archdeacon just referred to, was published in *L'Aérophile* for August 1906, and was preceded by a revealing statement from the President of the Aéro-Club de France, L.-P. Cailletet, in which he said that the purpose of the manifesto was to shake the members out of their inexcusable torpor ("pour secouer notre inexcusable torpeur"), Archdeacon, who refused to admit the Wrights' flights, exhorted his friends to overtake the "slight advance (légère avance) which the Americans have made". He then reminded them of the existence of the famous 'Prix Deutsch-Archdeacon' for the first kilometre circle (on offer since 1904, and not to be won until January 13th 1908!); but he said nothing of the two other prizes, also offered in 1904, for the even more modest distances of 25 and 100 metres respectively, which were at last to be won this year by Santos-Dumont. Archdeacon concluded his manifesto by declaring, with italicised emphasis: "the discovery of aerial navigation is imminent, and there is just time for us in France to make the first public demonstration".

It is surprising that it was not until August 1906 that the Aéro-Club made this appeal: it was still, as it had been since 1903, a case of making haste slowly. No wonder that the more enlightened members of the Club were becoming ever more fretful and frustrated. It was now the late summer of 1906: no European powered aeroplane had yet flown, and no powered machine seemed within sight or hope of flying. The only hope was that a few hops might be achieved with the Vuia monoplane or the new Santos-Dumont biplane (see below). Ferber had been launched into the air last year in his tentative powered machine, and had reduced the angle of glide by the action of his engine and propeller; but that was all. The more honest Europeans realised that the position was well-nigh ridiculous, and as the President of the Aéro-Club said, "inexcusable".

The most important achievement of the year was the perfecting by Leon Levavasseur of his two Antoinette aero-engines (named after Antoinette Gastambide, daughter of the firm's chief), of 24 h.p. and of 50 h.p. His first engine was fitted to his abortive bird-form monoplane of 1903; then, with outstanding success, his motors powered motor-boats from 1904 onwards. Now, from this year 1906, Antoinette motors were to become the chief power-standby of European aviation until 1909: Antoinette motors might even be said to have made early European flying practicable. There was no comparable advance in European propellers, which remained primitive devices until Chauvière's sophisticated airscrew of 1909.

In March appeared a prophetic and influential machine by a Paris-domiciled Transylvanian, Trajan Vuia, a tractor monoplane on a four-wheeled undercarriage powered by a Serpollet carbonic acid motor (Pl. XI), with a rear rudder, and later a long spreading rear elevator. It was not successful, but made some 11 hops between March of 1906 and March of 1907, the best being of 24 metres in August 1906. But it was probably this Vuia monoplane—which ranks as the first full-size conventionally shaped monoplane in history[1]—which influenced Blériot to abandon biplanes and take to monoplanes.

[1] It also has the curious distinction of being the first European aeroplane with pneumatic-tyred wheels.

It was virtually a misspent year for Blériot, who again collaborated with Voisin and built a powered biplane (his *No. III/IV*) derived from the 1905 float-glider; but it was a failure. He altered it drastically during the year, and it appeared with—in varying combinations—elliptical tail-unit, elliptical wings, conventional wings; with one 24-h.p. Antoinette motor driving two airscrews, then with two such motors. The machine was tested on floats on the Lake d'Enghien, and finally on wheels at Bagatelle in November, where it crashed without having flown: it was in this last form that it bore two small between-wing ailerons, the third machine in history to be fitted with these surfaces. But it was time wasted for all concerned (Pl. XXII).

The Man of the Year in the eyes of all air-minded Europeans was undoubtedly the rich Paris-domiciled Brazilian, Alberto Santos-Dumont, who had done more than anyone to make Europe air-minded since 1898, with his series of odd-shaped little airships which sometimes flew excellently, but were apt to crash gracefully and safely on Parisian roof-tops or trees. Then, when he visited the United States for the St. Louis Exposition in 1904, he heard from Octave Chanute—whom he met there—about the Wrights' success with their first two powered *Flyers* of 1903 and 1904: it was evidently this which turned Santos toward powered aviation, tentatively in 1905 with a helicopter (which could not fly), then in 1906 with an aeroplane proper. The latter was his *14-bis*—so called because it was at one time flight-tested beneath his airship No. 14—which became one of the most famous aeroplanes of history (Pl. XII). The *14-bis* was a sterile creature that led nowhere: it had cellular box-kite wings of 52 square metres area, set at a pronounced dihedral angle, which derived from the Wrights and Hargrave *via* Voisin: but instead of longitudinal stability being obtained by a tail-unit, he transferred the front elevator outrigger into a long covered fuselage with a single large box-kite cell on the end (front) which acted as a combined elevator and rudder, later only as an elevator. There was no tail, and the first engine was a 24-h.p. Antoinette which lay on the lower planes and drove a crude pusher propeller. In July it was tested suspended beneath Santos' airship *No. 14*, after being tried out suspended from a trolley running on an overhead wire. Then, on September 13th, at Bagatelle (where all subsequent tests were made) it made its first free take-off, but covered only 7 metres, and made a bad landing. Repairs were accompanied by the fitting of a 50-h.p. Antoinette. On October 23rd, it made one hop-flight of 60 metres and won the Archdeacon prize for a 'flight' of 25 metres. Then Santos fitted octagonal ailerons—one in each outer box-kite cell—and on November 12th flew it (on one of several hops) of 220 metres in 21 ⅕ seconds: he thereby won the Club's 1,500 francs prize for the first flight of 100 metres; being officially observed and approved, the *14-bis* was accredited as having made the first powered flights in Europe. This event, which was indeed modest enough, caused a sensation in Europe, and was even taken by some to herald the 'arrival' of the powered aeroplane: "une ère nouvelle commence!" exclaimed Ferber. But the machine was a freak by any standards; was nowhere near being a practical aeroplane; and although it added *éclat* to aeronautics, it did nothing to promote or influence aviation, except perhaps to draw fleeting attention to dihedral at a time when European investigation of control in roll was virtually non-existent. The *14-bis* was abandoned after one more brief hop (April 4th 1907). One of the more interesting results of Santos' first European hops was the offer, by the Reims champagne firm of Ruinart, of a prize of 12,500 francs for the first aviator to fly the English Channel.[1]

On September 12th, a Danish engineer, J. C. H. Ellehammer, had made a 'hop-flight' of some 42 metres in an odd biplane on the island of Lindholm, which is sometimes claimed as the first European flight: but this claim is quite invalid, as this Ellehammer *II* 'flew' tethered to a central post, and it had a fixed rudder and automatic (pendulum) longitudinal control, thus making the pilot a passive passenger (Pl. XII). It made no free flights. The engine was an excellent 3-cylinder air-cooled radial of 18 h.p. designed by Ellehammer.

Finally, it is the historian's duty—and a melancholy duty indeed if he is an Englishman—to record the continuing neglect of practical aviation in Britain, a neglect as deplorable and inexcusable as it is still inexplicable, in view of the wealth of technological talent then present in the country. Here is a serious statement from a well-known authority of those days, Patrick Alexander (quoted in the *Daily Mail* of November 24th 1906):

"Great Britain and the British Empire stand easily in the van of progress. We know more about the science of aeronautics than any other country in the world. As yet, we have not attempted to apply our knowledge, but silently and quietly we have been studying the subject, exhausting every possible theory and fact, until today our scientists may lay claim to have conquered the air on paper. To achieve the victory in practice will not be a difficult matter."

Comment on such an incredible *obiter dictum* would be superfluous.

The list of powered aircraft that took off the ground, or attempted to, in 1906 was as follows:

§ Vuia *I* and *I-bis*. Best distance was 24 metres (say 80 ft.);

§ Blériot *III/IV*. Never left the water, or the ground;

§ Ellehammer *II*. No free flights; but best of tethered 'hops' was 42 metres (say 140 ft.);

§ Santos-Dumont *14-bis*. Best distance and time was 220 metres in 21⅕ seconds (say 720 ft.):

1907

The year 1907 witnessed the true, but still tentative, beginnings of practical powered flight in Europe, following the 'false dawn' of 1906. Three important configurations, all confirming the European inherent stability idiom, became well defined during the year; but only one machine achieved significant flights. These configurations were as follows:

(*a*) The pusher biplane, Wright-cum-Hargrave-derived, with forward

---

[1] This prize was not won by the first Channel-crossing (1909) as was the intention, but by the second, in 1910 (see footnote on page 152).

elevator, 'open' biplane wings, and box-kite tail-unit, but with no control in roll. This type was represented by the first two successful Voisin machines, the *Voisin-Delagrange I* and the *Voisin-Farman I*; the latter, after important modifications by Henri Farman, was the first European aeroplane—and the only one in 1907—to achieve productive flying (October 1907 onwards), and the first to stay in the air for a single minute (November 9th).

(b) The tractor biplane, derived from Ferber, but with no surfaces forward of the propeller: this was first seen in December in the De Pischof machine which, although itself not successful, was to exert much influence later.

(c) The tractor monoplane with main wings, fuselage, and tail-unit, developing from the Vuia (which itself made some hops in 1907), seen in the promising *Blériot VII* and the diminutive *Santos-Dumont 19*, both of November, but both only tentative.

Starting with the monoplane, we find Blériot—having abandoned the biplane—attacking the problem of practical aviation with extraordinary energy and intrepidity: but he dissipated his energy by changing from one configuration to another. He first built his *No. V* 'tail-first' canard monoplane, in which he only managed some 4 take-offs in April before it crashed and was abandoned. Then came his *No. VI*, a Langley-type tandem monoplane named *Libellule* (Dragonfly), fitted with wing-tip elevons and a 24-h.p. Antoinette (Pl. XXII): he made a number of short hop-flights in this during July and August at Issy before it, too, crashed and he narrowly escaped death. He had modified it en route, and in September exchanged the 24-h.p. for a 50-h.p. 16 cylinder Antoinette;[1] his best hop was 184 metres.[2] Then "avec infatigable ténacité", he built a third monoplane (Pl. XII) which was of vital importance. For, at one stroke, Blériot established the 'modern' tractor monoplane configuration with long enclosed fuselage (also enclosing a 50-h.p. Antoinette engine) with the main wings forward and a rear tail-unit, the machine resting on a two-wheeled undercarriage with a third wheel near the tail. Long to remain indecisive about his control systems, Blériot curiously decided to make this *No. VII* inherently unstable, with only the rudder and elevons forming the tail-unit. He made some six flights in all at Issy during November and December; on the last hop-flight he crashed the machine and abandoned it: the best flights were two each of about 500 metres (say 1,640 feet), one including some tentative turns.[3]

Also new in the monoplane field was Esnault-Pelterie, who built the first of his tapered-wing bird-like tractor monoplanes, powered by his own

[1] This was the first 16-cylinder Antoinette engine to become airborne.   [2] Say 604 feet.

[3] There has always been doubt about the amount of credit due to Blériot for the actual design and construction of his aircraft. Dollfus, who knew Blériot well, has made a study of this vexing subject. He has established that Blériot himself decided upon the small 'canard' No. V of 1907 the basic idea of which came from Santos-Dumont's *14-bis*. The tandem monoplane No. VI—derived from Langley—was designed and built by Louis Peyret, probably as a result of a general suggestion by Blériot. The prophetic No. VII was due entirely to Blériot; and the VIII and IX also seem to have been his ideas, along with the abortive biplane (No. X). The famous cross-Channel No. XI was, however, designed by another friend, Raymond Saulnier. The No. XII (and XIII) were probably Blériot's own design.

excellently designed 25-h.p. 7-cylinder fan-type engine. This *REP No. 1* (REP were his initials) was particularly interesting for its designer's return to a primitive version of the Wrights' wing-warping which he had done so much to discourage. The machine made short flights at Buc in November and December, the best being 600 metres, but it had little influence on contemporary design, its very short fuselage providing poor longitudinal stability. But his later machines were to fly well in 1908 and 1909.

Vuia made further short hops with his *No. I* monoplane in March, and tested his *No. II* briefly and unsuccessfully in June–July at Bagatelle, when he abandoned it, and ceased to play an important part in aviation.

Santos-Dumont, after his new biplane had failed to fly in March (see below), also abandoned the biplane and next built a combined aeroplane and airship (his *No. 16*); but this curiosity was destroyed on the ground during its first test in June. Then, in the winter, he turned his attention seriously to the monoplane and built the first of his remarkable miniature machines which in 1909 were to become famous by the strange name of *Demoiselle*. The new machine, the *No. 19* was tested in only three 'hops' (November) before being abandoned: it was a tractor monoplane built of bamboo poles, with a wing span of only 5 metres; a supporting area of 9 square metres, and a 20 h.p. two-cylinder Dutheil-Chalmers engine lying on the jointure of the wings: the pilot sat under the wings and controlled the machine by means of a combined rudder and elevator at the rear, two rudders at the side, and a forward elevator: it had a pronounced dihedral angle on the wings, but no control system for control in roll except leaning his body from side to side. It was damaged on November 21st at Buc, and not revived as a type until the end of 1908. It had made only three take-offs, the best covering 200 metres.

Turning now to the biplane, one must again mention Santos-Dumont, who completed a small biplane based on the *14-bis*, his *No. 15*, but working the other way round, as a tractor biplane. Its wings were covered in plywood, but the most interesting feature should have been the pair of small rectangular ailerons mounted ahead of the wings on short outriggers.[1] It was intended to fit a 16 cylinder 100-h.p. Antoinette, but that was not yet available, and a 50-h.p. was installed. This machine was damaged when taxy-ing on March 27th. After repairing it, and fitting the 16 cylinder engine, he still could not make it fly. Santos now turned to the monoplane, as we have seen.

Meanwhile the most important practical steps in aviation were being taken by the Voisin brothers at their Billancourt factory. As a result of the experience with their two 1905 float gliders, and having briefly flown (in May this year) a modified type of Chanute hang-glider with box-kite tail, they came to standardise a type of machine which was to persist until the year 1910. This was a stable pusher biplane with forward elevator, and tail-unit containing the rudder, but with no form of control in roll.[2] In its

---

[1] Although the ailerons were included in the designs, they were not fitted to the machine when built. The idea came from the Blériot *IV* of 1906.

[2] The form of these early Voisin biplanes which is most familiar had the so-called 'side-curtains' added both to the ends of the main wings and also inboard, thus making the wings

first form, it showed its origins clearly in the Wright biplane wings and forward biplane elevator (the latter soon reduced to monoplane form), and the Hargrave box-kite tail-unit. The Voisins built two similar machines, one of which was for Henry Kapferer: this never flew. The other—with a 50-h.p. Antoinette motor—was for Delagrange: it made six hops in March (Pl. XII): it was then tried on floats on Lake d'Enghien, without success; and finally, fitted with wheels again, it made two take-offs at Issy in November 1907, and crash-landed on the second.

Neither of these first two Voisins was a success; but in the summer a third machine was built for a newcomer to aviation, the English-born—but not English speaking—Henri Farman. Farman, who was the son of a prominent English journalist domiciled in France, was an artist turned motor-racer, and came to exert a far-reaching influence on the whole sphere of aviation. He first flew his new Voisin—the *Voisin-Farman I*—also with a 50-h.p. Antoinette in September; and thereafter pursued his new profession with a vigour and pertinacity only matched by Blériot. He proceeded to modify and improve his Voisin; he went on altering it right to the end of 1908, and by the end of that year had become the most successful and famous of the European pilots. On October 26th (1907) he had won the Archdeacon Cup with a flight of 771 metres in 52³⁄₅ seconds. In November he made turns, and on the 9th an unofficial circle of some 1,030 metres in 1 minute 14 seconds. This was the first European flight longer than the Wrights' 59 seconds in 1903. It was obvious now that he would soon win the Deutsch-Archdeacon prize of 50,000 francs offered for the first man to fly a kilometre circuit, i.e. to round a post placed 500 metres away from the start, and return (see later). By the end of the year he had already made important alterations to his Voisin, especially the exchange of the huge box-kite tail-unit for a similar but much smaller unit, the fitting of a monoplane elevator, and the rigging of his wings at a slight dihedral angle (Pl. XIII).

A. de Pischof built a biplane which he tested without much success at Issy (1907–08) (Pl. XII) its chief role being further to consolidate the tractor biplane tradition started by Ferber in 1905; it was, in fact, de Pischof who was the first to dispense with all forward control surfaces, and so crystallise the modern tradition, although in a somewhat primitive form, with a cruciform tail-unit 'sprouting' from the rear of the centre section: de Pischof used a 3-cylinder 25-h.p. Anzani fan-type engine, driving the first sophisticated propeller in Europe, a Chauvière. In England, where interest in aviation was beginning to grow, an important exhibition of model aeroplanes was held at Alexandra Palace in April: no first prize was awarded, but the second was given to A. V. Roe for his 8-foot span Wright-type model.

It was also in this year that the ageing Horatio Phillips made the first tentative hop-flight in Britain in a strange and quite impractical machine incorporating a large number of his high aspect ratio aerofoils in four

---

into giant box-kites, with a box-kite tail-unit. The tail-unit was in this form from the start, but the 'side-curtains' on the wings did not start appearing until about May (one curtain each side of the pilot), and did not appear fully-fledged (four in all) until July–August 1908. These standard Voisins disappeared in 1910 after ailerons or warping had become universal.

tandem frames, and powered with a 20–22 h.p. engine driving one tractor propeller. Phillips succeeded in becoming airborne for about 500 feet. It was his last appearance in aviation.

At Farnborough, S. F. Cody took the intermediate step between kites and aeroplanes by fitting a 12-h.p. Buchet motor to one of his modified man-lifting kites, and 'flying' it suspended from a wire at Farnborough, without anyone on board. Cody then commenced construction of his *British Army Aeroplane No. 1* (see under 1908). Meanwhile, J. W. Dunne, working in great secrecy for the British Government, had built his first swept-wing biplane (the *D.1*) in search of inherent stability, inspired by the form of the winged seed of the Zanonia plant: it was tested only once—when it was damaged—this year as a glider at Blair Atholl (Scotland). It was next fitted with two 12-h.p. Buchet motors, but was damaged on the ground at its first take-off attempt, and abandoned.

One of the important events of the year in aeronautics took place with the publication of an erudite book, *Aerodynamics*, by Frederick W. Lanchester, well-known as an automobile engineer, who next year issued his second book, *Aerodonetics*. Lanchester is recognised as one of the great figures of aeronautical history (Fig. 65). Although the profundity of Lanchester's theory of sustentation is universally recognised, his books were very difficult to understand, even by specialists; consequently his theory was not applied by anybody and his books made no impact on practical aviation. The German engineer Ludwig Prandtl (1875–1953) had evolved an essentially similar theory, expressed in a much clearer mathematical form, and, largely through translations and expositions of Prandtl's work, the theory of lifting wings was made known to the scientific world, and thence made its impact on aeroplane design and construction. It was not until 1915, in a paper which he read to the Institution of Automobile Engineers, that Lanchester re-cast his theory in a form more capable of application to practical aircraft design. The circulation theory of wings is today referred to as the "Lanchester-Prandtl Theory"; but as communication is the key to technological influence, one must pay primary tribute to Ludwig Prandtl and to the school of aeronautical research workers which he established at Göttingen.

The Wright brothers had been continuing their complex negotiations for the sale of their aeroplanes on both sides of the Atlantic; and although both Wilbur and Orville visited Europe this year, a satisfactory conclusion of their affairs was not to be reached until early in 1908. But during 1906 and 1907 they had been building some half dozen improved engines, and two or three improved and 'finalised' aircraft, one of which was to make aviation history. This finalised type of Wright biplane, which we will call the type A, was a two-seater, basically similar to the *Flyer III*, and with a Wright 30-h.p. engine: it is illustrated in Pl. XIII. In expectation of a French manufacturing agreement, the new Wright was shipped to France in July 1907, and remained in store at Le Havre until the summer of 1908. The brothers had also taken stock of European aviation and found it so backward that they felt they had nothing to fear from Continental progress; which indeed proved correct.

Also, in 1907, there appeared the first tentative man-carrying helicopters.

After some six centuries of experiments with models, this type of machine arrived at the stage of lifting a man for the first time in history. There are two claimants for this 'first', Paul Cornu and the Breguet brothers, but the French authorities have established that the Breguet-Richet machine— Richet collaborated—was the first to take off with a man (September 29th at Douai); but it was not a free flight, in that four men steadied it, and although not helping to lift the machine, they certainly aided its stability in the air. The Cornu helicopter, on the other hand—a much more compact two-rotor machine—was the first to fly freely with a man without any connection with, or help from, the ground (November 13th, near Lisieux: Pl. XXI). So, although the matter is somewhat academic, the proper 'first' should go to Paul Cornu. Both machines had Antoinette engines, the Breguet a 50-h.p. and the Cornu a 24-h.p., but the flights—although genuine enough—can only be regarded as extremely tentative, the practical helicopter not appearing until the 1930's.

Machines off the main lines of influence which merit inclusion here were the following: 1. The Tatin-de La Vaulx monoplane built by Mallet with a 50-h.p. Antoinette driving two pusher propellers: it took off twice at St. Cyr in November 1907, but was abandoned when it crash-landed after the second take-off; 2. The tailless monoplane by I. Etrich and F. Wels, with swept-back wings, intended to be powered by a 24-h.p. Antoinette, but tested at Oberalstadt (Bohemia) only as a glider: this machine ultimately led to the famous *Taube* monoplanes of 1909–13. The first man-carrying triplane of history, which Ellehammer introduced—his *No. III*—this year, with an excellent 5-cylinder 30-h.p. Ellehammer radial: the machine made many hops, but was not successful.

To sum up for 1907, it may be said that, despite the talented men who were now growing up in European aviation—many of them attracted away from automobilism—the same basic attitudes and habits of mind possessed them now as had possessed them in 1903. The 'chauffeur' philosophy was still dominant, and still no one realised that mastery of glider construction and control—which they could easily have accomplished within a year of Chanute's revelations in 1903—would have led rapidly to mastery of powered flight. The main reason for this neglect was their basic mistake of regarding flight-control as only passive and corrective—as an extension of inherent stability—and not as both corrective and as a positive dynamic means of manoeuvre (see page 139). They also failed to realise that even the corrective function of flight-control needed a control system which would be instantly effective about all three axes: hence their neglect of proper control in roll. In view of Chanute's partial revelations of 1903, and the explicit revelations in the Wright patent published in 1906, it is well-nigh incredible that this dual function of flight-control was not properly comprehended, let alone appreciated and utilised, by the Europeans until they saw Wilbur Wright's display of mastery in France, from August to December of 1908.

Nor had the Europeans progressed beyond the most primitive of ungeared propellers, revolving at engine speed, despite the modest presence of the Chauvière propeller on the de Pischof biplane. No one came forward, in this important but neglected sphere, to initiate proper research and development. Yet again we meet this incomprehensible stagnation.

Continental pioneers were understandably unwilling to risk any effective catapult, or other launching methods, with their embryo machines: they would certainly not have known how to control them if they found themselves suddenly committed to the air, and would assuredly have suffered many a casualty. Not having had to face the problems of flight-control in gliders, they underestimated or neglected flight-control in general—especially control in roll—in their powered machines; they therefore concentrated on forcing them into the air in small straight-line hops. Henri Farman alone had begun to acquire the 'airman's' attitude by the end of 1907; Blériot was to embrace this attitude next year.

The only strong suit of the Europeans was their traditional pursuit of inherent stability, and their correct insistence on the adoption of a tailplane to bring it about longitudinally, and wing dihedral for lateral stability. But this persistent pursuit of stability was largely nullified by their equally persistent refusal to appreciate the vital role of flight-control. This neglect of control—one of the two chronic European diseases—was worse confounded by the second disease, the refusal by the European pioneers to think out and adopt any definite configuration and pursue it through test and modification, until success was reached. Blériot's production of no less than three basic configurations in this one year, 1907, with no proper testing and development of any of them, was typical of the Continental attitude. It was again a question of time-wasting 'slapdashery'. Blériot had been working at the problem of flight since mid-1905; but only at the end of 1907 had he even arrived at a promising configuration: he was to labour until mid-1909—two more years—before he could achieve a practical aeroplane. Here we have a typical, and incomprehensible, case-history of European pioneering. Equipped with all the information and clues that anyone could wish for, and with ample funds, a talented and fearless man took no less than four years—forty-eight months, two hundred and eight weeks—to progress from an unsuccessful (but feasible) float-glider to a practical powered machine; and, even then, he had others to aid him in the designing of his aircraft.

The case-history of the Voisin machines is equally extraordinary. Gabriel Voisin was tentatively piloting Archdeacon's Wright-type *No. 1* glider in the spring of 1904; but it was not until November of this year, 1907, that the powered machine he built for Henri Farman (and modified by him), could remain in the air for sixty consecutive seconds; and not until November 1907 and January 1908 that this same machine could make its first two wavering circles, yawing round on rudder alone. The standard Voisins were indeed never to have any control in roll, right to the end of their days in 1910.

There was, therefore, only one European aeroplane—the *Voisin-Farman 1*—which, by the end of 1907, could remain airborne for a single minute. But at least it was a beginning, and Europe had to be content with small mercies.

1908

January to July

The year 1908 was an *annus mirabilis* in aviation history, for the Wright brothers first flew in public—Wilbur in France in August, and Orville in the United States in September—and revealed in dramatic fashion the true nature of the aeroplane and its control in the air. They revealed a type of flying-machine whose every part and feature had grown out of masterly design and experimentation, a machine inspired by a clear vision of the nature of mechanical flight, and of the proper kind of vehicle to accomplish it. This vision and this experimentation were seen to have conditioned and unified the whole aircraft, its aerodynamic qualities, its construction, motor, propellers and—above all—its flight-control system.

The Wrights also revealed themselves, not only in their consummate skill as pilots, but in their personal modesty and integrity in the midst of their triumphs. Where the Europeans chauffeured their machines cautiously and doggedly, as if they were steering winged automobiles through the alien air, the Wrights rode their aircraft as if man and machine were one; rode them with perfect ease and assurance; rode them with the mastery of born airmen. They were, indeed, the mythical 'hommes oiseaux' come to life, as François Peyrey described them.

In Europe, little realising that one of the machines which was to bring about this revolution was lying in a crate some 100 miles away, the French aviators acclaimed "la mémorable victoire" of Farman when he won the Grand Prix d'Aviation for the first circle at Issy on January 13th: the prize was donated by Henry Deutsch de la Meurthe and Ernest Archdeacon, two of the most generous and far-sighted benefactors of early aviation. Farman flew the prescribed kilometre circle and, owing to his having to make such a wide turn (on rudder alone), he probably covered 1,500 metres (nearly a mile). He was airborne for 1 minute 28 seconds. This was by far the longest and most impressive flight yet made in Europe (Pl. XIII); last year—1907— it was also Farman who had been the first European to fly for over a minute.

The period from January to August saw only modest technical advance in European flying, but some interesting achievements. The Voisin biplane remained throughout these months the only near-practical European aeroplane, and Farman and Léon Delagrange shared the duration honours between them, the former re-naming his machine *Henri Farman No. 1-bis* in March, after having the wings covered with rubberised fabric and the engine changed temporarily to the new 50-h.p. Renault, but changed back rapidly to the 50-h.p. Antoinette. Delagrange, who had taken delivery of his new Voisin—the *Voisin-Delagrange II*, soon modified to become the *III*, with two side-curtains—started to make some good flights, and on June 23rd had flown over 14 kilometres (8¾ miles) in 18 minutes 30 seconds at Milan. Farman on July 6th had flown for 20 minutes 20 seconds at Ghent. The first passenger flight had been made on May 14th by Wilbur Wright, taking C. W. Furnas; and the first passenger flight in Europe was then made by Farman, taking Archdeacon, on May 29th. The first woman to fly in an

PLATE XIII

a Farman's *Voisin-Farman I-bis* flying the first European circle at Issy: January 13th 1908

b The first A.E.A. machine, the *Red Wing*: 1908

c The A.E.A. (Curtiss) *June Bug*: 1908

d The *Wright A* (*France*), which revolutionised European aviation by its manoeuvrability: 1908

e Esnault-Pelterie's *REP. 2* monoplane: 1908
10+A.

f Cody's *British Army Aeroplane No. 1*: 1908

PLATE XIV

a A standard Voisin biplane: 1909

b Farman's *Henry Farman III*,
one of history's classic
aeroplanes: 1909

c The Curtiss Reims machine,
seen at the Reims meeting:
1909

d A standard two-seat *Wright A*
biplane: 1909

aeroplane was Madame Thérèse Peltier, when Delagrange took her up at Turin on July 8th: the same lady became the first of her sex to fly solo soon after, but she did not become a qualified pilot.

Captain Ferber reappeared briefly with a promising stable 50-h.p. tractor biplane, the *Ferber IX* (also called *Antoinette III*, as Ferber had joined the firm) which made a number of hops and short flights from July to September at Issy, the best covering 500 metres: it had a front elevator, wing-warping, fixed rear tailplane and fin, and wing-tip rudders (later exchanged for a single tail rudder): this machine certainly added to Ferber's influence in leading Europe towards the practical tractor biplane type, but was not itself a success. This was Ferber's last machine. He next bought a standard Voisin.

In the European monoplane field there was much activity and promise of things to come. First tests were made in February with the new *Gastambide-Mengin I* (Pl. XII) designed by Levavasseur from which—after making important alterations to it—he was to develop his famous *Antoinette* monoplane at the end of the year. Blériot built his *No. VIII* on the lines of the enclosed monoplane of 1907, then modified it radically until it emerged as the *No. VIII-bis* and flew in June: this Blériot had a 50-h.p. Antoinette engine and was the first of his machines to have the typical "Blériot look", with open trellis fuselage supporting the tail-unit: Blériot had also given serious but inadequate attention to control in roll by equipping it with two flap-type ailerons—the first in the world—but unwisely abandoning them later in the summer for still inadequate pivoting wing-tip ailerons on the same machine—a reversion to the practice on his Langley-type *Libellule* of 1907: this final revision of *No. VIII* was numbered the *VIII-ter*, which flew well in the latter months of the year (see later). Meanwhile Esnault-Pelterie made a number of flights in his *REP No. 2*, still using his simplified wing-warping, but with greater fin area.

Amongst other projects and attempts of this period should be mentioned three curious failures, each bearing a well-known name in aviation, and each proving still-born when completed. In 1907 Levavasseur had made a model of a pusher monoplane, with deep wing curvature, a long tapering fuselage with rudder, tailplane, fin and tail-propeller, and—forward of the wings—a horizontal stabiliser flanked by elevators (or elevons): he built a full-size version of this (the *Antoinette I*), and then abandoned it. The Voisins built for Henri Farman the English-titled *Flying Fish* with a long fuselage, four sets of small wings in tandem (three at the front and one at the back), fixed tailplane and rudder, and Renault engine driving a tractor propeller; this—called also the *Henri Farman II*—was also abandoned. And Henry Kapferer built another tractor tandem-wing monoplane with two sets of wings, a forward elevator and fixed tailplane, powered by an REP engine; this, too, was abandoned. It is hard to say why the last two men temporarily neglected the promising types of aircraft under development for what were aeronautical freaks, fruitlessly derived from Langley.

In England S. F. Cody had, in the Spring, completed his *British Army Aeroplane No. 1* at Farnborough (Pl. XIII), with the assistance of Colonel Capper, which had been commenced in the winter of last year. It was a Wright-derived biplane with forward elevator and rear rudder, with another rudder on top of the wings, and small between-wing ailerons (which were abandoned before the machine finally flew): it was powered by a 50-h.p. Antoinette engine driving two propellers between the wings: but it was not to be tested until September (see later).

Incidentally there also occurred at Farnborough that May an event of considerable aeronautical importance when successful ground-to-air wireless transmissions were made to the free balloon *Pegasus*, 20 miles away.

Also in England, A. V. Roe built a full-size aeroplane based on his prize-winning Wright-type model of 1907: tests were made at Brooklands in June, a few flights were made towed by a motor car, and a few hops were made, almost certainly after downhill runs. In later years it was alleged that free powered hops were also made, but Roe's claim to be the first Briton to fly a powered machine in Britain—the American Cody was not yet naturalised—has been disallowed in favour of J. T. C. Moore-Brabazon. (See page 149).

In the United States, aviation—apart from the Wrights—may be said to have revived with the work of the Aerial Experiment Association based on Hammondsport (N.Y.), Lake Keuka, an organisation founded by Mrs. and Dr. Graham Bell, Glenn Hammond Curtiss, and others. They completed the first of their series of biplanes—they referred to them as 'aerodromes' following Langley—in March: this was the *Red Wing* (Pl. XIII), designed by Lieut. T. Selfridge (who in September was to be the first to die in an aeroplane); it made only two short hops (on March 12th and 17th) before crashing. The first four machines from this 'stable' had a general family resemblance—derived from both Wright and European forms—and were to lead to an important and influential stream of aviation design, especially in America. The biplane wings were curved toward one another in a slight double bow; there was a forward elevator, and a tail-unit comprising tailplane and vertical rudder: the first three machines had Curtiss-designed 30-h.p. engines. As the Association came thus late into the aviation field, their machines could take full advantage of the lessons learnt in Europe, and were growingly successful with each new aircraft. The *Red Wing* had no control in roll; but the second machine, the *White Wing* (designed by F. W. Baldwin), was fitted with four small ailerons outboard of the wing-tips, the first ailerons to be used outside Europe[1]: *White Wing* made five take-offs in May, the best being for 1,017 feet. The third, the *June Bug* (Pl. XIII), was designed by Glenn Curtiss—it also had the wing-tip ailerons—first flew in June, and won the *Scientific American* magazine's prize for the first official public flight in the United States of more than a kilometre (July 4th): this covered 5,090 feet at 39 m.p.h. in 1 minute 42½ seconds. The last machine of the year (*No. 4*), called the *Silver Dart*, was designed by J. A. D. McCurdy and followed the same lines as the others, including ailerons: it first flew at Hammondsport in December 1908. The considerable success of these aircraft led direct to the excellent Curtiss machines of 1909, which will be noted later.

[1] It is now known that Lawrence J. Lesh fitted ailerons to his Chanute-inspired biplane hang-glider and flew it near Montreal in September 1907: see paper by K. M. Molson in *Journal of the Canadian Aviation Historical Society*, Vol 12 No 2, 1974.

Meanwhile the Wrights had secured agreement to have their machines built in France, and an official acceptance test was also at last to be made before the U.S. Army authorities. In April the Wrights took their 1905 *Flyer III* to the Kill Devil Hills in order to regain their skill as pilots[1]: it was modified to take the pilot and one passenger sitting upright on the wing; on May 6th they flew for the first time since 1905, and from May 6th to 14th made twenty-two flights for practice. On May 14th Wilbur and Orville made the world's first two passenger flights, each taking C. Furnas, the second covering about 2½ miles in 3 minutes 40 seconds.

By the end of May, Wilbur had arrived in France to remove the new *Wright A* from store and prepare it for its first public flights. At the invitation of Léon Bollée he assembled the machine in Bollée's factory near Le Mans. Interest in France mounted high as Wilbur made his preparations, and scepticism mounted with it when the time dragged on owing to the many renewals and adjustments which had to be made on the machine after its last year's journey and long storage at Le Havre. Meanwhile Orville surveyed the ground at Fort Myer, Washington, D.C. and a new machine was constructed for the military trials which he was to conduct there in September.

In July Orville heard that Curtiss was using ailerons on his *June Bug*, and wrote to him alleging infringement of the Wright warping patents: this was the first shot in a protracted and bitter legal battle with Curtiss and others, and the primary cause of Curtiss later adopting between-wing ailerons in an effort to avoid further infringement.

August to December

After the delays noted above, Wilbur at last completed the assembly of his machine, which incidentally included new types of control lever. Intense and widespread interest, suspicion, and scepticism, was focussed on Wilbur by both the French aviators and the Press. Therefore, when Wilbur announced his first flight in public—he had so much confidence in the machine that he made no secret flight tests—the most critical of technical audiences assembled on August 8th 1908 at the small local racecourse at Hunaudières (5 miles south of Le Mans). The spectators whom Wilbur Wright faced on that day comprised the most combative audience imaginable; these were the aviators and would-be aviators of France who, in their own uncertain hopes, were the only aviators in the world.

On that memorable day, Wilbur took off, made two graceful circles and landed smoothly: he was in the air for only 1 minute 45 seconds, but he had revolutionised European aviation. It is hard for us today to realise the shock, and almost stunned amazement, which greeted Wilbur's effortless mastery of control, his graceful banks, turns, and circles (Pl. XIII).[2]

---

[1] They first 'warmed up' on their 1902 glider, now fitted with a double rudder.

[2] In recent years a somewhat novel myth has been put about on both sides of the Atlantic concerning the Wrights. As one French writer put it, "The Wright aircraft was never able to leave the ground under its own power until the 1908 period, when it was fitted with a French engine, built in France by the firm of Bariquand and Marre of Paris." For the record, it should be

His audience was by turns astounded, dismayed and—to give them credit—repentant; repentant of their six years of disbelief, and dismayed at the memory of their six years aeronautical fumbling. With no proper control in their hands, and indeed no image of true flight in their minds, they were now experiencing a painful moment of truth. The veteran pioneer Léon Delagrange spoke for all his honest countrymen when he exclaimed, "Well, we are beaten! We just don't exist" ("Eh bien, nous sommes battus! Nous n'existons pas!"). "No one can estimate", said one French spokesman, "the consequences which will result from this new method of locomotion, the dazzling beginnings of which we salute today." "For us in France," exclaimed Blériot, "and everywhere, a new era in mechanical flight has commenced . . . it is marvellous". "It is a revelation in aeroplane work," said René Gasnier, "who can now doubt that the Wrights have done all they claimed? . . . We are as children compared with the Wrights." "Mr. Wright has us all in his hands," said Paul Zens. The French aviation press was equally repentant, and enthusiastic; "One of the most exciting spectacles ever present in the history of applied science." *Le Figaro* wrote, "Ce ne fut pas un succès, ce fut un triomphe!" "I had the good fortune," wrote François Peyrey, "to find myself at Hunaudières on August 8th, 1908, the date of the memorable demonstration. I shall try to give an idea of the incomparable mastery of the American aviators in the marvellous act of imitating the birds. For a long time—for too long a time—the Wright brothers have been accused in Europe of bluffing; perhaps even in their own land. Today they are hallowed (consacrés) by France, and I feel an intense pleasure in counting myself among the first to make amends for such flagrant injustice. . . . It would also be just as puerile (puéril) to challenge the first flight of December 17, 1903 in North Carolina as it would be to deny 'les expériences' in La Sarthe (the Department in which Le Mans is situated). . . . From the stands (on the race course) an immense acclamation goes up from the witnesses of this prowess. . . ."

The London *Times* said "All accounts . . . published in this morning's papers from the correspondents on the spot, attest the complete triumph of the American inventor . . . the enthusiasm was indescribable . . . all accounts agree that the most admirable characteristic of yesterday's flight was the steady mastery displayed by Mr. Wright over his machine." The Europeans, until this moment, had virtually no notion of flight-control: now they acquired that notion properly for the first time, and it effected the revolution necessary to bring about the final conquest of the air. The world—not only of aviation but of politics and power—soon endorsed the now famous statement of Major B. F. S. Baden-Powell, the Past-President of the (later Royal) Aeronautical Society: "that Wilbur Wright is in possession of a power which controls the fate of nations, is beyond dispute".

said that, (a) the outstanding flights made in the U.S.A. by Orville Wright in 1908 were made with a Dayton-built Wright engine; (b) Wilbur Wright flew brilliantly in France from August 8th to October 30th, also with a Dayton-built Wright engine; (c) after that date he used a standard Wright engine built under licence by the Paris firm named above. At no time did the Wrights use any engines other than those they designed themselves; in fact, they were not at all satisfied with the work done for them by Bariquand and Marre in the early days.

Between August 8th and 13th Wilbur made nine flights, the longest lasting just over 8 minutes. Then he received permission to use the Camp d'Auvours, the great military ground 7 miles east of Le Mans. Here from August 21st to the last day of December 1908, he made over 100 flights, and was airborne for about 25½ hours. When Wilbur was established at Auvours, both his flying and his personality proved irresistible; the Europeans flocked there as the Faithful flock to Mecca. Those who went 'to pray', as distinct from those who went 'to stare', paid special and sustained attention to two particular features of Wilbur's flying; his mastery of flight-control and manoeuvre, especially the co-ordinated use of warping and rudder, and his sophisticated, efficient propellers, geared-down to produce optimum thrust, as opposed to the primitive direct-drive 'paddles' used by the Europeans. The Comte de La Vaulx was to write of this Wright aircraft as "the machine which has just revolutionised (revolutionner) the aviator's world".

When Wilbur got into his stride, so to say, at Auvours, the effect on the whole world of aviation was indeed revolutionary. It was not just the achievement of duration and height records that made such an impression: it was the flying of an aeroplane as it should be flown, smoothly, expertly, and with complete mastery of manoeuvre. Climbing, banking, turning—with rapid and graceful circles and figures of eight—and even glides with the engine off, displayed both an aircraft and a flying technique undreamt of in Europe. There was no limit to the astonishment, no end to the praise and adulation. An English authority wrote that the machine described circles "in a manner that was altogether unknown to Europe". As the flights continued, the repentant French aviation writers could scarcely find words adequate to express their amazement: "au Camp d'Auvours, Wilbur Wright continue la série de ses merveilleuses performances"; "les glorieuses performances"; "les performances sensationnelles"; and so on. Nor was praise wanting for Wilbur himself, whose quiet charm and modesty became a legend. "I know of only one bird, the parrot, that talks," he said at a dinner, "and it can't fly very high."

As the first excitement died down, and as the world of aviation treated the Camp d'Auvours as a new Mecca, the European designers and engineers made some wise and rueful assessments of their own efforts since 1903. One of the earliest realisations that dawned upon them was that the Wrights could never have attained such perfection without years of prodigious labour and experimentation: they thereupon investigated the previous history of the Wrights' machines, and publicly accepted the facts of the early flights as we know them.

Wilbur's flying at Auvours drew every serious aeronautical investigator to examine the aircraft and watch its performance; to discuss aviation with him; and to fly with him when possible.[1] Wilbur divided his flights between

[1] The first British pilot was, of course, Farman. The first 'resident' Briton to fly as a passenger was Griffith Brewer, who first flew with Wilbur on October 8th, followed during the same day by the Hon. C. S. Rolls, Frank Hedges Butler and Major Baden-Powell, who were already well-known balloonists. Wilbur had considerable trouble with his three women passengers owing to the aerodynamic (and moral) hazards of their skirts, which had to be tied round with string below the knees; the first was Mrs. Hart O. Berg who was taken up on October 7th.

taking passengers—on some 60 of the 104 flights—and performing endurance and height tests for record and prize-winning purposes. He made his first major endurance flight on September 21st, when he was in the air for over an hour and a half, and covered 41 miles. Of the seven flights in 1908 lasting over an hour, three lasted for over 1½ hours, and one lasted 2 hours 20 minutes, in which he covered 77 miles (December 31st), which broke all his own records and won the Michelin prize of 20,000 francs. On October 10th he had taken a passenger for the record 'two-up' flight of 1 hour 9 minutes, and covered about 45 miles. On December 18th, he broke all altitude records—his own, Orville's and Henri Farman's (see below)—by reaching 360 feet.

It is fitting that a French historian (Charles Dollfus) should sum up: "The first flight [by Wilbur Wright] took place on August 8th 1908. Numerous flights followed, which revolutionised aviation by the quality of the pilotage, and by the manageability and versatility of the machine. The mechanism of wing-warping was also a revelation. Finally, the "haute personalité" of Wilbur Wright, his reserve and his sureness, the nobility of his character, culminated in conquering the world of aviation and the general public'."

Meanwhile triumph and tragedy attended Orville Wright's U.S. Army acceptance trials at Fort Myer. He made ten flights, starting on September 3rd, which included four of over an hour, and two which created altitude records of 200 and 310 feet. The flight of 1 hr. 2 min. 15 sec., on September 9th, was the world's first flight of an hour, a duration not to be achieved by a European until Paul Tissandier flew for 1 hr. 2 min. 13 sec. on his Wright biplane on May 20th 1909. On September 17th Orville was making his third flight with a passenger—this time with Lieutenant T. E. Selfridge—when the machine crashed from a height of 75 feet, and was wrecked. Lieutenant Selfridge was killed and Orville injured: it was the first fatality in powered aviation.[1]

The robust and sophisticated aircraft which thus brought the first period of powered flying to a close were of what is now known as the Wright type *A*: it had a span of 41 feet and a wing area of 510 square feet. They were efficient two-seaters which, despite the low-powered 30-h.p. engine, had an ample power margin, thanks to the overall excellence of design of both airframe and propellers, and to satisfactory gearing. The records show that at least seven of these machines were built, all similar except for small details. Illustrations may be seen in Pl. XIII and XIV. These seven machines—reduced to six after the Fort Myer crash—were the Wrights' 'ambassadors' and brought about a proper understanding of their technique and achievements, as well as the disadvantage, for general use, of their inherent instability. Wilbur's machine, as assembled and flown in August 1908, was also the first aeroplane to be fitted with dual control; it was designed with an eye to instruction.

[1] A blade of the starboard propeller developed a longitudinal crack which caused it to flatten and lose its thrust, thereby setting up an imbalance with the good blade: the consequent violent vibration loosened the supports of the propeller's long shaft, causing the latter to 'wave' to and fro, and thus enlarge the propeller disc: the good blade then hit, and tore loose, one of the four wires bracing the rudder-outriggers to the wings, the wire winding itself round the blade and breaking it (the blade) off. Orville cut the motor and tried to land; but the rudder canted over and sent the machine out of control, despite Orville's near-successful effort to right it.

Although completely overshadowed by the Wrights' performances, the Europeans—and Curtiss in America—were making steady headway in endurance flights. Delagrange, Blériot and Farman set the pace. Delagrange covered 24·7 kilometres (15 miles) at Issy on September 6th; Farman flew for 40 kilometres (nearly 25 miles) at the Camp de Châlons, on October 2nd. It was Farman who made the first true cross-country flight in history on October 30th, when he flew from Bouy to Reims, 27 km. (16¾ miles) in 20 minutes. On October 31st Farman also won temporarily the official height record at 80 feet, although Wilbur Wright had already flown higher and was soon officially to beat all records by a large margin. Blériot made a celebrated cross-country flight—using his *VIII-ter* with pivoting wing-tip ailerons—from Toury, around Artenay, and back on October 31st (with two landings en route), a distance of about 28 km. (some 17 miles) in about 22 minutes flying time. Delagrange continued successfully flying his Voisin at Issy and at Port Aviation (Juvisy), and both he and Farman had now the full quota of four 'side-curtains' on the main wings of their Voisin.

Farman had been first to follow the Wrights' lead on control in roll, and had taken a great step forward by fitting four large flap-type ailerons (Pl. XXII) in time for his cross-country flight of October 30th. This started the European tradition of large effective ailerons, which he was to establish fully and successfully on his own self-designed 1909 biplane. In November of this year he added another small wing on top of his well-tried and much modified Voisin, thus converting it uselessly into a triplane: he sold this famous machine in spring 1909, and thereafter designed his own machines.

Amongst a growing amount of experimentation—much of it naïve and fruitless—there are a number of important aircraft to note. The leading pioneers had been building new machines, some with the intention of exhibiting them at the first Salon de l'Aéronautique,[1] which was held in Paris for a few days at the end of December. Some of the machines shown had not flown at all, some only waveringly.

Among the aeroplanes which had been completed and flown promisingly by the end of the year, the most important were the first two of Levavasseur's true *Antoinette* monoplanes, the *Antoinettes IV* and *V*. They were the first members of an outstanding aircraft family which flourished in 1909 and 1910, and grew out of the *Antoinette I* and the Gastambide-Mengin of early 1908. Both the new *Antoinettes* had flap-type ailerons, a form of control in roll which was abandoned on all subsequent *Antoinettes* in favour of the Wrights' wing-warping.

Also tested in only four short hop-flights from September to December (before being abandoned) were the Goupy and de Caters triplanes built by the Voisin brothers. The Goupy was illustrated in the aeronautical press earlier in the year when under construction: in the tractor tradition, it was to lead directly—in 1909—to another and more famous triplane made and

[1] Strictly speaking it was the aeronautical section of the Salon de l'Automobile and, apart from balloons, airships, and Ader's historic *Avion III*, comprised sixteen aeroplanes including the Blériot monoplanes (*Nos. IX* and *XI*), the Blériot biplane (*No. X*), the incomplete *Antoinette VI*, the *REP 2*, Santos-Dumont's *Demoiselle* (*No. 20*), two standard Voisins, and a standard type A Wright: the rest were mostly unflown or unflyable machines of some interest but little importance.

flown by A. V. Roe in England.

Santos-Dumont now returned briefly to aviation with another version—the Santos-Dumont '*19-bis*'—of the small *Demoiselle* with the engine now below on the undercarriage driving an outside propeller by a long belt; but this machine was a failure and never left the ground. But the idea of the *Demoiselle* was sound and was to flourish later.

Esnault-Pelterie had been making flights on his *REP 2* (Pl. XIII) and had by the year's end built and flown an improved machine, the *REP 2-bis*, one of the machines to adopt the Wrights' wing-warping, although inadequately. Various and somewhat vague claims have been made for the *REP* machines, but although they possessed some degree of streamlining, a semi-metal construction, a practical control column, and an excellent engine, there was nothing either particularly outstanding or original about them; the same qualities—and better—had been developing elsewhere and, despite considerable later success, these aircraft stood to one side of the main productive stream of aviation.

In England the main event of this period was the first official aeroplane flight by Cody: he put his machine through a number of tests at Farnborough starting properly on September 19th; its ailerons were removed after the tests of September 29th; and on October 16th—having already made some hops—it achieved its first proper flight (1,390 feet) at the end of which it crashed: this is now recognised as the first official powered aeroplane flight in Great Britain. Cody was a colourful, ingenious and intrepid pioneer, who helped materially to make Britain air-minded, but technically he did not influence aviation (Pl. XIII).

In November–December, the new swept-wing Dunne *D.4* powered biplane was tested in Scotland; but the 30-h.p. REP motor (giving only 21–23 h.p.) was not strong enough to fly it. In December, England saw her first resident to become a qualified aeroplane pilot, in the person of J. T. C. Moore-Brabazon (later Lord Brabazon), who learnt to fly in France on a standard Voisin, two of which he was to purchase, and one of which he was to bring back to England in the new year.

Aviation in countries other than America, France and Britain, got off to a slow start, despite the presence of so much activity nearby. The first hop-flights in Germany took place on June 28th at Kiel, when J. C. H. Ellehammer, made two—of some 11 seconds each—in his No. *IV*, a biplane. But Germany herself was at last awakening to a science she had once done so much to promote, and her first true aviator, Hans Grade—Karl Jatho can scarcely qualify—was making preliminary ground tests with his triplane *à la* Ellehammer at Magdeburg in October. Delagrange had made the first aeroplane flights in Italy in May, at Rome.

Away from the main stream of aeronautics, but of importance, was a suggestion this year by a French artillery officer and engineer named René Lorin, which was published in *L'Aérophile* (September 1st) in Paris and was followed by other articles which continued up to the period of the First World War. It concerned a new method of jet propulsion which, although not itself practicable, was to exert considerable influence on workers to come. Lorin suggested a slender streamlined aeroplane to be propelled by two in-line petrol engines—one on either side of the fuselage—which were to be fitted with special exhaust nozzles on each cylinder, and thus form two intermittent reaction propulsion units. An interesting feature of the design was the provision of a hinged mounting to direct the jets downward for a near vertical take-off, and then gradually straighten up for horizontal flight. Lorin later developed the idea of this manned "aéroplane à grande vitesse" into an unmanned, radio-directed and catapult-launched flying bomb, powered by a ram-jet, a scheme in which he failed to interest the French military authorities in the First World War.

On December 28th, an isolated American pioneer, Matthew B. Sellers, first tested his quadruplane in Kentucky. He never made more than brief hops, but his aircraft was probably the first to use a retractable wheeled undercarriage: it took off on wheels, and landed on skids.

This remarkable year of 1908 saw a major turning point in aviation history. The European configuration of the stable tailed biplane had been born in 1904–05 from the example of the Wrights' gliders—whose structure was poorly imitated and whose *raison d'être* and management were misunderstood—and was thereupon married to the box-kite of Hargrave. Lacking personnel of sufficient insight and pertinacity, it had moved forward over the years 1905, 1906, 1907 and half of 1908, with an uncertain and often blundering gait, unorganised and confused in its ideas, and relying on a technique of hit and miss for its unsteady progress. In 1906, this tradition had been joined by the first petrol engines designed specifically for aeroplanes, which from then on were to achieve an ever-improving power-weight ratio. Then, still neglecting aerodynamic research, the practical problems of flight-control, and the true ethos of aeroplane flight, the pioneers of the European flying-machine had slowly succeeded in dragging their vehicles into the air by brute force of engine and airscrew, so that by January of this year 1908—after nearly five years of prodigal exertion—they could just keep an aeroplane flying for one and a half minutes at a few feet off the ground, and steer it perilously round in a circle by rudder alone, thereby winning the acclaim of the world for such a "mémorable victoire". These pioneers, some by the end of this year, had seen Wilbur Wright not only keeping his aeroplane in the air for 2 hours and 20 minutes, but flying like a bird. Such an impact of achievement, and of the ideas that lay behind it, was now to establish a new and mature conception of the aeroplane as a practical flying vehicle.

*   *   *   *   *

Note on Aircraft Speeds. The average air speeds of the first aeroplanes are difficult to arrive at accurately. On December 17th 1903 the Wrights flew at about 30 m.p.h.: in 1904 and 1905 at about 40 m.p.h. In 1906 Santos-Dumont made his short flight at about 25 m.p.h. At the end of 1907 and beginning of 1908 Henri Farman was flying his Voisin at some 30 m.p.h. At the end of 1908, Wilbur was still flying at about 40 m.p.h. and the Farman-modified Voisin at some 40 m.p.h., but it should be borne in mind that the Wright machines in use in 1908 were two-seaters, and their speed was easily maintained with 'two up'.

Fig. 64. Principal drawing of the Wright patent of 1903 (granted in 1906), showing the wing-warping, rudder, and elevator system

Fig. 65. Diagram of a wing-tip vortex, from Lanchester's *Aeronautics*: 1907

Fig. 66. Santos-Dumont light monoplane, *Demoiselle*: 1909

Fig. 67. *Valkyrie* canard-type monoplane: 1910

Fig. 68. Wright *Model B* biplane, with wheeled undercarriage: 1910

13. *The Aeroplane as an Accepted Vehicle:*
1909

DURING 1909 the aeroplane came of age, and became accepted as the world's new practical vehicle. This acceptance was particularly signalised by two events, Louis Blériot's Channel crossing on July 25th, and the first great air meeting at Reims in August. The former was a splendid feat of daring, aided by good luck, performed in an unsuitable machine; it fired the public's admiration—and imagination: it shook the confidence of governments in the invincibility of navies; and it cast a long and ominous shadow across the minds of many sober men, filling them with dread and apprehension for the future of mankind.

The Reims meeting, with its prizes for distance, speed, altitude and passenger-carrying, was an outstanding success—socially, officially, and above all, technically. It reinforced the message of the Channel crossing by bringing together the best in machines and pilots in an effective concentration, and exhibiting the variety and possibilities of the new vehicle: the impact on public and governments alike was formidable.

It was inevitable that the eyes of the world would remain fixed on the Wrights for much of 1909; for the brothers continued to make spectacular flights in France (at Pau), Italy, Germany and the United States, and at last received the universal honour and acclaim they deserved. But significant developments in Europe were soon attracting attention. Having been put firmly on the right 'control' road by the Wrights' example, European aviation—and Curtiss in America—developed and blossomed into mature success during 1909.

Two general achievements soon emerged as dominant in aviation, and came to condition all future flying. The first was effective control in the air, control in three dimensions—in pitch, yaw and roll. This stemmed direct from the Wrights, and involved the understanding of control in roll and its co-ordination with both directional and longitudinal control, not only to preserve equilibrium, but, equally important, the dynamic employment of this co-ordinated control to *initiate* manoeuvres. Until Wilbur Wright flew in France in 1908, the Europeans had looked upon flight-control in a spirit of passivity; as a technique of simply remaining intact in the air by corrective action.[1] It had been the chauffeur's attitude, so often noted before, in which the pilots saw themselves as driving their winged automobiles off the ground

---

[1] Dollfus agrees with this view: in *Les Avions* (1962) he says of the Wright machine of 1908, "The ease of its flight came from the fact that its lateral control—wing warping—was utilised not, as were the primitive ailerons of the French machines, to right the aircraft, but as a means of control for turning."

and keeping them in equilibrium on the aerial highway; and only steering them cautiously to right or left when necessary. Then, in 1908, the Europeans saw Wilbur using his flying controls actively and dynamically as an airman. Translated into the sphere of equitation—an analogy which Wilbur himself had favoured—it meant the difference between a rider whose whole effort is devoted passively to staying on the horse's back, and one who actively rides and commands the horse, and bends it to his will.

The second achievement was the successful marriage of control and manoeuvrability with the inherent stability which had been a concept fostered by the Europeans (in models and full-size attempts) ever since Cayley advocated it in 1809: with this union, having now matched their mentors in control, the Europeans were henceforth to make their own major contribution to aeronautical history.

Deliberate inherent instability, which the Wrights had seen as an essential factor in their development and mastery of flight-control, meant that the aircraft had to be actively pilot-controlled during every second in the air: hence Wright pupils had to acquire considerable skill before they felt confident to fly successfully. The training time was not long by our standards, but it was rather discouraging to the average would-be pilot, who rightly demanded a reasonable amount of repose and security when airborne. The stable aeroplane—not to appear in its fully-fledged form until the British *B.E.2c* of 1913—increased safety, and reduced the measure of skill necessary to fly an aeroplane, thus increasing the number of potential pilots, and allowing the less skilful a wider margin in their pilotage; and all this without sacrificing controllability.

The next important feature of the first half of the year was the rise of the monoplane, a class of flying-machine till then regarded as a tentative and doubtful proposition. It was the successful emergence, with steadily improving performances, of Levavasseur's two graceful *Antoinettes* (the *IV* and *V*), and of Blériot's small *No. XI*, that put the monoplane squarely in the public eye, a position of prominence greatly enhanced by these aircraft being the only protagonists in the "battle of the Channel" (Pl. XV).

Despite the growing success of the monoplane, it was the biplane which in the eyes of professional and amateur alike, still represented the only fully tried and reliable species of aeroplane during the first six months of the year; but even here, only two makes were fully established, the manoeuvrable two-seat Wright, with its rightful aura of fame; and the limited but reliable single-seat Voisin, already obsolescent, on which almost anyone in their right mind could become safely airborne in straight hop-flights in calm weather, after the briefest of briefings on the ground (Pl. XIV).

But, by the close of the Reims meeting, a newcomer, the *Henry Farman* biplane (basically the *Henry Farman III*), had blazed its way into acceptance as the leading biplane of the day—and the morrow—with a highly attractive compromise between Wright-like manoeuvrability and Voisin-like stability, and an overall look of flyability and reliability. Close runner-up in this class of biplane, and superior in speed, was the Glenn Curtiss 'Reims machine', which was soon to become, so to say, the Farman of the U.S.A. (Pl. XIV).

There also appeared two tentative tractor biplanes, which were later to condition the form of the modern biplane: these were the *Goupy II*, with its staggered wings, and the *Breguet I*, both of which had sensibly eschewed the Wright-derived forward elevator (Pls. XV, XVI).

A passing tribute—perhaps coupled with a retrospective sigh—should be paid to the many inventors on both sides of the Atlantic who designed a multitude of aircraft during 1909. Few of them ever left the ground, few possessed true originality, and fewer still combined originality with any degree of practicality. In short, there was in 1909—along with the few successful aeroplanes—a prodigious amount of wasted aeronautical energy.

In the sphere of propellers, the year saw at last one European product, the Chauvière, to rival the Wrights; it appropriately came to propel the Farman and Blériot machines. In the matter of engines, the aviators of the day had little difficulty in agreeing that it was in these prime movers that the chief weakness of aviation lay: it was now not the heaviness, but the unreliability of the engines, which was the bugbear of early flying, despite the many excellent qualities of the ubiquitous Antoinette, the Vivinus, the Anzani, the REP and the revolutionary rotary Gnome. But still the most reliable of all was the 30-h.p. Wright motor, soon to be rivalled by the Gnome.

The collective identity of the aeroplane as revealed at Reims showed the world's new vehicle as capable of conveying two men through the air in comparative safety at some 40 m.p.h.; of being kept in satisfactory aerial equilibrium; of being adequately controlled and manoeuvred; and of being able to fly reliably for two or more hours at a time. It was now evident to the world that the flying machine had truly 'arrived', and that the way was open to rapid progress.

*   *   *   *   *

Public attention was still focussed on the Wright brothers. In January Wilbur moved to Pau in south-west France, where he set up the first 'powered' flying school, and taught the three Frenchmen who his contract with the French manufacturers called for.[1] Orville, now fully recovered, had come over from the United States and, together, the brothers were honoured and fêted throughout Europe. Wilbur—using a new type *A* machine built in Dayton and assembled at Pau—then gave demonstrations and lessons (to Lieutenant Calderera and another Italian lieutenant) at Centocelle, near Rome, from April 15th to 25th, to great acclaim. While at Centocelle, Wilbur took up the first aerial cinematographer (on April 24th).[2] Then Wilbur and Orville returned to America in May to make further demonstration flights, and receive the acclaim of their own countrymen. In August, Orville returned to Europe and made spectacular flights in

[1] The machine which Wilbur used in France in 1908–09—*the Wright A (France)*—was the first in history to be fitted with dual controls.

[2] This year also saw the first still photographs taken from aeroplanes. After one or two tentative shots by unknown operators, M. Meurisse, flying in an *Antoinette* piloted by Latham, took a series of photos in December of Mourmelon airfield and its surroundings. There is now some evidence that Wilbur Wright may have taken up a cinematographer at Auvours in early September 1908.

Germany during September and October. Meanwhile Wright machines were being built under licence in France and England (by Shorts) and proved successful, popular and robust, despite their inherent instability (which made piloting them quite an accomplishment), and their take-off technique. The first Short-built Wright—made for the Hon. C. S. Rolls—flew in October 1909 (Pl. XIV). Incidentally, it was on a standard Wright *A* machine that the first flight of an hour was made by a European (Paul Tissandier) on May 20th in France.

The European airmen, with the Wrights' achievements and technique to emulate, now started to come into their own. They unreservedly acclaimed the Wrights' superiority in flying, but did not trust their inherently unstable machines for general use. But they had at last learnt from the Wrights the lesson of proper control in roll, Farman taking to ailerons, Blériot to warping; and Levavasseur at first fitting ailerons to his *Antoinettes*, and then taking to warping. Only the Voisins remained stubbornly unaffected, with no form of control in roll. The Wrights, on the other hand, clung to their instability and—somewhat irrationally—to their weight, derrick and rail launching, although during the year some owners of Wright machines added wheels to the skids,[1] the first Wright machine with wheels being the *Wright A* (*Schreck*) which made its first wheeled take-off on September 20th 1909 at Port Aviation (Juvisy).

During the first half of this year, there arose a growing number of aviators, designers, and amateurs, and the forms of their aircraft began to multiply. There was still also much wasted effort and wasted construction by a surprisingly large eccentric 'fringe'. However, the dominant types of aeroplane became more efficient and reliable, and now set the general style for some years to come. The 'message' of powered flying began spreading over the world, and the beginnings of national aircraft industries, as well as Government concern with aviation, were now to be seen throughout Europe.

In France, which naturally remained the aeronautical centre of affairs in Europe, the five more important producers of aircraft were Farman, Blériot, Levavasseur, the Voisins, and the Wrights (by proxy). Whereas the Wright biplane remained basically the type *A*, the Europeans pressed ahead. Blériot developed his small *No. XI* monoplane (Pl. XV), on which he exchanged his first engine, a 30-h.p. REP, for the new 25-h.p. 3-cylinder Anzani: the machine was fitted with efficient Wright-type wing-warping, with his patented control column ending below in the *cloche*, to which warping and elevator cables were attached. With the success of the *XI*, he soon abandoned his two other new types shown in the Salon, the *No. IX* which was a long-fuselage variation of the *VII-ter*, designed to take the 16 cylinder 100-h.p. Antoinette; and also his biplane (*No. X*), a type which he now eschewed; but he also persevered with his two-seat *No. XII* (Pl. XV).

A new and popular aviator appeared in the handsome person of Hubert Latham—half French, half English—who always flew *Antoinettes*, and whose

---

[1] The Wright machines were manhandled about the aerodromes on two single-wheel dollies, one under each wing. They sometimes took off from the rail without the derrick and weight, but not often, owing to the short length of the rail.

skilful pilotage did much to advertise the type. The *Antoinettes* were in many ways the finest of the early monoplanes, with advanced construction, and the fine 50-h.p. Antoinette engine; they were also by far the most elegant machines of this period (Pl. XV). By mid-year, the *Antoinettes IV* (Latham's machine), *V*, and *VI* were all flying successfully, the *IV* and *V* fitted with ailerons, the *VI* and *VII* (nearing completion) with wing-warping, with which all subsequent *Antoinettes* were to be fitted.

Santos-Dumont introduced in March the world's first successful light aeroplane, his new (*No. 20*) machine which became the standard *Demoiselle*, with one of various engines placed again on the wings; there was a robust three-boom bamboo fuselage—in place of the single boom—a combined rudder-cum-elevator, and body-operated wing-warping (Fig. 66). It found a small but enthusiastic market on into the year 1910.

With Esnault-Pelterie improving his *REP* monoplanes, but not making significant advances, and the Voisin brothers continuing to produce their stereotyped box-kite machines (Pl. XIV), we come to the next—and very important—innovation, the self-designed and constructed biplane of Henri Farman's, which was named the *Henry Farman III*.[1]

This *Henry Farman* biplane (Pl. XIV) was to become even more popular as a safe sporting machine than that of the Wrights, as he gladly learned from them, but not they from him—in the matter of stability. This first true Farman showed its Wright, Hargrave and Voisin parentage plainly enough; but Farman had transformed his modified Voisin type into a light, robust, and handsome machine with a single front elevator carried on a slender outrigger, four ailerons instead of the sterile non-aileroned and side-curtained wings of the Voisin, and an open biplane tail-unit sporting twin rudders; he also fitted a light four-wheeled undercarriage, with turned-up skids added for safety in nose-down landings. It was first fitted with a 50-h.p. Vivinus motor, and then with a completely new power plant, the 50-h.p. 7-cylinder rotary Gnome[2] which had been developed by the end of 1908; with its descendants, this machine was to become one of the classic aeroplanes of history. The *Henry Farman III* first flew in April of 1909.[3]

In America, Curtiss had meanwhile produced an outstanding aeroplane in his *Golden Flier*, the second of which (un-named) was soon to be seen at Reims (Pl. XIV): these started the main rival tradition to the Wrights in the U.S.A. Developed from his *June Bug*, with his 30–40-h.p. engine, these

---

[1] The Farman brothers, Henri and Maurice, were now in business as constructors; but each brother designed his own distinctive machines. Maurice also tested during this year his modification of the Voisin type, but it was not successful: it was later that he became a powerful rival to his brother with the famous 'Longhorns' and 'Shorthorns'.

[2] The Gnome was designed by the brothers Seguin, and first "flew" when it powered Paulhan's Voisin in June 1909.

[3] Farman himself—"Monsieur Henri" as he was always called—was Europe's outstanding pilot from the autumn of 1907 to well into 1910, and one of the most prominent manufacturers in France from 1909 to 1937. Son of British parents living in France, he retained British nationality until 1937, although he could scarcely speak any English. He was an art student who became successively a champion cycle-racer and champion automobile racer, before he turned to aviation. He was a delightful man, of "un courage tranquille" as Dollfus put it, who developed a remarkable mastery of both pilotage and the technical problems of aviation.

biplanes had a forward biplane elevator, large between-wing ailerons, fixed rear fin and tailplane, and tricycle undercarriage. They represented, with the Farman, the new and successful compromise between stability and controllability. Curtiss fitted one of his new 50-h.p. engines in the Reims machine.

Back in Europe, as I have said, are two other machines of note, which—although not at first outstandingly successful—established once and for all the basic tractor biplane form of the future. First was the Goupy biplane—the *Goupy II*—which was designed by Ambroise Goupy and the Italian naval Lieut. A. Calderera, Wilbur Wright's first pupil at Centocelle in 1909: it was built in the Blériot factory, and was the world's first tractor biplane with fuselage and tail-unit: it first 'hopped' in March (Pl. XVI): the Goupy had staggered biplane wings with elevons (first at mid-wing position then pivoting on the wing-tips), a long fuselage, and a biplane tail-unit: it already possessed the familiar modern 'biplane look' and clearly influenced A. V. Roe in his successful biplanes of 1911 and after. The second of these influential machines was Louis Breguet's biplane, which first flew in June; in this first of his long line of biplanes he was feeling his way with a somewhat maladroit design (Pl. XV), and it was not until next year (1910) that he produced a clean 'modern' type machine (see Fig. 69).

The outstanding aeronautical event of the year was Louis Blériot's flight across the Channel on July 25th, thereby winning the *Daily Mail* £1,000 prize. By rights he should not have won it: for Latham, in his aileroned *Antoinette IV*—a robust aircraft with a suitable engine—set off from Sangatte (near Calais) on July 19th (Pl. XV); but he had engine failure when seven or eight miles out and had to 'ditch' in the Channel, being rescued by the escorting French destroyer. Others also had it in mind to attempt the Channel crossing, including the Comte de Lambert (Wilbur Wright's first pupil) and even Wilbur himself. But success was to attend Blériot, who—feeling none too fit after a recent accident—took off from Les Baraques (near Calais) at 4.41 a.m. and landed in the Northfall Meadow by Dover Castle at 5.17½ a.m. on July 25th after a devious and perilous flight of about 23½ miles in his frail and quite unsuitable *No. XI* monoplane, with its 3-cylinder 25-h.p. Anzani motor.[1] "No pilot of today," says Dollfus, "no matter how great, could repeat this exploit in such an aircraft and with such an engine." But luck was with him, and he triumphed: it was a fitting climax to a courageous career. This flight had as vivid and profound an effect on Kings and Governments as it had on the general public. "The day that Blériot flew the Channel," wrote Sir Alan Cobham, "marked the end of our insular safety, and the beginning of the time when Britain must seek another form of defence besides ships." Although the writing on the wall was clear enough to most of those who controlled the destinies of Europe, there were still many military commanders who could not stomach the idea of an aeroplane being of any more service in war than a flying observation post.

Two days after Blériot's Channel-crossing—on July 27th—Latham again started from Sangatte in the *Antoinette VII* (with wing-warping) and again

---

[1] The times of take-off and landing are those given by the official observers.

PLATE XV

a The Blériot *No. XI* (*modified*) which was first to fly the English Channel on July 25th 1909

b The first machine to attempt the Channel crossing (and to fail); Levavasseur's aileroned
Antoinette IV,
Latham piloting:
July 19th 1909

c The *Antoinette VII*,
with warping, which
(with Latham piloting)
also failed to cross
the Channel:
July 27th 1909

d The trend-setting *Breguet I* tractor biplane: 1909   **e** The *Blériot XII* monoplane: 1909

PLATE XVI

a The *Goupy II* tractor biplane: 1909

b A. V. Roe's second triplane: 1909

c The first seaplane, Fabre's float plane: 1910

f De Havilland's Farnborough *B.E.2* biplane, later to develop into the stable *B.E.2C*, the world's first properly stable aeroplane: 1912

d Prototype of all fighters, the Farnborough *B.S.1*: 1912

e The revolutionary *Deperdussin-Monocoque*, incorporating monocoque construction in its fuselage:: 1913 suffered the ill fortune of engine failure, this time only a mile from England (Pl. XV): this was the first occasion on which the 16-cylinder 100-h.p. Antoinette engine was used in a sustained flight.

The fame which attended Blériot's flight had an immediate effect on the embryo aviation industry; for Blériot, it resulted in orders for over a hundred aircraft, and the type *XI*—in various modifications—became known the world over, and remained in service even into the First World War.

If the Channel-crossing made the greatest impact on the public, it was the Reims aviation week which provided the greatest technical and governmental stimulus to aviation, and proved to officialdom and the public alike that the aeroplane had indeed 'arrived'. The first great aviation meeting of history was held from Sunday August 22nd to Sunday August 29th in the year 1909, on the plain of Bétheny, three miles north of Reims, the scene (in 1901) of the military review in honour of the Tsar. The full official title of the meeting was "La Grande Semaine d'Aviation de la Champagne", and was under the patronage of the President of the Republic; the whole event was initiated, promoted and financed by the Champagne industry, and managed by a "comité d'organisation" under the presidency of the Marquis de Polignac. As an added inducement to the world of aviation, the Champagne industry offered a number of highly generous prizes which resulted in highly creditable performances. The aeroplane was thus finally ushered into civilisation by courtesy of the most civilised, urbane and sophisticated industry of France. The meeting was an unqualified success, both technically and officially (in the way of its later influence), financially, and even socially. Many military and political chiefs, including Lloyd-George—who was then Chancellor of the Exchequer—attended and were deeply impressed. "Flying machines are no longer toys and dreams," said Lloyd-George, "they are an established fact. The possibilities of this new system of locomotion are infinite. I feel, as a Britisher, rather ashamed that we are so completely out of it."

The final list of entries numbered thirty-eight machines, but only twenty-three took off during the eight days—some only briefly—with twenty-two pilots flying them, some sharing aircraft and some flying more than one. There were over 120 take-offs, which resulted in eighty-seven flights of over 5 km. (3 miles), and some seven of 100 km. (62 miles) or more, the longest being 180 km. (112 miles). The best speed obtained was nearly 48 m.p.h., and the best height 155 metres (508½ feet). The types of machine (with numbers of each which flew) were:

BIPLANES		MONOPLANES	
Breguet	1	Antoinette	3
Curtiss	1	Blériot type XI	2
Henry Farman	3	Blériot XII	1
Voisin	7	Blériot XIII	1
Wright	3	REP	1

The figures may be summarised as follows:

§ Machines finally entered 38

§ Machines which were airborne (15 biplanes and 8 monoplanes) . 23

§ Aircraft types which were airborne (5 biplanes and 4 monoplanes) 9

§ Engine types used 12

§ Pilots who were airborne 22

§ Take-offs made . . . . over 120

§ Flights made of more than 5 km. (3 miles) 87

§ Greatest timed distance flown (Farman) 180 km. in 3 hr. 4 min. 56⅖ sec.

§ Highest speed over a 30 km. course (Curtiss) 75 km.p.h. (46⅗ m.p.h.)

§ Highest speed over a 20 km. course (Curtiss) 75·7 km.p.h. (47 m.p.h.)

§ Highest speed over a 10 km. course (Blériot XII) 76·95 km.p.h. (47⅕ m.p.h.)

§ Greatest altitude (Antoinette VII) . . . 155 m. (508½ ft.)

There were some excellent performances, with the distance Grand Prix being won by Farman—having just previously exchanged his Vivinus engine for a rotary Gnome—with 180 km. (112 miles) in 3 hours 4 minutes 56⅖ seconds; the 30 km. and 20 km. speed contests were won by Curtiss with 46⅗ and 47 m.p.h. respectively, and the 10 km. by Blériot at 48 m.p.h. Latham won the height prize with 155 metres (508½ feet). There were some crashes—including the burning of Blériot's *XII*—but no serious injuries; but what struck observers as strongly as the fine performances was the general unreliability of the engines. The Reims meeting was an unqualified success, and its influence was profound and far-reaching over the whole field of aviation. It led to a great expansion of aircraft and aero-engine design and construction, and was to set the fashion for many future meetings of the kind in Europe and America. Reims marked the true acceptance of the aeroplane as a practical vehicle, and as such was a major milestone in the world's history.

Shortly after, on September 7th, aviation saw its first pilot killed when Eugène Lefebvre crashed at Port Aviation (Juvisy) when test-flying a new type *A* Wright. And on September 22nd the veteran pioneer Captain Ferber was killed at Boulogne, when his Voisin hit a ditch when taxy-ing at speed.

*   *   *   *   *

The practical powered aeroplane had taken exactly one hundred and ten years to emerge from idea to reality. The process started when Sir George Cayley first formulated its basic nature in 1799, and came to fruition in 1909 at Reims, when the aeroplane was finally exhibited as a practical and accepted vehicle. Before 1799 there had been an age-old desire to fly; bold but misguided attempts to fly by means of wings attached to the body; speculation at all levels of intellect; some few fine flashes of reason or intuition; and—in 1783—the achievement of air voyaging by balloon.

The hundred and ten years from 1799 to 1909 may accurately and conveniently be divided into two periods; there was first a century-full of fore-runners (1799 to 1899), who laboured to bring powered aviation to the threshold of accomplishment; and then ten years in which the practical machine was finally achieved, primarily by the achievement of flight-control on gliders, prior to the introduction of power.

Although a considerable variety of configurations had appeared since 1903, including triplane, tandem, canard, and even annular, aeroplanes, only two basic types of practical aircraft had crystallised: these were the pusher biplane with forward elevator, represented by the Wright, Voisin, Farman and Curtiss machines; and the tractor monoplane, represented by the *Antoinettes* and two types of Blériot. All these machines flew at Reims.

Waiting in the wings, so to speak, and still not matured enough to succeed when it appeared at Reims, was the prophetic tractor biplane, with all control surfaces aft of the propeller, represented by the *Breguet* (Pl. XV); and the still tentative *Goupy* which was not seen at the meeting.

Each of the successful aircraft types at Reims, except the Voisin, possessed the following characteristics:

(a) a pair of cambered biplane or monoplane wings as its main lifting surfaces;

(b) a horizontal elevator for control in pitch, placed forward of the wings on the biplanes, aft on the monoplanes;

(c) a vertical rudder (aft) for control in yaw, which also provided one component in satisfactory directional steering;

(d) a helical twisting ('warping') of the wing-tips, or hinged ailerons, to provide control in roll in combination with the rudder, either for preserving lateral balance or to effect banked turns;

(e) a light petrol engine driving one or two propellers—pusher on the biplanes, tractor on the monoplanes—to provide the necessary thrust for forward propulsion;

(f) a robust but light construction, including a strong wheeled undercarriage on all but the Wright machines, which had skids;

(g) an airspeed of between 35 and 45 m.p.h.;

(h) a flight duration of between one and two hours;

(i) the ability to maintain satisfactory flight—except as yet in strong winds—and to bank, turn and circle safely in the air.

All these types, including the Voisin, but excluding the Wright—which was designed as inherently unstable—had a considerable amount of inherent stability built into them, including fixed tail-surfaces, and were thus comparatively simple to fly in favourable weather. The Voisin—safe, slow, but sterile—was alone in possessing no form of control in roll.[1] The prevailing weakness in all the aircraft was the unreliability of the engines, and it was to be many years before this menace to aerial safety and efficiency was remedied.

One other important characteristic to be noted was the ability of the

[1] The Voisins could only be flown in dead calm weather.

aircraft to carry passengers; among the machines at Reims which showed themselves capable of carrying passengers, the Wright and the Blériot *XII* were the only machines specifically designed for, and capable of, carrying a passenger in comfort as a regular part of their duties.

* * * * *

Aviation, in this year 1909, was now seriously embarked upon in other countries of Europe. But it is curious and unhappy to note how backward Britain still was in practical aviation, despite her important contributions made by former generations, and the technical leadership she now held in other branches of applied science. A particular blow was the Report of the Sub-Committee of the Committee of Imperial Defence on 'Aerial Naviga- tion', which was approved in February 1909. This Sub-Committee had to report on the dangers to which Britain could be exposed from the air; the naval or military advantages to be gained from the use of airships or aeroplanes; and the amount of money to be allocated to aerial experiments. It was perhaps the most deplorable Committee ever to sit on aeronautical matters: it was appointed in October 1908, when Wilbur Wright was at the height of his triumphant demonstrations; and when Farman, Blériot, Delagrange and others, were forging ahead. It did not take evidence from a single pilot; and it was mesmerised by airships. Where aeroplanes were concerned, the Report stated that "The Committee have not been able to obtain any trustworthy evidence to show whether great improvements may be expected in the immediate future, or whether the limit of practical utility may have already been nearly attained." It was therefore decided to help airship-building, to which private enterprise would not be attracted, by allocating £45,000 for their construction; and to stop all the money at Farnborough which was being spent on aeroplanes—which was £2,000!— and put all responsibility for aeroplanes on to private manufacturers. Can one wonder, in the face of such monumental ineptitude, that Mr. Winston Churchill "thought that there was a danger of these proposals being considered too amateurish. The problem of the use of aeroplanes was a most important one, and we should place ourselves in communication with Mr. Wright himself, and avail ourselves of his knowledge." Mr. Churchill was then President of the Board of Trade.

It was no wonder that, after Blériot's crossing of the Channel, H. G. Wells let fly in the *Daily Mail* in these words:

"What does it mean for us? One meaning, I think, stands out plainly enough, unpalatable enough to our national pride. This thing from first to last was made abroad. . . . Gliding began abroad when our young men of muscle and courage were braving the dangers of the cricket ball. The motor-car and its engine was being worked out 'over there', . . . Over there, where the prosperous classes have some regard for education, . . . where people discuss all sorts of things fearlessly and have a respect for science, this has been achieved. . . . It means, I take it, first and foremost for us, that the world cannot wait for the English. It is not the first warning we have had. It has been raining warnings on us—never was a slacking, dull people so liberally served with warnings of what was in store for them. . . . In the men of means and leisure in this island there was neither enterprise enough, imagination enough, knowledge, nor skill enough, to lead to this matter. . . . Either we are a people essentially and incurably inferior, or there is something wrong in our training, something benumbing in our atmosphere and circumstances. That is the first and gravest intimation in M. Blériot's feat. The second is that, in spite of our fleet, this is no longer, from the military point of view, an inaccessible island."

However, despite the general malaise, in 1909 the country was becoming slowly more air-minded. The indefatigable Cody—still not naturalised and therefore deprived of various British 'firsts'—flew a mile in May, made a cross-country flight of nearly 6 miles in August, and flew 40 miles in September on his *No. III*. A. V. Roe, abandoning his unsuccessful type of 1908 biplane, and following the Goupy triplane of 1908, built two triplanes this year; on the first he could 'hop' for 900 feet by July, and by December he could fly half a mile on the second (Pl. XVI). Dunne was improving his stable V-wing biplane; the first 'full-size' British exhibition had been held at Olympia in March; the first aviation meetings in Britain were held at Doncaster and Blackpool (in October). The firm of Short Brothers had an order to build six standard type *A* Wrights, and the first flew in October piloted by its owner, the Hon. C. S. Rolls, who was to buy a second—French-built—Wright next year. Frank McClean was another who bought a Short-built Wright. Other British citizens were favouring—or about to favour—Farmans, Voisins and Blériots.

It has already been noted that J. T .C. Moore-Brabazon had (late in 1908) learnt to fly in France on a Voisin, and later brought a second one to England. On this Voisin which he called *The Bird of Passage*, Moore-Brabazon had made the first flights in Britain by a British-born Briton, during the last days of April and the first of May, at Shellbeach (Leysdown). He now went on to win the *Daily Mail* £1,000 prize for the first circular mile on an all-British-built machine (October 30th): this flight was made on the second machine which the Short brothers constructed to their modified Wright design at their new works at Shellbeach. This hybrid machine did not really quite merit the fame it won: it was constructed basically on the Wrights' ideas but with Cody–Curtiss between-wing ailerons. It was not a success; but the Shorts were later to produce admirable machines of their own design.

Although there were many experimenters in this country during the year, little of basic importance took place; the few new aircraft were mainly variations on French or Wright themes, and almost all of the practical flying in England was done on foreign-designed aircraft. But a word should be said about the Alsatian painter José Weiss, French educated and English domiciled, who for many years had been experimenting with stable model gliders based on bird forms; in 1909 he built, and G. England flew, an interesting full-size glider designed on the same principles. The Weiss glider gave rise directly to the first aeroplane of a newcomer to aviation, Frederick Handley Page, who in this year built his *Blue Bird* with Weiss-type swept-back wings; it was not successful, but was to lead thereafter to a famous line of British machines.

British tardiness in aviation had been more than matched elsewhere on the Continent of Europe. Germany at last saw her first native pilot, Hans Grade, briefly fly his triplane—derived from Ellehammer—at Magdeburg in January; then Grade built a *Demoiselle*-like machine which flew well at Borck in September. Austria saw her first flight in April at Vienna (the French Legagneux on a Voisin); and the Austrian Igo Etrich—who had made and flown an interesting glider in 1907—first flew his powered aeroplane *Taube* in November at Wiener-Neustadt. Legagneux on his Voisin made the first flight in Sweden at Stockholm in July. Blériot made the first flight in Rumania, at Bucharest, in October. In Russia, Van den Schkrouff flew a Voisin at Odessa in July, followed by Cattaneo, Legagneux and others at Moscow and St. Petersburg. De Caters, Blériot and Zipfel flew in Turkey: and Mamet in Portugal.

A word must be said here about the Comte Charles de Lambert, Wilbur Wright's first pupil, who was not only the first man to fly in the Netherlands (this year) but performed one of the memorable feats of early aviation when he was the first to fly over a city. On October 18th (still in this year) he took off from Port Aviation at Juvisy on the Wright A (Brancsy)—his own Wright had been damaged—and made straight for Paris where he flew directly over the top of the Eiffel Tower; then returned to Juvisy after a flight of about 50 minutes. This event caused almost as great a sensation as Blériot's channel crossing in July.

The flying of powered aeroplanes had become an established and popular activity in 1909, although passenger carrying—an everyday practice of the Wrights—was only slowly making headway on the Farmans, *Antoinettes* and Blériots. Aviation, having been transformed by the example of the Wrights in 1908, had now reached its first maturity and was settling into well-defined moulds. Having learnt the basic lessons of flight-control, the Europeans and Curtiss had rejected the Wrights' concept of inherent instability and had aimed at, and were attaining, excellent manoeuvrability with an increasing degree of inherent stability, thus making their machines comparatively safe and easy to fly. The biplane was for the present standardised as a machine with forward elevator, pusher propeller, aileron control, fixed horizontal tailplane(s) and one or more rear rudders, as in the new Farmans. But already, in this year 1909, there were embryo biplanes of great future importance which had already—and rightly—eschewed the Wrights' forward elevator idiom, and transferred this means of control in pitch to the rear: notable among such machines were the Breguet and Goupy biplanes. The monoplanes had, of course, adopted the age-old rear elevator by 1908.

The removal of the front elevator, and the idiom of the tractor airscrew and long fuselage, had been accomplished by Goupy and Breguet, but was not to exert its full influence until 1911. Produced from time to time, but never to prove a strong favourite, was the triplane, which—descended from Stringfellow—had emerged with the *Goupy I* of 1908 and the A. V. Roe of this year 1909. The monoplane form, however, was firmly and finally established in Europe as a type with tractor propeller, main wings with ailerons or warping, and a fuselage and tail-unit, as seen in the *Antoinettes* and Blériots.

The direct influence of the Wright brothers was now virtually at an end. Having created the practical aeroplane, having successfully first germinated and then rejuvenated—or rather recreated—European aviation, their designs from now onwards were not to influence the coming aeroplanes: rather were the Wrights to follow European trends and influences. Interestingly enough, the brothers were never to experiment with the monoplane.

Propellers and engines had also been slowly developing into practical forms, and by the end of 1909 the engines were divided mainly into the single bank in-lines (such as the Wrights), the Vees (such as the Antoinettes), the fan-types (Anzani, etc.), and the rotary (the Gnome). Horsepower ranged from 25 h.p. (the Anzani) to the 100 h.p. (the Antoinette); this last motor—with 16 cylinders—was powering the two-seater *Antoinettes* being built in the latter half of the year.

In view of the dangers of flying, it is interesting to note the casualties which were sustained in heavier-than-air flying up to the end of this important year 1909. Since the beginning of the 19th century there had been five men and one woman killed on parachutes; and Letur (1854) and de Groof (1874) killed in their curious and miscellaneous craft, one of which might be called a parachute-type glider, the other an ornithopter. But since the proper inauguration of fixed-wing flying with Lilienthal, there had only been seven fatalities, six of them pilots, as follows:

§ 1896 Lilienthal: glider.

§ 1899 Pilcher: glider.

§ 1905 Maloney: Montgomery glider.

§ 1908 Selfridge: passenger on a type A Wright.

§ 1909 Lefebvre: type *A* Wright.

§ 1909 Ferber: Voisin.

§ 1909 Fernandez: biplane of his own design.

By the end of 1909 the aviation records stood at: 47·85 m.p.h. for speed (Blériot, on a Blériot *XII*, at Reims); 145·59 miles for distance (Henry Farman on a Farman at the Camp de Châlons); and 1,486 feet for height (Latham on an *Antoinette* at the Camp de Châlons).

14. *Practical Powered Flying: 1910–1914*

1910

THIS year saw the wide popularisation of flying, with exploits, meetings, races, competitions and demonstrations staged to meet the new public demand to see aeroplanes, and even to fly in them. This great popular interest led to a rapid expansion of aviation, and to a proliferation of aeroplane types. But, despite a growing reliability of aircraft and engines, basic technical progress was slow. The increase in joy-riding directed attention to the aeroplane as a possible passenger vehicle, and its ability thus to carry 'cargo' also drew attention to potential uses in war. In both these respects it is interesting to note the contemporary state of the dirigible airship, particularly the Zeppelins—the first of which flew in 1900—which this year started their remarkable passenger flights between various German cities, a service in which—between 1910 and 1914—five of these craft carried over 35,000 passengers some 170,000 miles without a single fatality or injury. As for the airship's military possibilities, the world had recently been made unpleasantly aware of the German army's interest in Zeppelins, and all which that implied.

Despite the large number of newly designed aircraft, most of the popular and productive flying was performed on the well-tried Wrights, Blériots, *Antoinettes*, Henry Farmans and Curtiss machines which were being produced in quantity, and steadily improving in construction and performance.

Taking the monoplane first, it was on a Blériot that the first night flights were made by a Frenchman Emil Aubrun, when on March 10th he made two flights of about 20 km. each from—and back to—Villalugano, a suburb of Buenos Aires (Argentine). In Europe there was Louis Blériot producing mostly improved type *XI* machines, but also a new two-seat version. Blériot machines won particular successes when de Lesseps made the second Channel-crossing in May,[1] and the Franco-American J. B. Moisant made on August 17th the first Channel-crossing (Calais to Dover) with his mechanic as passenger, in a two-seater Blériot.[2] More spectacular was the Peruvian

[1] This second Channel-crossing on May 21st, by Jacques de Lesseps, won him the Ruinart prize, originally offered in 1906 for the first Channel-crossing. Through an oversight, Blériot failed to make formal entry for the Ruinart prize before he flew the Channel; the authorities—rather obtusely to our way of thinking today—refused to award him the prize on this technicality. So, contrary to the basic intention, the second crossing won it.

[2] It has often been said that a tabby cat, 'Miss Paris', was carried across the Channel, on this trip. Unfortunately this is not true, as the cat in question was only taken on board the machine from the point where it landed (near Dover) for the journey to London, which necessitated no less than five stops. It is not yet known when the first animal crossed the Channel by air. The first animal to be carried in an aeroplane at any time was probably the pig that Moore-Brabazon took

Georges Chavez' flight from Brig over the Simplon Pass on September 23rd, but it ended in tragedy when he crashed fatally on coming in to land at Domodossola.

It was also Moisant who built, this year, the first aeroplane entirely of metal: it was a monoplane, mostly of aluminium; but it could not fly.

Blériot's 1909 Channel crossing not only led to many orders for his own machines, but to many imitators. The year saw directly Blériot-derived monoplanes in the Humber, Lane, Nicholson, Lascelles *Ornis*, Neale, *Avis*, Deperdussin and Nieuport. This first Nieuport must be singled out because, although it was derived from the Blériot, it also broke new ground: it was a single-seater, with fully enclosed and streamlined fuselage, and could be fitted with a number of engines: with a 20-h.p. Darracq it could fly at about 45 m.p.h.

Also standing somewhat by itself, and derived from the Etrich-Wels glider of 1907, with a touch of Blériot added, was the Etrich *Taube* (pigeon) in Austria which, under the licensed maker's name of the Rumpler *Taube*, was later to develop into a famous First World War reconnaissance aircraft: it had large rearwards extending wing-tips—for warping—and gave the machine its bird-like appearance. It should be said here that the name *Taube* became applied to various types of monoplane similar to the original Etrich machine with its swept-back wing-tips.

The *Antoinette* inspired the *Star* and—combined with Blériot influence—the Hanriot, which became one of the more popular machines. The *Avis* grew out of the Blériot and the Santos-Dumont *Demoiselle*; then the latter, on its own, gave rise to an enlarged offspring in the first of the long line of Blackburn aircraft; and Blériot-influence also helped Handley Page in the production of his new monoplane. Two canard-type monoplane types, with more complex ancestry, were the *Valkyries A*, etc. (Fig. 67), and the ambitious Gnome-powered float-plane of Henri Fabre, which made the first seaplane flight in history (March 28th) at Martigues, near Marseilles (Pl. XVI) followed by flights of up to nearly two miles by September. Levavasseur continued to produce his excellent *Antoinettes* at Mourmelon, all now being fitted with his distinctive pivot-twist type of warping. The majority of monoplanes were now equipped with normal 'twist' warping. As a class, the monoplane also did particularly well competitively at many of the meetings, especially the second Reims meeting in July.

Amongst the biplanes, the most successful and popular was undoubtedly the Henry Farman; it now flew in two forms, the standard '1909' (*No. III*) type, and a new version with extended upper main planes which bore the only two large ailerons: these machines were to be seen at every aviation meeting, and they too inspired close imitators in such makes as the Sommer, Zodiac, Neale, Howard Wright (no relation to the Wright brothers), Euler, Bristol, and the new Short. It was the multiplication of Henry Farman-type biplanes that led to the common appellation 'box-kite', such as the Bristol

---

up in 1909 to show, as he said, that "pigs can fly". The carrying of inanimate mascots soon became popular with pilots, one of the best-known being the soldier puppet carried by Grahame-White which he tied to a strut of his *Henry Farman*.

'box-kite', a popular and persistent, but incomprehensible, misnomer, since it was the Farman machines and their progeny that deliberately abandoned the box-kite structure of wings and tail-units.[1] A famous Farman occasion was when two Henry Farmans fought out a chance duel for the *Daily Mail*'s £10,000 prize for the first flight, with or without stops, from London to Manchester in April; the Frenchman Louis Paulhan won against Claude Grahame-White, but the latter had the distinction of making a short night flight—the first in Europe—between two stops (March 28th). Grahame-White later won the Gordon Bennett speed contest at the Belmont Park meeting in the U.S.A. with an average speed of 61 m.p.h. The Maurice Farman biplane, with its characteristic swept-up skid-cum-outrigger support for the front elevator, was flying successfully, but was not yet widely used.

Both in Europe and the United States the Wrights were still popular; but their popularity, like their influence, was now slowly on the wane. This year the Wrights made important changes in their control system: first of all they equipped their modified standard type with a fixed tailplane aft of the double rudder; and then, soon after, converted it into a rear elevator working in concert with the front elevator. Then appeared the Wright *Model B*, which for the first time showed the Wrights abandoning the front elevator (Fig. 68), with a proper wheeled undercarriage. But the brothers also produced in this year their fine little racing biplane, the *Model R*, which appeared in two forms—both without a forward elevator—the *Baby Wright* (with a span of 26 feet 6 inches), and the *Baby Grand* (with a span of 21 feet) which flew at over 70 m.p.h. at the Belmont Park meeting in October.[2] The most noteworthy flight by the old Wright *A* type was the Hon C. S. Rolls' double crossing of the English Channel, without landing in France, on June 2nd. All the Wright types were still pusher biplanes with warping.

One of the most influential biplanes flying successfully in 1910 was the *Goupy III* of 1909, which was demonstrated at meetings both in France and England, and so reinforced its design 'message' to the more far-sighted constructors. Breguet had also cleaned up his biplane design, and now produced an excellent machine which became even more important than the Goupy in establishing the tractor biplane type in rivalry to the pusher (Fig. 69).

The familiar side-curtained Voisin biplanes soon became outmoded, and they disappeared from serious flying early in the year; the Voisin company, after trying a type with no front elevator, then commenced the construction of aileroned types, but did not achieve success during the year. They also showed an interesting military machine at the Salon in October, in which the familiar nacelle supported a large machine-gun: it was not successful.

It was during this year that Sir Hiram Maxim returned to aviation, driven

---

[1] The modern pilot's slang term 'kite' for any aeroplane—now fallen out of use—possibly derives from this period, although Cody called both his actual powered kite of 1907, and his first full-size powered aeroplane of 1908, a 'power kite': this term gained considerable temporary currency by the publication, in the *Aeronautical Journal* of January 1909, of Cody's December 1908 lecture to the Aeronautical Society, in which he used the term 'power kite' both in the text of his lecture and the captions to his photographs.

[2] This machine was powered by a unique Wright 50-h.p. V-8 engine (comprising two standard 'fours'): it was not used again.

Fig. 69. Breguet tractor
biplane: 1910

Fig. 70. Standard Curtiss
biplane: 1910

Fig. 71. Levavasseur's
Monobloc Antoinette: 1911

Fig. 72. First Avro biplane
(type D), with wing-
warping: 1911

Fig. 73. First practical
seaplane, by Curtiss: 1911

Fig. 74. Béchereau *Monocoque*
Deperdussin: 1912

155

on, it would seem, by his experience in the Sub-Committee of 1908–09, with a curious biplane showing Wright and Curtiss-derived forward and rear elevators, three pusher propellers, an arched dihedral on the wings, and Wright warping: it was greeted with much acclaim by the press—one technical journal devoting to it 8 pages and 21 illustrations—but it never left the ground. This was the last that was heard from Maxim in practical aviation.

Another unsuccessful, but prophetic, machine was the Coanda biplane (strictly speaking a sesquiplane) exhibited at the Paris Salon in October. It was of all-wood construction, with fully cantilevered wings—which, however, did not look very robust—and an *Antoinette*-like fuselage with obliquely cruciform tail-unit; it was equipped with a reaction propulsion unit consisting of a 50-h.p. Clerget engine driving a large ducted fan in front of it, the latter enclosed in a cowling which covered the nose of the machine and part of the engine: the fan was a simple air-fan driving back the air to form the propulsive 'jet'. Although inevitably earth-bound, this aircraft stands as the first full-size attempt at a jet-propelled aeroplane.

In the United States, the now standardised Curtiss biplane—closely similar to the 1909 type—was earning as high a reputation as the Wright machines (Fig. 70) and was establishing itself successfully in the popular and official mind with such flights as that from Albany to New York City on May 31st (by Curtiss himself), and that from New York to Philadelphia and back on June 13th (by C. K. Hamilton). Even more remarkable was the flight, on November 14th, by Eugene Ely when he safely took off from the American cruiser *Birmingham* in Hampton Roads: the warship had had an 83-foot platform built over the fore-deck for the take-off. Two months later, on January 18th 1911, Ely bettered this performance by flying 13 miles out to sea from San Francisco, and landing on the cruiser *Pennsylvania*; then taking off and returning to the city. Curtiss himself was the first man to carry out bombing tests, when he dropped dummy bombs on the shape of a battleship marked out by flagged buoys on Lake Keuka on June 30th.

Some other biplanes remain to be mentioned: Cody was making some excellent flights, and in December won the British Empire Michelin Cup with a flight at Farnborough of 185·5 miles in 4 hours 47 minutes; but he was always to keep somewhat doggedly apart from the main and advancing stream of the biplane, and—despite his long flights—did not contribute technically to aviation. The Dunne tailless *No. 5* was flying well at Eastchurch, and the type was to develop even more successfully later. Two biplanes were built and tested by a newcomer to aviation, Geoffrey de Havilland, who had, as he said, been attracted away from the motor car industry to aviation by Wilbur Wright's flying at Auvours in 1908: the first 'D.H.' was a curious machine with a long fuselage reaching out fore and aft of the aileroned wings, with elevator on the front and rudder at the back: this *No. 1* crashed on the first take-off. Then came his second machine, of the *Henry Farman* type, which flew well and was acquired—along with its creator—by the Government factory at Farnborough[1], which now by

---

[1] This aircraft was purchased for £400, and was designated the *F.E.1*.

ingenious subterfuge began unofficially to renew aviation research. Thus, in December, de Havilland became both the first Farnborough designer and test pilot under the new aeroplane 'regime', and started one of the most distinguished careers of aviation history.

To the many famous names of flying was also now added that of T.O.M. Sopwith, who took his pilot's licence in November at Brooklands.

First flights were made in Spain and Switzerland,[1] the latter also producing her own first aeroplane in the Dufaux biplane, which flew across Lake Geneva on August 28. Aviation also reached both South America and Asia: first flights were made in the Argentine (on a Voisin), and Brazil (on a *Henry Farman*), and the first flight in Asia took place at Saigon, in Indo-China, on a *Henry Farman*, followed soon after by a flight in China.

Public enthusiasm for flying was well reflected in the large number of aviation meetings held during the year, and the static exhibitions such as the Paris Salon and the show at Olympia in London. On the Continent there took place over twenty flying meetings, including those at Barcelona, Berlin, Bologna, Brussels, Budapest, Cannes, Copenhagen, Florence, Geneva, Le Havre, Lyons, Milan, Munich, Nice, Reims, Rouen and St Petersburg. In Britain there were meetings at Blackpool, Bournemouth, Burton, Cardiff, Dublin, Doncaster and Lanark. There was also a meeting at Heliopolis in Egypt. Three important meetings took place in the U.S.A.; at Los Angeles in January; the Harvard-Boston meet at Boston Harbour, in September; and the Belmont Park meet at Long Island, New York, in October. The Belmont Park meeting merits special attention, as its quality and venue attracted influential attention from American financial, military and social spheres: it was also an international occasion, with overseas teams from England and France, and helped—more than any other occasion—to popularise flying in the country, as well as stimulating technical development. It was just before the Belmont Park meeting that Grahame-White, already having flown at the Harvard-Boston meeting, made his spectacular landing on the roadway near the Capitol in Washington when he paid a flying visit from the Benning Race Track, on October 14th 1910.

Often passing unnoticed, but of great historical importance, was a patent granted in February to a then obscure German engineer named Hugo Junkers: it was for "an aeroplane consisting of one wing, which would house all components, engines, crew, passengers, fuel and framework". Although the 'flying wing' aircraft envisaged here by Junkers was never to be fully exploited, this patent marked the origin of the deep cantilever wing which was to be made and first used by Junkers in 1915, and then widely employed in aircraft construction.

With the spread of flying, the toll of accidents and deaths inevitably rose. The first mid-air collision took place on October 2nd at Milan, when an *Antoinette* collided with a *Henry Farman*, both pilots luckily surviving the resulting double crash.[2] Chavez, as already noted, was killed after flying

[1] The first flights were made by the German Captain Engelhardt on his Wright *A*, from the ice-covered lake at St. Moritz, on March 13th 1910.

[2] The *Antoinette*, which was piloted by Thomas, dived into the top of the *Farman* piloted by Captain B. Dickson, who was seriously injured. It is sometimes said that the first collision

over the Simplon Pass; Delagrange was killed flying a Blériot (January 4th); and the Hon. C. S. Rolls was killed at the Bournemouth meeting on July 12th, after fitting wheels, and an outrigger surrounding his tail-unit bearing an auxiliary elevator, to his standard French-built Wright *A*: this elevator was torsionally unstable, and, under stress when diving, gave way and wrecked the machine. This was England's first loss of a powered pilot. Twenty-seven other pilots and two passengers were also killed in 1910, making a total of thirty-two aviation fatalities for the year.

On August 27th, radio was used for the first time between the ground and an aeroplane in flight when McCurdy both sent and received messages from a Curtiss at Sheepshead Bay (New York State), using an H. M. Horton wireless set. Late in the year, the first practical airspeed indicator was invented by the French Captain A. Étevé, which was tested in January 1911: this was a plate, blown back against a spring by air pressure.

Another 'first' of the year was the first woman to become a qualified pilot: she was the French *soi-disant* Baroness de Laroche, who received her "brevet de pilote d'aéroplane" on March 8th.

Aerodromes were now becoming established in Europe, apart from the many open spaces that lent themselves informally to flying. By the end of the year the best-known in France was still the historic military ground at Issy-les-Moulineaux, a suburb of Paris, where flying inconveniently shared the space with the army; then there was the Camp de Châlons (Mourmelon, etc.), near Reims, where the *Antoinette* works had been set up; Pau, which was monopolised by the Wright and Blériot schools; Nice; Port Aviation (Juvisy), near Paris; and Croix d'Hins, near Bordeaux. In England the most popular aerodromes were at Brooklands and Hendon, with other flying fields at Wembley, Park Royal, Hounslow Heath, Wormwood Scrubs, Fambridge (Essex), Maplin Sands (Essex), Dagenham, Camber Sands (near Rye in Sussex), as well as the Royal Aero Club grounds at Shellbeach (Leysdown) on the Isle of Sheppey, and at Eastchurch.

The year 1910 stands out as the last well-defined period of early flying history, in which one can say that the aeroplane, having matured technically in 1909, achieved an international popularity. With that in mind, it must still be wondered at that the whole sphere of aviation—after so many years—was still moving in such a haphazard manner, with virtually no organised and systematic research, planning and development, and no adequate financial or scientific support. Perhaps the reason for this strange state of affairs, even as late as 1910, lay in the intransigent attitude of those ultra-conservative Army and Navy circles which, despite the prophecies of many enlightened men, conditioned the view of politicians and financiers.

Records for 1910 stood at 68·2 m.p.h. for speed (A. Leblanc of France on a 100-h.p. Blériot at New York); 10,476 feet for height (G. Legagneux of

---

occurred at Wiener-Neustadt (Austria) on September 8th 1910: the machines involved were two *Autobiplanes* (a development of the *Henry Farman*), each piloted by one of the brothers Warchalowski: but a reading of the contemporary account makes it clear that even at the time, it was not certain whether the machine which crashed, did so after getting into the disturbed air of the other, or whether they just touched: one pilot broke a leg.

France on a 50-h.p. Blériot at Pau); and 363.34 miles for distance in a closed circuit (Tabuteau of France on a 60-h.p. Maurice Farman at Buc).

1911

Basic progress was again slow in 1911. But this year saw the first long-distance flights, the growing popularity of joy-riding, an added apprehension and concern about aerial warfare, the first actual use of the aeroplane in war, and a number of innovations in practical flying.

Long-distance flying came into its own when Pierre Prier flew non-stop from London (Hendon) to Paris (Issy) on a Blériot (April 12th) 250 miles in under 4 hours; and continued in the form of races (with stops), such as those from Paris to Madrid (won by Vedrines on a Morane); Paris to Rome (won by Conneau—whose pseudonym was André Beaumont—on a Blériot) which should have continued to Turin; the first European Circuit Race of some 1,000 miles from Paris back to Paris, *via* Brussels, London and Amiens (also won by Conneau); the German national circuit race (won by Koenig); and the *Daily Mail* British national 1,000-mile circuit race (again won by Conneau). In America McCurdy flew a Curtiss 90 miles over water from Key West to Havana, in January; H. N. Atwood flew a Wright biplane from St. Louis to New York *via* Chicago in August (1,266 miles in 28 hours 53 minutes); and in September–November C. P. Rodgers made a remarkable and adventurous flight in a Wright *EX* biplane across the U.S.A. from Long Island to Long Beach (California), *via* Chicago and San Antonio (Texas), covering some 4,000 miles in 82 flying hours and in 82 stages: it took him 49 days—he was followed by a special train with spares and also his wife and mother—and as the machine crashed nineteen times, it was virtually rebuilt by the time it reached California. Other notable flights were Latham's crossing of the Golden Gate at San Francisco on his *Antoinette* on January 7th; and Lincoln Beachey's hazardous flight on a Curtiss over Niagara Falls and under the nearby suspension bridge on June 28th.

The aircraft in use during the year included ever-improving versions of tried machines, with new machines also coming from both famous and unknown makers. The manufacture of aircraft was also steadily expanding despite a lack of large-scale investment in the industry. The three basic types of aeroplane—pusher biplanes, tractor biplanes and tractor monoplanes— were becoming more specialised and efficient, and benefiting from a steadily increasing volume of aerodynamic research. Aero-engines, too, were undergoing a similar improvement in power, lightness and efficiency.

Metal was entering more frequently into aircraft structures, and it is fruitless to pursue too far the question of priorities in this controversial field of 'firsts', except to repeat here that the full-size Langley *Aerodrome* of 1903 had a main structure of steel, but did not fly, and various aeroplanes thereafter incorporated metal parts. Most aeroplanes were still made substantially of wood, generally spruce, and were braced with wire: coverings were of silk or linen. But another feature of aircraft construction, cantilevered wings,[1] comes into special prominence this year with Levavas-

[1] The first full-size aeroplanes with cantilevered wings—though primitive—were the Blériot

seur's revolutionary monoplane the *Latham* (also called the *Monobloc Antoinette*) shown at the Reims 'Concours Militaire' (Fig. 71). This remarkable three-seater had fully cantilevered wings, completely enclosed and streamlined fuselage, and 'spatted' undercarriage: two engines were tried at different times—the engine was also enclosed—the 50-h.p. and 100-h.p. Antoinette. Owing to hasty construction, lack of power and other faults, it only succeeded in flying a few yards, and was a failure: but it exerted a powerful influence on later designers. Streamlining, which had already been carried out in some measure by a number of builders, was taken a step further in the Tatin-Paulhan torpedo-shaped monoplane—it was called the *Aéro-Torpille*—with a pusher propeller at the tail-tip of its long fuselage, driven by a shaft from the 50-h.p. Gnome enclosed amidships. As tailpieces to these remarks on construction, it should be recorded here that the second retractable undercarriage[1] appeared this year on the otherwise unimportant German Wiencziers monoplane: it was a primitive affair consisting simply of fitting each 'leg' with a hinge so that the wheels came up rearwards to lie flush beside the fuselage. Secondly, the first oleo-undercarriage appeared, fitted by the Frenchman Esnault-Pelterie (to be followed next year by that fitted to the Farnborough *B.E.2*). Farnborough also fitted an airspeed indicator to an aeroplane; this was the first to utilise the differential pressure in a pitot-static tube.

In the monoplane sphere there were developments of the standard types, as well as new machines, by such makers as Bristol, Handley Page (the so-called *Yellow Peril*), Blackburn, Vickers, Blériot, Nieuport, Morane, Deperdussin, Esnault-Pelterie (who now had a conventional fuselage on his new machine) and Hanriot; but no basically new departures were made except in those aircraft already noted.

Amongst biplanes there was more real progress, especially in England, where two important machines set the style for many tractor biplanes to come. First the Avro biplane (Fig. 72) with a 35-h.p. Green engine, which was to lead to the famous line of type *504* trainers: the 1911 machine had an interesting feature in its wing-warping, which next year was to give way to ailerons. Second, the *B.E.1* biplane produced in the Government factory at Farnborough to the designs of F. M. Green and Geoffrey de Havilland: this famous type, with its sharply slimming fuselage, was to grow into a successful reconnaissance machine of the First World War (Pl. XVI). Amongst the other British biplanes it may be said that Shorts produced what has been claimed as the first twin-engined aeroplane in history in their *Triple-Twin* biplane with an independent engine at either end of the nacelle,[2]

'canard' and Blériot *Libellule*, both of 1907. Both Ader's machines—*Eole* of 1890 and *Avion III* of 1897—which have been described as fully cantilevered structures, in fact incorporated struts. But the practical application of cantilevered wings was to wait until the *J.1* monoplane of Hugo Junkers in 1915.

[1] See page 137 for the first.

[2] Strictly speaking, this claim is not valid, as both Maxim and Ader built twin-engine machines, but neither of these ever flew: Blériot's 1906 biplane also once had twin-engines: the Coanda biplane of this year 1911 had twin Gnome engines driving one airscrew. This Short machine may perhaps stand as the first to fly, having two independent engines and two or more propellers.

one driving a single airscrew, the other driving two: the *Tandem Twin* soon followed, with each motor driving a single airscrew.

On the Continent a number of successful biplanes were produced, such as the new Maurice Farman (the precursor of the so-called *Longhorn* with its skid-outrigger support for the front elevator), the three-seat military Breguet with various engines, and the *Albatros* in Germany. The Voisin firm curiously reverted to a 'canard'-type biplane, which was then fitted with additional floats by Fabre and became the world's second amphibian: it was flown by Colliex from Issy and landed on the Seine, and then made the return journey (in August): but it cannot be classed as a practical machine.

One of the outstanding achievements of the year was the introduction by Curtiss (in January) of the first practical seaplane of history: it was basically a standard Curtiss land-plane with a large single float beneath the centre section, and small auxiliary floats beneath the wings (Fig. 73): it first flew at San Diego (California) on January 26th. But there is little doubt that he was strongly influenced by a development of the seaplane which Fabre had tentatively introduced after his pioneering machine of 1910. On February 25th Curtiss took up the first passenger to fly in a seaplane. And also in that February of 1911, Curtiss fitted wheels to this machine, and thus created the first amphibian. Curtiss soon became the world's leading pioneer and promoter of seaplanes.

The role of the aeroplane in warfare came in for much attention during the year, probably as a result of Germany's Zeppelin programme. The concern of governments became reflected in various ways. Although some prophetic statements were voiced about the aggressive role of the aeroplane, it was not considered by most authorities to extend much further than observation and a little light bombing or incendiary dropping. In England, money was at last voted in some quantity for aviation—when wiser heads reversed the absurdities of the 1909 Report—and official interest in the aeroplane was also shown at the Hendon meeting in May which was attended by leading military and political figures, including Mr. Winston Churchill, who had long been convinced of aviation's important future. In France, the first 'Concours Militaire' took place at Reims (October–November) for the display of aircraft that could be utilised in war. In America, as noted before, Ely both landed and took off from a warship at sea in January: then, also in January, the first live bomb test was made by the U.S. army from a Wright biplane at San Francisco, shortly followed by the first bomb-sight, made by the United States Lieutenant Riley Scott (who next year won the Michelin prize for bomb-dropping). Rifles and machine-guns were being carried experimentally in various aircraft, and it is impossible to say which machine was the first to be designed or adapted for warlike use, although the two-seater Nieuport of this year, with its machine-gun, was one of the earliest. Some of the most interesting machines for which the makers had a military use in mind are noted later. Needless to say, the armies of Europe were paying their compliment to the aeroplane by equipping troops and transport with machine-guns for anti-aircraft use.

It was in October that the aeroplane first saw service in war, when the Italian Captain Piazza, in a Blériot, made a reconnaissance flight of about an hour from Tripoli to observe the Turkish positions near Azizia (October 22nd). After this, the aeroplane was used in various campaigns prior to the First World War, primarily for reconnaissance.

Somewhat trivial in themselves, but popular indications of what an aeroplane could perform, were the three 'mass' passenger flights in France in February and March when a special Blériot (a freak machine which was not repeated) lifted ten, a Breguet eleven, and an outsize Sommer thirteen: this impressive progression of numbers became less impressive when close examination of the photographs revealed a number of boys among the passengers! But these flights served to direct attention to the prospect of multi-place and transport aircraft.

Another small sign of things to come was seen in the first airmail flights—they were little more than stunts—which took place at Allahabad in February (by the Frenchman Pequet); between Hendon and Windsor in September by Gustav Hamel, C. H. Greswell and E. F. Driver; and at various places in the United States in September and October.

Gliding and soaring, which had been practised experimentally since the Wrights' flights of 1900–02, was put on a new and sounder basis by Orville Wright, who in October set up a world soaring record of 9¾ minutes at the Kill Devil Hills, a record that stood for a decade: the flights were made on a new biplane glider, based on the powered Wright *Model B*, with rear rudder and elevator, and the addition of a forward fixed vertical fin and an 8-lb. bag of sand placed 7 feet out in front on a pole.[1] One of the main and significant reasons for this short Wright gliding 'season'—the last ever to be held at the Kill Devil Hills—was to test an automatic stabiliser; but the tests were not carried out.

It was the Swiss inventor Ruchonnet, domiciled in France, who first introduced 'monocoque' construction in 1911; but it was not until next year that it was successfully applied in the Deperdussin (see pages 163–164).

Miscellaneous but interesting happenings in aviation during the year which deserve mention are the following: the Assistant Superintendent at Farnborough (Lieutenant T. Ridge) was killed on the factory's *S.E.1* (in August) in one of the first clear cases of spinning (the first recovery from an unintentional spin was F. P. Raynham's on September 11th)[2]: a sign of the times at Farnborough was the change of its title, in April, from the Balloon Factory to the Army Aircraft Factory; this followed the Balloon School of the Royal Engineers being retitled the Air Battalion: the first aeroplane-to-ground radio transmissions in England were made by Dorrington Bangay from a Flanders monoplane at Brooklands: the French pilot R. Grandseigne, on a Caudron, made a successful night flight over Paris in February; the Dutchman Anthony Fokker, at the age of eighteen, built his first aeroplane which made tentative flights: the first air-sea rescue took place when Hugh Robinson in a Curtiss seaplane landed on Lake Michigan in August and rescued another pilot who had crashed in the lake: the United

[1] Photographs of this aircraft are sometimes published by mistake for the 1900–02 gliders: the difference is easily detected in the lack of a forward elevator and the presence of a rear elevator in this 1911 glider.

[2] For early spins, see *The Aeroplane*, January 30th 1953, and *Aeronautics*, July 1960.

States saw as her first qualified woman pilot the dramatic critic Harriet Quimby (also the first woman to fly the English Channel, in 1912), although Miss Blanche Scott and a Dr. Bessica Raiche had made some informal flights before her. Montgomery was killed this year when testing one of his gliders.

World records for 1911 stood at 82·73 m.p.h. for speed (E. Nieuport of France on a Nieuport monoplane at Châlons); 449·2 miles for distance over a closed circuit (A. Gobé of France on a Nieuport monoplane at Pau); and 12,828 feet for height (R. Garros of France on a Blériot *XI* at St. Malo).

1912

This year was marked by a large-scale, and official, concern with the aeroplane's role in warfare; and by several important technical advances, including the introduction of monocoque construction, the first flying-boat, the first flight at over 100 m.p.h., and the extended use of metal in aircraft structures.

The year also saw the growing ascendancy of the biplane—especially the tractor biplane—and the beginnings of the monoplane eclipse. This eclipse, despite some notable exceptions, was due partly to the obvious advantages in lift, strength, compactness and lightness possessed by the biplane as opposed to the weakness and inefficiency of large braced monoplane surfaces at a time when thin wing sections were regarded as obligatory; although Junkers, Levavasseur and others had proposed thicker, and internally strong enough, monoplane wings. Aerodynamics and structure research was still proceeding only slowly, and without any proper co-ordination.

The standard type of tractor biplane was even more firmly established by the improved, aileron-equipped, *Avro*, and the Farnborough *B.E.2* of this year; the *B.E.1* of last year was also still flying productively. But it was the arrival of the Farnborough *B.S.1* (Pl. XVI) which was of paramount importance. Designed chiefly by Geoffrey de Havilland, it was the first single-seat scout of history, and ancestor of every scout and fighter thereafter.[1] One of its more immediate progeny was the excellent *S.E.5* of the First World War. The *B.S.1* was a single-bay biplane of 27·5 feet span, powered by a 100-h.p. Gnome: this remarkable and handsome little aeroplane, with excellent streamlining, had a speed of 92 m.p.h. In April, the Army Aircraft Factory became the Royal Aircraft Factory.

The most important structural innovation was the monocoque[2] fuselage, in which the skin (or shell) carried all or most of the loads, as opposed to a framework fuselage left open, or covered in with wood or textile material.

[1] This distinction is often, but wrongly, claimed for another excellent machine, the Sopwith *Tabloid*, which did not make its first real trial flight until November 1913. It is highly probable, if not inevitable, that it was the *B.S.1* which directly inspired the *Tabloid*. The comparative neglect of the *B.S.1*, and the fame of the *Tabloid* at its expense, poses an important problem of aviation history: the answer, as we see it today, lies chiefly in the deplorable attitude adopted by certain early writers—and others—who sought to denigrate the Farnborough products, coupled with the lack of channels available to Farnborough to "blow its own trumpet".

[2] Monocoque: from the Greek *monos* (single) and the French *coque* (egg-shell). Considerable confusion has arisen in historical studies over the meaning of 'monocoque' and 'stressed-skin' construction: these words are discussed in the Appendix on page 171.

This first wood monocoque structure was designed by the Swiss Ruchonnet and applied by Béchereau in the Deperdussin monoplane called the *Monocoque Deperdussin* (Fig. 74), an admirable streamlined machine, powered by a partially enclosed 140-h.p. Gnome, on which Jules Védrines won the Gordon Bennett Cup and the world's speed record of 108·18 m.p.h. at Chicago on September 9th. This invention of monocoque construction stands as one of the milestones in aviation, but although certain other makers soon followed—even with experiments in metal monocoque—the practice did not become widespread; and even by the end of the First World War only a handful of Allied and German machines were built with monocoque fuselages, the latter being the most original and advanced. Another structural experiment was the adoption, by H. Reissner, of corrugated aluminium wings (without fabric covering) in his canard-type monoplane, thus anticipating the practice of Junkers. Still more ambitious were the first tentative flights by an all-metal aeroplane in history, the French *Tubavion* monoplane of Ponche and Primard; but a fatal accident put an end to its tests.

The seaplane came properly into its own this year, and it was Curtiss who figured as its most important pioneer and exponent. Having established the float-plane last year, he had turned to the flying-boat, and (still in 1911) had built an unsuccessful machine, virtually a modification of the float-plane, with an enlarged float to house the pilot. Now (1912) he built the first successful flying-boat, a further modification of his 1911 float-plane. This machine led to a curious chain of events, as it prompted the French designer Denhaut to build his *Donnet-Lévêque* pusher flying-boat with a nacelle-type hull (which was stepped), with the tail-unit on booms, and with no front elevator: he thus set the basic style for future flying-boats and was soon paid the compliment of partial imitation by Curtiss himself who—still in this year—produced a long hull type with no front elevator, a flying-boat which was the first of a long line of successful Curtiss boats. On Nov 12th, at the Washington Navy Yard, the U.S. Navy's Curtiss float-seaplane *A-1* was the first aeroplane to be successfully launched from a powered catapult. The catapult, driven by compressed air and mounted on an anchored barge, was invented by Captain W. I. Chambers, and the pilot was Lieut. T. G. Ellyson. An earlier attempt to devise a method of launching an aeroplane from the limited space available on a ship was tested at Hammondsport in September 1911, when Ellyson successfully took off in a Curtiss float-plane suspended from a trolley running on an inclined wire cable rigged from high up on the beach down to the shore.

The first seaplane meeting was held at Monaco in March, at which seven machines competed: all were biplanes, and all at this time were, of course, float-planes, including one or two amphibians. The first prize was won by Fischer who flew a *Henry Farman*.

Both old and new biplanes and monoplanes were appearing in 'cleaned up' and sophisticated forms, and the ideals of streamlining were slowly gaining acceptance, though impeded by the still ubiquitous struts and wiring on most machines. Amongst the many new machines of the year was the Bristol monoplane (designed by Coanda); and the world's first enclosed cabin aeroplanes, the Avro cabin monoplane and the Avro cabin biplane[1]: the latter established another small title to fame when Lieut. Parke successfully pulled it out of a spin, the second earliest example of such survival (Fig. 75). Also, a robust machine developed out of the already familiar Maurice Farman types, powered by a 70-h.p. Renault engine, and having the characteristic swept-up skids supporting the front elevator—hence *Longhorn* (Fig. 76): this type became famous among World War I pilots, many of whom were trained on them.

Military aviation now became the serious concern of the leading European nations. In Britain the Royal Flying Corps was founded in April, with both a Military and Naval wing, and a Central Flying School was later established at Upavon. The first Military Aeroplane Competition was held at Larkhill, Salisbury Plain (in August), in which some thirty British and French machines took part. Marking was for a variety of characteristics and abilities—including landing in a ploughed field—and S. F. Cody won with his new biplane, powered by a 120-h.p. Austro-Daimler engine. But this success was not truly deserved, as the Farnborough *B.E.2* (Pl. XVI) piloted by de Havilland, won the highest marks; but it was obliged to fly 'hors concours', as it was a Government aircraft and the Farnborough Superintendent (Mervyn O'Gorman) was one of the judges. In September a Military and Naval review of aircraft took place at Hendon, and a similar heightened interest in the aeroplane's role in warfare—without much advanced thinking on the subject—was witnessed on the Continent and in the United States. Despite the traditional army view that the main use of aircraft was observation, limited tests were continued with airborne machine-guns and light bombs, as well as the more enthusiastically encouraged experiments with radio, including the first successful artillery spotting carried out by the *B.E.1* over Salisbury Plain. Naval flying added ship-board aircraft to its armoury when, after a take-off on January 10th 1912 (not in December 1911) by Lieutenant C. R. Samson in a Short biplane[2] from a trackway on the forecastle of H.M.S. *Africa* (at anchor). Take-offs were also made in this year 1912 from H.M.S. *Hibernia* and H.M.S. *London* when under way, flights which led the way to many similar achievements, and later to the aircraft carrier proper.

On the Continent, the year saw the same rising official concern with aviation. Germany, impressed and bemused for some years by her Zeppelins and other airships, suddenly awoke to the importance of the aeroplane, and a public campaign led the way to governmental action and the setting up of a military flying school. France, already alarmed by the German airships, and aware of the potential usefulness of the aeroplane, increased her production of aircraft, experimented with new bombing gear, and sent aircraft to take part in the great military manoeuvres of September, at Poitou.

A curious situation concerning military monoplanes should be mentioned here. Owing to two crashes in England, and a report by Blériot in France on the structural weakness of certain monoplanes, a temporary ban on all

[1] Later this year, Etrich's high-wing cabin monoplane—the 'Taube-Limousine'—flew successfully in Austria.

[2] The modified 1910–11 Short *S.38*. See *Sheerness Guardian*, January 13th 1912.

monoplanes was foolishly imposed by the army authorities in both countries, which undoubtedly aided the eclipse of the monoplane and retarded research into the aerodynamic and structural problems which would have promoted the type.[1]

Two more important technical 'firsts' during the year were the first parachute drop from an aeroplane, using a static line, made (March 1st) by Captain Albert Berry at St. Louis in the U.S.A.; and the first automatic pilot built by Lawrence Sperry and successfully demonstrated on a Curtiss float-plane at Hammondsport on Lake Keuka, in New York State.

Among the exploits of the year should be mentioned the first cross-Channel flight by a woman, the American Harriet Quimby in a Blériot from Deal to Cape Gris-Nez (in April); and Frank McClean's flight through Tower Bridge on his Short float-plane, and his landing on the Thames at Westminster (in August), a double feat for which he was rightly reprimanded by the police and—just as rightly—acclaimed by the public.

Finally must be recorded the tragic death from typhoid fever of Wilbur Wright on May 20th: "This morning at 3.15", wrote Bishop Wright, "Wilbur passed away, aged 45 years, 1 month and 14 days. A short life, full of consequences. An unfailing intellect, imperturbable temper, great self-reliance and as great modesty; seeing the right clearly, pursuing it steadily, he lived and died", a fitting epitaph for the greatest man in aviation.

Records of 1912 stood at: 108·18 m.p.h. for speed (by J. Védrines of France on a *Deperdussin*[2] at Chicago, after first passing the 100 m.p.h. mark in February at Pau); 628·15 miles for distance over a closed circuit (A. Fourny of France on a Maurice Farman at Étampes); and 18,405 feet for height (by R. Garros of France on a Morane-Saulnier at Tunis).

1913

French historians refer to 1913 as "La Glorieuse Année" and indeed it was a memorable year in various departments of aviation. Most spectacular perhaps were the first intentional aerobatics—including loops and upside-down flying—by the Frenchman Adolphe Pégoud on his Blériot in September, which formed an unconscious prelude to the necessary manoeuvres of wartime flying.[3] Although Pégoud was the first true exponent of these new 'stunts', he was not the first to loop the loop, this distinction belonging to the Russian Nesterov who performed the feat in a Nieuport monoplane on August 20th, at Kiev. Looping now became a popular feat and soon passed into the normal repertoire of flying. Pégoud also made the first parachute jump from an aeroplane in Europe, on August 19th.

A number of impresive long-distance flights were also made, including those by Védrines on a Blériot (November–December) from Nancy to Cairo via Prague, Vienna, Belgrade, Sofia, Constantinople, and Tripoli, with a number

[1] It is said that Mr. Churchill, then First Lord of the Admiralty, wisely refused to allow the ban to apply to the Naval wing; but I have been unable to confirm this.

[2] His mascot was a reproduction of Leonardo da Vinci's *Mona Lisa* on the fuselage.

[3] At Brooklands, at the end of September, Pégoud performed a vertical S (a bunt followed by a half loop), an inverted loop, a bunt-and-roll-out, and a tail-slide. He had made his first loop at Buc on September 21st.

of stops, a distance of some 2,500 miles; by Bonnier and Barnier on a Nieuport (November–December) from Paris to Cairo over a similar course, but more to the east and via Bucharest; and by Garros on a Morane-Saulnier (September) in the first non-stop flight across the Mediterranean, from St. Raphael in the South of France to Bizerta in Tunisia. Such performances, especially the long-stage flights, said much of the growing reliability of engines and airframes.

One of the lasting achievements of the year was the first true and proper inherently stable aeroplane—i.e. a practical manoeuvrable and 'all-round' stable machine—at Farnborough. It was the *B.E.2*, now modified according to the research work of E. T. Busk who had come to the factory in 1912 and was tragically killed in a crash in 1914: designated the *B.E.2c*, it became one of the most successful and early reconnaissance machines, of which nearly 2,000 were subsequently built. Another pioneer product of the Farnborough factory was the prototype *F.E.2a* pusher biplane fighter, which can perhaps be claimed as the first aeroplane designed specifically to fight in the air, that is to say to attack other aircraft: it was based on the Maurice Farman tradition and subsequent Farnborough variations, but the design was not to be produced— in the shape of the Vickers *Gunbus* and Farnborough *F.E.2b*—until 1915–16. Farnborough was now rapidly becoming the foremost of the world's aeronautical research establishments; it was developing both aircraft and aero-engines, methods of inspection and testing, and aircraft accessories, as well as conducting basic aerodynamic research.

Two outstanding fast machines were built and flown during the year. The Sopwith *Tabloid* (Fig. 77)—designed by Harry Hawker and F. Sigrist—was a small two-seat biplane with a single wing-bay, inspired by the Farnborough *B.S.1*; it was powered by an 80-h.p. Gnome, had a top speed of 92 m.p.h., and could climb to 15,000 feet in 10 minutes. The *Tabloid* was spectacularly flown and publicised by Harry Hawker, and showed officialdom and public alike what extraordinary manoeuvrability a well-designed small biplane could achieve; it undoubtedly helped, with the *S.E.2* (*B.S.2*) and its successors, to revolutionise the concept and design of biplanes in general, and scouts and fighters in particular: it also played a large part in finally killing the monoplane, as no monoplane of the period—or of the foreseeable future—could hope to match the *Tabloid*'s powers of climb and manoeuvrability.

The second of the fast aeroplanes worthy of special mention was the improved monocoque *Deperdussin*, with a completely enclosed 160-h.p. Gnome (Pl. XVI) on which Prévost broke the world's speed record three times during the year at Reims, the final figure being 126·67 m.p.h. This *Deperdussin* is one of the 'classic' forward-looking aircraft of history, and had it not been for the virtual disappearance of the monoplane within a year or two, might well have led to a rapid development of monoplane fighters. Curiously enough, both the *Tabloid* and the *Deperdussin* employed wing-warping, although the *Tabloid* changed to ailerons on the later production machines.

A number of other important aircraft were produced during this year. A. V. Roe built his first Avro type *504* biplane, with staggered wings, developed from his 1911–12 biplanes—with a large debt to Goupy—which

Fig. 75. First cabin
biplane, an Avro: 1912

Fig. 76. Maurice Farman
Longhorn; first built in 1912

Fig. 77. Sopwith *Tabloid*
designed by Hawker and
Sigrist: 1913

Fig. 78. Avro type 504 biplane;
first built in 1913

Fig. 79. Sikorsky four-
engine *Bolshoi*: 1913

became one of the most famous and widely used aeroplanes in history, especially as a 2-seater trainer (Fig. 78). It was first powered by an 80-h.p. Gnome and had a speed range of 35–82 m.p.h.: in slightly modified forms and with a number of engines, it continued in service, after many thousands had been built, until the early 1930's. The Dunne *No. 8* swept-wing tail-less biplane, built in 1912, and now powered by an 80-h.p. Gnome, made a notable flight in August from Eastchurch to Paris: the aerodynamic research embodied in this remarkable aircraft was to inspire many followers: one of the machines directly inspired by Dunne was Hill's *Pterodactyl* of 1926. Russia now entered aeronautical history with the precursor of all large multi-engined aircraft, the four-engined *Bolshoi* (Russian for 'The Great'), a cabin biplane designed by Igor Sikorsky who had earlier been concerned with helicopter experiments which he had temporarily abandoned for conventional type aircraft: he was afterwards to leave Russia and become the leading helicopter pioneer in the U.S.A. The huge *Bolshoi* (the span was 28·2 m., say 92½ ft.) when its nature and performance became understood, struck the world of aviation as a highly remarkable aerial phenomenon, without rival or precedent. Powered by four 100 h.p. Argus engines—at first arranged in two tandem tractor-pusher groups, then four separate tractors—made its first flight on May 13th 1913 at St. Petersburg, piloted by Sikorsky himself. Among its achievements was a flight (with 8 on board) of 1 hour 54 min. The *Bolshoi* included a large cabin, fully glazed, in which there were four armchairs, a sofa and a table, with the pilot and co-pilot's seat up front fitted with dual control (Fig. 79). The subsequent history of this outstanding aircraft is noted in the next section.

The second seaplane meeting at Monaco drew a selection of float monoplanes, float biplanes, and biplane flying-boats, all of which were established as successful types: the main event was the first race for the new Schneider Trophy in April, which was won by Prévost on a *Deperdussin* float-monoplane at an average speed of 45·75 m.p.h.

Night flying, after its tentative beginnings in 1910, was carried a stage further at Hendon when a *Henry Farman* biplane was fitted with two rows of electric lamps (on the leading edges of upper and lower wings), and was taken off, flown, and landed successfully in a series of tests.

On August 7th, when testing his new biplane carrying W. H. B. Evans the cricketer as a passenger, S. F. Cody and Evans were killed when the machine broke up in the air and crashed over Laffan's Plain, Aldershot. Overrated by some, underrated by others, Cody had played a human, rather than a technical, role in aviation history: the Farnborough authorities, where he had done so much of his work, wrote his epitaph in the words: "History accords him the prime virtues of courage and perseverance." Perhaps Cody's most valuable contribution, when viewed in the historical perspective of today, was in creating much valuable air-mindedness in Britain at a time when both the Government and the public were lamentably apathetic about flying in general, when the land of Cayley, Wenham and Pilcher was all but aeronautically asleep.

Records for 1913 stood at: 126·67 m.p.h. for speed (M. Prévost of France on a *Deperdussin* at Reims); 634·54 miles for distance over a closed circuit (A.

Seguin of France on a *Henry Farman* at Buc); and 20,079 feet for height (G. Legagneux of France on a Nieuport at St. Raphael).

1914

The traditional lull before the storm found only a few important events in aviation to record, with the major powers actively preparing for war, but only secondary attention being paid to military aeroplanes. Sikorsky in Russia started productive flying with the second of his great four-engined cabin machines: this was the *Ilia Mouriametz*, a development of the *Bolshoi* which was powered by four 100 h.p. Mercedes engines and was fitted successfully at different times with skis, wheels and floats. It first flew in January 1914; on February 11th it flew well with 16 on board; and in June made a record flight—partly at night—from St. Petersburg to Kiev and back, with several stops, a distance of some 2,560 km. (say 1,590 miles).[1] Some 75 machines of this type were produced in Russia during the War. But perhaps the most important point about these Sikorsky giants was that they directly inspired Count von Zeppelin to play a leading role in the design and limited production of large aeroplanes. An American, P. E. Fansler, opened the first scheduled airline in history in Florida, between St Petersburg and Tampa (22 miles) employing A. Jannus to pilot a Benoist flying-boat, and carrying both passengers and freight; this airline continued successfully for some weeks, but Fansler's enterprising example was not followed up at the time. Also in America, Curtiss was testing successfully his twin-engined flying-boat *America* for a projected trans-Atlantic flight to be undertaken by the Englishman Lieutenant J. C. Porte; but the war put a stop to it. In France, Lawrence Sperry of the U.S.A. demonstrated his new gyroscopic stabiliser for aeroplanes (installed in a Curtiss flying-boat) and with it won the Concours de la Sécurité en Aéroplane at Buc.[2] Sperry later invented the turn and bank indicator, and did more than any other inventor to bring about safety in flying, and automatic piloting of aircraft. A converted Sopwith *Tabloid* on floats, piloted by C. H. Pixton, won for Britain the second Schneider Trophy speed contest at an average speed of 86·78 m.p.h., and raised the speed record for seaplanes to 92 m.p.h.

The speed and other records noted on previous pages give a somewhat misleading idea of the performances of work-a-day production aircraft carrying a productive load. The position in mid-1914, regarding aircraft performance in Britain, France, Germany and the United States, was that one or two machines such as the *Tabloid* and *Deperdussin* had a maximum speed of about 90 m.p.h., but most of the available aeroplanes had a maximum speed of some 65–75 m.p.h. Individual aircraft, engines and performances will be noted in the next section.

The aeroplane was now to enter its first major war, in which it would benefit greatly from the intensive research and experience expended by the

[1] Culinary history here combined with aeronautical, as there was served aboard the *Ilia Mouriametz* the first full meal to be eaten in the air.

[2] The judges decided not to award the Grand Prix to any of tne competitors, but Sperry was given the next highest award and so won the 'Concours'.

combatant nations, all of which would later benefit the whole field of flying. Also for the first time the name of the aeroplane was to be unjustly darkened by its association with warfare.

APPENDIX

Monocoque and Stressed-Skin Construction

Owing to the misunderstandings which have in the past surrounded the terms "monocoque" and "stressed-skin", I asked one of my technical advisers to clarify the meaning of these terms. Dr. P. B. Walker, the former Head of Structures Department at the Royal Aircraft Establishment (Farnborough), feels that this is a question of semantics, and has to be looked at in realistic terms of what was actually practised, rather than of theoretical definitions.

The term "monocoque" represents an idealised concept of a hollow shell-like structure: in fact, like the egg-shell itself (i.e. 'coque', egg-shell). The first use of such a "pure" monocoque structure—and of the word "monocoque"—was that employed in the wooden fuselage of the *Monocoque Deperdussin* monoplane of 1912; it was then used in a few other aircraft soon after: in this construction, which was not applied to the wings, the shell itself—with no internal bracing—bore all the structural loads in addition to the local air pressure. It was not long before such monocoque fuselages were forced, for weight considerations, to become too thin to bear the main loads, and were therefore reinforced with a few stiffening members: but the construction was basically "monocoque", as the loads were still borne by what was essentially a shell structure, i.e. without internal bracing or multiple bulkheads to take the primary loads. The use of the term "semi-monocoque" for such stiffened structures is, Dr. Walker feels, both unnecessary and confusing, since "pure" monocoque construction is so rare in history as to make the use of two terms unjustifiable.

In 1919 Dr. Adolph Rohrbach introduced the concept of "stressed-skin", and he was probably the first to use this actual term, in 1924. It is here that, I believe, confusion started to creep in, as the term mistakenly came to be used, where fuselages were concerned, for stiffened monocoque construction; whereas it was chiefly the wings that were in question. For Rohrbach's great contribution was to combine a smooth—in contrast, for example, to the Junkers corrugated—metal skin for the wings and tail-surfaces, which was laid over metal spars, the skin bearing a share of the load. As wings at that time, and for long after, were customarily built up of spars and ribs (wood or metal), and the surfaces formed of fabric stretched over the spars and ribs, this newly-suggested practice of Rohrbach's of making the spars and ribs share some of the primary load with the actual surface of the wings, appeared as revolutionary; but it came to influence the whole course of aircraft construction. Thus the concept of so-called "stressed-skin" construction is properly confined to an aeroplane's wings and tail-surfaces, and not to its fuselage; whilst 'monocoque' was appropriate for the fuselage. Today there are scarcely any other joint practices than these, so the terms themselves have died out.

15. *The First World War: 1914–1918*

WAR was declared in July and August, and the opening of hostilities found the Allies with a combined total of some 208 aircraft on the Western Front (48 British,[1] 24 Belgian and 136 French are the approximate figures), with the Germans possessing about 180 machines. In addition a considerable number of training and other miscellaneous aircraft remained at home bases on both sides.

The general pattern of aircraft development in the war followed naturally upon the duties expected of the machines. The aeroplane started the war as an aerial intelligence agent or scout, for visual and then photographic reconnaissance—it was soon fitted with radio—and then added spotting for the artillery as another of its tasks. This was taken at first to demand a slow and stable two-seater, although one or two types of fast single-seat scout were available from the start. As anti-aircraft fire improved, speed and climb became growingly important, qualities which became even more vital when the machines had to defend themselves from attack by other aircraft. This in turn led to specially fast and highly manoeuvrable aircraft to defend the reconnaissance machines, the vulnerable observation balloons, and later the bombers; and, of course, to shoot down those same types—along with airships—when flown by the enemy, as well as the enemy fighters. And so, out of the fast single-seat scout there was born the single-seat fighting scout, or simply the 'fighter'. When bombing was introduced, it was at first carried out by the slow reconnaissance machines and later by the specialised medium and long-range bombers. But in between these categories, and superseding the old two-seat reconnaissance type, arose the general purpose machine, which grew out of the two-seat reconnaissance type—often known as a fighter-reconnaissance aircraft—which could spot, spy, fight, 'strafe' targets on the ground and, in a small way, bomb. In addition, certain more specialised types were produced for special duties (see below).

Typical of the early operational two-seat reconnaissance machines was the British *B.E.2C* (Fig. 80), with an R.A.F. (Royal Aircraft Factory) 8-cylinder, 90-h.p. V-type engine: it had staggered wings—giving a good view up and down—a span of 37 feet, and a maximum speed of 75 m.p.h.,[2] it could climb to 10,000 feet in 45 minutes, and stay up for about 3¼ hours. Armament

---

[1] The British types available at the outbreak of war included the *B.E.2*, *2A*, *2B*, Avro *504*, Sopwith *Tabloid* scout, and Bristol scout. Trainers included various Farmans, as well as Blériot monoplanes.

[2] From now onwards, aircraft speeds will be given to the nearest 5 m.p.h., or in approximate ranges, where machines have a top speed below about 250 m.p.h. Where speeds above that figure enter history, the figure will be given to the nearest 10 m.p.h. or even more approximately, according to circumstances. Aircraft speeds are governed by so many factors, and are listed differently by so many apparently reliable sources, that published figures can

was at first a revolver or rifle, and later, a sideways-firing machine-gun: as one R.F.C. officer put it, "the early war pilot went into battle armed more as a sportsman than as a soldier". Other British reconnaissance types were the *B.E.2*, *2*A and *2*B, and the famous Avro *504*. Analogous types were the French Henry and Maurice Farmans, and the German *Albatros*, L.V.G., and Rumpler *Taube*, the last being a monoplane with swept-back birdlike wings.

The early fast single-seat scouts were typified by the Sopwith *Tabloid* and the Bristol *Scout* of 1913 and 1914. The latter was powered with various rotary engines, including the 80-h.p. Gnome and the 100-h.p. Mono-soupape, with a speed range of 40–105 m.p.h. French equivalents were the Nieuport and Morane scouts, the latter a monoplane; and the German Fokker monoplane (*Eindecker*). This type of aircraft was revolutionised as soon as a fixed forward-firing gun was devised, thus converting it into a piece of flying artillery aimed at the enemy, a development which is described below.

It was soon realised that the reconnaissance aeroplanes, both fast and slow, must be able to defend themselves from, and destroy, the enemy's similar machines; but as the propeller was revolving at the front of the fuselage, this feat was almost impossible for the tractor machines, except for 'pot-shots' from the side with small-arms. The available single-seat scouts were admirable in performance but helpless without a forward-firing gun. So the two-seat pusher biplane was revived, and in 1914 and early 1915, the two-seat Vickers *F.B.5 Gunbus* (Fig. 81) went into action, the observer seated right in the front of the nacelle and wielding a machine-gun on a pedestal. Although slow (70–80 m.p.h.) and somewhat cumbersome, they dealt severely with the German reconnaissance machines, such as the Rumpler and other *Taube* types, when they could reach them. Similar types were the *D.H.1* and *2*, and later the *F.E.2*B and *6*: the *D.H.2* and the *F.E.8* were single-seaters.

Then, on April 1st 1915, the famous French ace Roland Garros, in J. M. Bruce's words, "opened the era of true fighter aircraft", when he first shot down a German *Albatross* by firing a machine gun through the propeller disc of his *Morane-Saulnier L* (Fig. 82) which was fitted with metal deflector plates. Unfortunately, after five such victories in less than three weeks, Garros was himself shot down by ground fire and captured, along with his machine, which he tried to destroy, but failed: the secret was now out. A team of three German designers examined this device, then rapidly improved on it: they produced a gun properly synchronised to fire past the blades when they were not in line with the muzzle.[1] Fokker was commissioned to produce this interrupter gear, and he seems later to have taken credit for its invention. By July 1915, some Fokker (*Eindecker*) *E.1* scouts (Fig. 83) were operational with

---

seldom be considered accurate except in highly specialised cases where complete data is available, and provided for a given aircraft operating under a given set of conditions.

[1] Ideas for firing a synchronised machine-gun between the propeller blades had been developed by Schneider in Germany (1913–14), and by Saulnier and Peyret in France (1913–14): the two latter proceeded to an advanced test stage, but tests were abandoned because of hang-fire troubles with the ammunition. Saulnier then simply fitted metal deflector plates to the propeller; the first exponent of this technique was Garros, as narrated above.

the new gun, and the first Allied machine was shot down with it on August 1st. Thus developed the so-called "Fokker scourge", which continued until Allied aircraft could be similarly equipped. The Fokkers were by no means as efficient as they should have been, but the lack of effective opposition lent them fame. The first Allied machine to rival the Fokker was the French Nieuport with a machine-gun fixed on the top wing; it soon incorporated a synchronised gun, and with this it went into action in January of 1916. By April 1916, when the British *F.E.2*B became fully effective, the Fokker ascendency was neutralised, and was soon in eclipse. From then onwards, there was to be a constantly alternating superiority of fighters, as new designs were produced in quick succession by the Allies and by Germany.

The British single-seat fighting-scout, developed from the Farnborough *B.S.1*, the Sopwith *Tabloid*, and another remarkable Farnborough prototype the *S.E.4* (of 1914), produced a line of formidable and famous aircraft. The *Tabloid* grew into the Sopwith *Pup* (1916), the Sopwith triplane (1916) and the Sopwith *Camel* (1917), all with rotary engines. The *Pup* (Pl. XVII), with a 100-h.p. Monosoupape motor, had a top speed of 110 m.p.h., a ceiling of 18,500 feet, and an endurance of 1¾ hours: the *Camel*, with a 130-h.p. Clerget, had a top speed of 120 m.p.h., a ceiling of 19,000 feet and an endurance of 2½ hours. The outstanding in-line motored fighter was Farnborough's *S.E.5*A (1917) which was powered by a 200-h.p. Hispano-Suiza, had a top speed of 130 m.p.h., a ceiling of 22,000 feet and an endurance of 3 hours (Fig. 84). These, and most fighters, were fitted with progressively more powerful motors, of which the latest type is given here. The most notable French fighter was the *S.P.A.D.* (1916) which many American, and some British, pilots flew. The German single-seat fighters, which were equally successful, included the *Albatros D.III* (1917), the Pfalz *D.III* (1917), the Fokker triplane (1917) and the Fokker *D.VII* (1918) (Pl. XVII): the last was perhaps the finest all-round fighter of the war: it incorporated a type of semi-cantilever wing system, a 160-h.p. Mercedes engine (amongst others), a speed of 125 m.p.h. and a ceiling of 21,000 feet: its superiority lay in a combination of qualities, especially its rate of climb and its manoeuvrability. Performance figures for the various contemporary versions of these machines were similar; and by the end of the war the best fighters on either side had a service ceiling of some 25,000 feet, a top speed (low down) of 155 m.p.h. and of 140 m.p.h. at 10,000 feet, to which they could climb in about 10 minutes.

Meanwhile the two-seat reconnaissance machine was developed to defend itself and also fight, thus becoming the so-called fighter-reconnaissance type, the first successful example of which was the Sopwith *1½-Strutter* of 1916 (named for its centre-section strut arrangement), with a fixed forward-firing synchronised gun and a movable rear gun mounted on a Scarff ring for the observer[1]: this machine, which had a top speed of 100 m.p.h., was also fitted with ingenious air-brakes,[2] one of the earliest uses of them in production aircraft. Later in 1916 came the *R.E.8*, and (in 1917) the famous and

---

[1] The first practical 2-seater was the Caudron *G-4* (1915).
[2] These air-brakes were placed at the rear of the lower centre-section, close to the fuselage: they hinged upwards and could be moved to stand vertically, at right-angles to the air-flow.

Fig. 80. Farnborough-
designed reconnaissance
biplane, *B.E.2*c: 1914–15

Fig. 81. Vickers *F.B.5*
Gunbus pusher biplane:
1914

Fig. 82. Morane-Saulnier
L, with forward-firing gun
utilising airscrew deflector
plates: 1915

Fig. 83. Fokker *E.1*
(*Eindecker*) scout, with
interrupter gun gear: 1915

Fig. 84. Farnborough-
designed *S.E.5*A fighter:
1917

Fig. 85. Junkers low-wing
cantilever monoplane
fighter *J.10*: 1918

formidable Bristol Fighter (Pl. XVII) with a speed of 115 m.p.h. at 10,000 feet, and a service ceiling of 20,000 feet: it was fitted with various in-line engines including the 250-h.p. Rolls-Royce Falcon, and could scout, fight and defend itself with success. Analogous German machines were the L.V.G. (1916), *Aviatik* (1916) *Hanoveraner* (1917) and *Halberstadt* (1917).

The bomber developed from the slow reconnaissance aircraft—three Avro *504*s raided the Zeppelin works at Friedrichshafen in November 1914—and the two-seat reconnaissance fighter became the first light bomber. Then specialised light bombers were produced, the most effective of which were the De Havilland *D.H.4* (1917), the *D.H.9* (1917) and the *D.H.9A* (1918), the latter carrying a bomb-load—under the wings—of 450 lb. at over 100 m.p.h., and remaining airborne for 4 hours.

The heavy bomber, developed for both tactical bombing and assault on cities, was typified by the twin-engine Handley Page *O/400* (Pl. XVII) and the similar German *Gotha*, which were both in active operation from 1917 onwards. The *O/400* flew at 60–80 m.p.h. for 8 hours with a bomb load of 1,800 lb. carried internally.[1] The *Gotha*, on which the Germans relied for long-range bombing after the Zeppelins had proved too vulnerable, had a slightly lower performance and bomb-load, but was an excellent machine: perhaps the best—and certainly the widest used of the German 'giant' bombers—was the 4-engine Staaken *R VI* and its developments, the *R XIV* being shown in Fig. 86. By the end of the war Handley Page had built a number of 4-engined *V/1500* bombers which were prevented by the Armistice from bombing Berlin: these had a speed of 70–90 m.p.h., a radius of action of 1,300 miles, and a bomb load of 7,500 lb.

The seaplane quickly came into its own for reconnaissance, bombing and torpedo-dropping, and particularly successful were the Short float-planes and the *Felixstowe F.2* flying boats (Pl. XVII), the latter being the excellent creations of John Porte. Airships were quite extensively used during the war: the British, French, and Italian Navies used mainly small non-rigid airships (colloquially called "blimps") for anti-submarine patrols; but the Germans concentrated on the development of the rigid airship. The majority of these were built by the Zeppelin company, and they were used both for long-range bombing and for naval scouting. Countering the German airships was a major task of the Royal Naval Air Service, and one result of this was the development of an entirely new type of warship, the aircraft carrier, by a process of evolution. Initially, seaplane tenders were in use, from which the aircraft were off-loaded by crane to take-off from the sea, alongside the ship. In 1915, one of these ships, H.M.S. *Vindex*, was fitted with a small flight deck forward; and, on November 3rd, Flight-Lieutenant H. F. Towler took-off in a Bristol *Scout* from the moving ship. Several seaplane tenders were thus equipped, and at least one attack on a Zeppelin was launched from H.M.S. *Vindex*. In another attempt to develop a Zeppelin-interceptor, one of *Vindex*'s Bristol *Scouts*, flown by Flight-

---

[1] It has often been stated that it was the capture by the Germans of an intact *O/400*—it had the misfortune to land by mistake on a German aerodrome—which inspired the Germans to build the *Gotha*: this is, of course, quite untrue, as the *Gotha* was already in production when this event occurred.

L⸏⸏⸏⸏⸏ Day, was carried aloft on the large Porte *Baby* flying-boat on May⸏⸏⸏⸏⸏ ⸏, and successfully launched in mid-air.

To av⸏⸏ ⸏he delays associated with launching flying-boats by crane, H.M.S. *Campania* was fitted with a longer flight-deck, and specially-built Fairey float-planes mounted on a detachable wheeled trolley were flown off this from mid-1916. The first landing on a moving ship was made by Squadron-Commander E. H. Dunning on August 2nd 1917 in a Sopwith *Pup* on the 228-foot long fore-deck of H.M.S. *Furious*: he was killed repeating the exercise a few days later, and the experiments ceased until H.M.S. *Furious* had been fitted with a 284-foot long after-deck, equipped with a primitive arresting-gear, in March 1918. From this, it was a short step—though a revolution in warship design—to H.M.S. *Argus*, which appeared in September 1918 with a completely unobstructed full-length flight deck. An operational squadron of torpedo-carriers was embarked in October, but saw no active service.

Short flying-off decks were also provided on a considerable number of British cruisers and battleships from June 1917 onwards. Although the U.S. Navy had continued its pre-War experiments with catapults, and a British version was tested on H.M.S. *Slinger* from September 1917, this technique was not regularly used until after 1922. Successful experiments were also conducted with single-seat fighters launched from flat-topped lighters towed behind destroyers: on August 11th 1918, Lieutenant S. D. Culley, flying a Sopwith *Camel* from one of these lighters, shot down the Zeppelin *L.53* off the Belgian coast.

In many departments of aviation and its accessories, important advances and experiments were made. Radio communication with aircraft became universal: aerial photography, many instruments, and armament all made great strides. Even glider-bombs, as well as powered radio-controlled aerial bombs—virtually small pilotless bombers—were pioneered during the War. On September 12th 1916 the first demonstration of a pilotless radio-guided bomb was made—the Hewitt-Sperry biplane[1]—which had a 40 h.p. motor and was capable of carrying an explosive charge of about 140 kg. over a distance of some 80 km. (Pl. XXI). A similar machine was produced in England at Farnborough, called the *Aerial Target*, which was tested in 1917. In Europe the first was the Siemens glider bomb which was tested in October 1916, with an improved design of the same machine (not exploited) in 1917. There was also a biplane glider bomb which made a test-flight from Zeppelin *LZ.12* on April 27th 1917. This type of weapon remained relatively neglected and undeveloped until the Second World War. A variety of other special developments were also encouraged including, for example, the fitting of Le Prieur rockets to Allied fighters for dealing with enemy observation balloons, although incendiary bullets were satisfactory enough for bringing down these balloons, which at first were widely used for artillery spotting until superseded by aeroplanes. The Royal Aircraft Factory at Farnborough played a leading part in other inventions, and developed the following, most of which were not to be properly exploited

[1] Built by Curtiss.

for years to come: the first flaps, giving a variation of 5 m.p.h., fitted to the experimental *S.E.4* (1914), bubble cockpit covers (1914), corrected bomb-sights (1915), the application of superchargers to aero-engines (1916), tail-trimming (1917), a two-pitch airscrew (1918), as well as complete design and prototype construction of various aircraft, including the outstanding *S.E.5* fighter (designed by H. P. Folland) in 1917, which were mass-produced by numerous firms outside the aircraft industry.

One invention, however, was conspicuous by its absence, and that absence reflects great discredit on both enemy and Allies alike, especially, one regrets to record, on the British: the invention was, of course, the free pack-type parachute for escape from aeroplanes.[1]

Basic aerodynamic research and development centred chiefly on the production of improved wing sections of high lift and low drag, most of the productive work being carried out at the National Physical Laboratory and at Farnborough in England, and the Aeronautical Laboratory at Göttingen in Germany under Professor Prandtl. Apart from the all-important military aircraft (see below), surprisingly little attention was paid to improving aircraft structures. The traditional fabric-covered framework of wood or metal persisted, and only in Germany was monocoque construction developed in a progressive way, the *Albatros, Roland* and *Pfalz* scouts having excellent monocoque fuselages of wood.

Aero-engines advanced from the small in-line and rotary types of 1914–15, such as the 80-h.p. Gnome, Le Rhône and Oberursel rotaries, and the 90-h.p. V-type R.A.F. and 100-h.p. Daimler, to the large in-line motors of 1917–18, which included the 12-cylinder 360-h.p. Rolls-Royce Eagle VIII, 12-cylinder 400-h.p. American Liberty, and the 8-cylinder 240-h.p. Mercedes.

Flying techniques naturally depended on the strength and manoeuvrability of the aircraft available, and, where fighters were in question, designers were also concerned with the necessity of varying the degree and nature of inherent stability to allow of greater sensitivity to the controls. Both the exigencies of aerial combat and the ever-improving effectiveness of anti-aircraft gunnery forced the aeroplane to climb quicker and higher, and to manoeuvre with extreme agility: what had once been thought of as dangerous stunt aerobatics became normal flying tactics, and part of the everyday training of the pilot.

---

[1] The parachute, which had been in use since 1797, was inadequately developed in the war for the use of observation balloon and airship crews—the canopy being pulled out of a fixed case—and used on a few German aeroplanes in the War. But no British or French aeroplane crews were allowed parachutes in 1914–18 (although tests were permitted at the end of the War), for the disgraceful reasons (a) that the balloon type was not reliable enough, and (b) that pilots would be encouraged to abandon their machines. There was no excuse whatever for not having produced a satisfactory pack parachute, the problem being relatively simple and already having been tentatively solved and published by an American showman, Leo Stevens: as early as 1908 he had dropped from a balloon with his free-type pack parachute, opened at will by a rip-chord when falling. In October 1912, F. R. Law made a similar safe descent from a Wright biplane, using Stevens' improved "Life-Pack" parachute: this parachute was described and illustrated in the American magazine *Aeronautics* (October 1912), and could easily have been located by the Allied authorities.

It was in Germany that one of the most vital and far-reaching aeronautical innovations took place during the war years. It has already been noted that Hugo Junkers had in 1910 patented his thick-section cantilever wing, without external bracing with struts or wires. It was not until 1915 that this epoch-making invention was successfully applied in aviation, and then in conjunction with metal construction. With his *J.1* (Pl. XVII) Junkers produced an all-metal (iron and steel) fully cantilever-wing monoplane, which made its first successful flights in December 1915, powered by a 120-h.p. Mercedes motor: it attained a speed of 105 m.p.h. The German authorities, however, were sceptical of such a revolutionary step,[1] and proved obstructionist in face of both Junkers' achievements and proposals. But although progress was slow, he pressed on: in 1917 the improved *J.2* appeared, still constructed of iron and steel, and in the same year he produced the remarkable *J.4* (Pl. XVII). The latter was an all-metal cantilever sesquiplane for ground attack, chiefly constructed of duralumin, and heavily armed and armoured: it was a two-seater, powered by a 200-h.p. Benz motor, with a top speed of 95 m.p.h., and was produced in quantity. Then came the first low-wing cantilever monoplane fighters; the first was the *J.7/9* of 1917, the second the *J.10* of 1918 (Fig. 85), which was later to lead to the successful small passenger machine, the *F.13* (*J.13*) of 1919. These first of the world's low-wing cantilever monoplanes represented a complete innovation, and were at first looked upon with suspicion, owing chiefly to the high centre of gravity and its possibly adverse effect on lateral stability: but the fears were proved groundless. It is interesting to note that one of Junkers' main reasons for adopting the low wing position was to minimise injury to the crew in a crash, as the wings would be the first to hit the ground and thus absorb a large part of the initial shock.

The influence of Junkers was to affect the whole course of aircraft evolution. He may be fully and fairly credited with the design and construction of (*a*) the first practical cantilever wing aeroplanes, (*b*) the first practical all-metal aeroplanes, and (*c*) the first practical low-wing monoplanes, all of which he continued to develop successfully over the years.

The aircraft industry in Europe and America had, of course, expanded enormously. To take Britain as an example; from the handful of machines available in 1914, through all the losses of the intervening years, the number in service in 1918 was some 3,300; and the number built reached the huge total of 55,000. The few hundreds of men employed in the industry in 1914 had been swelled by 1918 to nearly 350,000 men and women.

War in the air had been envisaged for centuries, and had even been prophetically described by Francesco de Lana in 1670. When the balloon was invented in 1783, there was a new outburst of aggresive prognostications, and balloons were in fact used passively for military observation from the eighteenth century onwards, with one balloon bombing-raid (by the Austrians against Venice) in 1849. As the powered aeroplane came nearer to achievement, two camps of speculators arose; those who prophesied and advocated the use of the aeroplane in war, such as Maxim and Ader, and

[1] The main criticism was that the steel structure was impractically heavy.

those who felt that the aeroplane's power would neutralise itself when both sides possessed this destructive potential, such as the Wrights, who were proved wrong. The aeroplane has, of course, transformed the whole conduct of warfare; and one unfortunate but understandable result of the early successes in this field became its role—in the eyes of many—as a symbol of destruction. It took the rise of the light aeroplane and the development of air transport in the 'between wars' period to mitigate the flying machine's evil reputation in the world's mind, and establish its parallel but peaceful role as a productive and often life-saving carrier of passengers and cargo. As Cayley prophesied, "We shall be able to transport ourselves and our families, and their goods and chattels, more securely by air than by water."

16. *Between the Wars: The First Period* *1919–1929*

THIS period was one of spectacular and prophetic flying achievements, as well as steady technical progress in aviation. Acceptance of the importance of flying was also being gradually extended in the public mind, and air transport began to establish itself as a means of public transport.

The tone of high adventure was set in 1919 by the first flights across the Atlantic. In May, Harry Hawker and Mackenzie-Grieve had attempted a direct crossing in a single-engined Sopwith biplane, but they had to force-land in the Atlantic, and were given up for lost until they arrived a week later on a Danish steamer which had no radio to announce their rescue. The first completed crossing was accomplished (May 16th–27th) in stages by the U.S. Lieut.-Commander A. C. Read and his crew in the Curtiss *NC-4* flying-boat (Fig. 87), the only one of three similar aircraft to stay the course: it flew from Newfoundland to Lisbon with two landings in the Azores. The first *direct non-stop crossing of the Atlantic* was by the British Captain J. Alcock and Lieutenant A. Whitten-Brown in a converted twin-engine Vickers *Vimy* bomber (Pl. XVIII): they left St. John's, Newfoundland on June 14th and crash-landed safely in a Galway bog near Clifden the next day, after flying the 1,890 miles non-stop from coast to coast in 15 hours 57 minutes at an average speed of 118 m.p.h.: the total flying time, from take-off to landing (some 1,950 miles) was 16 hours 27 minutes.

Also in 1919, and of far-reaching importance, was the almost unnoticed publication of a now classic work entitled *A Method of Reaching Extreme Altitudes* by an obscure American scientist named Dr. R. H. Goddard: this book marked the birth of modern rocketry, as it dealt with the liquid fuel rocket, the first of which was successfully launched by Goddard in 1926. It is historically important to note that Goddard specifically stated that it was a reading of Jules Verne's *From the Earth to the Moon* that inspired him to take to rocketry. Significantly enough, the end of the decade saw the first flights by rocket-propelled aeroplanes in 1928–29 (see page 190).

Leaving for a moment the record of great exploits, of which these years saw so many, it is important to trace briefly the trends in aircraft construction. From the functional and structural point of view these ten years saw the monoplane enter into full rivalry with the biplane in the field of transport aircraft, and to a lesser degree in the small light aeroplane class, and amongst racing machines, where its low drag characteristics were vital. This development was due almost entirely to the cantilever wing policy of Junkers, and its successful application by him, and by the German Reinhold

Fig. 86. Zeppelin-Staaken R. xiv
five-engine bomber: 1918

Fig. 87. Curtiss *NC-4*
flying-boat, which made
the first Atlantic crossing,
by stages: 1919

Fig. 88. Handley Page
patent slotted wing: 1920

Fig. 89. Airco *D.H.*4A
passenger transport: 1919

Platz, who designed the Fokker-type wing. The cantilever wing grew more efficient as the strength and lightness of materials increased, but continued for some years in the familiar Junkers and Fokker-type wings, which were thick-sectioned and of large chord at the roots, tapering in thickness and chord towards the tips. Junkers mostly favoured the metal low-wing application, which necessitated a pronounced dihedral angle to provide lateral stability; and Platz the high-wing of wooden construction, which he laid horizontally across the top of the fuselage, lateral stability being aided by the pendulum action of the fuselage and undercarriage. The Junkers practice was to pay handsome aerodynamic dividends in the future, when retractable undercarriages became the rule, as the low-wing arrangement allowed of a much shorter, and therefore lighter, undercarriage which could be retracted into the wings or engine nacelles.

Of particular long-term importance was another German designer, Dr. Adolph Rohrbach. He realised that the Junkers corrugated metal surfaces produced high drag, and that they could not bear sufficient of the stresses involved, especially where the wings were concerned. So, in 1919, he started building smooth-skinned metal surfaces, with metal box-spar construction in the wings, thus allowing the primary loads to be borne by the surfaces (Fig. 91). This was the beginning of the modern stressed-skin concept—Rohrbach was probably the first to use the term 'stressed-skin', in 1924—which was further evolved and improved by H. A. Wagner, who worked with Rohrbach. It was also Rohrbach, in a lecture in the U.S.A. in 1926, who helped materially to inspire the first, and revolutionary, American transport machines of the 1930s (see page 171).

The monoplane was not yet to make much headway in the military field, even as a bomber, where it could have been employed with advantage. For fighters, the high-drag but extremely manoeuvrable biplane was still preferred to the low-drag monoplane, a state of affairs which was to be transformed in the next decade.

The ever-growing use of metal—steel and aluminium alloys—in all parts of the aircraft structure, was another vital development, with the gradual adoption—not to become general until the 1930's—of monocoque construction carried out in both wood and metal, or the two combined. A particularly ambitious machine with duralumin monocoque fuselage was the all metal Short *Silver Streak* (at first called the *Swallow*) of 1920, but its example was not to be followed in this country for some years (Fig. 94).

It should, perhaps, be said here that British construction, both of civil and military aircraft, was strangely conservative and unprogressive compared with the Continent, and later the United States. This lack of progress was worsened by the British practice of "redesigning biplanes of the wood era in high strength alloy steel", as Professor N. J. Hoff put it: this basic idea, he goes on to say, "was incorrect from the structural standpoint. It did not utilise the inherent lighter strength of the metals which makes them suitable for the construction of cantilever wings." This particularly applied to the rebirth of British military aircraft construction about 1924, when the Air Ministry—with Britain's scant supply of suitable woods in mind—ruled that the vital parts of the structures of all new service aircraft were to be made of

Fig. 90. First French
airliner, a modified
Goliath bomber: 1919

Fig. 91. Zeppelin-Staaken
E.4/20 four engine airliner,
designed by Rohrbach: 1920

Fig. 92. Handley Page
*W.8*B airliner: 1921

Fig. 93. Dayton-Wright
R.B. racer, with retractable undercarriage: 1920

184

metal. Even so, some remarkable machines, particularly fighters, were produced during this period.

A major innovation in aircraft construction in the mid-1920's was the high-wing single-engined transport monoplane, to carry a pilot and some six to eight passengers, with a cruising speed of 100 m.p.h. upwards, and a range of 500 miles and up. This type derived originally from the Fokker high-wing monoplane of the immediate post-war years, such as the *F.II*, but it was both revolutionised and crystallised in the United States by the Lockheed *Vega* of 1927 (Fig. 100). With a radial engine of either 220 h.p. or 425 h.p. the *Vega* could cruise with a pilot and six passengers at 100 to 135 m.p.h. and had a range of 550 or 900 miles: it had fully cantilevered wooden wings, and a wooden monocoque fuselage of an advanced streamlined shape built in two moulded sections. Of particular importance was its practical demonstration that a stressed-skin structure allows the same interior height and breadth of fuselage as that of a framework structure, at a saving of 35% of the cross-sectional area, thus greatly reducing drag and saving much weight and material. The *Vega* set the fashion and the pace for this general-purpose type of aircraft, and inspired a world-wide development, and its influence spread also to the design of larger transport aircraft.

The military aeroplanes of the decade kept, with some notable exceptions, to the biplane form which, as already mentioned, offered a good performance at a time when speeds were not high enough to encourage designers to exploit the cleaner lines of the monoplane. The English biplane fighters, paralleled by similar machines in other countries, included many successful types, such as the Fairey *Flycatcher* and *Firefly*, Gloster *Grebe* and *Gamecock*, Armstrong-Whitworth *Siskin*, and Bristol *Bulldog*, and reached their zenith at the end of the decade in the Hawker *Fury* (1929), which had a top speed of over 200 m.p.h., the first military aircraft to exceed this figure (Fig. 102). Exceptions to the biplane fighter tradition included the remarkable Bristol monoplane racer (1922), an experimental mid-wing machine with retractable undercarriage (Fig. 95); the Dewoitine *D-27*; and the Junkers *K-47* two-seat fighter which was built in Sweden and became the ancestor of the firm's *Stuka* dive-bomber. Comparatively few bombers were built during this period, but fast single-engine types such as the Fairey *Fox* were made in England, with Fairey and Blackburn machines being built for torpedo-carrying. The Americans kept alive the large biplane bomber such as the twin-engined Martin *NBS-1* and the Curtiss *B-2*; and their courageous Colonel 'Billy' Mitchell strove—at the expense of his career—to focus attention on the bomber as the future's most powerful weapon of war over both land and water: his successful sinking of a so-called unsinkable ex-German battleship in 1921, and his outspoken criticisms of American air policy in 1925, had a decisive influence on the future of United States military aviation. In 1928 Britain produced two interesting machines, one an experimental aircraft—the Beardmore-Rohrbach *Inflexible*, an all metal three-engined cantilever monoplane—and the large Fairey monoplane, with one 500-h.p. Napier engine, which was not specifically designed as a bomber but as a long-range record-breaker aircraft. After the first of the latter had crashed, the second (in 1933) flew non-stop for 5,309 miles in 57½ hours.

An interesting military 'side-line' was experimenting with airships in the role of aircraft carriers. There had been unsuccessful tests during the war, but in 1918 a Sopwith *Camel* was successfully released from the British airship *R.23*. Later in the decade other successful tests, both of releasing and taking-on fighters, were made both in Britain and America: but all such work ceased when both countries abandoned large airship construction after the succession of disasters to these lighter-than-air aircraft in the 1930's.

The development of the small fast aeroplane, which was to lead directly to the modern fighter, was a prominent feature of the 1920's, and was mostly due to the encouragement of air-racing, especially the Pulitzer Trophy races in the U.S.A., and the international Schneider Trophy races for seaplanes. One of the most important of these early racers was the Dayton-Wright R.B. high-wing monoplane which competed for the Gordon-Bennett trophy in France in 1920; for this machine was the first to incorporate a modern-type fully retractable undercarriage[1] (Fig. 93), a device which was to see much slowness of development, since retractable undercarriages were not to be widely used until the 1930's. At first the more advanced disciplines of streamlining were applied to the biplane, and the 1925 Schneider race was won by the American, J. Doolittle, on his little Curtiss *R3C-2* at 232·5 m.p.h. (Fig. 97). But a monoplane—an Italian Macchi—won the next year's race, and monoplanes won all subsequent contests. The 1927 Schneider race was especially significant for Britain, for it was won by the Supermarine *S.5* at 281·65 m.p.h.: the *S.5* was a low-wing float monoplane designed by R. J. Mitchell and powered by an 800-h.p. Napier Lion engine, and was the ancestor of Mitchell's *Spitfire*. In 1929, Mitchell's Supermarine *S.6*, with a Rolls-Royce engine, won the Schneider contest at 328·63 m.p.h. and later raised the world's speed record to 357·7 m.p.h. These high-speed float-planes—chiefly British, American and Italian—laid the foundations for the fighters of the future, and provided ideal opportunities for developing strong and light metal structures, streamlining, and powerful engines.

The non-military sphere of flying saw the most dramatic developments during the decade. European air transport, in the form of properly scheduled airlines, started in 1919, after an interlude of military transport flying which grew out of the immediate needs of official travel after hostilities had ceased.[2] The first civil airline for passengers started on February 5th 1919, when the German Deutsche Luftreederei opened a service between Berlin, Leipzig and Weimar. On February 8th, the French Farman Company opened a tentative Paris–London service with converted *Goliath* bombers (Fig. 90).

After some pioneering passenger flights from May to August, the world's first daily commercial scheduled air service opened on August 25th with the first flight—in an Airco *D.H.4A*—from London (Hounslow) to Paris (Le

[1] It was also the first to have variable camber.
[2] A remarkable transport service for official passengers and mail was carried on, amongst others, by the R.A.F. between Hendon (later Kenley) and Buc near Paris, from January to September 1919, with a regularity of 91%. (See Peter Masefield's now famous paper *Some Economic Factors in Air Transport Operation*, to which I am indebted for these and other details of British air transport.)

Bourget), making it in 2½ hours (Fig. 89). The line was operated for passenger and light freight by the short-lived Aircraft Transport and Travel Ltd.: the single fare to Paris was £21. Also on August 25th, the Handley Page Co. opened an *ad hoc* service to Paris from Cricklewood, using a converted *O/400* bomber.

In France, England and America the first transports, both small and large, were adapations of wartime bombers: all such machines were biplanes. In the smaller class, they were conversions of such single-engined bombers as the *D.H.4* and *D.H.9*, to carry three or four passengers. By about 1922 the British airlines had specially designed single-engined aircraft such as the *D.H.34*, with a 500-h.p. Napier Lion engine, which carried eight passengers.

The larger transports—soon called 'airliners'—were adapted twin- or four-engined bombers like the Handley-Page *O/400*, *V/1500*, the Vickers *Vimy* (converted into the *Vimy Commercial*), or the Farman *Goliath* bomber, which became the first French airliner (Fig. 91).

Air transport then spread erratically and sporadically throughout Europe, and a number of other airlines were opened in 1919, including the Dutch K.L.M. The British company, Imperial Airways Ltd., in which various companies were merged, was formed in 1924. Strangely enough, the United States were slow to open airlines, and it was not until 1927 that a passenger service was inaugurated over one of the various contract mail routes which had been operating since the war: this first passenger service was started in April between New York and Boston, and was operated by Colonial Air Transport.

In the early days of the airliners, there appeared two broad categories of transport aircraft, the single-engined machine taking some three to five passengers, and the larger multi-engined airliner for bigger loads and longer routes.

In both types of machine, Junkers and Fokker made themselves pre-eminent, both favouring monoplanes. They soon came to represent the most influential trends in world design, a position they held until the late 1920's, when the United States began taking the initiative, especially with smaller machines such as the Lockheed *Vega* already described. In 1919 Junkers had produced his single-engine *F-13* transport which carried two crew and four passengers (Pl. XVIII): with its low-set cantilever wings it derived directly from the *J.7/9* and *J.10*, and was in many respects the miniature prototype of the modern airliner. Following the *F-13*—which could, like its successors, be fitted with floats—Junkers went on to build an ever-improving series of low-wing cantilever machines culminating in one of the most successful of the larger European transports, the three-engined *G-31* (1926), the precursor of the *Ju 52 3m* transport: the *G-31*, with three 450-h.p. radial engines, carried a crew of two and sixteen passengers at a cruising speed of 90 m.p.h. This development was paralleled by Fokker—he had set up a factory in the U.S.A. as well as in Holland—who during this period produced excellent single-, twin- and three-engine high-wing transports (Fig. 96). Directly competitive with the three-engine Fokker came, in June 1926, the first successful American transport, the all-metal Ford *4-AT*, designed by William B. Stout; with three 220 h.p. engines, it carried ten passengers at a cruising speed of 105 m.p.h.

Then, in 1920, came the first successful large British transport, the twin-engined Handley Page *W.8* (derived from the *O/400* bomber) which carried a crew of two and twelve passengers (Fig. 92).

With the developments of the long Empire air routes, Britain was soon building larger machines for such services, and the De Havilland *Hercules* and Armstrong-Whitworth *Argosy*—both biplanes with three engines— appeared in 1925–26. The *Argosy* was powered by three 420-h.p. Jaguar radial engines, and carried twenty passengers and their luggage at a cruising speed of 95 m.p.h. for over 5 hours.

By the end of this decade, the larger three-engined airliners—biplanes and monoplanes—could carry some fifteen to twenty passengers, a crew of two or three, and a small amount of freight, at cruising speeds of 90–110 m.p.h. over stages of about 500 miles.

A measure of the growth of air transport over the years were the world totals of miles flown on scheduled airlines, China and Soviet Russia excluded: in 1919 the figure was approximately a million; in 1929, 57 million. World passenger figures are also available for the period, and show 5,000 for 1919, rising to 434,000 in 1929.

The flying-boat also became a popular type of airliner, and after much research into hull-shapes, and methods and materials of construction, such excellent machines as the three-engined Short *Calcutta* biplane boat were available for the Empire routes; this carried fifteen passengers at a cruising speed of 90 m.p.h. Similar machines, such as the Short *Singapore*, were produced for the R.A.F. In Germany, the Dornier Company was producing successful monoplane flying-boats, with one or more engines set above the fuselage-hull; and the same firm, in 1929, completed a giant monoplane flying-boat, the *Do X*, with a span of 157 feet 5 inches, twelve 525 h.p. engines and a cruising speed of 110 m.p.h.: three of these were built, and one of them once took up 169 passengers. But the *Do X* can only be called an ambitious freak (Pl. XVIII); all other seaplanes were of much more modest capacity, with passenger accommodation for up to 20. Most countries were building flying-boats and float-planes in a variety of forms, for both civil and military use, the biplane still holding its own in both these classes of seaplanes.

This decade also saw the rebirth and growth of the glider as a sporting aircraft, and the rise of the light aeroplane. The Germans were responsible for the revival of gliding owing to the Peace Treaty restrictions on military flying, and used the glider both for sport and for undercover training of their future air force (Pl. XVIII). This revival also paid aerodynamic dividends, as much valuable work on reducing drag resulted from it.

The light aeroplane movement started in the mid-1920's, principally in England and Germany, where it was officially encouraged, before spreading to the U.S.A., and both biplane and monoplane types became popular for club and private flying. Symbol of the whole movement, which offered powered flying for pleasure even to the man and woman of modest means, was the admirable, ubiquitous little two-seat biplane named the *Moth* (Pl. XVIII), first produced by Geoffrey de Havilland in 1925, with a 65-h.p.

Fig. 94. Short *Silver Streak*, of monocoque construction: 1920

Fig. 95. Bristol monoplane racer, with retractable undercarriage: 1922

Fig. 96. Fokker *F. VII-3m* three-engine airliner: 1925

Fig. 97. Curtiss *R3C-2* racing float-plane: 1925

Fig. 98. Cierva *Autogiro* C.6 c: 1926

189

Cirrus engine and a speed of 90 m.p.h. It was light but robust, cheap and easy to fly, and—in various subsequent versions—was to remain in universal use for private flying and service training for over thirty years. De Havilland's light *D.H.71 Tiger Moth* monoplane of 1927 (not to be confused with the *Tiger Moth* biplane) was another remarkable little machine built for racing, which set up a record of 186·4 m.p.h., over 100 kilometres.

The helicopter, a dream of engineers since the eighteenth century, began to approach practical form in the 1920's. Many inventors had been at work since Cornu and the Breguet brothers had first risen from the ground in 1907. Productive suggestions had been made by such men as C. Renard, who suggested flapping rotor blades, but for the wrong reasons (1904); G. A. Crocco, who first suggested cyclic pitch control (1906); and Ellehammer, the Dane, who demonstrated the latter in a tentative machine (1912). Between 1919 and 1925 the Argentinian Marquis de P. Pescara built a number of helicopters in France and Spain which, although unstable and unsatisfactory in other ways, incorporated cyclic pitch control for the first time, and also provided for auto-rotation in case of engine failure. On May 4th 1924 the French Oehmichen No. 2 made the world's first helicopter flight of a closed kilometre circle.

Back in 1923, the Spanish Juan de la Cierva made his first successful flights in a gyroplane, the *C.4*, called an *Autogiro* (Fig. 98), at Getafe (Spain) then at Madrid. In 1925 he came to continue his work in England. The *Autogiro* was half-way towards the helicopter: it consisted of a conventional aeroplane fuselage and tail-unit, with a tractor airscrew, above which was a freely turning rotor which provided the machine's lift. The *Autogiro* could take off with a very short run, and could land almost vertically. Cierva's most important invention and improvement, however, was (in 1922) to cure the machine's tendency to roll over in flight—due to unequal lift between the retreating and advancing rotor blades—by providing a flapping hinge for each blade: the advancing blade automatically moved up as its increased airspeed gave it more lift, but the movement of the air relative to the blade was changed, the angle of attack reduced, and the lift decreased: meanwhile, the opposite process was at work on the retreating blade; whereupon the lift forces on all the blades were balanced and the system rendered stable. In 1933 Cierva first achieved successul 'jump-starts' by gearing the engine to the rotor for take-off. It was the growing success of the *Autogiro* during the 1920's and 1930's that undoubtedly spurred on research into the helicopter proper, and Cierva's introduction of flapping blades was to prove a major contribution to the success of the practical helicopter.

Isolated from other programmes of development, but ingenious and prophetic, were the first true aeroplane flights in history in which man-carrying aeroplanes were propelled and sustained in the air by reaction propulsion. On June 11th 1928, F. Stamer piloted a canard-type glider propelled by rockets from the Wasserkuppe, one of the Rhön mountains in Western Germany: the venture was promoted by Max Valier, and financed (in part) by Fritz von Opel, the rockets made by F. W. Sander, and the experiments were directed by the well-known German aerodynamicist. A. Lippisch. After model tests, the full-size aeroplane made only one—but a successful—flight of about a mile after a ground-towed launch, the aircraft being damaged after landing. On September 30th 1928, von Opel himself flew a specially built glider powered by rockets (Fig. 101): it was launched from a rocket-propelled cradle, and a successful flight of some ten minutes was made, in which the speed at one point reached 100 m.p.h. These experiments were not continued, but—loosely speaking—they mark the first successful aeroplane flights in history by reaction propulsion (see Glossary).

In 1924, Burnelli pioneered a biplane in which the fuselage was aerofoil-shaped (with engines buried in it) to augment the wing-lift, a move toward the flying-wing ideal of Junkers; Burnelli later built a number of monoplanes on the same principles (1928, etc.), but little came of these machines.

In 1926, the British Professor G. T. R. Hill produced the first of his swept-wing tailless *Pterodactyls* (Fig. 99) to secure, like Dunne, a machine which would be easily controllable and which would not stall: but the *Pterodactyls*—and Dunne—did not contribute significantly to the swept-back and delta configurations of today.

After the first trans-Atlantic flights there was a continuous succession of notable flying exploits throughout the decade, many of them acting as 'prospecting' flights for future airline routes. Amongst the more important flights were the following: in November–December 1919, Ross Smith and his crew flew in a Vickers *Vimy* from London to Australia, over 11,000 miles in 27 days 20 hours; in May 1923, Lieutenants Kelly and Macready made the first non-stop flight across the U.S.A. in a single-engined Fokker, 2,516 miles in 26 hours 50 minutes; in April–September 1924, two U.S. Army Douglas biplanes (fitted alternatively with floats or wheels) made the first round-the-world flight, 27,500 miles in about 15½ days' flying time; and in July 1924, the first U.S. transcontinental air mail service was started. In November 1925, Alan Cobham made the first of his fine pioneering flights when he flew in a *D.H.50* from London to Cairo: in 1926, he flew the same machine to India, Australia and South Africa, thus helping to lay the foundations for the British Empire air routes. On May 9th 1926, Lieutenant-Commander Richard Byrd, in a Fokker trimotor, was the first to fly over the North Pole, from Spitzbergen; and in 1929, on November 28th, he was the first to fly over the South Pole, a double success for America.

One exploit might be said to have transformed the entire picture of American air transport and private flying: this was, of course, Charles Lindbergh's solo flight direct from New York to Paris, on May 20–21st 1927—3,600 miles in 33 hours 39 minutes—at an average speed of 107·5 m.p.h. in his single-engined Ryan monoplane *Spirit of St. Louis* (Pl. XVIII). The United States was already well advanced in service and racing aircraft, and in the operation of mail routes; but it took the romantic impact of Lindbergh—similar in its tremendous impact to Blériot's Channel crossing of 1909—to make the nation truly air-minded, and so create the financial and technical climate necessary for the large-scale development of aviation.

In April 1928, the first East to West crossing of the Atlantic was made by a Junkers monoplane, the *Bremen* (H. Koehl and others), from Ireland to Newfoundland; in May–June 1928, a Fokker monoplane the *Southern Cross*

Fig. 99. Hill swept-wing tailless *Pterodactyl*: 1926

Fig. 100. Lockhead *Vega* passenger transport, first built in 1927

Fig. 101. Glider fitted with rockets, flown by Opel: 1929

Fig. 102. Hawker *Fury* biplane fighter: 1929

Fig. 103. Lippisch tailless research monoplane: 1931

Fig. 104. Outright winner of the Schneider Trophy, the Supermarine *S6B*: 1931

PLATE XVII

a The first significant all-metal cantilever aeroplane, the Junkers *J.1*: 1915

b One of the outstanding fighting scouts of World War I, the Sopwith *Pup*: 1916

c The two-seat *Bristol Fighter*, which could scout, fight and defend itself: 1917

d The first British heavy bomber, the twin-engine Handley Page *0/400*: 1917

e The Felixstowe *F.2A* flying-boat, for naval reconnaissance and anti-submarine patrol: 1917

f One of the most successful of German fighting scouts, the Fokker *D.VII*: 1918

g A pioneer among armoured ground-attack aircraft, the all-metal semi-cantilever Junkers *J.4*: 1918

14 + A.

PLATE XVIII

b One of the ancestors of the modern airliner, the German Junkers *F-13* four-passenger transport: 1919

c A German glider of the 1930's, when Germany came to lead the world in this form of flying

f The 12-engine German Dornier *Do X* flying-boat, carrying 70–80 passengers: 1929

a The start of the first direct transatlantic flight, from Newfoundland to Ireland (Alcock and Brown in their Vickers *Vimy*): 1919

e The Ryan monoplane *Spirit of St. Louis*, in which Charles Lindbergh made the first solo Atlantic crossing: 1927

d The most successful light aeroplane in history, the De Havilland *Moth*: 1925

(Sir C. Kingsford Smith and C. Ulm) flew the Pacific from California to Australia via Hawaii and Fiji; also in 1928, a Savoia flying boat (A. Ferrarin and C. P. Del Prete) flew non-stop from near Rome to Brazil, 4,500 miles. As a tail-piece it should be said that in 1929 the German Zeppelin *Graf Zeppelin* flew round the world, 21,500 miles in 21 days, including 7,000 miles non-stop from Friedrichshafen to Tokyo—an outstanding achievement.[1]

In research laboratories and workshops, the science of aerodynamics was being extended and deepened by workers in many countries. Much of the basic research on lift and drag, which would be incorporated in new wing shapes and sections, appropriate aspect ratios, etc., in the aeroplanes of the thirties, was being mathematically formulated and developed in this period 1919–29. Of particular importance now was the development and fuller understanding of the theory of circulatory motion, and the problems of drag, by the Germans Ludwig Prandtl and M. W. Kutta, the Russian-born N. E. Joukowski, and the Hungarian-born American, Theodore von Kármán: their work had been in progress since before the war, but formulation and availability for practical application date chiefly from the immediate post-war decade. Another worker who profoundly influenced subsequent aircraft design was the British Professor B. Melvill Jones, with the publication of his paper *The Streamline Aeroplane* (1929). From now on, the science of aerodynamics was to play a major role in the world's scientific institutions.

Also the subject of basic formulation and experiment at this time was propulsion by means of the gas turbine, and it was at the Royal Aircraft Establishment at Farnborough in 1926–28 that Dr. A. A. Griffith made the first practical proposals and experiments. After further research and experimentation, the project was unfortunately shelved and not revived until the mid-1930's, when the R.A.E. at Farnborough and Frank Whittle were working on parallel lines. It is important to note that Dr. Griffith did not envisage propulsion by 'pure jet', but by propeller-turbine (turbo-prop). It was Whittle who pioneered the turbo-jet engine in this country (see later).

Of particular inventions and improvements, one of the most important was the slotted wing, matured in 1919, with the patenting of the device by Handley Page Ltd. It was a device consisting of a curved slat (at first manually operated and then automatic) which was made to project from the leading edge of the wing and thus force air through the resulting slot and over the upper surface of the wing: the effect was to smooth out the air flow over the wing and reduce turbulence at large angles of attack, and so postpone stalling: it therefore increased the speed range of the aircraft and all but eliminated the stall-and-spin type of crash. In 1928, the Air Ministry ordered slots to be fitted to all British service machines, and the adoption of the device for both large transports and light aircraft materially decreased the accident rate, and increased the general confidence in flying (Fig. 88).

Instrument flying began to be practical by the end of the war, but it was during the years 1919–29 that blind flying became successful and practical, chiefly as a result of Sperry's work in the United States; Sperry perfected the

---

[1] This journey included the first flight over the Pacific Ocean.

gyro horizon[1] and directional gyro, and on September 24th 1929, Lieutenant James Doolittle, in a Sperry-equipped Consolidated *NY-2* biplane, was able "to take off, fly a specific course, and land without reference to the earth". During the next decade, instrument flying was to become a routine accomplishment for all commercial and military pilots.

Many other inventions, improvements and adaptations occurred during the years 1919–29: the flap, which had first been used tentatively in the war, was being experimented with; the retractable undercarriage was successfully pioneered on a few machines[2]; the metal propeller came into its own—but not with variable pitch—together with electric and other powered engine-starters; superchargers for aero-engines came into use; wing-folding—already in use during the war—became standard practice on certain types of aircraft, especially carrier-borne machines and on light aeroplanes, for ease of transport and storage; the aircraft carrier was further developed as well as catapult-launching from warships; and the refuelling of aeroplanes in flight was pioneered in America (1923). The aeroplane became used for an ever-growing variety of purposes, including ambulance work, crop-dusting and freight-carrying.

In the sphere of aero-engines the most far-reaching development was the perfecting of the air-cooled radial engine and its all important low-drag cowling. This type of engine, light and powerful, soon rivalled the liquid-cooled in-line motors, and shared with them the power-unit market until the arrival of jet propulsion. The radial engine came to power the majority of the world's medium and large transport aircraft, and continued to do so until the jet age started. There were also a few compression ignition (heavy oil) engines now being developed, the only one of significance being the Junkers Jumo, which was first built in 1926, and first fitted to an aircraft in 1929; but the main task of propulsion fell to the conventional four-stroke petrol motor. By 1929 there was a large range of aero-engines available for the many types of aircraft: there were in-line engines, from the small type suitable for light aeroplanes, such as the 4-cylinder 120-h.p. De Havilland Gipsy III, to the 12-cylinder, 450-h.p. Napier Lion, and the 12-cylinder 525-h.p. Rolls-Royce Kestrel.[3] Radial engines included such types as the 7-cylinder 215-h.p. Armstrong-Siddeley Lynx in the lowest power range, and the 9-cylinder 550-h.p. Bristol Jupiter in the larger class.

Performance records for 1929 were 357·74 m.p.h. for speed (British Supermarine *S-6*); 41,794 feet for height (German Junkers *W.34* with a Bristol Jupiter engine); and 4,912 miles for distance in a straight line (French Breguet 19).

---

[1] Mr. Brooks tells me that, although seldom recorded in history, artificial horizons were fitted in the giant German bombers of World War I.

[2] The first primitive, retractable undercarriages were used by Sellers (1908) and Wiencziers (1911). The first modern-type fully retractable undercarriage, as previously noted, appeared in 1920 on the American Dayton-Wright R.B. high-wing racing monoplane which competed in the Gordon-Bennett race of that year: the wheels retracted into the fuselage (Fig. 93). The year 1922 saw the first machine with undercarriage retracting into the wings, the American Verville-Sperry Racer, a low-wing monoplane sometimes designated the R-3.

[3] The term 'in-line' is here loosely—but quite usefully—taken to include not only the single bank types, but those with cylinders in V or W arrangements.

17. *Between the Wars: The Second Period 1930–1939*

THIS second between-wars decade saw the full maturing of the propeller-driven aircraft, the virtual eclipse of the biplane, and the beginnings of practical jet propulsion. It also saw the aeroplane established as a universal and accepted means of transport, as well as its renaissance as a weapon of war—a prelude to its becoming the decisive military weapon—and then in our own day slowly giving way in face of the rocket missile.

Research over the whole field of fluid mechanics, of which aerodynamics is a part, progressed rapidly in Europe and America. One of the most significant events was the flight (in 1931) of the first practical near-delta-wing aeroplane designed by the German Dr. Alexander Lippisch: it was a small machine powered by a 32-h.p. Bristol Cherub engine (Fig. 103) incorporating trailing-edge ailerons and elevators—not elevons—as well as wing-tip fins and rudders. He had been experimenting in the 1920's with swept-wing tailless designs on parallel lines with Dr. Hill's researches, which resulted in the *Pterodactyls*, but more with a view to high-speed flight. Lippisch was the chief pioneer of the delta-wing aeroplane, although many other scientists in related fields were contributing important theoretical research; but the true flourishing of Lippisch's conceptions had to wait for the practical jet-engine. The delta, or near delta, forms—if made large enough—would produce the ideal of many designers to have a 'flying wing', a machine which would have no drag beyond that of the wing itself, in which all the engines, crew and pay-load would be enclosed: the Northrop *N1M* of 1940 came near to this ideal but was not altogether successful. In smaller high-speed aircraft, the delta form provides a strong and low thickness-to-chord ratio wing, which helps delay the effects of compressibility set up at transonic speeds, especially by curbing the displacement of the centre of pressure: the delta wing can also be made longitudinally stable, thus avoiding the addition of a separate tailplane, the combined 'elevons' being hinged to the wings. But the ideal of the all-enclosing flying-wing will later be paralleled by the choice of a conventional fuselage and very thin wings for supersonic flying.

The science of aerodynamics was strongly augmented by ever-improving methods and processes of manufacture, and the strides taken in metallurgy, especially the production of better steels and light aluminium and magnesium alloys. By the late 1930's the all-metal stressed-skin aeroplane became the rule rather than the exception.

Engine development kept in step with the other technical advances in aviation and took advantage both of aerodynamic and metallurgical research, as well as progressing in mechanical design and efficiency. The air-cooled radial engine grew in popularity, and in America almost ousted the liquid-cooled in-line types; and the adoption of more successful low-drag cowling, and the twin-row cylinder arrangement, helped to bring the radial to a high state of efficiency. By 1939 there were such radials in service as the British 9-cylinder, 1,000-h.p. Bristol Pegasus and the American 14-cylinder Pratt and Whitney Twin-Wasp of 1,200 h.p. The in-line engine, cooled for so many years by water, exchanged this early system for high-temperature cooling by ethylene glycol, which, with its low freezing and high boiling points—and only needing a small radiator—proved more efficient and economical. By 1939 there were in-line engines of 1,000 h.p. such as the 12-cylinder Rolls-Royce Merlin, and similar types in Germany. Most of the smaller in-line engines—made by several European firms—for light aircraft were air-cooled. Although small air-cooled in-line engines continued in production in Europe to power a wide variety of light aircraft, there developed in the United States during the 1930's the flat horizontally-opposed configuration of light air-cooled aero-engine. These proved highly successful and eventually displaced the older in-line type almost completely for powers up to about 300 horse-power.

As aircraft speeds mounted by virtue of this multiple progress, the aerodynamic problems were met and dealt with in various ways: streamlining was aided not only by improved airframe design, but by better layout of engines, low-drag engine cowlings, and retractable undercarriages; the latter came into general use in the mid-1930's.

In single-engine types, the wheels were retracted into the wings, and in multi-engine machines into the engine nacelles. To allow of slower landing-speeds, the trailing-edge flap in its various forms was universally adopted to preserve maximum lift at minimum speeds.[1]

One of the most important inventions rendered practical in this period, and one of the most important developments in the whole history of aviation, was the introduction of the practical variable-pitch propeller (1932) and, developing out of it, the constant-speed propeller (1935), inventions which allowed the airscrew to give the optimum thrust for all conditions of flying, from take-off to landing, by variations in the pitch of the blades. The former had been achieved in a tentative way during the First World War, and at various times since; and the latter had even been patented in England in 1924 by Dr. H. S. Hele-Shaw and T. E. Beacham, and test-flown in 1926–27. Both types were ultimately put into practical production in the U.S.A., and were in service in the years noted above. The sequence of events leading to this production followed a complex international pattern.

Amongst other special developments during this period were the pressurisation of aircraft cabins[2] for flying beyond the 'comfortable' height

---

[1] It was the ageing Orville Wright who, with J. M. Jacobs, invented the important split flap in 1920, a form of flap which came into general use in the mid-1930's.

[2] There were a few machines prior to the Lockheed *XC-35* which were fitted with experimental pressure cabins, but none was successful. The earliest was a *D.H.4* which was flown at Wright Field (U.S.A.) about 1922. This was followed by a Farman machine which was test-flown on July 21st 1932, but later suffered a fatal crash.

for breathing (about 8,000 feet), the first machine to be fully equipped for this being the Lockheed *XC-35* in 1937; the use of tricycle undercarriages, which began to appear in the late 1930's; the further development and perfecting of refuelling in flight; the perfection of the automatic pilot to keep aircraft on a pre-determined course; instrument flying and approach; and various radio aids to flying.

Our solution to the problem of getting a heavily-loaded aircraft into the air was the Short-Mayo Composite, tested by Imperial Airways in 1938; the small four-engined float-plane *Mercury* was launched in mid-air from the flying-boat *Maia*. On 8 October, Captain D. C.T. Bennett flew *Mercury* non-stop from Scotland to South Africa, a distance of 5,997·3 miles. The air-launching of a small aircraft from a larger had been pioneered at Felixstowe in 1916 (see page 176), and taken further by the Russians in 1931–4. In their experiments, as many as four small fighters were carried on a TB-3 bomber.

The helicopter, which had been a popular toy since the 14th century, as we have seen, and already showing signs of feasibility in this century, at last arrived in a practical form, although it was to remain undeveloped for some years more. In 1935, Louis Breguet flew his twin-coaxial-rotor machine successfully, but it was neither a practical helicopter nor a properly controllable one. Then, in 1936, after other inventors had also made tentative experiments, came the German Focke-Achgelis *FW-61*, which may be described as the first practical helicopter of history (Pl. XXI): it was a twin-rotor machine which could stay up for 1 hour 20 minutes, attain a speed of 76 m.p.h. and reach an altitude of 11,243 feet. The success of the *FW-61* was not to be fully exploited, although a development of the machine, the *Fa 223*, was to fly in 1940 and go into production: the *Fa 223* was therefore the world's first production helicopter. The design and construction of helicopters in general was to remain in abeyance until the 1940's, when the greatest progress was to take place in the United States (see next section).

Reaction (jet) propulsion, which had been a favourite dream since the 18th century, also now became a reality; and despite the pioneer work of Frank Whittle[1] and his successful engine of 1937—his first patents were taken out in 1930—it was the Germans who produced the first tentative turbojet of history, the Heinkel *He 178*, which flew on August 27th 1939 (Fig. 116): it was powered by a centrifugal flow turbojet engine designed by Dr. Hans von Ohain.[2] It has often been assumed, since Whittle's early patents were published, that it was his invention which led the German engineers to

[1] The difficulties, thwartings and disappointments faced by Frank Whittle are detailed in his book *Jet* (1953); and in this connection it is interesting to find the British Under Secretary of State for Air, writing to the British Interplanetary Society as late as 1934: "We follow with interest any work that is being done in other countries on jet propulsion, but scientific investigation into the possibilities has given no indication that this method can be a serious competitor to the airscrew-engine combination. We do not consider that we should be justified in spending any time or money on it ourselves."

[2] This engine, the He S3b, had an axial inductor, a centrifugal compressor, reverse flow combustion chambers, and a one-stage inflow turbine. The *He 178*, which only made a few flights, was, however, a successful test vehicle.

develop their jets. This view is not borne out by the facts. Schlaifer, in his detailed study, *Development of Aircraft Engines*, etc. (1950), showed that von Ohain was also absorbed by the challenge of jet propulsion in the early 1930's, and was "completely unaware of Whittle's patent of 1930, and his engine was different in almost all its details".

A special tribute should be paid to the high-speed flying of the time. In 1931, Britain won her third successive victory in the Schneider Trophy contest and thus secured the Trophy permanently: the winning aircraft was the Supermarine *S.6B* (Fig. 104) which won at 340·6 m.p.h., a machine which led to Mitchell's single-seat land monoplane built to an Air Ministry specification, which was not successful, and then to his own individual design of the *Spitfire* of 1936. In America, one of the world's best racing aircraft, the *Gee Bee 7–11 Super Sportster* (Fig. 106), set up a record for land-planes in 1932 of 294·4 m.p.h. and also won the Thompson Trophy. In 1934 came the MacRobertson Air Race from Mildenhall, England, to Melbourne, Australia, which was won by a specially designed twin-engine De Havilland machine named the *Comet*, which flew the distance in 2 days 23 hours (time in the air 2 days 15 hours 52 minutes) at an average speed of 180 m.p.h.: the *Comet* was the direct ancestor of the *Mosquito* of World War II

The transport aeroplane in Europe was led by Fokker and Junkers during this period, until the sudden flourishing of American civil aviation in the mid- and late 1930's. The three-engine monoplane transports of Germany and Holland provided the backbone of the Continental airlines, and after the three-engine Junkers *G-31* of 1926 there came another distinguished machine, the Junkers *Ju 52/3m*, a three-engine transport which appeared in 1931–33 and was later mass-produced to provide the Germans with their standard military transport and invasion work-horse for freight and troop-carrying, and for parachute dropping: it could carry up to seventeen passengers at a cruising speed of 130 m.p.h. (Fig. 107). The Fokker tri-motors of this period can be typified by the *F.XVIII* of 1932 which took fourteen passengers at a cruising speed of about 155 m.p.h. In 1931 the Junkers firm had put into service for the Berlin–London Lufthansa route their giant four-engine *G-38*, with its deep-section wings in which the engines were buried, carrying a crew of seven and thirty-four passengers at 115 m.p.h. (Fig. 105). This machine was the precursor in Europe of such four-engine airliners as the Junkers *Ju 90* and the Focke-Wulf *Fw 200 Condor*, which were usefully converted to military purposes soon after.

England kept a very conservative tradition of biplanes in her air transport during most of this period, and Imperial Airways seem to have adopted the slogan "slow but sure". Most famous of British airliners were the four-engine Handley Page *H.P. 42* and *45* biplanes[1] which went into service in 1931 and became some of the most dignified and reliable aircraft in our

---

[1] All eight of these aircraft are generally described as of the *H.P. 42* type. In fact, although structurally they were basically the same, the *H.P. 42 Hannibal* class was fitted for the Empire routes, and the *H.P. 45 Heracles* class for the European service. The *Heracles* itself had "carried well over 100,000 passengers by the outbreak of war. This was nearly a fifth of the total number of passengers carried by Imperial Airways during 16 years of operation" (Peter Masefield in the paper already cited).

Fig. 105. Junkers *G-38*
airliner: 1929 (in service 1931)

Fig. 106. *Gee-Bee 7-11*
Super Sportster racing
monoplane: 1932

Fig. 107. Junkers *Ju 52/3m* airliner:
first built in 1931

Fig. 108. First modern
airliner, the Boeing *247*:
1933

Fig. 109. The Lockheed
Electra airliner: 1934

Fig. 110. Boeing *Model 299* four-engine heavy bomber: 1935

Fig. 111. Junkers *Ju 87A Stuka* dive-bomber: 1935

Fig. 112. Stinson *Reliant*, small passenger transport: 1937

Fig. 113. De Havilland *Albatross*: 1937

Fig. 114. Boeing *314 Clipper* flying-boat: 1938

Fig. 115. First four-engine transport, the Boeing *307 Stratoliner*: 1938 flying history: they carried forty passengers in comparatively quiet comfort at 100 m.p.h. (Pl. XIX). Eight of these aircraft were built, including the well-known *Hannibal* and *Heracles*: they flew more than ten million miles and were in the air for over 100,000 hours without a fatality. But the *H.P. 42/45* was a somewhat backward-looking design, as was another large Imperial Airways machine the Short *Scylla*, with its four engines, forty passengers and cruising speed of just over 100 m.p.h. The Armstrong Whitworth *Atalanta* of 1932 was the first four-engine transport monoplane to go into regular service as a British airliner; like its biplane companions it was particularly useful for the long-haul Empire routes: it carried up to twenty passengers, and cruised at 125 m.p.h.: this, however, fell a good deal short of contemporary Dutch, German and American machines.

Smaller commercial machines in Britain included the De Havilland biplane *D.H. 84 Dragon* of 1932, which grew into the famous *Rapide* of 1934, carrying eight passengers at a cruising speed of 130 m.p.h. for 550 miles.

But it was in the United States that the modern airliner was born, and many of the basic features arrived at in the first years of design and operation are still in force today.[1] The first 'modern' type airliner was the Boeing *247*, which first flew in February of 1933 (Fig. 108); and the second was the Douglas *DC-1* which first flew in July of 1933. In February 1934 there flew for the first time the Lockheed *Electra* which, although not as important as the others, nevertheless had a considerable influence on subsequent aircraft. These three machines, and their immediate progeny, revolutionised the whole sphere of air transport. The dominating features of these first machines were: (*a*) low-wing, all-metal, monocoque monoplane construction; (*b*) two powerful, well-cowled, and supercharged air-cooled radial engines mounted in the wings, allowing level flight on either engine alone in an emergency; (*c*) variable-pitch propellers; (*d*) retractable undercarriage; and (*e*) wing flaps, which allowed of increased wing-loading with a slow stalling speed. The Boeing *247* was the only one of the trio without flaps.

The Boeing *247* was developed out of the Boeing *B-9* bomber of 1931, which in turn developed from the Boeing *Monomail* of 1930, the basic ideas for which owed much to a lecture given in America by Adolph Rohrbach in 1926 (published January 1927), which seems to have originally 'sparked' the Boeing engineers. The *247* carried 10 passengers, was powered by two 550-h.p. Pratt and Whitney Wasp radials, and had a cruising speed of 155 m.p.h. Although the *247* had fixed-pitch propellers, the *247 D* (in service in 1934) had variable-pitch propellers, more powerful engines, and a stage length of 750 miles: it was also the first transport to have wing and tail-unit de-icing (inflatable rubber 'overshoes').

The Douglas Company, alive to possible airline demands, rapidly designed their twelve-passenger *DC-1*, and the one and only machine flew in July of 1933, some six months after the *247*. It was so promising that a

[1] The following information is taken, with kind permission, from articles in *Flight* (April–May 1958) by Mr. Peter W. Brooks, entitled 'Origins of the Modern Airliner'. These articles have now been revised and enlarged, and published under the title *The Modern Airliner* (see Bibliography): this book is already a classic of aeronautical history.

slightly longer version (the *DC-2*), to take fourteen passengers, was immediately put into production, and the first of them flew in May 1934. The *DC-2* was an outstanding machine, with two 710-h.p. Wright Cyclones, a cruising speed of 170 m.p.h. and a stage length of 1350 miles: thus it was faster, and had a longer range than the *247*. The incorporation of flaps (split), allowing a higher wing-loading, and the long enduring multi-spar wing construction, did much to give it a commercial advantage, which led to world-wide sales.

In February of 1934 the Lockheed *Electra* first flew, and started another but smaller line of successful transports (Fig. 109). The *Electra* carried eight passengers, had two 450-h.p. Pratt and Whitney Wasps, and a cruising speed of 160 m.p.h. Its configuration differed from the others in that it had twin fins and rudders in place of their single units. In 1937 appeared the *Electra*'s offspring, the Lockheed *14*, which not only introduced the Fowler-type flap (which increased the wing area), but was the first airliner in service to have two-speed superchargers and constant-speed-cum-feathering propellers.

In December 1935 there had flown for the first time the Douglas *DC-3* (Pl. XIX), by far the most famous and successful airliner in history. The *DC-3* was similar to, but slightly larger than, the *DC-2*, with greater wing-area, span and length, and of course, different engines. It carried twenty-one passengers, was powered by two 1,000–1,200-h.p. Cyclones or Twin-Wasps, had a cruising speed of 170 m.p.h., and a stage length of 500 miles. Known also by the name *Dakota* (or the designation *C-47* among others) the *DC-3* achieved success so rapidly that by 1938 it was carrying the bulk of American domestic air traffic. It came to fly in the service of virtually every nation and airline, and to perform Herculean tasks under the most varying and exacting of conditions in wartime. When production ceased in 1945, some 13,000 of this unrivalled machine and its derivatives had been built.

Soon after the details of the Boeing *247* had been published, other nations began designing similar machines, but without much commercial success in the face of the highly competitive and rapidly expanding American aircraft industry. Inspired by the *247* was the British Bristol *142* (the 'Britain First') of 1935, which was the prototype of the Bristol *Blenheim* bomber; and the German Junkers *Ju 86* and the Heinkel *He 111*, both of which flew in 1935 and were soon developed as bombers. Various other nations constructed machines directly or indirectly inspired by the Boeing *247*.

Two large British airliners merit inclusion here, although few were produced, and the types were not developed. One was the Armstrong Whitworth *Ensign* of 1938, a large four-engine all-metal high-wing monoplane carrying forty passengers. The other was the remarkable and aerodynamically advanced De Havilland *Albatross* of 1937, a four-engine low-wing monoplane of wooden construction seating twenty to thirty passengers.

Although Europe had pioneered the four-engine low-wing transport, the preparations for war, and then war itself, put an end to projects and construction which might well have led to machines which could keep abreast of the U.S.A. It was, therefore, in America that the modern large four-engine airliner for long-haul service saw its beginnings. In June 1938 there flew the one and only Douglas *DC-4E*, to carry some forty passengers: but it was a failure: it had triple fins and rudders, and incidentally, was the first large transport to have a tricycle undercarriage, and the first to have power-boosted controls. The 'classic' *DC-4*, with single fin and rudder, which has given its name to the so-called '*DC-4* generation', was an entirely different design and did not fly until 1942 (see in next section).

The second important aircraft, which was the most influential of the 4-engine transport era to go into airline service, was the Boeing 307 *Stratoliner* (Fig. 115), derived from the Boeing *B-17* bomber, which first flew on the last day of 1938. An improved version, the *307B*, was the first to go into airline service (with Trans-Continental and Western Air) in April of 1940: it flew on long-haul internal American routes, carried thirty-three passengers, and was also the first airliner to go into service with a pressurised cabin.

Of vital importance to the success of transport aircraft in general during this period was the inclusion as standard equipment of such instruments and equipment as the artificial horizon and directional gyro (both of which were being fitted to airliners in the early 1930's), the vertical speed indicator, the barometer scale-setting sensitive altimeter, efficient radio communication, de-icing devices, and—in the mid-1930's—variable pitch propellers. These, and other improvements, allowed of reliable all-weather flying, and created, as Mr. Brooks says, "a complete revolution in operating techniques".

Seaplane development progressed steadily through the years, in what was to become its last successful phase before the near-eclipse of boat and float planes in our time. The most important arrivals in the field were the four-engine flying-boats—dates are prototypes—the Martin *Model 130* and Sikorsky *S–42* (both of 1934), the Boeing *314 Clipper* of 1938 (Fig. 114), and the Short *Empire* boat (Pl. XIX) of 1936; this was an all-metal four-engine monoplane boat (four Bristol Pegasus 815-h.p. radials) with a cruising speed of 165 m.p.h., accommodation for twenty-four passengers and a considerable load of luggage and mail, and a range of 800 miles. In 1937 two of these boats, with extra fuel tanks, made five successful experimental crossings of the north Atlantic. The Short *Sunderland* R.A.F. patrol flying-boat of 1937, which served right through World War II and beyond, was the military adaptation of the *Empire* boat. The successful American Boeing 314 *Clipper* flying-boat of 1938–39, which flew on a regular trans-Atlantic air-route during the Second World War, was of a similar type to the Short boats. In Germany the monoplane was well established, and the Dornier boats, and Blohm and Voss float-planes, performed valuable pioneer services to aviation: these machines were often catapulted from ships and made many mail-carrying flights across the north and south Atlantic between 1937 and 1939.

Float-planes were produced in large numbers during the decade, and were often simple adaptations of land aircraft: they were widely used in naval air services and in countries like Canada—where lakes abound—for communications, air charter, forest patrol and other purposes.

The single-engine light aeroplane, both biplane and monoplane, was produced in great numbers in nearly every country to serve the private airman of business concern, as well as flying clubs and the training branches of the air forces. The D.H. *Moth* remained typical for biplanes, and for monoplanes the American Taylor *Cub*, Model E.2 (the ancestor of the British-built *Auster* of later on) may be singled out; the Taylor *Cub* was a two-seat high-wing machine produced in 1931–32, with a 37-h.p. engine, with a cruising speed of 74 m.p.h., and a range of 210 miles. The light aeroplane was also to become the army observation machine and light ambulance of the Second World War. Some formidable achievements stand to the credit of the light aeroplane during this period, including Miss Amy Johnson's solo flight from England to Australia in 19 days (1930) and James Mollison's from England to Australia (1931), both in De Havilland *Moths*, and Mollison's crossing of the Atlantic—the first solo east–west crossing—in a De Havilland *Puss Moth* monoplane (August 1932), this last a remarkable achievement.

There was naturally a great variety of 'in-between' types of aeroplane being produced for special uses; one such type may be described, the single-engine American Stinson *Reliant* of 1937 (Fig. 112), a high-wing monoplane, descended from the *Vega*, Ryan and other types of the 1920's, with a 285-h.p. radial engine, seats for a pilot and four passengers, a cruising speed of 100 m.p.h. and a range of 300 miles: such aircraft were admirable for general business, charter, or feeder-airline operations.

The coming to power in Germany of Adolf Hitler in 1933, and his obviously aggressive intentions, resulted in other governments preparing a large design programme of aircraft intended solely for warfare. So intense and efficient was this sudden drive, that during the years 1935 and 1936 the prototypes of many of the world's finest fighting aeroplanes were first flying. Amongst the fighters were the Hawker *Hurricane* (1935), Supermarine *Spitfire* (1936) (Pl. XIX), and Messerschmitt *Me 109* (1936): amongst the bombers were the Bristol *Blenheim* (1936)—which grew out of the Bristol *142*—the Vickers-Armstrong *Wellington* (1936), Armstrong Whitworth *Whitley* (1936), the Handley Page *Hampden* (1936), Heinkel *He 111* (1936), and Junkers *Ju 86* (1936): in 1935 came the Junkers *Ju 87 Stuka* dive-bomber (Fig. 111).

The advent of such outstanding military aircraft, and the experience of actual warfare in Abyssinia (1935) and Spain (1938) which became testing grounds for our future enemies, gave a great impetus to aircraft design and production in general, along with subsidiary equipment and instruments. By the time these aircraft had passed into the production stage in the late 1930's, a new epoch of flying and fighting was inaugurated. By 1940 the monoplane single-seat fighter was fully established, and the *Spitfire II* of that year may be taken as a criterion: it was of all-metal stressed-skin construction, had a 1,250-h.p. Rolls-Royce Merlin engine, a top speed of about 350 m.p.h. at 18,000 feet, a cruising speed of 250 m.p.h. and armament of eight ·303 machine-guns in the wings firing outside the airscrew disc. It is interesting to compare this great early monoplane fighter with the last of our biplane fighters, the Gloster *Gladiator*, which first flew a year before the *Spitfire*. The *Gladiator* had a 840-h.p. Bristol Mercury radial motor, a top speed of 250 m.p.h., a service ceiling of 33,000 feet, and six machine-guns (two in the fuselage, four in the wings): it performed excellent service in the early part of the war. Another notable biplane was the Fairey *Swordfish* (first flown in 1934) which continued as a bomber, torpedo-carrier and rocket attacker throughout the war.

The twin-engined *Wellington I*A may be taken to represent the heavy bombers of the day: it had two 1,000-h.p. Bristol Pegasus radials, a cruising speed of about 200–250 m.p.h., a radius of action of some 1,000 miles, a crew of five, defensive armament of six ·303 machine-guns, and a bomb load of 4,500 lb.: the *Wellington* also incorporated the interesting geodetic structure.

Although several four-engine monoplane bombers were produced in the 1930's, such as the French Bordelaise *A.B.20* and the Russian *ANT-6*, the modern conception of the long-range heavy bomber was first crystallised in the American Boeing *Model 299* of 1935 (Fig. 110); again in 1930, a De Havilland *Moth* flew from England to Australia in 19 days (Amy Johnson, solo); in 1931 a Lockheed *Vega* encircled the world, 15,500 miles in 8 days 16 hours (Wiley Post and H. Gatty); in April 1933 two Westland biplanes flew over Mount Everest (the Marquess of Clydesdale and others); also in 1933 24 Italian Savoia-Marchetti *SM-55* flying-boats flew from Italy to Chicago and back (General Balbo and others); still in 1933 (July) the first solo flight round the world, 15,600 miles, was made in a Lockheed *Vega* in 7 days 19 hours (Wiley Post); in 1934 the MacRobertson race to Australia took place (see earlier in this section); in 1937 a Russian *ANT-25* monoplane flew from Moscow to Seattle over the North Pole (V. Chkalov and others); in 1938 a Focke-Wulf *Condor* flew non-stop from Berlin to New York, 3,950 miles, and from New York back to Berlin (Captains Henke and von Moreau).

Civil air transport figures for miles flown (excluding China and Soviet Russia) were 57 million in 1929 and 185 million in 1939.

The speed record for 1939 was 469·142 m.p.h. (German Messerschmitt *Bf 109R*)[1]; there were no height and straight-line distance records for 1939, but the figures for 1938 were 56,046 feet (Italian Caproni *161*) and 7,158 miles (British Vickers *Wellesley*).

---

[1] The commoner usage would be *Me 109*R, but it appears that the use of 'Bf' (Bayerische Flugzeugwerke) is technically correct.

18. *The Second World War: 1939–1945*

THE Second World War witnessed an enormous development in aviation, in aero-engines, and in every type of equipment used in connection with flying, as well as the arrival of the practical jet-propelled aeroplane, the production helicopter, the winged pilotless missile, and the long-range rocket. In addition, the glider took on a new function as troop-carrier, being towed by powered aeroplanes. Although the world's aviation industries were almost wholly turned over to war production, the great variety of aircraft required by the fighting services included many machines which were not built for actual combat; hence the transport and the light-plane in all their forms were developed intensively for troop and other transport, and for training, army spotting and ambulance work; and so were ready by the end of the war to provide highly developed peace-time airliners and smaller private and commercial machines. This transport production—under an Allied agreement—fell almost entirely to the United States.

Military aircraft in the war came to be resolved into a number of basic types, but each took over or exchanged a variety of functions as time went on, and strategic and tactical considerations dictated: thus fighters became light bombers, ground attack and reconnaissance machines; and light bombers became long-range fighters, and so on. The main types of manned aircraft may be classified as heavy bombers, medium bombers, light bombers, fighters, night-fighters, fighter-bombers (including ground attack), transports, liaison aircraft, reconnaissance and photo-reconnaissance aircraft, light observation aircraft, primary trainers, basic trainers, advanced trainers, training gliders, transport gliders, seaplanes (boat, float and amphibian), target towers, and helicopters. In addition there were a number of winged pilotless missiles, as well as long-range wingless rocket missiles, the last being exploited only by the Germans; also small wingless 'artillery' rockets.

Some idea of the immense labour extended during this period on the production of aircraft may be had from the approximate combined total of aeroplanes of all kinds manufactured by Britain and America during the years they were at war: the figure stands at over 380,000.

The versatility of a given aeroplane type may be gauged by such a machine as the De Havilland *Mosquito*—of wooden construction—which was used for bombing, photographic reconnaissance, long-range day fighting, night fighting, and ground attack (Pl. XX). In the following notes the progress achieved in various aircraft types during the war will be suggested by comparing the speeds and other factors at the beginning and end of the period: the figures given can only be approximate.

The single-seat, single-engine fighter had a top speed of some 350 m.p.h.

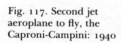

Fig. 116. First jet
aeroplane to fly, the
Heinkel *He 178*: 1939

Fig. 117. Second jet
aeroplane to fly, the
Caproni-Campini: 1940

Fig. 118. Hawker
Hurricane fighter

Fig. 119. Messerschmitt
Me 109 (*Bf 109*) fighter

Fig. 120. Junkers *Ju 88* bomber

Fig. 121. Vickers-Armstrongs *Wellington* bomber

Fig. 122. Boeing *B-29 Superfortress* heavy bomber

Fig. 123. Short *Sunderland* reconnaissance flying-boat

Fig. 124. Messerschmitt *Me 262* jet fighter

PLATE XIX

a The British Handley Page *H.P.42* four-engine airliner, carrying 40 passengers: 1930

b The most famous transport of history, the twin-engine Douglas *DC-3* of 1935; some 13,000 of these machines were built

The British four-engine Short *Empire* class flying-boat *Cambria*: 1937

d The prototype of the British Vickers Supermarine *Spitfire*, a single-engine, single-seat all-metal fighter: 1938

e The first British jet-propelled aeroplane, the experimental Gloster *E.28/39* with a Whittle engine: 1941

PLATE XX

a The twin-engine De Havilland *Mosquito* (Great Britain)

b The four-engine Avro *Lancaster* heavy bomber (Great Britain)

c The single-engine North American *P-51 Mustang* fighter

d The four-engine Boeing *B-17 Flying Fortress* heavy bomber (U.S.A.)

in 1939–40, and in this class were the Supermarine *Spitfire* and the Messerschmitt *Me 109*, with the Hawker *Hurricane* (Fig. 118) a little behind. By the end of the war the fighter could make 450 m.p.h., and this speed was shared by such machines as the later varieties of *Spitfire*, the Hawker *Tempest*, the *Me 109* (Fig. 119), the Focke-Wulf *Fw 190* and the North American *Mustang* with a Rolls-Royce engine (Pl. XX). (The jet fighters, although operational by the end of hostilities, had no appreciable effect on the war effort, and will be noted later.) Ceiling heights for fighters rose to between 35,000 and 40,000 feet, with a rate of climb of up to 5,000 feet a minute. The fighter was soon being made also to bomb and to photograph, and the variety of armament was considerable. The fighter of 1939 with eight ·303 machine-guns had, by 1945, two 20-mm. cannons and four machine-guns; or it carried both guns and rockets; or guns and up to 500 lb. of bombs.

The twin-engine long-range fighter, or night fighter, such as the Bristol *Beaufighter* and Messerschmitt *Me 110* in 1939–40, had a top speed of around 330 m.p.h. and a radius of 650 miles: they, too, became light bombers, ground attack aircraft or photographers, and could carry 750 lb. of bombs or the equivalent in rockets. By 1945 the latest De Havilland *Mosquito* and the Messerschmitt *Me 410* were flying at 400 m.p.h.: if bombing, the *Mosquito* could carry 4,000 lb. of bombs for a radius of action of 750 miles; or unarmed, with cameras, make 1,000 miles and back.

The twin-engine medium bomber at the outset of the war was capable of a speed of 200–270 m.p.h., and a radius of up to 1,000 miles with a bomb load of 1,000–1,500 lb. The Bristol *Blenheim* and Bristol *Beaufort* were in this class, with the Junkers *Ju 88* half-way towards what one might call then the 'medium heavy' (Fig. 120), with a speed and radius comparable with the first two, but with a larger bomb-load. The typical medium heavy bomber that bridged the peace-war period was the twin-engine Armstrong-Whitworth *Whitley*, with a speed of 190–220 m.p.h., a normal bomb-load of 3,500 lb. and a radius of 1,000 miles. The classic heavy bombers of the early war years were the Heinkel *He 111* (Pl. XX) and Vickers-Armstrong *Wellington* (Fig. 121): their performances were similar, with speed of 200–250 m.p.h., bomb load of 4,500 lb. and radius of up to 1,250 miles, the *Wellington* having the greater range. Each machine had a crew of five with defensive armament of some six machine-guns. At the end of the war the latest North American *B–25 Mitchell* was typical of the medium bomber class, and could carry 2,000 lb. of bombs at above 300 m.p.h. over a 500 mile radius; whereas the final light bomber version of the *Mosquito*—unarmed—could carry a bomb-load of 4,000 lb. at 400 m.p.h. for 750 miles and return. The heavier medium bomber had disappeared in favour of the four-engine heavy bomber.

The concept of the four-engine night bomber had been maturing long before the war, both in Britain and the U.S.A., and in 1939 there flew for the first time the Short *Stirling*, the first—but not entirely successful—heavy bomber of this war: it went into service in 1940, and into action in 1941. Also first flown in 1939, it was also in 1941 that the successful Handley Page *Halifax* went into action, followed by the Avro *Lancaster* in 1942. These two machines were designed for night bombing without escort, and the *Lancaster* became, perhaps, the 'classic' in this field: with a crew of seven, and four

1,280-h.p. Rolls-Royce Merlins, this famous machine could c
load of 12,750 lb. at about 160 m.p.h. for 1,200 miles and retu.
22,000 lb. for shorter distances: defensive armament was ten ma
and the ceiling was 20,000 feet. The 'classic' four-engine day bom
American Boeing *B-17E Flying Fortress* (Pl. XX) which, although ⱨ
flown on other duties by the R.A.F., came into its own in the America.
daylight raids of 1942; it had a crew of six to ten, four 1,200-h.p. Wɪ ̯nt
Cyclone engines, a speed of 225–300 m.p.h., a ceiling of 35,000 feet and a
bomb-load of 6,000 lb. for long sorties, 12,800 for medium raids, and 20,800
for very short trips, with a normal radius of some 2,500 miles: defensive
armament was up to thirteen machine-guns. The *B-17* was followed by the
B-29 Superfortress (Fig. 122) which first saw action in 1944, in the Far East: it
dropped the first atomic bombs on Japan in 1945[1]; it had a speed of
300–350 m.p.h. and a radius of over 2,000 miles, with a maximum
bomb-load of 20,000 lb. The Germans did not need long-range heavy
bombers until it was too late to produce them in quantity, but they had a
number of large aircraft under development, such as the *Me 264* and *He 177*,
which, if they had been properly exploited, could have been formidable
attackers. The same was true of Russia and Japan, the former building one
large bomber, the *TB-7*, and the latter the Nakajima G5N (*Liz 2*).

A large variety of other military aircraft were developed during the war
for use both from land bases and from aircraft carriers, the only type which
remained relatively neglected being the seaplane. The only large flying-boat
in full service by the British was the four-engine Short *Sunderland* which did
excellent reconnaissance work, with its radius of 1,500 miles and speed of
150–210 m.p.h. (Fig. 123). Other nations had comparable flying-boats, and
the Americans in particular an outstanding medium-sized amphibian
flying-boat, the Consolidated PBY *Catalina*, with two engines and a radius of
1,800 miles. Limited use was made of small float-planes for reconnaissance.

The glider experienced a surprising revival, and many large troop-
transport types were produced, and played an important part in the
invasion of Europe: they were towed by bombers or large transport aircraft.
Typical of these were the British Airspeed *Horsa* which carried two pilots
and 15–20 fully-armed troops (or their equivalent in freight), and the
American Waco *CG-4A*, which took fifteen troops. An interesting transport
glider which was experimented with by the Germans—before appearing in a
six-engine version—was the huge Messerschmitt *Me 321 Gigant* (Giant) which
could carry up to 130 armed troops: it was towed by three *Me 110*'s.

The helicopter, comparatively neglected since the success of the Focke-
Achgelis, came rapidly to a mature, fully controllable and practical form in
the U.S.A., and soon became an indispensable type of aircraft.[2] In Germany,
as noted before, the *Fa 223* had flown in 1940 and had then been built in
limited numbers: it was thus the first production helicopter of history. But
the subsequent and sudden development of the mature helicopter—which

---

[1] The first atomic fission bomb to be used against the enemy was dropped on Hiroshima on
August 6th 1945; the second (and last) on Nagasaki on August 9th 1945.
[2] A curious war-time application of the rotating-wing principle was the *Fa 330* single-seat rotor
kite, used experimentally by German submarines for observation.

put an end to the *Autogiro* family—was due largely to the work of the Russian-born American Igor Sikorsky, who had abandoned his concern with multi-engine aeroplanes and returned to the subject of his earliest enthusiasm, the rotating-wing aircraft, first inspired by Da Vinci.

From the first, Sikorsky concentrated on the single-rotor configuration for his helicopters—with the small anti-torque rotor at the tail—and in 1939 the first of his machines, the *VS-300*, was completed and tested tethered: it had full cyclic-pitch control and a 75-h.p. engine, but was not successful.[1] In 1940, the cyclic-pitch control was temporarily abandoned, and two small horizontal rotors on outriggers were provided for fore-and-aft control (including forward motion) and lateral control: this machine made its first successful free flight on May 13th 1940; in May 1941, with a 90-h.p. engine, it set up a world's endurance record for helicopters of 1 hour 32 minutes and 26 seconds. Then in June 1941, the *VS-300* was again improved by providing cyclic-pitch lateral control and a single horizontal rotor at the tail for fore-and-aft control. Finally, in December 1941, full cyclic-pitch control with the single main rotor was achieved successfully. The small anti-torque rotor had been retained throughout. In 1942 the *VS-300* proved itself the first fully practical and successful single rotor configuration machine (Pl. XXI). In the same year was produced the *XR-4* with a 175-h.p. engine, as well as the production version (the *R-4B*) which went into service with the U.S. Army. The 'classic' Sikorsky helicopter, the *R-5* (*S-51*) went into service in 1946: it had a 450-h.p. engine, a cruising speed of 85 m.p.h., endurance of 3 hours, and carried a pilot and three passengers. It distinguished itself particularly in the Korean war, as well as in a variety of civil and military roles before and after.

Thus it was 1942 that can be marked as the year in which the helicopter 'arrived' as a fully practical flying machine. Thereafter it developed so rapidly—with new constructors continuously entering the field—that within a decade there were to be some thirty types flying. In 1943 appeared the first helicopter with a jet-propelled rotor, the Austrian Doblhoff *No. 1*, in which compressed air and petrol vapour were fed through the rotor blades and burnt in combustion chambers at the tips, where it was expelled through nozzles; this system obviated the use of the anti-torque rail rotor.

Perhaps it should be emphasised here that the helicopter proper—as the word is used today—implies a machine which uses its powered rotor(s) for vertical take-off and landing, hovering stationary in the air, and progressing through the air: it should also be capable of flying backwards and sideways, as well as forwards. The *Autogiros*, on the other hand, had freely revolving rotors which only supported the aircraft in flight, and allowed of vertical descent (until near the ground when the machine had to move forward as well) and a steep take-off, all propulsion being supplied by a conventional tractor propeller.

The obsolescent biplane not only survived the impact of war, but in a limited way performed valuable services, especially in naval warfare, where

[1] It has been said that this first version of the *VS-300* made a single free flight in 1939, but there is some doubt about this claim. In any case, the machine in this form was not successful and the point is academic.

such machines as the Fairey *Swordfish* and *Albacore* acted as torpedo-droppers and maids-of-all-work. The excellent Gloster *Gladiator* also fought manfully in Norway, Malta and North Africa. In training, too, the biplane remained in service in all countries, and a number of pre-war biplanes flew throughout the war on communications and other duties.

The most important aeronautical development of the Second World War—although it did not materially affect the conflict—was the inauguration of practical jet propulsion. After the Heinkel *He 178* first flew in 1939, the next development—short-lived and abortive—came in Italy where the second jet, the Caproni-Campini monoplane, first flew in 1940 with limited success: this aircraft employed a piston engine to operate a ducted fan, acting as an air compressor: fuel was injected into the resulting air stream, burnt continuously, and expanded through the rear nozzle: it was therefore a jet, but not a turbojet machine. It had a speed of some 200–300 m.p.h., and was abandoned after a few flights in 1940 and 1941 (Fig. 117).

Meanwhile, in Germany and Britain, research and development were pressed ahead, and Frank Whittle (now Air Commodore Sir Frank Whittle) had his first airborne success in 1941 when on May 15th the Gloster *E.28/39*, driven by a Whittle centrifugal flow turbojet engine, made its first flight (Pl. XIX). The second aircraft powered by a Whittle engine—two of them—was the only Allied aircraft to see operational service in the war, the Gloster *Meteor*, which was a single-seat twin-jet fighter with a maximum speed of 480 m.p.h. and a ceiling of 40,000 feet. The *Meteor* first flew in 1943 and was in action against German flying-bombs in August 1944, before going overseas with the Allied invasion forces.

But it was in Germany, with her growingly desperate need for fighters to attack the mass Allied raids, that were produced the most spectacular and varied war-time jet aeroplanes. Outstanding was the twin-jet Messerschmitt *Me 262* (Fig. 124), which first flew in 1942. However, it was not until 1944 that the *Me 262* was in production and service as a fighter, and later—perhaps misguidedly and for political reasons—as a light bomber. It was powered by two axial-flow Jumo engines, had a maximum speed of 525 m.p.h. (as against the *Meteor's* 480 m.p.h.) and a service ceiling of 40,000 feet, and was in every way a remarkable aircraft. It was the world's first operational jet-propelled combat aeroplane. Thus the two basic classes of turbojet engine—centrifugal and axial flow—were in service from the earliest days.

In Britain, the prototype De Havilland *D.H. 100* (later to be named the *Vampire*) had flown on September 20th 1943, with a centrifugal-flow gas turbine designed by Major F.B. Halford.

It is curious to find that the United States took little interest in jet propulsion before 1941,[1] although her excellent nickel alloys had helped to give longer life to Whittle's jet engines. In October 1941 a Whittle engine was flown to U.S.A., and by 1942 a number of American copies had been built. Two American-built Whittle *W.2B* engines powered the Bell *XP-59A*

---

[1] This was all the more curious in view of the American development of the turbo-supercharger, which incorporated an exhaust-driven turbine, a device which might have led the designers to the turbojet.

Fig. 125. Messerschmitt
Me 163 Komet rocket
fighter

Fig. 126. First American
jet aeroplane, the Bell
*XP-59*A fighter: 1942

Fig. 127. Douglas *DC-4*
Skymaster airliner: 1942

Fig. 128. Lockheed
Constellation airliner: 1943

Airacomet, the first American jet, first flown in October 1942 (Fig. 126). In 1943 a De Havilland centrifugal-flow engine was also despatched to the Americans, and fitted with an original D. H. engine, the prototype of the successful and shapely Lockheed *XP-80*, later to become the *Shooting Star*, first flew: this aircraft did not see combat until the Korean War. So it was that the entire turbojet engine industry of the United States grew directly from the acquisition of two British engines.

Meanwhile in Germany there appeared in some quantity the little so-called 'Volksjäger' jet fighter—the Heinkel *He 162 Salamander*—which first flew operationally in 1945, and could reach 520 m.p.h.; and also the prototype of the world's first heavy jet bomber, the Junkers *Ju 287*, with swept-forward wings, four engines and auxiliary take-off rockets, which had a maximum speed of over 500 m.p.h. with a bomb-load of 8,800 lb. Even more remarkable was the production by the Germans of the world's first practical rocket-powered aeroplane, the Messerschmitt *Me 163 Komet* fighter (Fig. 125), which first flew in action against Allied bombers in 1944: it had swept-back wings, a Walter liquid-fuel rocket motor, and a speed of 590 m.p.h. and could climb to 30,000 feet in 2½ minutes; but the duration (under power) was only 8–10 minutes—which could be extended by intermittent gliding—and it was often towed by another aircraft to the scene before release. Fortunately for the Allies, all these developments of the jet aircraft arrived on the scene too late, and in too small quantities, to influence the course of the war: great historical credit is here due to Germany.

German pioneering in the jet-propulsion field was of the highest order, and the enemy was also the first to utilise the swept-back and swept-forward wing forms for high-speed aircraft. What is more, they did not stop at conventional aircraft. In 1944 they launched against England the first of some 8,500 so-called 'V-1 Flying Bombs' (the *FZG-76*), which were in effect small aeroplanes of 17½ feet span, with a 1,870-lb. war-head, a pulse-duct jet motor which gave them a speed of 390–410 m.p.h. and a range of 150 miles, after being power-launched at 200 m.p.h. from a ramp, and kept gyroscopically on a predetermined course. A few of the flying bombs were carried and launched from aircraft after the ground launching sites were overrun by the Allied invasion forces. In all, some 20,000 flying bombs were launched against the Allies (Pl. XXI).

Analogous to the flying bomb, but piloted—as were one or two of the German bombs for test purposes—was the rocket-propelled Japanese suicide machine, the *Oka 11*, which was a winged bomb released from a parent aircraft and flown direct at its target by the pilot. These, along with full-size machines flown in the so-called *Kamikaze* suicide attacks by Japanese pilots, sank a number of American ships in the Pacific (1944–45).

Another remarkable German machine under test at the end of the war was the single-seat Bachem *Ba 349-A Natter* (Viper): this consisted of a multi-rocket-filled nose, the pilot's section, and the rocket-motor section: it was equipped with wings and a simple control system, and was launched vertically. It was designed to climb at the speed of over 35,000 feet per minute: the pilot was to level off amongst a bomber formation, fire the rockets in one salvo and then intentionally dismember his aircraft, his own section and the rocket-motor descending on its own parachute, the nose being jettisoned as expendable. After unpiloted launchings, one piloted *Natter* was launched, but the machine crashed and was destroyed (1945).

Also in 1944 arrived an even more ambitious weapon, the second of the 'Vergeltungswaffen' (Revenge weapons—hence 'V' weapons) in the A-4 liquid-fuel rocket colloquially called the 'V-2'. This remarkable weapon marked the most decisive step taken towards the conquest of space. It was the publication of 1919 of Dr. R. H. Goddard's *A Method of Reaching Extreme Altitudes* which had marked the birth of modern rocketry, and it was the 'flying' in 1926 of Goddard's first liquid-fuel rocket which may be said to have actually "ushered in" the rocket era.

However, it was the first successful 'flight' of the German A-4 (V-2) rocket-bomb at Peenemünde on October 3rd 1942 that provided the pivotal achievement in practical rocketry, and was to confront the world for the first time with the reality of space travel. For the A-4, during its normal performance, reached a height of 60 miles, and attained an upward airspeed of some 3,600 m.p.h. It weighed about 12½ tons at take-off—including a 2,000-lb. war head—and landed at about 2,000 m.p.h. anywhere up to 220 miles from the firing point after 'flying' for 5 minutes (Pl. XXI). A stub-winged version (the A-7) was under development at the war's end as a test missile for a projected winged vehicle of far greater range.

In addition to these two ingenious weapons, the Germans were making great strides with winged rocket missiles, one of which, the Henschel *Hs 293* glider-rocket-bomb which was launched from an aircraft, was in action in small numbers. Most of the missiles, however, were designed as anti-aircraft weapons, and only one or two had already been successfully test flown by the time Germany surrendered. All modern developments in guided missiles and rockets derive direct from these German inventions; and German personnel, both in the U.S.A. and Russia, have been prominent in producing them.

With the far-reaching development of combat aircraft, and the complicated equipment necessary for their flying and communicating, went a comparable development of the civil transport, especially by the United States. Light and medium transports were following a steady progress, but the backbone of Allied transport aircraft throughout the war remained the twin-engine Douglas *Dakota* (*DC-3*), paralleled in Germany by the three-engine Junkers *Ju 52*. It was in the sphere of the large four-engine transport that the particularly significant development took place, and the U.S.A. produced aircraft which were to set the whole style of modern heavy transports, and virtually to monopolise the traffic on the world's long-haul airlines for a decade after the war, making such flights as the Atlantic crossing a mere routine performance. Most important of the new four-engined airliners was the Douglas *DC-4 Skymaster* (military *C-54*), which set the standard for four-engine transports for a generation (Fig. 127). The *DC-4* first flew in February 1942, and went into military transport service during 1943: it was smaller than its predecessor with the confusingly similar designation noted before, had a span of 117½ feet, a single fin and rudder, and four 1,350-h.p. Pratt and Whitney radial engines; it carried a crew of six and forty-two passengers at a cruising speed of some 200 m.p.h. for stage lengths of over 1,500 miles. Oddly enough no *DC-4*'s were pressurised. The *DC-4* was an immediate success and provided the backbone of Allied long-haul transport, as it did of civil airlines the world over after the war's end.

The *DC-6* was a 'stretched' and pressurised development of the *DC-4*, with reversing propellers for ground braking, which first flew in February 1946, and went into airline service in April 1947.

Second in importance was the Lockheed *049 Constellation* (*C-69*) (Fig. 128), one of the most graceful aircraft ever to fly, with its sinuous fuselage and triple tail-unit: it first flew in January 1943, went into partial military service in April 1944, and full service in April 1945. The *Constellation* was pressurised, had four 2,200-h.p. radial engines, and carried fifty-one passengers at a cruising speed of 280 m.p.h. for stage lengths of over 2,000 miles: like the *DC-4E*, the *Constellation* had reversing propellers. Both machines were first employed as military transports. After the war, being well-suited to fuselage 'stretching' and other developments, they had a numerous progeny which were consistently successful.

Another large airliner which should be mentioned here was the bulbous Boeing *Stratocruiser*, which was built in small numbers as a civil transport and in considerable quantity as a military transport (*C-97*): it was developed out of the *B-29* and *B-50 Superfortress* bombers; first flew in November 1944; and went into military service in 1945.

By the time that the post-war commercial airlines had got into their stride, and then with constant improvement of airframes and engines, it can well be realised what formidable—and indeed unrivalled—transports these machines were to prove.

We can barely mention the vast and intricate development of instruments of all kinds that were to make aircraft more effective as weapons of war, and safer for the crews who operated them, including navigational and locating aids such as radar, and the systems for safe-take-off and landing under all weather conditions. Almost all these devices were later to be successfully applied to peace-time aircraft, making them more secure against hazard and more reliable in operation.

In the field of aero-engines the piston engine reached its near-final state, and various practical jet power-plants were born. The large liquid-cooled Vee engine may be exemplified by two Rolls-Royce engines: at the beginning of the war the 12-cylinder Merlin X had a maximum power output of 1,030 h.p.; this was later raised to 1,650 h.p. in the Merlin 63, and to 2,035 h.p. in the Griffon 65. For the air-cooled radial engine, two 14-cylinder Bristol engines may be taken as typical, one at either end of the war: the Hercules III, which gave 1,380 h.p,; and the Centaurus X, which had an output of 2,520 h.p. These engines were paralleled in the United States and Germany, with the former making comparatively little use of the Vee liquid-cooled types, and the latter extensive use of both radials and Vee motors. In general it may be said that the advantage of the in-line engine lay in its small frontal area—with consequent saving in drag—and the radial in its better power–weight ratio and the absence of the vulnerable cooling liquid.

PLATE XXI

a The first man-carrying helicopter to make a free vertical flight: 1907 (Cornu, of France)

b The first practical helicopter, the Focke-Achgelis *FW-61*: 1936 (Germany)

c The first practical single-rotor helicopter, the Sikorsky *VS-300*: 1941–42 (U.S.A.)

f The German *A-4* (so-called V-2) rocket bomb, which became the prototype vehicle on which space travel has been based: first in action, 1944

d The Sperry experimental guided missile: 1914–18 (U.S.A.)

e The so-called 'V-1 Flying Bomb' (*FZG-76*): first in action 1944 (Germany)

15*

PLATE XXII

a Wing-warping in action: a British-built Wright glider of 1909, showing the Wrights' system, invented in 1899

b The first use of ailerons: Esnault-Pelterie's glider: 1904

c Cody's kite-glider: 1905

d Blériot *No. IV* biplane: 1906

e Santos-Dumont *14-bis* biplane: 1906

f Blériot *No. VI* tandem-wing *Libellule*: 1907 (showing the pivoting wing-tip elevons)

g Cody *British Army Aeroplane No. 1*: 1908

h Blériot *No. VIII-bis* mono-plane: 1908

i A.E.A. (Curtiss) *June Bug* biplane: 1908

j Henri Farman's modified Voisin biplane: 1908

k Levavasseurs *Antoinette IV*: 1909

l Curtiss Reims biplane: 1909

m *Henry Farman III* biplane: 1909

The turbojet engine, even in the short period of its war-time development, was seen in both axial and centrifugal types; the pulse-duct jet was used on the 'Flying Bomb'; and the liquid-fuel rocket engine powered the *Me 163*, the A-4 rocket, and some of the experimental guided missiles.

The smaller piston engines, like the larger, improved in power and refinement, and the horizontally-opposed flat air-cooled engine emerged as the dominant type. Engines of all classes benefited not only from mechanical research and development but from the advances made in metallurgy. The turbojet and rocket engines in particular owed an especial debt to metallurgy, as they depend more than the piston on metals which can stand up to the very high temperatures involved.

Finally, a word about the men who flew these war-time aeroplanes. For the second time in a generation the flying-machine was sent to war, and this time it became the final and decisive weapon. Again it demanded of its crews exceptional human qualities, and became a vehicle in which exhilaration, endurance, bravery and heroism were called out in every form and degree. "However we may try to analyse it", wrote Lord David Cecil, "their superhuman heroism is an elemental attitude of human nature; and, as such, must always evade analysis. It is better to accept it as a fact of existence, happily not so infrequent as might be expected; and to offer it in humility, our tribute of admiration."

Quotations on Flying

Quotations on Flying

If the heavens then be penetrable, and no lets, it were not amiss to make wings and fly up; and some new-fangled wits, methinks, should some time or other find out.

ROBERT BURTON (1621)

The judge, . . . when it was alleged that the prisoner could fly, remarked that there was no law against flying.

THE DICTIONARY OF NATIONAL BIOGRAPHY
(on Jane Wenham, accused of witchcraft in 1712)

The time will come, when thou shalt lift thine eyes
To watch a long-drawn battle in the skies,
While aged peasants, too amazed for words,
Stare at the flying fleets of wond'rous birds.
England, so long the mistress of the sea,
Where winds and waves confess her sovereignty,
Her ancient triumphs yet on high shall bear,
And reign, the sovereign of the conquered air.

Translated from Gray's *Luna Habitabilis* (1737)

'If men were all virtuous', returned the artist, 'I should with great alacrity teach them all to fly. But what would be the security of the good, if the bad could at pleasure invade them from the sky? Against an army sailing through the clouds neither walls, nor mountains, nor seas, could afford any security. A flight of northern savages might hover in the wind, and light at once with irresistible violence upon the capital of a fruitful region that was rolling under them.'

SAMUEL JOHNSON (1759)

I would . . . make it death for a man to be convicted of flying, the moment he could be caught. . . . Historians would load my memory with reproaches of phlegm, and stupidity, and oppression; but in the mean time the world would go on quietly, and if it enjoyed less liberty, would at least be more secure.

WILLIAM COWPER
(in a letter to the Rev. W. Unwin)

221

The whole problem is confined within these limits, viz.—To make a surface support a given weight by the application of power to the resistance of air.

SIR GEORGE CAYLEY (1809)

I may be expediting the attainment of an object that will in time be found of great importance to mankind; so much so, that a new era in society will commence from the moment that aerial navigation is familiarly realised. . . . I feel perfectly confident, however, that this noble art will soon be brought home to man's convenience, and that we shall be able to transport ourselves and families, and their goods and chattels, more securely by air than by water, and with a velocity of from 20 to 100 miles per hour.

SIR GEORGE CAYLEY (1809)

An uninterrupted navigable ocean, that comes to the threshold of every man's door, ought not to be neglected as a source of human gratification and advantage.

SIR GEORGE CAYLEY (1816)

I suppose we shall soon travel by air-vessels; make air instead of sea-voyages; and at length find our way to the moon, in spite of the want of atmosphere.

LORD BYRON (1822)

For I dipt into the future, far as human eye could see,
Saw the Vision of the world, and all the wonder that would be;
Saw the heavens fill with commerce, argosies of magic sails,
Pilots of the purple twilight, dropping down with costly bales;
Heard the heavens fill with shouting, and there rain'd a ghastly dew
From the nations' air-navies grappling in the central blue;
Far along the world-wide whisper of the south-wind rushing warm,
With the standards of the peoples plunging thro' the thunder-storm;
Till the war-drum throbb'd no longer, and the battle-flags were furl'd
In the Parliament of man the Federation of the World.

LORD TENNYSON (1842)

'Well, gentlemen, do you believe in the possibility of aerial locomotion by machines heavier than air?' . . . 'You ask yourselves doubtless if this apparatus, so marvellously adapted for aerial locomotion, is susceptible of receiving greater speed. It is not worth while to conquer space if we cannot devour it. I wanted the air to be a solid support to me, and it is. I saw that to struggle against the wind I must be stronger than the wind, and I am. I had no need of sails to drive me, nor oars nor wheels to push me, nor rails to give me a faster road. Air is what I wanted, that was all. Air surrounds me as water surrounds the submarine boat, and in it my propellers act like the screws of a steamer. That is how I solved the problem of aviation. That is what a balloon will never do, nor will any machine that is lighter than air.'

JULES VERNE (1886)

But we must admit the possibility that continued investigation and experience will bring us ever nearer to that solemn moment, when the first man will rise from earth by means of wings, if only for a few seconds, and marks that historical moment which heralds the inauguration of a new era in our civilization.

. . . . .

It must not remain our desire only to acquire the art of the bird; nay, it is our duty not to rest until we have attained to a perfect scientific conception of the problem of flight.

OTTO LILIENTHAL (1891)

It seems, therefore, not unreasonable to entertain the hope that man may eventually achieve a mechanical success (if not a commercial one) in the attempt to compass a mode of transportation which so strongly appeals to the imagination, and that it may result in greater speeds than pertain to our present journeyings.

OCTAVE CHANUTE (1893)

The alighting upon the ground is likely to prove the most difficult and dangerous of the problems to be solved. It has been much too little considered by would be inventors and patentees of flying machines, and it may long prove a bar to the success of such apparatus, for nothing but direct experiment, and that of a perilous kind, will determine how this operation can be successfully performed.

OCTAVE CHANUTE (1893)

Upon the whole, the writer is glad to believe that when man succeeds in flying through the air the ultimate effect will be to diminish greatly the frequency of wars and to substitute some more rational methods of settling international misunderstandings. This may come to pass not only because of the additional horrors which will result in battle, but because no part of the field will be safe, no matter how distant from the actual scene of conflict . . . a chance explosive dropped from a flying machine may destroy the chiefs, disorganize the plans, and bring confusion to the stronger or more skillfully led side.

. . . . .

So may it be; let us hope that the advent of a successful flying machine, now only dimly foreseen and nevertheless thought to be possible, will bring nothing but good into the world; that it shall abridge distance, make all parts of the globe accessible, bring men into closer relation with each other, advance civilisation, and hasten the promised era in which there shall be nothing but peace and good-will among all men.

OCTAVE CHANUTE (1894)

223

During a gliding flight taken from a great height this was the cause of my coming into a position with my arms outstretched, in which the centre of gravity lay too much to the back; at the same time I was unable—owing to fatigue—to draw the upper part of my body again towards the front. As I was then sailing at the height of about 65 feet with a velocity of about 35 miles per hour, the apparatus, overloaded in the rear, rose more and more, and finally shot, by means of its vis viva, *vertically upwards. I gripped tight hold, seeing nothing but the blue sky and little white clouds above me, and so awaited the moment when the apparatus would capsize backwards, possibly ending my sailing attempts forever. Suddenly, however, the apparatus stopped in its ascent, and, going backward again in a downward direction, described a short circle and steered with the rear part again upwards, owing to the horizontal tail which had an upward slant; then the machine turned bottom upwards and rushed with me vertically towards the earth from a height of about 65 feet. With my senses quite clear, my arms and my head forward, still holding the apparatus firmly with my hands, I fell towards the greensward; a shock, a crash, and I lay with the apparatus on the ground.*

OTTO LILIENTHAL (1895)
(the first account in history of an aircraft crash by the pilot)

"The object of experimenting with soaring machines is to enable one to have practice in starting and alighting, and controlling a machine in the air. . . . They are excellent schooling machines, and that is all they are meant to be, until power, in the shape of an engine working a screw propeller, or an engine working wings to drive the machine forward is added; then a person who is used to sailing down a hill with a simple soaring machine will be able to fly with comparative safety."

PERCY PILCHER (1897)

I have not the smallest molecule of faith in aerial navigation other than ballooning.

LORD KELVIN (1896)

I believe that simple flight at least is possible to man and that the experiments and investigations of a large number of independent workers will result in the accumulation of information and knowledge and skill which will finally lead to accomplished flight.

WILBUR WRIGHT (1899)

What is chiefly needed is skill rather than machinery.

WILBUR WRIGHT (1900)

There are only two ways of learning to ride a fractious horse: one is to get on him and learn by actual practice how each motion and trick may be best met; the other is to sit on a fence and watch the beast awhile, and then retire to the house and at leisure figure out the best way of overcoming his jumps and kicks. The latter system is the safer, but the former, on the whole, turns out the larger proportion of good riders. It is very much the same in learning to ride a flying machine; if you are looking for perfect safety you will do well to sit on a fence and watch the birds, but if you really wish to learn you must mount a machine and become acquainted with its tricks by actual trial.

WILBUR WRIGHT (1901)

Success four flights thursday morning all against twenty one mile wind started from Level with engine power alone average speed through air thirty one miles longest 57 seconds inform Press home Christmas. Orevelle Wright.[1]

ORVILLE WRIGHT
([1] THE TELEGRAM AS RECEIVED BY HIS FATHER, DATED DECEMBER 17th 1903: through errors in transmission '57' appeared for '59' and 'Orevelle' for 'Orville')

When we arose on the morning of the 17th, the puddles of water, which had been standing about camp since the recent rains, were covered with ice. The wind had a velocity of 22 to 27 m.p.h. We thought it would die down before long, but when 10 o'clock arrived, and the wind was as brisk as ever, we decided that we had better get the machine out. . . . Wilbur having used his turn in the unsuccessful attempt on the 14th, the right to the first trial belonged to me. Wilbur ran at the side, holding the wings to balance it on the track. The machine, facing a 27-mile wind, started very slowly. Wilbur was able to stay with it until it lifted from the track after a forty-foot run.

The course of the flight up and down was exceedingly erratic. The control of the front rudder was difficult. As a result, the machine would rise suddenly to about ten feet, and then as suddenly dart for the ground. A sudden dart when a little over 120 feet from the point at which it rose into the air, ended the flight.

This flight lasted only twelve seconds, but it was nevertheless the first in the history of the world in which a machine carrying a man had raised itself by its own power into the air in full flight, had sailed forward without reduction of speed, and had finally landed at a point as high as that from which it started.

ORVILLE WRIGHT (1903)

It is not extravagant to say that the 17th December 1903, when the Wright brothers made the first free flight through the air in a power-driven machine, marks the beginning of a new era in the history of the world.

SIR WALTER RALEIGH (1922)

The demonstration that no combination of known substances, known form of machinery, and known forms of force can be united in a practicable machine by which men shall fly seems to the writer as complete as it is possible for the demonstration of any physical fact to be.

SIMON NEWCOMB (1906)

I know of only one bird—the parrot—that talks; and it can't fly very high.

WILBUR WRIGHT
(in declining to make a speech in 1908)

Pendant une dizaine de minutes, je suis resté seul, isolé, perdu au milieu de la mer écumeuse, ne voyant aucun point à l'horizon, ne percevant aucun bateau.

LOUIS BLÉRIOT
(on his cross-Channel flight, July 25th 1909)

Blériot did not get up in any blare of trumpets. In the cold, grey dawn of the morning, before the sun had warmed up things, before it had dissipated the dew-drops, he was in our country. It marks a new era in the world.

LIEUTENANT SHACKLETON
(in the *Daily Mail*, 1909)

It is vital to the safety of the nation, that Britain should become a nation of aviators. In matters of defence, we live on an island no longer. The day that Blériot flew the Channel marked the end of our insular safety, and the beginning of the time when Britain must seek another form of defence beside its ships.

SIR ALAN COBHAM

The engine is the heart of an aeroplane, but the pilot is its soul.

SIR WALTER RALEIGH

The ground was very rough and hard, and as we tore along, at an increasing pace that was very soon greater than any motor I had yet been in, I expected to be jerked and jolted. But the motion was wonderfully smooth—smoother yet—and then—! Suddenly there had come into it a new, indescribable quality—a lift—a lightness—a life! Very many there are now who know that feeling: that glorious, gliding sense that the sea-bird has known this million years, and which man so long and so vainly envied it, and which, even now, familiarity can never rob of its charm. But picture, if you can, what it meant for the first time; when all the world of Aviation was young and fresh and untried; when to rise at all was a glorious adventure, and to find oneself flying swiftly in the air, the too-good-to-be-true realisation of a life-long dream. You wonderful aerial record breakers of today and of the years to come, whose exploits I may only marvel at and envy, I have experienced something that can never be yours and can never be taken away from me—the rapture, the glory and the glamour of 'the very beginning'.

GERTRUDE BACON
(writing of her flight with R. Sommer in August 1909)

The cavalry, in particular, were not friendly to the aeroplane, which, it was believed, would frighten the horses.

SIR WALTER RALEIGH
(writing of the year 1910)

I am bound to confess that my imagination supplied me at every moment with the most realistic anticipations of a crash, . . . However, we descended in due course with perfect safety. I have no compunction in relating the apprehensions which surrounded my first taste of the glorious sensations of flying. I am sure that when the secrets of all hearts are revealed, they will be found to have been shared by a good many others. . . . Having been thoroughly bitten, I continued to fly on every possible occasion when my other duties permitted.

WINSTON S. CHURCHILL
(writing of 1912)

This morning at 3:15, Wilbur passed away, aged 45 years, 1 month and 14 days. A short life full of consequences. An unfailing intellect, imperturbable temper, great self-reliance and as great modesty, seeing the right clearly, pursuing it steadily, he lived and died.

BISHOP MILTON WRIGHT
(in his diary, dated May 30th 1912)

First Europe, and then the globe, will be linked by flight, and nations so knit together that they will grow to be next-door neighbours. This conquest of the air will prove, ultimately, to be man's greatest and most glorious triumph. What railways have done for nations, airways will do for the world.

CLAUDE GRAHAME-WHITE and HARRY HARPER (1914)

When my brother and I built and flew the first man-carrying machine, we thought that we were introducing into the world an invention which would make further wars practically impossible.

ORVILLE WRIGHT (1917)

In 1492 Christopher Columbus sailed across the Atlantic and discovered America. I cannot help feeling that this afternoon we are to some extent in contact with that event, and that when we welcome our guests, the heroes of today, who have come back from the other side, come to us from America in something less than 16 hours—we are in the presence of another event of something like the same order as that stupendous event which revealed to Europe and Asia the boundless glories and possibilities of the new world across the Atlantic Ocean.

WINSTON S. CHURCHILL
(speaking at a luncheon in 1919 to honour Alcock and Brown)

The air service still flourishes; its health depends on a secret elixir of immortality, which enables a body to repair its severest losses. The name of this elixir is tradition, and the greatest of all the achievements of the air service is that in a very few years, under the hammer of war, it has fashioned and welded its tradition, and has made it sure. Critics who speak of what they have not felt and do not know have sometimes blamed the air service because, being young, it has not the decorum of age. The Latin poet said that it is decorous to die for one's country; in that decorum the service is perfectly instructed.

SIR WALTER RALEIGH

High spirits they had: gravity they flouted.

CECIL DAY LEWIS

I took her in and landed. I was drunk with air. I was wild and driving home sang and shouted, full of realization that we have found a new freedom—a new Ocean. For thousands of years we have crawled or run on the earth, or paddled across the seas, and all the while there has been this great ocean just over our heads in which at last we sail with joy. The longing for the sea: the call of the sea, one has heard of that, and that was the natural adventure in the past. But now it is a longing for the air, to go up. The air is more marvellous than any sea, it holds more beauty, more joy than any Pacific swell or South Sea lagoon.

DAVID GARNETT

En plein vol. . . . Plus haut, toujours plus haut, plus loin, plus loin toujours.

BERNARD LAFONT

Before take-off, a professional pilot is keen, anxious, but lest someone read his true feelings, he is elaborately casual. The reason for this is that he is about to enter a new though familiar world. The process of entrance begins a short time before he leaves the ground and is completed the instant he is in the air. From that moment on, not only his body but his spirit and personality exist in a separate world known only to himself and his comrades.

As the years go by he returns to this invisible world rather than to earth for peace and solace. There he also finds a profound enchantment although he can seldom describe it. He can discuss it with others of his kind, and because they, too, know and feel its power they understand. But his attempts to communicate his feelings to his wife or other earthly confidants invariably end in failure. Flying is hypnotic and all pilots are willing victims to the spell. Their world is like a magic island in which the factors of life and death assume their proper values. Thinking becomes clear because there are no earthly foibles or embellishments to confuse it. Professional pilots are, of necessity, uncomplicated, simple men. Their thinking must remain straightforward, or they die—violently.

E. K. GANN

This is earth again, the earth where I've lived and now will live once more. . . . I've been to eternity and back. I know how the dead would feel to live again.

CHARLES A. LINDBERGH
(on sighting Ireland after his solo Atlantic crossing in 1927)

The more man can enlarge the frontiers of mystery, the better for his health of mind. Storm and lightning cater generously for our sense of wonder, and those who travel from one city to another by the Valkyrie's route find still subtler, yet more awe-inspiring Valhallas opening up to the imagination.

JEAN COCTEAU

Our descendants will certainly attempt journeys to other members of the Solar system . . . By 2030 the first preparations for the first attempts to reach Mars may perhaps be under consideration. The hardy individuals who form the personnel of the expedition will be sent forth in a machine propelled like a rocket.

LORD BIRKENHEAD (1930)

Scientific investigation into the possibilities [of jet propulsion] has given no indication that this method can be a serious competitor to the airscrew-engine combination.

THE BRITISH UNDER-SECRETARY OF STATE FOR AIR (1934)

It is one thing to have an idea. It is another to have the technical and executive ability to give it flesh. It is another to have the tenacity of purpose to drive through to success unshaken in confidence, in the face of discouraging opposition. Whittle, whose name in the annals of engineering comes after those of Watt, Stephenson, and Parsons only for reasons of chronology or alphabetical order, had these things.

LORD KINGS NORTON (1947)

It is impossible to over-estimate the importance of the ground staff; reliability, safety, and economy—three foundation stones on which the goodwill of aviation must be erected—depend on their efficiency. It is true to say that the man on the ground keeps the machine in the air.

P. T. ETHERTON

Table of Powered Take-offs and Flights

Table of Powered Take-offs and Flights
(c. 1874–1908)

ON the following pages is a table showing *the best airborne duration times* achieved by every man-carrying powered aeroplane which can be said to have made one or more successful take-offs from about 1874 to the end of 1908. Flight duration was the best indication of sustentation and controllability—thus of success—in those early days; but distances are also given when known. In the case of some well-known machines, two or more entries are given to show their progress.

As may be imagined, the incompleteness and unreliability of contemporary records have made exact details often hard to come by; but after a scrutiny of the circumstances in each case, the calibre of achievement emerges clearly enough, and minor discrepancies do not affect the overall picture.

In assessing the historical importance of many of the early performances (from 1903 onwards), it could be argued that the achievements were so minuscule that they do not even merit the bare inclusion in such a table as this. The reason for their inclusion here is to show the number of machines constructed which were brought to the stage of being at least able to take-off. Thus those take-offs which lasted for less than 15 seconds—they were in no sense proper flights—have not been excluded, but recorded simply as large black dots on the zero line: their times or distances are also recorded. Even in terms of distance travelled through the air, none of these take-offs represented more than about 200 metres (say 650 feet) at most: the majority of them were much less.

The durations have been shown in the table to the nearest half minute in flights of up to half an hour; then, after that, to the nearest minute.

The last column on each left hand page gives the approximate number of take-offs made by each machine, taken to the end of 1908.

The entries are numbered in case it was thought of interest to add a note: these notes will be found following the table pages.

The abbreviations used in the table are as follows:

B	Biplane	MP	Multiplane
SB	Semi-biplane (i.e. what later would have been termed a sesquiplane)	P	Passenger flight (i.e. pilot plus one passenger)
ctd.	continued (i.e. a further flight by an aircraft already included in the table)	T	Triplane
		ST	Semi-triplane
		ft.	ft.
M	Monoplane	m.	metre(s)
TM	Tandem-monoplane	min.	minute(s)
		ml.	mile(s)

233

NOTE   If the pilot of a machine was not the man whose name the aircraft bears (i.e. Blériot, Esnault-Pelterie etc.) his name is recorded immediately beneath the name of the aircraft.

List letter	Date	Location	Dur-ation	Distance	Type	Aircraft and Pilot
a	c. 1874	Brest (France)	—	—	M	Du Temple (a sailor)
b	1884 (or 1882)	Krasnoye Sélo, near St. Petersburg (Russia)	—	20–30 m. (65–98 ft.)	M	Mozhaiski (unknown)
c	1890 (Oct. 9)	Armainvilliers (France)	—	50 m. (164 ft.)	M	Ader
d	1894 (July 31)	Baldwyns Park, Kent (Britain)	—	—	B	Maxim (Maxim and two assistants)
e	1898 (Oct. 10 & 22)	St Joseph, Michigan (U.S.A.)	—	15 & 22 m. (50 & 73 ft.)	B	Herring
f	1903 (Oct. 7)	Widewater, on the River Potomac (U.S.A.)	—	—	TM	Langley Aero-drome A (Manly)
g	1903 (Nov.)	Vahrenwalder Heide, near Hanover (Germany)	—	60 m. (197 ft.)	ST	Jatho
h	1903 (Dec. 8)	Widewater, on the River Potomac (U.S.A.)	—	—	TM	Langley Aero-drome A (Manly)

NOTES

(a) This steam-powered French tractor monoplane took off for a few metres after a down-ramp take-off.

(b) Also steam-powered (with a British engine) this Russian machine also ran down a ramp, and was said to have been airborne for some 20–30 metres.

(c) This was the world's first powered aeroplane take-off from level ground; but it was not a flight in any sense of the term, the machine being incapable of sustaining itself, or of being controlled.

(d) This was really a giant biplane test-rig, rather than an aeroplane: it sustained itself for a second or two—until it fouled the restraining rails—but also did not make a flight in any sense of the word: its flight-control was primitive to a degree.

(e) A foot-launched hang-glider assisted by a compressed-air motor (see page 290).

(f) This famous tandem monoplane fouled the catapult launching mechanism and plunged into the river: it was both underpowered and weakly constructed, with inadequate flight-control.

(g) This very primitive machine probably took off downhill.

(h) This machine again fouled the launching mechanism, or suffered a structural breakage, and again plunged into the Potomac. Manly was luckily rescued unhurt on both occasions.

Notes

(The numbers are the List Numbers in the tables)

1, 2 These two entries refer to the first and last—of four—flights which constitute the world's first powered, sustained and controlled flights in an aeroplane: 'Orville' and 'Wilbur' refer, of course, to the two Wright brothers. All four of these flights were made from level ground, under engine power alone, and were not assisted either by a down-hill run, or by any form of assisted take-off. The Wrights' weight-and-derrick assisted take-off device was not introduced until 1904.

3 On September 20th 1904, this machine made the world's first circle by an aeroplane, at the Huffman Prairie, near Dayton.

4–6 This machine was the world's first fully practical aeroplane, which could bank, turn, circle and do figures of eight, all with ease, and could remain airborne for over half an hour at a time; it was the first to fly for half an hour.

7 Although not itself successful, this machine initiated the revival of the monoplane, and strongly influenced both Blériot and Levavasseur.

8 This Ellehammer machine has often been proclaimed as having made the first powered flight in Europe, antedating Santos-Dumont. This claim cannot stand; it did not even make free hop-flights, but was tethered to a central pole: it incorporated automatic control, with no rudder, and the 'pilot' was virtually a passenger.

9, 11 The difference between these two was chiefly the important one of the Antoinette engine, the 14-*bis* having a 24 h.p., and the 14-*bis* (mod.) a 50 h.p. engine: the modified machine also incorporated octagonal ailerons in the outer wing-bays. This modified version made the first official hop-flights in Europe, in October and November 1906, of which entry No. 11 was the best.

12 The start of the first classic tradition of European powered biplanes, with forward (Wright-derived) elevator, pusher airscrew, and tail-unit on an outrigger: the Voisin-built biplanes had no control in roll.

13 This was a 'canard' pusher monoplane of very flimsy construction.

14 Phillips' machine might, with its multiple slats in a frame, be described as a test-rig: it may be said to have made the first tentative hop-flights in Britain.

16 A Langley-derived tandem-wing monoplane with a 24 h.p. Antoinette engine.

17 This was the modified version of this tandem monoplane, now with a 16-cylinder 50 h.p. (not 100 h.p.) Antoinette engine, which was the first 16-cylinder Antoinette to be airborne.

18 The first flight in Europe of over half a minute duration.

19 The first flight in Europe of over one minute.

235

20   The letters REP. stand for Robert Esnault-Pelterie, the designer, builder and pilot.

21   Although unsuccessful itself, this represented the first modern configuration tractor monoplane, with enclosed fuselage, tail-unit, etc.

22   The first "light aeroplane" of history, to be developed later into the *Demoiselle*.

24   Although itself unsuccessful, this became influential as the first biplane with no surfaces or controls forward of the wings.

29   Levavasseur's first conventional monoplane design, and the parent of his famous Antoinettes.

30   The first proper American aeroplane other than the Wrights—and derived from them—with forward elevator and rear rudder. The letters A.E.A. stand for Aerial Experiment Association.

32   This was the world's first passenger flight.

34   Curtiss touched down momentarily after 614 ft.

37   This was the first hop-flight made in Germany.

38   The first Blériot monoplane having the typical "Blériot look".

40   The first flight in the U.S.A. after the Wrights.

44   The first Wright machine to fly in public, which revolutionised European aviation by its display of flight-control, and its all-round manoeuvrability and efficiency.

47   The world's first flight of over an hour. This machine caused the first fatality in powered aviation when it crashed at Fort Myer on September 17th 1908, killing the passenger, Lieutenant Selfridge, and injuring Orville Wright.

49   The first European machine to fly for half an hour.

52   The world's first flight of over 1½ hours.

54   The world's first passenger flight of over half an hour.

55   The world's first passenger flight of over one hour.

56   The first powered flight in Britain.

61   The first German-designed and German-piloted machine to make hop-flights in Germany.

63   The first of the "typical" Antoinette monoplanes, soon to become famous.

71   The world's first flight of over 2 hours.

A Chronology of
Aviation
from Antiquity to 1945

A Chronology of Aviation
from Antiquity to 1945

B.C.

c. 852	Legendary King Bladud of England is said to have been killed when attempting to fly
c. 400	Archytas of Tarentum is reported to have made a steam-jet-propelled pigeon

A.D.

c. 1010	Eilmer of Malmesbury attempts to fly from Malmesbury Abbey
12th cent.	Windmills of the post (or tower) type are in use in Europe
c. 1100	First use of rockets (in China, as artillery)
c. 1250	Roger Bacon speculates about mechanical flight
c. 1325	First known illustration of a helicopter model (string-pull type), in a Flemish MS.
1326–27	First illustration in the Western world of a kite, and of an aerial bomb (Milemete MS.)
1379	First mention of rockets in Europe (Muratori), which are war-rockets
1483–86	Da Vinci designs the first parachute
c. 1485	Da Vinci designs finned projectiles
1485–1500	Da Vinci designs various types of ornithopters
1495–97	Da Vinci designs the first powered aeroplane of history
1498	G. B. Danti attempts to fly, with wings attached to him, at Perugia
1505	Da Vinci writes his treatise on bird-flight
1507	Damian attempts to fly with wings from the castle walls at Stirling (Scotland)
1560	First mention of kites in Europe (Schmidlap)
1589	First description of a kite in Europe (della Porta)
c. 1600	Guidotti attempts to fly at Lucca
1618	First illustration of a conventional plane surface kite in Europe (in a Dutch engraving)
c. 1620	Veranzio publishes his design for a parachute based on a ship's sail
1638	Works of moon-travel fiction published by Bishops Godwin and Wilkins

1639	Desmarets publishes an illustration of a sail-derived parachute
1647	Burattini makes his model 'flying dragon'
1655	Hooke tests his model ornithopter
1670	Lana publishes his *Prodromo*, with his design for a lighter-than-air *Flying Ship*
1673	Bernoin attempts to fly at Frankfurt-a-M., and is badly injured
1678	Besnier attempts to fly with flappers at Sablé
1680	Borelli publishes his *De Moto Animalium*, in which he demonstrates the inadequacy of muscle-power for human ornithopter flight
1709	Gusmão designs, and probably tests, a model glider version of, his *Passarola* flying-machine
1714–15	Swedenborg describes his ideas for an aeroplane
c. **1742**	De Bacqueville attempts to fly with wings across the Seine at Paris
1746	First use of the whirling arm (for ballistic tests, by Robins)
1752–53	Whirling arm used for testing windmill sails (Smeaton)
1754	Lomonosov is said to have flown his helicopter model in Russia
1764	Bauer designs his fixed-wing monoplane
1768	Paucton suggests his 'ptérophore' machine, the first idea for a convertiplane with a helicopter screw and a propulsive screw
1772	Desforges builds his 'voiture volante'
1781	Meerwein tests his ornithopter-cum-glider
	Blanchard builds his 'vaisseau volant'
	Restif de la Bretonne publishes his *La Découverte Australe*
1782	The Montgolfier brothers fly their first model hot-air balloons
1783	
June 5	First public demonstration (at Annonay) of a Montgolfier hot-air balloon, unpiloted
Sept 19	Animals ascend in a Montgolfier hot air balloon at Versailles
Oct	Joseph Montgolfier suggests jet propulsion (by hot air) from a balloon, the first idea for reaction propulsion for aircraft
Nov 21	THE FIRST AERIAL VOYAGE IN HISTORY (de Rozier and d'Arlandes in a Montgolfier hot-air balloon at Paris)
Dec 1	First voyage in a hydrogen balloon (Charles and Robert), also at Paris
1784	Re-invention of the model helicopter (Launoy and Bienvenu)
	First test of a full-size propulsive airscrew (Vallet, on a river boat)
	Designs for ornithopters by Renaux and Gérard
	Aries attempts to fly with wings at Embrun
Sept 15	First aerial voyage in Britain (Lunardi, in his balloon)
Oct 16	First attempt to propel a full-size aircraft with an airscrew (Blanchard on his balloon at London)
1785	Meusnier designs his prophetic airscrew-driven airship
Jan 7	First Channel crossing by air (Blanchard and Jeffries in a balloon)
June 15	First ballooning fatalities (de Rozier and Romain) in a combination hot-air-cum-hydrogen balloon, near Boulogne
1794	First military aerial reconnaissance by the French army (from a hydrogen balloon at Mauberge)
1796	Cayley flies his model helicopter, adapted from that of Launoy and Bienvenu (see 1809)
1797	
Oct 22	First human parachute descent from the air (Garnerin, from a balloon)
1799	First design of a modern configuration aeroplane, incorporating fixed wings, tail-unit control surfaces, and an auxiliary method of propulsion (Cayley)

1799	British army invading India is attacked by rockets from Tipu Sultan's rocket brigade; this news, when it reaches London, leads directly to Congreve's revival of the European war rocket
1804	Aerofoils first tested on a whirling arm (Cayley)
	First modern configuration aeroplane flies (Cayley's model glider)
1805	First modern rocket missiles tested (Congreve)
1807	Partial destruction of Copenhagen by Congreve rockets fired from ships of the British Royal Navy
1807–17	Degen attempts to fly with his flap-valve ornithopter, supported by a balloon (he claims most attention in 1809), when he was the direct cause of Cayley publishing his classic paper (see below)
1808	Invention of the cycle-type tension-wheel (Cayley)
1809	Cayley flies his first full-size glider (unmanned)
	Cayley designs a solid of least resistance, based on the trout
1809–10	Cayley publishes his classic triple paper on aviation, which lays the foundations of modern aerodynamics; in this, his 1796 helicopter model is also illustrated, and thereafter leads to all subsequent helicopter development
1811	Berblinger attempts to fly at Ulm, with a Degen-type ornithopter
1815	First tandem-wing aeroplane design (Cayley), but it is not published
1816	Cayley attempts to found an aeronautical society
	Degen flies his clockwork helicopter model
1818	De Lambertye designs his ornithopter and helicopter, with a helicopter 'tender'
c. **1822**	Pocock flies his tentative man-lifting kite
1827	Pocock's kite-drawn carriage (char-volant) travels a road successfully
c. **1830**	Artingstall tests his steam-powered model ornithopter
1831	Walker publishes his tandem-wing designs, which are the first to be published, and influence later inventors
1837 July 24	Cocking killed in his dihedral parachute, derived from a published design by Cayley
1842	Phillips' steam-driven (from rotor tips) model helicopter flies
1843	Bourne's helicopter models fly, powered by watch-springs
	Illustration of Miller's man-powered ornithopter design published
March	Henson publishes his design for an *Aerial Steam Carriage*, which has a far-reaching influence owing to its widespread and continuing publication; it is also the first design in history of an airscrew-propelled fixed-wing aeroplane
April	Cayley publishes his design for a convertiplane, which is also the first biplane design in history
1847	First powered aeroplane model tested (Henson's steam-powered monoplane); it is also the first airscrew-propelled fixed-wing aeroplane in history; but it cannot sustain itself
1848	Stringfellow's near-successful steam-powered model aeroplane tested; it could not sustain itself
1849 Aug 22	First bombing raid in history (Austrian pilotless hot-air balloons, carrying bombs, are sent against Venice)
	Cayley's full-size 'boy-carrier' glider makes tentative flights
1852	First aeronautical society founded (in France)
Sept 24	First tentative flight by a manned full-size airship (Giffard), including the first aero-engine—a steam engine—to power an airborne aircraft

1853	First proper man-carrying flight—but not under control by the occupant—by an aeroplane (Cayley's 'coachman-carrier' glider)
	Loup designs his monoplane, the first consistent design in France for an airscrew-propelled aeroplane
c. **1853**	First design for stretched rubber motor for models (Cayley)
1854	
June 27	Letur is killed on his 'parachute-type' glider
1856	Carlingford designs his monoplane, in Ireland, which he later built and flew as a kite
1856–68	Le Bris tests his two full-size gliders, based on the albatross
1856–96	Mouillard tests his full-size gliders
c. **1857–58**	First successful powered flight by a clockwork-powered model aeroplane (Du Temple)
1858	First tentative aerial photo taken (by Nadar from a captive balloon over Paris)
	Jullien tests his rubber-driven model monoplane
c. **1858–59**	Wenham tests his multiplane glider, and demonstrates the superior lifting power of high aspect-ratio wings
1859	Cordner flies his tentative man-carrying kite
1860	Smythies designs his ornithopter-cum-fixed-wing aeroplane
	Invention of the gas engine (Lenoir)
1861	First 'aircraft carrier' in service (for balloon) in U.S. Civil War
1863	De La Landelle designs his fantasy helicopter
	Ponton d'Amécourt tests his steam-driven model helicopter
	Bourçart builds and tests a full-size man-powered multi-winged ornithopter
	Jules Verne publishes his *Five Weeks in a Balloon*
	Nadar founds La Société d'Encouragement pour l'Aviation
1864	Nadar founds the Journal *L'Aéronaute*, which becomes the most important aeronautical journal in the world
	D'Esterno publishes his *Du Vol des Oiseaux*
1865	First design for a jet-propelled aeroplane (de Louvrié)
1866	Foundation of the Aeronautical Society of Great Britain
	Wenham gives his lecture on *Aerial Locomotion* to the Society at its first meeting, in which he first announces the results of his 1858–59 tests: the publication of this lecture exerts a great influence on later inventors
1867	First delta-wing jet aeroplane designs (Butler and Edwards), which include both jet propulsion, and airscrew-jet propulsion proposals, the latter to be rotated by jets from the tips
1868	
June	First aeronautical exhibition in history (at the Crystal Palace, near London), where the most important exhibit, Stringfellow's model triplane, is tested (see next entry)
	First powered model triplane tested (Stringfellow); although unsuccessful, this model is to have great influence and, through widespread publication to lead direct to the first biplanes and triplanes
	Ailerons first designed, but in an unpractical form (Boulton)
	Kaufmann, in Britain, tests steam-driven fixed-wing-cum-ornithopter model, which is unsuccessful
	Bourçart tests his full-size ornithopter at Guebwiller
	Hunter suggests a jet aeroplane, which also incorporates jet lift
1870	Pénaud introduces twisted rubber to power models

1870	Harte designs modern flap-type ailerons, but not for proper control in roll
	Trouvé's gunpowder-driven model ornithopter flies
1870's	Danjard's tandem-wing model gliders fly
1871	Pénaud's powered model monoplane (called 'planophore') flies, and demonstrates inherent stability
	First wind tunnel used (Wenham and Browning)
1872	First internal combustion engine (gas) drives a full-size aircraft using envelope's gas (Henlein's airship)
1873	Marey publishes his *La Machine Animale*
	Renard tests his multi-wing model
1873–74	Brown tests longitudinal stability of tandem-wing models, which probably influence Langley
1874	
July 9	De Groof killed on his semi-ornithopter, at London
c. **1874**	First powered man-carrying aeroplane takes off (Dù Temple), but does not fly
1875	Moy successfully tests his large model tandem-wing *Aerial Steamer*
1876	Pénaud patents his full-size aeroplane design, which is also the first design for an amphibian
	Cayley's triple paper of 1809–10 is re-published by the Aeronautical Society in London
	Invention of the four-stroke petrol engine (Otto)
1877	Melikoff designs a gas-turbine helicopter model
	Forlanini's steam-driven model helicopter flies
	Cayley's triple paper of 1809–10 is re-published in *L'Aéronaute*
1879	Tatin's compressed-air-driven model monoplane flies
	Biot tests his full-size glider
	Brearey's model 'undulator' flies
	Dandrieux flies his 'butterfly' helicopter models
1881	Mouillard publishes his *L'Empire de l'Air*
1883	First electric motor to drive a full-size aircraft in flight (Tissandier's airship)
1883–86	Montgomery in U.S.A. tests his first gliders, which are unsuccessful
c. **1884**	Second powered man-carrying aeroplane takes off, but does not fly (Mozhaiski)
1884	First near-practical airship flies (Renard and Krebs *La France*)
	Phillips takes out first patents for his double-surfaced cambered wings, which are widely published and become very influential
	Invention of the steam turbine (Parsons)
	Daimler invents the light, high-speed petrol engine
1885	First practical petrol automobile (Benz)
1886	Daimler builds the second practical petrol automobile
	Jules Verne publishes *Robur le Conquérant* (trans. as *The Clipper of the Clouds*)
1888	First petrol engine to power a full-size aircraft in flight (Wölfert's airship)
1889	Lilienthal publishes his classic *Der Vogelflug als Grundlage der Fliegekunst*
1890	
Oct 9	First full-size piloted aeroplane to leave the ground under its own power (Ader's steam-powered *Éole*), but it does not fly
1891	Langley in the U.S.A. unsuccessfully tests his first steam-driven tandem-wing model

1891–96	First successful piloted gliding flights, which directly inspire the final phase of aviation which culminated in powered flight (Lilienthal)
1892	Invention of the Diesel engine
1893	Phillips tests his large powered multi-wing model aeroplane
	Parsons flies his steam-driven model aeroplane
	Invention of the box-kite (Hargrave in Australia)
	International Conference on Aeronautics is held at Chicago, at which Hargrave's box-kites are revealed for the first time
1894	First semi-practical man-lifting kites (Baden-Powell)
	Chanute publishes his *Progress in Flying Machines*, the first scientific and authoritative history of aviation to appear
June	Lanchester announces his theory of circulatory flow
July 31	Maxim tests his full-size steam-powered biplane test-rig, which just rises from its rails, but does not fly
1895	First piloted biplane gliders fly (Lilienthal)
	Automobile-Club de France founded, which greatly stimulates automobilisme on the Continent
1895–97	Means in the U.S.A. publishes three issues of *The Aeronautical Annual*, which disseminates much useful information
1895–99	First successful piloted glider flights in Britain (Pilcher; thus he is the first true British aviator)
1896	Chanute's biplane hang-glider flies successfully and incorporates the Pratt-truss method of rigging, which is to be copied by the Wright brothers
	Lilienthal is killed gliding, the publicity attending which, helps to precipitate the final phase in aviation. He crashes on August 9, and dies next day
	Automobiles are granted freedom of the roads in Britain, which gives great stimulus to automobilisme
	Langley obtains his first successes with two of his steam-powered tandem-wing models
1896–97	Tatin and Richet fly their steam-driven model aeroplane successfully
1897	Ader twice tests his *Avion III*, on October 12th and 14th, but it does not leave the ground, on either occasion
	First all-metal airship flies (Schwartz)
1898	Aéro Club de France is founded in Paris
Oct 10, 22	Herring makes brief hops at St. Joseph, Michigan on his biplane hang-glider fitted with a compressed-air motor
1899	Wilbur Wright invents his system of wing-warping for control in roll, and flies a kite incorporating it
	Hargrave visits England and gives a lecture demonstration on his box-kites
	Pilcher is killed on his *Hawk* glider; he crashes on Sept. 30, and dies on Oct. 2
1900	First Zeppelin flies tentatively
	The Wrights fly their *No. 1* glider at Kitty Hawk
1901	The Wrights fly their *No. 2* glider at the Kill Devil Hills, near Kitty Hawk
	Wilbur Wright gives his first lecture, on September 18 (in Chicago), in which he explains his wing-warping
	Santos-Dumont flies his airship No. 6 round the Eiffel Tower
	First petrol-driven model aeroplane flies tentatively (Langley)
	First full-size petrol-driven aeroplane destroyed when taxying (Kress' Seaplane) in Austria

1901	Cody's man-lifting box-kites are patented
	Aero Club (later Royal) founded in London
1902	The Wrights make nearly 1,000 glides on their *No. 3* glider, and invent co-ordinated warp and rudder control (i.e. combined control in roll and yaw)
	The Balzer-Manly radial engine is completed for the full-size Langley *Aerodrome* (see 1903)
	Ferber, after correspondence with Chanute, builds first European Wright-type glider, and starts the revival of European aviation
1902–03	First practical airship flies (Lebaudy, in France)
1903	Chanute visits France and greatly intensifies the European revival of aviation by lectures and articles on the Wrights
	Jatho, in Germany, tests his powered aeroplane, which is unsuccessful
Oct 7	Langley's full-size piloted *Aerodrome* crashes at take-off
June 24	Wilbur Wright gives his second lecture at Chicago
Dec 8	Langley's *Aerodrome* again crashes at take-off; it is then abandoned
Dec 17	THE FIRST POWERED, SUSTAINED AND CONTROLLED AEROPLANE FLIGHTS IN HISTORY (Wilbur and Orville Wright) at the Kill Devil Hills, near Kitty Hawk; the first of the four flights lasts for 12 sec., the last for 59 sec.
1904	Esnault-Pelterie unsuccessfully imitates a Wright glider
	Ailerons (elevons) first used (Esnault-Pelterie), but unsuccessfully
	Archdeacon's Wright-type glider is briefly tested
	Cody's man-lifting kites are adopted by the British army
	Ferber introduces the stable type of biplane glider with a tailplane
	First tentative glide with a passenger (Ferber)
May 26	Wrights start flying their powered *Flyer II* near Dayton
Sept 7	First use by the Wrights of their weight- and derrick-assisted take-off method
Sept 20	First circle flown (Wilbur Wright); this was witnessed and described by A. I. Root
Nov 9	First flight of over 5 minutes (Wilbur Wright)
1905	The box-kite concept is first incorporated in an aeroplane (the Voisin-Archdeacon, and Voisin-Blériot float-gliders, in France); this starts the stable box-kite aeroplane tradition of Europe
	Cody flies his aileron-equipped glider-kite
Feb	Exhibition of aeroplane models in Paris
Mar 16	First glider descent from a balloon (Maloney, on a Montgomery tandem-wing machine); he is killed this year, when flying the same glider
May	Ferber fits an engine and tractor airscrew to his stable tailed type of glider, but it cannot sustain itself
June	First fully-practical powered aeroplane flies (Wright *Flyer III*)
Oct 4	First flight of over half-an-hour (Orville Wright)
Oct 14	The Fédération Aéronautique Internationale (F.A.I.) is founded by La Vaulx
Oct 16	Wrights' last flight until May 6th 1908
1906	
Jan	The Wright patent, including description of simultaneous use of wing warping and rudder, is published in *l'Aérophile*
Mar	First tractor monoplane tested (Vuia), which, although unsuccessful, leads to Blériot and the whole European monoplane tradition
Sept 12	Ellehammer makes a hop-flight of 140 feet, but the machine is tethered

1906	to a central post, and no free flight is made
Oct–Nov	Santos-Dumont makes the first official powered hop-flights in Europe, but the best (Nov 12) covers 721 feet in 21⅕ sec.
Nov	Ader, as a result of Santos-Dumont's efforts, suddenly claims—for the first time—that he flew for 300 metres in 1897; this claim is now known to have been deliberately fabricated
1907	First tentative powered flight in Britain (Phillips), in his multi-slat aeroplane
	Lanchester publishes his *Aerodynamics*, which includes a detailed exposition of his theory of circulatory flow.
	Dunne's first swept-wing tail-less biplane tested, unsuccessfully
	Cody's unmanned engined kite flies along a wire
	First full-size powered triplane tested (Ellehammer) in Denmark
Feb–Mar	European pusher biplane configuration crystallised (Voisin-Delagrange), but the machine is not successful
April	Exhibition of aeroplane models at London
April and July	First primitive cantilever monoplanes tested (Blériot's 'canard' and *Libellule*)
Sept 29	First man-carrying helicopter rises (Breguet), but not in free flight
Oct–Nov	Henri Farman becomes the first successful European pilot
Nov	First 'light aeroplane' type tested (Santos-Dumont's *No. 19*), but is not successful
	Blériot introduces the modern-configuration tractor monoplane (his *No. VII*); although very influential, it is not itself successful
Nov 10	First flight in Europe of over 1 minute (Farman on a Voisin)
Nov 13	First man-carrying helicopter rises vertically in free flight (Cornu), but is not practical
1908	
Jan 13	First official circle flown in Europe (Farman, on his modified Voisin, at Issy)
May 6	Wrights fly for the first time since 1905, and first use upright seating at the Kill Devil Hills
May 14	First passenger flight (Wilbur Wright takes C. Furnas) at the Kill Devil Hills
May 30	First passenger flight in Europe (Farman takes Archdeacon)
May 30	First European flight of over ¼ hour (Delagrange on a Voisin)
June–July	First flap-type ailerons used (*Blériot VIII*), but only for stabilising
	Roe tests his biplane at Brooklands and makes brief hop-flights, almost certainly after down-hill runs
June 28	Ellehammer makes the first flight in Germany
July 4	First monoplane flight of 5 minutes (Blériot, on his *No. VIII*)
	Curtiss wins the *Scientific American* trophy for the first flight in public in the U.S.A. (1 minute 42½ seconds)
July 8	First woman to fly as passenger (Mme. Peltier, with Delagrange)
Aug 8	Wilbur Wright first flies in public (at Hunaudières, in France) in the first practical two-seat aeroplane, and transforms aviation, chiefly by his display of flight-control; he transfers to nearby Auvours and flies there from Aug 21st to Dec 31st
Sept	Lorin publishes in France the first of his designs for jet aeroplanes
Sept 3	Orville Wright first flies in public at Fort Myer (U.S.A.)
Sept 6	First European flight of about ½ hour (29 minutes 53 seconds) (Delagrange on a Voisin)
Sept 9	First flight of over 1 hour (Orville Wright)

246

Sept 17	First fatality in powered aviation (Selfridge, flying as passenger with Orville Wright, is killed)
Sept 21	First flight of over 1½ hours (Wilbur Wright)
Oct	Grade becomes first native German pilot
	First practical aileroned monoplane flies (*Antoinette IV*)
Oct 3	First passenger flight of over ½ hour (Wilbur Wright takes Reichel)
Oct 6	First passenger flight of over 1 hour (Wilbur Wright takes Fordyce)
Oct 8	First Briton to fly as passenger (G. Brewer, with Wilbur Wright)
Oct 16	First powered flight in Britain (Cody—still American—at Farnborough)
Oct 30	First cross-country flight (16½ miles, by Farman from Bouy to Reims)
Oct 31	Farman attains altitude of 80 feet
Dec	First Briton to become a pilot, excluding Farman (Moore-Brabazon)
Dec 18	Wilbur Wright attains altitude of 360 feet
Dec 31	First flight of over 2 hours (Wilbur Wright)
	Wilbur Wright finishes his season at Auvours, having made over 100 flights; having been in the air for over 25 hours, including making 6 flights of over ½ hour, 6 of over 1, and 1 of over 2 hours; he takes up passengers on more than 60 occasions
1909	Wright brothers are honoured and fêted throughout Europe
	First flights take place in Austria, Sweden, Rumania, Russia, Turkey, Portugal and Canada
	Weiss flies his bird-form gliders
	Gnome rotary engine first goes into service on *Henry Farman* (*type*) *III*
	First practical wing-warping monoplanes fly (*Blériot XI* and *Antoinette VII*)
Feb 23	First flight in the Commonwealth outside Britain (McCurdy on the *Silver Wing* in Canada)
March	*Goupy II* flies and establishes the modern tractor biplane configuration
April	First cinematograph photos taken from the air (from a Wright machine, near Rome)
April–May	First practical aileroned biplane flies (*Henry Farman III*)
	First Briton flies in Britain (Moore-Brabazon)
May 22	First monoplane flight of over ½ hour (Latham on *Antoinette IV*)
June 5	First monoplane flight of over 1 hour (Latham on *Antoinette IV*)
July 13	Blériot flies cross-country for 26 miles (Étampes to Chevilly)
July 19	Latham crashes in his first attempt to fly the Channel, on *Antoinette IV*
July 23	Roe covers 900 feet on his first triplane
July 25	First Channel crossing by aeroplane (Blériot), from near Calais to Dover, on his *No XI* monoplane; this flight has profound effect on world governments as showing that the sea can be conquered by aircraft
July 27	Latham crashes in his second attempt to fly the Channel on *Antoinette VII*
August	First great aviation meeting is held at Reims, and has widespread influence as showing that the aeroplane was now a practical vehicle
Aug 27	First flight of over 100 miles, which was also first lasting over 3 hours (Farman, at the Reims meeting)
Sept 7	First powered aeroplane pilot killed (Lefebvre, when testing a new French-built Wright)
Sept 8	First flight of over 1 hour in Britain (Cody)
Sept 22	Second powered aeroplane pilot killed (Ferber on a Voisin, when taxying, at Boulogne)
Oct	First Short-built Wright machine flies in Britain
Oct 2	First flight of above 1,000 feet altitude (Orville Wright)
Oct 30	Moore-Brabazon wins *Daily Mail* prize for first circular mile by a Briton on an all-British machine, i.e. a Short

1909

Dec	First successful air-to-ground still photos taken from an aeroplane (of Mourmelon, Camp de Châlons, from an *Antoinette*)
Dec 6	Third powered aeroplane pilot killed (Fernandez on a self-designed machine)
Dec 24	Roe flies ½ mile on his second triplane
Dec 30	First flight by a monoplane of over 100 miles, which was also the first by a monoplane to last over 2 hours (Delagrange on a *Blériot XI*)

1910

	Over 20 aviation meetings are held in Europe: also meetings in U.S.A. and Egypt
	First flights made in Spain, Switzerland, Argentine, Brazil, Indo-China and China
	First full-size (but unsuccessful) jet-propelled aeroplane is built by Coanda, the jet being produced by a ducted fan
	First air passenger service starts (Zeppelin airships in Germany)
	First practical airspeed indicator (Etévé)
	Official report on Ader's 1897 trials is released, showing he never flew at all
	Aviation fatalities for the year number 32; this makes 39 since (and including) Lilienthal
Jan	Los Angeles meeting (U.S.A.)
Jan 4	Delagrange killed when flying his Blériot
Feb	Patent granted to Junkers for a cantilever 'flying wing' aeroplane
Mar 8	First woman to become a qualified pilot (Baroness de Laroche)
Mar 10	First night flights (Aubrun on a Blériot, in the Argentine)
Mar 28	First flight by a seaplane (Fabre)
Apl 27–28	London to Manchester air race (won by Paulhan on a Henry Farman)
April 28	First night flight in Europe (Grahame-White on a Henry Farman)
June 2	First double crossing of the Channel, without landing (Rolls on a Wright)
July	First bombing tests made (Curtiss, with dummies over Lake Keuka)
July 12	First British pilot to be killed (Rolls, flying a French-built Wright, at Bournemouth)
Aug 17	First cross-Channel passenger flight (Moisant and his mechanic in a Blériot)
Aug 27	First air-to-ground radio, and vice versa, (by McCurdy, from a Curtiss in the U.S.A.)
Aug 28	Dufaux, the first Swiss pilot, flies across Lake Geneva
September	Harvard-Boston meeting (U.S.A.)
Sept 23	First flight over the Alps (Chavez on a Blériot, but he is killed when about to land at Domodossola)
October	Belmont Park Meeting, Long Island, U.S.A.
Oct 2	First mid-air collision (at Milan)
Nov 14	First take-off from a ship, marking the true birth of the aircraft carrier (Ely, in the U.S.A., on a Curtiss)
December	De Havilland is appointed designer and test-pilot at Farnborough

1911

	The year sees the rise of aviation as a popular sport and spectacle, and the establishment of many aerodromes
	First long-distance flights and long-distance races take place
	Military aviation meetings held in Britain and France: various aircraft fitted with guns
	Wright's win action against French manufacturers for patent infringement (see 1913)
	First oleo-undercarriages (Farnborough and Esnault-Pelterie)
	First airmail flights in various countries

1911	First bomb-sight introduced (Scott, in U.S.A.)
	Montgomery killed on one of his own gliders
Jan	First live bombing tests (U.S. Army, from a Wright, at San Francisco)
	First practical seaplane flies (Curtiss floatplane)
	McCurdy, in a Curtiss, flies 90 miles over water from Key West (Florida) to Havana (Cuba)
Jan 18	First landing on, and take-off from, a ship (Ely), in the U.S.A.
April 12	First non-stop flight from London to Paris (Prier on a Blériot)
Aug	Atwood, on a Wright, flies from St Louis to New York *via* Chicago by stages (1,266 miles)
Aug 3	First amphibian flies (Fabre-Voisin)
Sept–Nov	Rodgers flies his Wright across the U.S.A., from Long Island (N.Y.) to Long Beach (Cal.) covering some 4,000 miles in 82 stages
Oct 22	First use of the aeroplane in warfare (reconnaissance by the Italians, in a Blériot, against the Turks)
Oct 24	Orville Wright makes record soaring flight of 90 minutes, at the Kill Devil Hills (see Sept 13th 1921)
Oct–Nov	First "Concours Militaire", at Reims
1912	The Farnborough *B.S.1* biplane flies, the prototype of all single-seat scouts and fighters
	Monocoque construction introduced (by the Swiss Ruchonnet, in a French Deperdussin)
	First artillery spotting by aeroplane (*B.E.1*, in Britain)
	German military flying is inaugurated
	First flying-boat flies (Curtiss)
	Military monoplane construction restricted in France and Britain after crashes
	First enclosed cabin aeroplanes fly, monoplane and biplane (Avro)
	First all-metal aeroplane flies (the *Tubavion* of Porche and Primard)
	First use of corrugated aluminium wings (Reissner)
Feb	First to fly over 100 m.p.h. (Vedrines on a Deperdussin)
Mar 1	First parachute drop from an aeroplane (Berry in U.S.A., using a static line)
March	First seaplane meeting (at Monaco)
April 13	Royal Flying Corps founded (Royal Warrant signed April 13th, and implemented on May 13th)
May 30	Wilbur Wright dies of typhoid
August	First British military aeroplane competition, which is won by Cody
Nov 12	First successful catapult launch of a powered machine after the Wrights (Curtiss)
1913	The Sopwith *Tabloid* first flies, and thereafter has much influence
	First practical 'all-round' stable aeroplane flies (the Farnborough *B.E.2c*)
	First race for the Schneider Trophy for seaplanes
	First large multi-engine (four) aeroplane flies (Sikorsky *Bolshoi* in Russia)
	Wrights again win their action (in appeal)
	The *Avro 504* first flies, and becomes one of the classic aircraft of history
	The tail-less Dunne *No. 8* flies from Eastchurch to Paris
	Vedrines flies by stages from Nancy to Cairo (2,500 miles)
Aug 20	First looping the loop (Nesterov on a Nieuport, at Kiev)
Sept	Pégoud performs the loop, and other evolutions, and becomes the world's first master of aerobatics
Sept 23	First non-stop flight across the Mediterranean (Garros)
1914	First tentative scheduled air-line opened (by Fansler, in Florida, U.S.A.)

1914	First "Concours de la Sécurité" (held at Buc)
	First Zeppelin raid (on Antwerp)
	English air attack on Friedrichshafen, using *Avro 504*'s
1915	First Zeppelin raid on London
	First successful gun firing through propeller fitted with deflector plates (Garros, on his Morane, in April)
	First practical interrupter gear invented by the Germans and fitted to *Fokker E.1*'s (July)
	First all-metal cantilever aeroplane flies (Junkers *J.1*)
1916	
May 17	First aeroplane-from-aeroplane mid-air launch (Porte *Baby* caries Bristol *Scout*)
Sept 12	First pilotless radio-guided flying bomb tested (Hewitt-Sperry, in the U.S.A.)
1917	First mass aeroplane raid on London (June 13th)
	First low-wing cantilever monoplane fighter flies (Junkers *J.7/9*)
1919	First regular and scheduled commercial airmail and passenger lines opened
	International Air Traffic Association (I.A.T.A.) formed
	Junkers invents aerofoil wing-flaps
May	U.S. Aerial Mail Service inaugurated
May 16–17	First trans-Atlantic flight, by stages via the Azores (by the U.S. Read *et al.* in the *NC-4* flying-boat)
June 14–15	First direct non-stop trans-Atlantic flight (by the British Alcock and Brown, in a Vickers *Vimy*)
July 2–13	First direct trans-Atlantic crossing by an airship, and first double crossing by an airship (British *R.34*)
Nov 12–Dec 10	First flight from England to Australia (by Ross and Keith Smith *et al.*, in a Vickers *Vimy*)
1920	First aeroplane flies with practical retractable undercarriage (Dayton–Wright R. B.)
	Split-flaps invented by Orville Wright and Jacobs
Mar	First machine flies with Handley Page wing-slots
Sept–Oct	Completion, and firsts tests, of Zeppelin-Staaken *E. 4/20* four-engine all metal 18 passenger transport, the forerunner of the modern large all-metal airliner
1921	Record flying leap (40 feet) by pedal cycle equipped with wings (Poulain, Paris)
Feb 22–23	First coast-to-coast (San Francisco–New York) air mail flight
July 21	First battleship (ex-German) sunk by bombs, in test (Mitchell of U.S. Army, with Martin bombers)
Sept 13	Hirth, in Germany, breaks 1911 soaring record (established by Orville Wright) with flight of 21 minutes
1922	
Aug 18	First soaring flight of one hour (Martens, in Germany)
Oct 1	First air force to assume complete control of a military command (the R.A.F. in Iraq)
1923	Turnbull variable-pitch propeller demonstrated (in production by Curtiss in mid-1930's)
Jan 3	First soaring flight of over 5 hours (Floret in a Hanriot, at Biskra)
Jan 9	First flight of a practical gyroplane (Cierva's C.3 *Autogiro*, near Madrid)
May 2, 3	First non-stop coast-to-coast crossing of U.S.A. (Kelly and Macready in a Fokker T-2)

June 27	First complete pipeline flight refuelling (in U.S.A., between two D.H. 4Bs)
1924	Hele Shaw-Beecham variable pitch, constant-speed, propeller demonstrated (produced by Rotol in late 1930s)
	The Fowler wing-flap invented
	Trimotor era started by first flight of Junkers *G-23* three-engine all-metal monoplane airliner
Apr 1	Imperial Airways formed
Apr 7– Sept 28	First round-the-world flight (by American Smith, Nelson, *et al.*)
1925	
Feb. 22	D.H. *Moth* first flies, and heralds the popularity of the light aeroplane movement
July 26	First soaring flight of 10 hours (Massaux, in Belgium, on a Poncelet)
Nov 16– Mar 13	Cobham makes the first of his pioneering empire flights (to Cape Town)
Dec 17	Gen. 'Billy' Mitchell (U.S. Army) found guilty at court-martial of criticising state of U.S. military aviation
1926	Proposals for gas-turbine propeller propulsion, by Griffith, lead to a development programme at the Royal Aircraft Establishment at Farnborough
	Rohrbach, in U.S.A., gives his influential lecture on stressed skin construction
Mar 16	First flight of a liquid-fuel rocket, designed by Goddard in U.S.A., which marks the birth of practical modern rocketry
May 9	First flight over the North Pole (Byrd and Bennett, of the U.S.A., in a Fokker *F. VII/3m*)
1927	
May 20–21	First solo Atlantic crossing (Lindbergh in a Ryan, from New York to Paris)
July 4	Lockheed *Vega* first flies, and inaugurates a new era in commercial flying
1928	
Apr 12, 13	First east-to-west aeroplane crossing of the Atlantic (Koehl *et al.*, in a Junkers *W. 33*)
May 31– June 10	First flight across the Pacific (Kingsford Smith *et al.*, in a Fokker *F.VII 3m*, from U.S.A. to Australia)
June 11	First rocket-propelled aeroplane flight (Stamer, in an Opel-Stamer)
1929	Melvill Jones publishes his influential paper, "The Streamline Aeroplane"
Oct 23	Dornier *Do X*, 12-engine flying boat, carries 169 people
1930	Whittle takes out his first jet engine patents (published 1932)
May 5–24	Amy Johnson flies solo from England to Australia, in a D.H. *Moth*
1931	First practical delta-wing aeroplane flies (Lippisch)
	First application of jet propulsion to a full-size aircraft in flight (Italian airship *Omniadir*, with compressed air)
June 11	Handley Page *H.P. 42* biplane airliner enters service with Imperial Airways, and sets new standards of comfort
Sept 13	Britain wins Schneider Trophy outright with the Supermarine *S.6B*, flown by Boothman at 340 m.p.h.
1932	Imperial Airways open London–Capetown service
	Junkers *Ju 52-3m* transport first flies, which is to form the backbone of German military transport in the Second World War
	Cobham starts his flight refuelling experiments
May 21, 22	First solo Atlantic crossing by a woman (Earhart in a *Vega*)

1932
Aug 18, 19   First solo east-to-west Atlantic crossing (Mollison)
1933
Feb 8   First modern-type monoplane airliner flies (*Boeing 247*)
Apr 3   First flight over Mount Everest (Clydesdale *et al.*)
July 1   Douglas *DC-1* first flies
July 15–22   First solo flight round the world (Post)
1934   First practical constant-speed variable pitch propellers enter airline service
July   Douglas *DC-2* first enters airline service
Oct   MacRobertson air race (England–Australia)
1935
July   Prototype of the *B-17 Flying Fortress* first flies (*Boeing 299*)
July   Breguet helicopter flies successfully
1935–36   Prototypes of many fighters and bombers of World War II first fly
1936
June   Douglas *DC-3* twin-engine airliner enters service, and so starts the career of the greatest transport aircraft of history
June 26   First flight of the first really practical helicopter (Focke-Achgelis *Fa 61*)
July 4   Short *Empire* monoplane flying-boat first flies
1937   First helicopter flight of over 1 hour (Focke-Achgelis)
May   First fully-pressurised aeroplane flies (Lockheed *XC-35*)
May 6   Zeppelin *Hindenburg* crashes in flames in U.S.A., and brings virtual end to large airship operation
Aug   First modern-type, four-engine, transport flies (Junkers *Ju 90*)
1937–39   Experimental mail-carrying and survey flights across the North and South Atlantic
1937–38   Spanish Civil War becomes testing ground for German and Italian combat aeroplanes
1938
Dec 31   First flight of first pressurised transport aeroplane (Boeing *307*)
1939
June 30   First rocket-propelled (liquid fuel) aeroplane flies (Heinkel *He 176*)
Aug 27   First turbojet aeroplane flies (Heinkel *He 178*)
1940
May 13   First successful flight by a single-rotor helicopter (Sikorsky *VS-300*)
Aug 27   Caproni-Campini 'quasi-jet' first flies
1941
Jan 9   Avro *Lancaster* heavy bomber first flies
Feb   First British four-engine bomber enters services (Short *Stirling*)
May 15   First flight of first British turbojet aeroplane (Gloster *E.28/39*, with Whittle engine)
Sept   Whittle jet engine is flown from Britain to U.S.A., and provides the model for the first practical U.S. jet engines
1942   First fully-practical single-rotor helicopter flies (Sikorsky *VS-300*) and inaugurates the modern helicopter age
              Douglas *DC-4* first flies, and inaugurates a whole generation of four-engine airliners
July 18   First operational jet combat aeroplane, which was also first production turbojet aeroplane, first flies (Messerschmitt *Me 262*)
Oct 1   First U.S. turbojet aeroplane flies (Bell *XP-59*A, with two Whittle-derived engines)

Oct 3	First long-range rocket missile 'flies' (German *A-4*): this marks the birth of practical space flight
1943	First jet-propelled-rotor helicopter flies (Doblhoff)
Jan 9	Lockheed *Constellation* airliner first flies
June 15	Prototype of the first jet bomber flies (German Arado *Ar 234*B-2)
July 24	Prototype of the Gloster jet *Meteor* first flies
1944	First practical rocket-propelled aeroplane in service (German *Me 163*)
	First flying bombs in action (German *Fzg-76*)
	First long-range rocket bombs in action (German *A-4*)
1945	First atomic fission bombs dropped (on Japan)
	First turboprop aeroplane flies (Gloster *Meteor* with Rolls-Royce *Trents*)
1945–46	Regular transatlantic passenger services introduced, with only American machines involved

Glossary

Glossary

Aerobatics. Aerial acrobatics.

Aerodonetics. A term, now obsolete, used for the science of gliding and soaring.

Aerodrome (as aircraft). The word mistakenly first used by S. P. Langley, then by others, for their aeroplanes: the Greek word *dromos* can mean a course, a race, or running, or the place where such activities take place; but never the man, animal, or machine that runs or races.

Aerodrome (as airfield). This good old-fashioned word (see also above for etymology) is now slowly disappearing in favour of Airfield for all military aerodromes, and for the small civilian aerodromes; and Airport for the medium and large civilian aerodromes from which scheduled airlines are operated.

Aerodromics. An early term, used by Langley, for the construction and operation of flying machines (i.e. of 'aerodromes' in his usage).

Aerodynamic Missile. See Missile.

Aerodynamics. That field of dynamics concerned with the motion of air and other gaseous fluids; a branch of fluid mechanics.

Aerodyne. The seldom-used word for all types of heavier-than-air aircraft, excluding certain missiles and VTOL machines. See also Aeroplane.

Aerofoil (Airfoil in U.S.A.). A body designed to obtain an aerodynamic reaction normal to its direction of travel through the air (e.g. a wing, propeller blade, fin, etc.).

Aeronaut. Literally an "air sailor": today generally confined to either pilot, crew member, or passenger in a balloon or dirigible airship, especially the former: but the word has, in the past, been applied to airmen in heavier-than-air machines.

Aeronautics. The whole field of man-made aircraft, of whatever type.

Aeronef. An early word (French for "flying-ship") for any kind of aircraft.

Aeroplane (Airplane in U.S.A.). Any heavier-than-air aircraft supported by the dynamic reaction of air flowing over or about fixed or rotating plane surfaces; the term has slowly become synonymous with "powered aeroplane", and most people today would understand it in that sense. Historically, it is used in the first sense. "Aeroplane" originally meant simply a fixed wing, i.e. an *aero*-plane.

Aerostation. The whole field of lighter-than-air aircraft; as opposed to aviation. A lighter-than-air aircraft is an Aerostat, and the science is that of Aerostatics.

Ailerons. Movable surfaces to control the rolling movements of an aeroplane, now generally set in or by the trailing edges of wings (near the tips). Some early aeroplanes had between-wing ailerons. See also Differential ailerons; Wing-warping.

Air-Brake. Any flap or similar device for slowing down an aeroplane in flight, i.e. which increases drag, as opposed to a Flap (which see) which increases both lift and drag. See also Flap; Spoiler; Air-Brake (steering).

Air-Brake (steering). A term adopted in this book at the suggestion of the Farnborough authorities, for a device in which a part of either wing can be raised or lowered in order to retard the wing and slew the aeroplane round, thus changing its heading. This concept was never associated with control in roll.

Aircraft. Any kind of man-made airborne vehicle. The word is often used loosely as

257

a synonym for aeroplane, which can be misleading if the machine in question is not identified at first.

AIRFIELD. See AERODROME.

AIRFLOW. The relative flow of air around an object in flight.

AIRFOIL. The American spelling of AEROFOIL (which see).

AIRFRAME. An aeroplane without its engines and their accessories.

AIRLINER. An unsatisfactory word connoting a medium or large transport aeroplane.

AIRPLANE. The American spelling of 'aeroplane'. This form of the word was officially adopted in the U.S.A. in 1911, and also strongly advocated at the time for use in Britain.

AIR POCKET. See BUMP.

AIRPORT. See AERODROME.

AIRSCREW. A screw to effect propulsion through the air: an alternative word to propeller (which see). "Airscrew" is sometimes the word of choice when discussing the early history of the device, to distinguish it from the marine propeller.

AIRSCREW DISC. See PROPELLER DISC.

AIRSHIP. A power-driven lighter-than-air aircraft; but often used before 1912 for any kind of powered aircraft, including aeroplanes.

AIRSPEED (or AIR SPEED). See SPEED.

AIRSPEED INDICATOR (A.S.I.). A flight instrument showing the speed of the aircraft relative to the surrounding air. The ordinary A.S.I. comprises a pitot and a static tube which measure the difference between dynamic and static pressures. See also MACH METER.

ALIGHTING GEAR. An elegant but obsolete early term for the undercarriage.

ALL-UP WEIGHT. The total weight of an aeroplane together with everybody and everything aboard.

ALTIMETER. An instrument for indicating altitude, usually an aneroid barometer calibrated to read feet or metres in a standard atmosphere.

ALTITUDE. The elevation of an object above a given level: with aircraft, a given altitude is generally taken to be that above sea level.

AMPHIBIAN. An aircraft equipped to take off and land on either land or water.

ANGLE OF ATTACK. See ATTACK; INCIDENCE.

ANGLE OF INCIDENCE. See ATTACK; INCIDENCE.

ANHEDRAL. The generally accepted term for negative dihedral, although etymologically the word "anhedral" should mean "positive dihedral": it is not clear how this contradiction arose. See CATHEDRAL; DIHEDRAL.

ANNULAR WING. A cylindrical wing.

ANTI-TORQUE ROTOR. See ROTOR (Anti-torque).

ARTIFICIAL HORIZON. A gyroscopic flight instrument indicating to the pilot the pitching and banking movements of his aircraft.

ASPECT RATIO. The ratio of the span to chord of an aerofoil: a high aspect ratio wing is great in span and small in chord; a low aspect ratio wing is small in span and great in chord.

ASSISTED TAKE-OFF. Any method of accelerating an aircraft's take-off, apart from its integral engine(s). See also JET-ASSISTED TAKE-OFF.

ASTRONAUTICS. The field of space travel.

ATTACK (Angle of). American term of INCIDENCE (which see).

AUTOGIRO. A trade name (the Cierva Autogiro) for the first succesful type of gyroplane (which see). The name is often loosely applied to other gyroplanes.

AUTOMATIC PILOT (AUTOPILOT in U.S.A.). A gyroscopically operated control mechanism which maintains a pre-set course and altitude of an aircraft by making automatic corrections of the control surfaces.

AUTOROTATION. The free rotation of rotor blades without engine power: also used of an aeroplane when spinning.

AVIATION. The whole field of heavier-than-air aircraft, as opposed to aerostation. It is becoming increasingly used as a synonym for aeronautics (to include all "man-made" flying) which is to be deplored.

AVIATOR. The pilot of a glider, powered aeroplane or helicopter; sometimes loosely used of other members of an aircrew, who are better termed "airmen".

AVION. The French word for 'aeroplane' invented by Clément Ader.

AXIS. A straight line that passes through a body and about which that body may revolve. An aircraft is considered to have three mutually perpendicular axes, each of which passes through the centre of gravity. 1. The LONGITUDINAL AXIS, the nose-to-tail axis, about which the aircraft revolves in rolling; 2. the LATERAL AXIS, the side-to-side (spanwise) axis about which it revolves in pitching; and 3. the VERTICAL (or NORMAL) AXIS, which runs in the plane of symmetry (through top and belly), about which it revolves in yawing.

BALANCE. See EQUILIBRIUM.

BALANCING PLANES (or TIPS). An early term for ailerons.

BALLISTIC MISSILE. See MISSILE.

BALLOON. An unpowered aerostat, generally spherical or near-spherical.

BANKING. Inclining an aircraft laterally, usually when making a turn, to prevent skidding. Sometimes loosely used for "turning".

BARNSTORMING. An early term for itinerant exhibition flying (especially in U.S.A.) where pilots flew at fairs, etc.

BEAUFORT SCALE. A scale from 0 to 12 symbolising the strength of wind devised by Sir F. Beaufort (1774–1857).

BERNOUILLI THEOREM. When applied to a flow of air, the theorem states that as the velocity increases, the pressure decreases.

BIPLANE. An aeroplane with two main sets of wings, one above the other: the term was sometimes used, in early works on flying, for a tandem-wing monoplane. See also WING(s).

BOOST. To supply an engine with more air than it would ordinarily induct, to increase the power obtainable under appropriate conditions.

BOUNDARY LAYER. A thin layer of fluid adjacent to a surface, in which the viscous (friction) forces are not negligible.

BOX-KITE. A form of kite (see KITE), and applied in the early days of flying to many full-size biplanes, often (and unaccountably) those machines which had no trace of box-kite construction, e.g. the so-called Bristol "Box-Kite".

BRAKING PARACHUTE. See PARACHUTE (Braking).

BUMP. A violent movement of an aeroplane, generally up or down, due to turbulent air currents: formerly called, colloquially, an "air-pocket".

BUNT. A manoeuvre in which an aeroplane performs half an outside loop downwards and emerges upside down going in the opposite direction.

BURBLING. Separation in the boundary layer of air about a streamlined body, resulting in divergent velocities and pressures, and causing loss of lift and increase in drag.

CAMBER. The curve of an aerofoil section from leading to trailing edge, either the upper surface, lower surface, or mean line between them.

CANARD. The French word for "duck". The word unaccountably applied to a "tail-first" aeroplane, i.e. with the fuselage and elevator forward of the main wings.

CANOPY. See PARACHUTE.

CANTILEVER. A wing (or any other member) supported at one end only, without any external bracing.

259

CANTILEVER AEROPLANE. One with cantilever wings.

CATHEDRAL. A corruption of "Katahedral", sometimes used in early aviation for negative dihedral (anhedral). See ANHEDRAL.

CEILING. The maximum altitude attainable by an aircraft. SERVICE CEILING is the altitude at which the rate of climb falls below some specified value.

CENTRE OF GRAVITY. The point at which the combined force (resultant) of all the weight forces in a body are concentrated for any position of the body.

CENTRE OF LIFT. The point at which a body in equilibrium may be said to be supported.

CENTRE OF PRESSURE. The point on the chord of an aerofoil where the resultant of all pressure forces may be said to act.

CENTRE SECTION. The central panel or section of an aeroplane's wing(s), often extended to mean the portion of the fuselage involved.

CERTIFICATE OF AIRWORTHINESS (C. of A.). A certificate issued by the Air Registration Board (in Britain) respecting civil aircraft, permitting the machine in question to operate under given conditions, etc.

CHORD. The straight-line distance between the leading and trailing edges of an aerofoil (as opposed to SPAN).

CLOCHE. The French word for 'bell', used to describe the inverted bowl at the base of Blériot's control column, to the edge of which the elevator and warping wires were attached.

COCKPIT. The compartment from where an aircraft is controlled, seating the pilot and often other crew members: in large aircraft it is often referred to as the "flight deck"; sometimes found in early French manuals spelt "coke-pit".

C. of A. Abbreviation of "Certificate of Airworthiness" (which see).

COLLECTIVE PITCH CONTROL. The helicopter control in which the pitch of all the rotor blades is changed simultaneously for vertical ascent and descent. See also CYCLIC PITCH CONTROL.

CONSTANT SPEED PROPELLER. See PROPELLER (Constant Speed).

CONTROL. See STABILITY AND CONTROL.

CONTROL COLUMN. The pilot's control for working elevators and ailerons.

CONTROL SURFACE. Generally used to denote one of the main control surfaces of an aeroplane (i.e. rudder, elevator, or ailerons) but including flaps, tabs, etc.

CONVERTIPLANE. An aeroplane whose shape is mechanically changed during flight to enable it to land and take off vertically.

CONTROL LEVER(s). An early word for the control column, when one or more levers were sometimes used, or suggested.

CRASH LANDING. A forced landing resulting in a crash.

CRITICAL MACH NUMBER. See MACH NUMBER.

CRUISING SPEED. A level flight-speed resulting from a power-setting recommended by the makers for flying under a given set of conditions, usually the optimum compromise of speed and range.

CYCLIC PITCH CONTROL. A helicopter control by means of which the angle of attack of the rotor blades is changed, to produce a horizontal thrust component, and hence horizontal flight in any direction.

DEAD RECKONING. The method of estimating an aircraft's position in the air by a calculation involving earlier known position, elapsed time, speed, heading, effect of wind, etc.

DECK. An early word for a wing. See also FLIGHT DECK.

DELTA WING. An aeroplane's wings which in plan form resemble an isosceles triangle, with the trailing edges forming the base.

DIFFERENTIAL AILERONS. Modern usage confines this term to the special aileron linkage which results in the up-moving aileron travelling farther than the down-moving one. The mere fact of one aileron moving up whilst the other one goes down is best referred to as "contra-acting".

DIHEDRAL. The upward inclination of an aeroplane's wings from their roots, making a shallow V from the front view: hence DIHEDRAL ANGLE. Strictly speaking this is "positive dihedral", but the "positive" is generally omitted. Negative dihedral (downward inclination) is generally called "anhedral" (which see). Longitudinal dihedral is the angle formed by the chord-lines of the wings and tailplane to aid longitudinal stability.

DIRECTIONAL GYRO. A gyroscopic flight instrument indicating the aircraft's heading.

DIRECTIONAL STABILITY. See STABILITY.

DIRIGIBLE. A dirigible airship (i.e. powered).

DIVE BRAKE. A small retractable surface on wing, or fuselage, to retard an aircraft in a dive.

DORSAL. Of, or pertaining to, the back; hence "dorsal fin", etc., where "back" is envisaged as the top of the aircraft as distinct from the bottom, where the word 'ventral' would apply.

DOWNWASH. The downward deflection of air by an aerofoil relative to the undisturbed air.

DRAG. A resistant force exerted by the air upon a body, in a direction opposite to the direction of motion. In the early days of flying, drag was termed 'drift', or simply 'resistance'. PROFILE DRAG is a composite drag produced by the lifting surfaces, and comprises FORM DRAG (due to the shape of the aerofoil) and SKIN FRICTION. INDUCED DRAG is that due to the lift forces produced by the wings. PARASITE DRAG is that produced by parts of the aircraft other than the lifting surfaces. INTERFERENCE DRAG is that induced by the interaction of wings, fuselage, tail, etc.

DRIFT. A lateral divergence of an aircraft or missile from the projected line of its heading. Also an early term for drag.

DROOP. An early word for "anhedral" (which see).

DYNAMOMETER. An instrument for measuring the power, thrust or torque of an engine, rocket, etc.

ELEVATOR. A horizontal control surface to control the climb and descent of an aircraft. In early aviation it was usually called the "horizontal rudder".

ELEVON. A control surface combining the functions of elevator and aileron.

EMPENNAGE. The early term for an aeroplane's tail-unit, this French word being derived from *empenner*, to feather an arrow.

ENGINE. The power source of an aircraft (see also MOTOR).

EQUILIBRIUM (in flight). The stability achieved when the forces of drag, thrust, lift, and weight are acting so as to produce steady flight. See also STABILITY.

F.A.I. Abbreviation of Fédération Aéronautique Internationale.

FAIRING. An auxiliary member or structure shaped to reduce drag.

FAN-TYPE ENGINE. A radial engine having cylinders disposed over not more than half the arc of the circle.

FILLET. A fairing, generally where two surfaces join, to improve the airflow.

FIN. A fixed vertical aerofoil for stabilising purposes. The American term is 'vertical stabiliser'.

FLAP. Any control surface designed to increase the lift, or lift and drag combined, of an aeroplane (as opposed to an AIR BRAKE, which only increases drag); the term is usually applied to those surfaces which either hinge down at the trailing edge of the wings, or are projected to form an extension of the trailing edge, curving downwards (Fowler Flap): among other types are slotted, split, and leading-edge flaps.

FLAPPER. An ornithoptering winglet, or small beating surface, used to effect either propulsion-cum-lift, or propulsion only.

FLATTEN OUT. To level off an aircraft after a dive or climb

FLIER. See FLYER.

FLIGHT DECK. The take-off and landing deck of an aircraft carrier: also used for the cockpit of a large aircraft.

FLIGHT PATH. The path described by an aircraft, etc., in the air; i.e. the hypothetical hole bored by an aircraft through space.

FLIGHT SIMULATOR. A device (dummy cockpit, etc.) in which any or all of the conditions and feelings of flight are simulated, for training and other purposes.

FLOAT PLANE. A seaplane on a float or floats. See also AMPHIBIAN; FLYING BOAT; SEAPLANE.

FLUTTER. A vibrating or oscillating movement caused by aerodynamic forces acting on an aerofoil (etc.) having elastic or inertial qualities.

FLYER. The Wrights' name for their powered aeroplanes. The name was widely used for powered aeroplanes of any make until about 1909–10. First used by Cayley in 1813. Curtiss spelt the word 'Flier'.

FLYING BOAT. A seaplane with a hull on which it floats, takes off, and lands. See also AMPHIBIAN; FLOAT PLANE; SEAPLANE.

FLYING MACHINE. Strictly speaking all aircraft, whether powered or not, are machines (see MACHINE); but the term has been confined almost exclusively to powered aeroplanes in the past, but is now dying out of general usage altogether.

FLYING SPEED. See SPEED.

FLYING TAIL. A tail-plane, the whole of which can have its angle of incidence changed in flight.

FLYING WING. An aircraft consisting entirely (or almost so) of a single large aerofoil within which the engines, passengers, etc., are contained.

FLYING WIRES (LIFT WIRES in U.S.A.). Wires (generally external) of the rigging which are attached to a wing, etc., to support the weight of the fuselage during flight.

FORCED LANDING. An involuntary or emergency landing, which may or may not result in a 'crash landing'.

FORM DRAG. See DRAG.

FOWLER FLAP. See FLAP.

FUSELAGE. The body or hull of an aeroplane. See also NACELLE.

GAP. The distance between the two sets of wings of a biplane (or triplane, etc.).

GAS TURBINE. An engine in which air is compressed by a rotating COMPRESSOR, heat is added by burning fuel, and energy extracted from the gas stream by a turbine. Residual energy in the exhaust gas stream can be utilised to provide JET PROPULSION. In addition, the turbine may drive an airscrew—the combination forming a TURBOPROP engine—or a helicopter rotor, or other machinery.

GAUCHISSEMENT. See WING-WARPING.

GLIDER. An unpowered fixed-wing aeroplane, for gliding or soaring. A 'hang-glider' is one in which the pilot hangs by his arms, etc., and controls the machine by movements of his body and legs.

GLIDING ANGLE. The angle between an aircraft's flight path relative to the air, and the horizontal, when it is gliding.

GRAVITY (Centre of). See CENTRE OF GRAVITY.

GROUND LOOP. See LOOP (Ground).

GUIDED MISSILE. See MISSILE.

GYROPLANE. In English usage a rotorcraft with non-powered rotors, as in the Autogiro, which provide lift, but no propulsion. In American usage "gyroplane" may refer to any rotorcraft.

HANDED PROPELLERS. Propellers revolving in opposite directions to cancel out torque reactions.

HANGAR. A building for housing aircraft.

HANG-GLIDER. See GLIDER.

HELICOPTER. A type of rotorcraft that derives all its lift and thrust from engine-driven rotating aerofoils (i.e. rotor blades) mounted about an approximately vertical axis.

HIGH WING MONOPLANE. One with its wings attached near or at the top of the fuselage.

HORIZON (Artificial). See ARTIFICIAL HORIZON.

HORIZONTAL RUDDER. The early term for an elevator.

HORIZONTAL STABILISER. The American term for a tailplane.

HYDRO-AEROPLANE. An early term for a seaplane (translated from the French *hydroavion*): sometimes confusingly shortened to "hydroplane".

HYDROPLANE. (*a*) A hydrofoil supported in water by hydrodynamic action; (*b*) a motor-boat equipped with hydrofoils, by which it is supported when in motion; (*c*) a misnomer for a seaplane, as a contraction of 'hydro-aeroplane'.

INCIDENCE (Angle of). (1) The angle between the chord of a wing and the direction of the undisturbed airflow. Also referred to as the ANGLE OF ATTACK. (2) The angle between the chord and the horizontal—properly referred to as the RIGGING ANGLE OF INCIDENCE.

INDUCED DRAG. See DRAG.

INHERENT STABILITY. See STABILITY.

IN-LINE ENGINE. One in which the cylinders are arranged in one or more straight fore-and-aft rows, as distinct from the 'radial' or 'rotary' engines (which see).

INSIDE LOOP. See LOOP.

INTERFERENCE DRAG. See DRAG

JET-ASSISTED TAKE-OFF. A take-off assisted by one or more small solid, or liquid, fuel rocket units.

JET PROPULSION. See REACTION PROPULSION.

JET THRUST. See STATIC THRUST.

JOY-STICK. An early term for the control column.

KEEL SURFACE. The effective side surface of an aircraft influencing directional stability.

KING-POST. A vertical strut above the wing, from which bracing wires support it.

KITE. The earliest type of heavier-than-air aircraft, in which "propulsion" is supplied by the pull on the "tow-line", and lift is supplied by the kite being inclined to the wind. The box-kite (invented by Hargrave in 1893) comprises two four-sided "cells" joined by booms, or variations of this configuration. The word "kite" has also been used as slang for aeroplane (see footnote on page 154).

LANDING FLAP. See FLAP.

LANDING WIRES. Wires (generally external) of the rigging which support the weight of the wings when on the ground.

LATERAL AXIS. See AXIS.

LATERAL CONTROL. A term which is sometimes loosely used for control in roll, but should only be used for overall lateral control which involves control in roll, yaw and pitch.

LATERAL STABILITY. See STABILITY.

LEADING EDGE. The edge of an aerofoil (wing, propeller, etc.) which first meets the air in normal flight; as opposed to the "trailing edge" (which see).

LIFT. That component of the total aerodynamic forces acting on an aerofoil (or whole aircraft, etc.) perpendicular to the relative wind; in normal flight, it is exerted in an upward direction, opposing the pull of gravity.

LIFT (Centre of). See CENTRE OF LIFT.

LIFT/DRAG RATIO. The ratio of lift to drag.

LINK TRAINER. A synthetic training device, comprising a hooded cockpit, for training in instrument flying, radio aids, etc. See also FLIGHT SIMULATOR.

LONGERON. A longitudinal structural member of the fuselage.

LONGITUDINAL AXIS. See AXIS.

LOOP (Ground). A violent turn to left or right made by an aeroplane when on the ground (i.e. taxying, taking off, or landing).

LOOPING THE LOOP (or LOOP). A flight manoeuvre in which an aeroplane flies an approximately circular path in a vertical plane; an INSIDE LOOP is the normal way of looping the loop, with the top of the aeroplane inside the circle traced: an OUTSIDE LOOP is a loop in which the top of the aircraft is on the outside of the circle traced.

LOW WING MONOPLANE. One with the wings attached at or near the bottom of the fuselage.

MACHINE. In an aeronautical context, the word is used synonymously with 'aircraft'.

MACH METER. A special airspeed indicator registering the Mach number.

MACH NUMBER. The ratio of the airspeed of an aircraft to the speed of sound in the air surrounding it. Mach 1 is the speed of sound; Mach 2 is twice the speed of sound; and so on. The CRITICAL MACH NUMBER is that representing the speed of a given aircraft at which a Mach number of 1 is attained at any local point of that aircraft: the term has also been used to denote the point at which control is lost in a non-supersonic aircraft. The speed of sound is approximately 760 m.p.h. at sea level and approximately 660 m.p.h. in the stratosphere.

MAIN PLANE(s). The main lifting surface(s) of an aeroplane, *i.e.* the wings.

MASS BALANCE. A balancing weight attached to a control surface.

MID-WING MONOPLANE. One with the wings attached mid-way on the fuselage.

MILITARY AIRCRAFT (etc.). When used with a small 'm', "military" refers to all aircraft used by the armed forces, as distinct from commercial or private owners. When spelt with a capital 'M', "Military" refers to the Army as such.

MISSILE. Any object thrown, dropped, projected or propelled, for the purpose of hitting a target. An AERODYNAMIC MISSILE is one which is in effect an aeroplane with aerodynamically supporting surfaces; a BALLISTIC MISSILE is any missile that becomes a free-falling body in the latter stages of its "flight"; a GUIDED MISSILE is a missile directed to its target either by pre-setting or self-reacting devices, or by radio or wire command from outside the missile; a ROCKET MISSILE is one propelled and supported entirely by rocket power. In practice, missiles may combine the characteristics of all four of these classes.

MONOCOQUE CONSTRUCTION. From the French word meaning "egg-shell": an idealised concept of a completely hollow shell-like structure. See the special note on page 171; see also STRESSED SKIN.

MOTOR. A word generally synonymous with 'engine'.

MOVABLE TIPS. An early term for ailerons.

MULTIPLANE. A general term for any aeroplane with two or more sets of wings mounted one above the other.

NACELLE. The French word for "a small boat": a separate enclosure on an aircraft for housing crew, engine(s), or other objects. The early pusher biplanes would have their fuselages described as "nacelles", where the tail was carried separately on outriggers. The most usual modern use of the word is an "engine nacelle".

NEGATIVE DIHEDRAL. See ANHEDRAL.

NEUTRAL STABILITY. See STABILITY.

ORNITHOPTER. An aircraft sustained and propelled by flapping wings.

OUTRIGGER(S). A projecting structure to support (on an aircraft) such parts as an elevator, rudder, or complete tail-unit, etc. The word "boom" is almost synonymous.

PANELS. Another early term for SIDE-CURTAINS (which see).

PARACHUTE. A parasol-like aeronautical device for retarding the movement of whatever is attached to it. The man-carrying parachute is composed of the CANOPY, the RIGGING (or SHROUD) LINES, and the HARNESS. In a rip-cord parachute the main canopy is pulled out of the PACK by a PILOT PARACHUTE. Also used for a glider in last century.

PARACHUTE (Braking). A parachute opened behind an aeroplane to retard it.

PARASOL MONOPLANE. One with the wings mounted above, and clear of the fuselage.

PAYLOAD. That part of the load of a commercial aircraft that produces revenue (i.e. passengers and cargo).

PÉNAUD TYPE TAIL. An early term for a cruciform tail-unit, based on the mistaken belief that such a configuration was introduced by Alphonse Pénaud. It was first used by Cayley in 1804.

PILOT PARACHUTE. See PARACHUTE.

PITCH. The blade angle of a propeller or rotor blade.

PITOT-STATIC TUBE. See AIRSPEED INDICATOR.

PLANE. (*a*) Short for 'aeroplane'; (*b*) a wing; (*c*) a flat surface.

PLANE OF SYMMETRY. A vertical plane containing the longitudinal axis of a symmetrical object, such as an aeroplane, where such a plane would cut through the machine from nose to tail leaving the port side and wing on one side of the plane, and the starboard on the other.

PLANOPHORE. Alphonse Pénaud's name for his stable model monoplane of 1871; from the Latin *plano* (plane) and the Greek *phoros* (bearing).

PONTOON. An early term for a float.

POWERED GLIDER. See GLIDER.

POWER PLANT (or UNIT). In aircraft these terms are generally taken to include the engine, propeller, and accessories.

POWER/WEIGHT RATIO. The ratio of the power of an engine to its own weight; or, when used of the whole aircraft, the ratio of power to total weight.

PRESSURE (Centre of). See CENTRE OF PRESSURE.

PRESSURIZATION. The keeping of the interior of an aircraft at a higher air pressure than the atmospheric pressure outside.

PRIME MOVER. A source of mechanical power produced entirely from non-mechanical sources of energy, e.g. chemical, electrical.

PRODUCTION MODEL. Any of a batch of aircraft (etc.) manufactured under standard conditions.

PROFILE DRAG. See DRAG.

PROPELLER. This word, in aeronautical and marine parlance, only became synonymous with 'airscrew' from about 1845–55. Prior to that it referred to any propelling device.

PROPELLER (Constant Speed). One that tends to maintain the engine revolutions under any flight conditions by automatically increasing or decreasing the pitch of the blades.

PROPELLER (Contra rotating). A twin unit comprising two co-axial propellers rotating in opposite directions. "Counter-rotating" is generally applied to two propellers on separate axes, or to two propellers on the same axis but driven independently by two engines.

PROPELLER (Reversible Pitch). One whose blades can be turned to negative pitch to produce reverse thrust to retard an aircraft when landing.

PROPELLER (Variable Pitch). Any propeller the pitch of whose blades can be altered in operation.

PROPELLER DISC. The space covered by a rotating propeller.

PROPJET. See TURBOPROP.

PROTOTYPE. The first one (or more) complete and working aircraft (or other object) of a new type, class, or series. There may be more than one prototype of a given machine. See also PRODUCTION MODEL.

PUSHER PROPELLER. A propeller placed behind its engine, and generally behind the main wings of an aeroplane.

PUSH-PULL. An adjective applied to a combination of pusher and tractor propellers.

RADIAL ENGINE. One in which one or more rows of cylinders are arranged radially around a common crankshaft: the cylinders are stationary, as distinct from the "rotary" engine (which see).

RADIUS OF ACTION. The distance between the take-off point of an aircraft and its point of safe return, allowing for the various conditions en route, at its 'target', etc. applied chiefly to military aircraft.

R.A.E. Abbreviation of Royal Aircraft Establishment.

R.AE.C. Abbreviation of Royal Aero Club.

R.AE.S. Abbreviation of Royal Aeronautical Society.

R.A.F. Abbreviation originally of the Royal Aircraft Factory (Farnborough); later of the Royal Air Force, (formed 1918).

RANGE. The overall distance an aircraft can fly under a given set of conditions. See also RADIUS OF ACTION.

RATE OF CLIMB INDICATOR. A flight instrument to show the rate of climb or descent of an aircraft.

REACTION PROPULSION. Propulsion by means of reaction to a jet of gas or liquid projected rearward (hence "jet propulsion"), as by a turbojet or rocket engine: in modern usage the term "jet propulsion" is only applied to air-breathing engines, and not to rocket engines.

REP. The initials of Robert Esnault-Pelterie which he used as a generic name for his aeroplanes, and which was inscribed on his machines, followed by a numeral.

REVERSIBLE PITCH PROPELLER. See PROPELLER (Reversible Pitch).

R.F.C. Abbreviation of Royal Flying Corps.

RIB. A chord-wise structural member of a wing, etc.

R.N.A.S. Abbreviation of Royal Naval Air Service.

ROCKET ENGINE. A reaction propulsion engine whose fuel includes an oxidiser, thus making it independent of the atmosphere. Rocket engines may use solid or liquid fuels.

ROLL. (*a*) Any movement about the horizontal axis of an aircraft; (*b*) a deliberate manoeuvre in which an aeroplane is rolled over: also HALF-ROLL; (*c*) the American equivalent of "run"; i.e. take-off, landing, or taxying, roll; also used thus in the early days of British flying.

ROLL, CONTROL IN. Control in an aircraft about its longitudinal axis, usually effected by ailerons or wing-warping.

ROTARY ENGINE. One in which the crankshaft remains fixed, and the cylinders revolve about it, the propeller revolving with them.

ROTARY WING AIRCRAFT. See ROTORCRAFT.

ROTATING WING AIRCRAFT. See ROTORCRAFT.

ROTOR (of a rotorcraft). An assembly comprising generally two or more long narrow wings (called "blades") set in a hub on a vertical shaft which provide lift (or lift and thrust).

ROTOR (Anti-torque). A small rotor on a rotorcraft revolving in the vertical plane which generates thrust to oppose the torque effects of the main rotor.

ROTORCRAFT. An aircraft which employs rotating aerofoils to provide lift, or both lift and propulsion. In American usage, a "gyroplane" is the equivalent of a rotorcraft. See also AUTOGIRO; GYROPLANE; HELICOPTER.

RUDDER. A vertical control surface for guiding an aircraft in the horizontal plane.

RUDDER (Horizontal). "Horizontal Rudder" was an early term for the elevator.

RUDDER BAR (or RUDDER PEDALS). The foot-operated bar or pedals to which are attached the cables operating the rudder.

RUNNER. An early term for a skid.

SAIL. Word used by Cayley for an aircraft wing.

SAILPLANE. A glider designed specially for soaring.

SEAPLANE. Any aeroplane built to operate only from the water: seaplanes are either FLOAT PLANES or FLYING BOATS. The word "seaplane" was introduced by Sir Winston Churchill in 1913. See also AMPHIBIAN.

SERVO-CONTROL. A power-assisted control.

SESQUIPLANE. A biplane, in which one wing (pair of wings) is much smaller than the other, generally half the area, or less.

SHOULDER WING MONOPLANE. One with the wings attached high on the fuselage: in practice often the same as a high wing monoplane.

SIDE-CURTAINS. The vertical surfaces sometimes placed between the wings of early biplanes to improve lateral stability, and turning the wings into box-kite cells.

SIMULATOR (Flight). See FLIGHT SIMULATOR.

SKID. Flat or curved wooden (or other) member which may be part of an aircraft undercarriage (with or without the addition of wheels); or be in the form of a TAIL SKID.

SKIDDING. The sidewise sliding of an aircraft away from the centre of the curve when turning.

SKIN FRICTION. The friction of the air particles on a surface in motion. See also DRAG.

SLAT. See SLOT.

SLIPSTREAM. The flow of air driven backward by the propeller.

SLOT. A gap between the wing and a specially formed slat, through which air is directed over the upper surface of the wing to preserve a smooth airflow, generally at high angles of incidence; the same principle applied to ailerons, etc.

SLOTTED WING. See SLOT.

SONIC SPEED. The speed of sound. See also SOUND.

SOUND (Speed of). The speed of sound is approximately 760 m.p.h. at sea level, decreasing with height (owing to decrease in temperature): in the stratosphere it is approximately 660 m.p.h. Speed below that of sound is called SUBSONIC; at that of sound SONIC; and above, SUPERSONIC. See also MACH NUMBER; TRANSONIC SPEED.

SOUND BARRIER. A popular but misleading term loosely indicating the rapid rise of drag at transonic speeds.

SPAN (of wings). The spread of the wing(s), from tip to tip.

SPAR. A span-wise structural member of a wing, etc.

SPEED. FLYING SPEED is the speed necessary for a fixed-wing aeroplane to attain, or maintain, in order to become or remain airborne. AIRSPEED is the speed of any aircraft through the air, i.e. relative to the air through which it moves. GROUND SPEED is the aircraft's speed in relation to the ground. SONIC SPEED is the speed of sound, i.e. about 760 m.p.h. at sea level (see SOUND).

SPEED BRAKE. See AIR BRAKE; FLAP; SPOILER.

SPIN. An aerial manoeuvre, intentional or not, in which an aeroplane descends vertically in autorotation.

SPINNER. A streamlined fairing fitted over the hub of an airscrew.

SPOILER. A projecting member designed to break down airflow around a body, in order to retard its movement; hence an air brake.

STABILITY AND CONTROL

STABILITY. There are two aspects of aircraft stability, longitudinal stability for motion *in* the plane of symmetry, and lateral stability for motion *out of* the plane of symmetry; the former concerns rising, falling and pitching movements; the latter, rolling, yawing and side-slipping movements. Colloquially and descriptively, however, one may also speak of "directional stability" which is a component of lateral stability.

CONTROL. Where flight control is concerned, one may speak of "longitudinal control", which is control in pitch; and "lateral control" which comprises control in both roll and yaw. In practise the term "lateral control" is often used to refer to control in roll only, and the term "directional control" for control in yaw. In the present work I have used the term "lateral control" for control in roll, unless otherwise stated.

In early aviation (up to 1908) the Europeans were concerned to ensure: (*a*) LONGITUDINAL STABILITY; *via* a tailplane at the back; (*b*) LONGITUDINAL CONTROL; *via* an elevator for control in pitch; (*c*) DIRECTIONAL STABILITY; *via* a keel area and a vertical surface in the rear; (*d*) DIRECTIONAL CONTROL; *via* a rear rudder. As the Europeans neglected the proper function and use of warping and ailerons, they found it difficult to control their machines when they attempted to turn them on rudder alone, with the outer wings producing more lift on the turn than the inner; the pilots could only counteract the inwards rolling momentum by putting on opposite rudder to accelerate the lowered wings and lift them, and—in extreme cases—hoping that this rudder action would be in time to stop the machine heeling right over and crashing. (*e*) STABILITY IN ROLL; *via* a dihedral angle of the wings. Until Wilbur Wright started flying in France in August 1908, the use of ailerons or warping to effect control in roll was neither properly understood nor practised by the Europeans; this was initially due to their remaining ignorant of the necessity to achieve proper control in roll when turning, and their belief that the main function of ailerons or warping was to maintain lateral balance in level flight; then, as a result of these considerations, it was due to their ignorance of the use of the rudder to counteract aileron (or warp) drag. The Wright brothers, on the other hand, were not concerned with any kind of inherent stability, but much concerned from the first with full lateral control (control in roll, yaw and side-slip).

STABILIZER. Any aerofoil used to provide stability.

STAGGER. The placing of the upper wing in advance of the lower in a biplane (or progressively of the upper two in a triplane), called 'positive' or 'forward' stagger. If this arrangement is reversed, it is called 'negative' or 'backward' stagger, or 'back-stagger'.

STALL. The behaviour of an aeroplane when, owing to excessive angle of incidence—usually associated with loss of speed—the wings lose lift.

STEERING AIR-BRAKES. See AIR-BRAKES (steering).

STEERING FLAPS (or TIPS). Early terms for ailerons.

STEP ROCKET. A multi-stage rocket.

STICK. Short for 'control stick', 'control column', or 'joy-stick'.

STRATOSPHERE. The layer of the earth's atmosphere above the tropopause, extending up to approximately 18 miles.

STREAMLINING. The giving of a specially shaped and smooth contour to an object to decrease its resistance in a fluid flow.

STRESSED-SKIN CONSTRUCTION. The use of the outer skin of a structure to carry primary structural loads in addition to local air pressure. See the special note on page 171; see also MONOCOQUE.

STRINGER. A longitudinal stiffening member in stressed-skin construction.

STRUT. Connecting member, e.g. between the wings of a biplane, etc.; mainly to take compression loads.

STUB-WING. A short wing.

SUBSONIC SPEED. Speed below that of sound. See also SOUND.

SUPERCHARGER. A pump or compressor for forcing more air or fuel-air mixture into an engine than it would normally induct at the prevailing atmosphere pressure.

SUPERSONIC SPEED. Speed above the speed of sound. See also SOUND.

TAB. A small auxiliary control surface set in, or attached to, a larger control surface in order either to correct or aid the latter's movement or position: a TRIM TAB is one that is set to trim the aircraft.

TACHOMETER. An instrument indicating revolutions per minute of any rotating unit.

TAIL (Flying). See FLYING TAIL.

TAIL-ASSEMBLY. Another term for TAIL-UNIT (which see).

TAIL BOOMS. Outrigger members supporting the tail-unit.

TAILPLANE. The fixed horizontal stabilising plane(s) of the tail-unit. ·

TAIL-UNIT. The rear assembly of an aircraft comprising, fin, rudder, tailplane, elevator, etc. Also called "tail assembly" and "empennage" (which see).

TANDEM. An arrangement of units one behind the other.

TAPER. The narrowing of an aerofoil (or other object) either in chord-length or thickness, generally applied to the former.

TAXI. To drive an aircraft along the ground or water, other than in take-off or landing runs.

TERMINAL VELOCITY. The constant velocity of a falling body attained when the resistance of the air has become equal to the force of gravity acting upon the body.

THRUST. The driving force exerted on any aircraft, missile, etc., by its propeller, rotor blades, propulsive jet, or other means.

TORQUE. A moment that produces, or tends to produce, rotation, twisting or torsion.

TRACTOR PROPELLER. One that pulls, i.e. in front of its engine and generally to the front of the main wings of an aeroplane.

TRAILING EDGE. The rear edge of an aerofoil, i.e. over which the air passes last.

TRANSONIC SPEED. The speed of an aircraft in the region of sonic speed, where the surrounding airflow is simultaneously subsonic, sonic, and supersonic over various parts of the machine.

TRIM TAB. See TAB.

TRIPLANE. An aeroplane with three main (sets of) planes set one above the other.

TURBOJET. The recognised combine-word for a gas turbine jet propulsion engine; or (loosely) an aeroplane propelled by it: as distinct from a TURBOPROP.

TURBOPROP. The recognised combine-word for an airscrew/gas turbine engine combination; or (loosely) an aeroplane propelled by it: sometimes referred to as a "propjet". See also TURBOJET.

TURN AND BANK INDICATOR. A gyroscopically controlled flight instrument indicating the rate of turn of an aeroplane, and amount of skidding (if any).

UNDERCARRIAGE. The collective term for the wheels or other gear supporting an aircraft on land or water, generally the former: also termed "landing gear".

VARIABLE PITCH PROPELLER. See PROPELLER.

V (or VEE) ENGINE. One with banks of cylinders arranged in a V, seen from the end.

VENTRAL. See DORSAL.

VENTURI TUBE. A tube with a constricted throat which, when placed in an airflow, brings about (in the throat) an increase in flow velocity with a consequent diminution of pressure (see BERNOUILLI THEOREM).

VERTICAL AXIS. See AXIS.

VERTICAL STABILIZER. The American term for a fin.

269

VOLPLANE. An early term (used as a verb or noun) for "glide".

VORTEX. A rotating airflow.

WARPING. See WING-WARPING.

WASH-IN and WASH-OUT. "Wash-in" is an increase in the angle of incidence of a wing towards, or at, the tip; "wash-out" is a decrease in the angle of incidence towards or at, the wingtip. "Wash-in" on one side, and "wash-out" on the other, was provided on the wings of early aeroplanes to counteract the torque effects of propellers and rotary engines. "Wash-in" is also incorporated at the tips of glider wings to give early warning of a stall.

WING(s). The main lifting aerofoil(s) of an aeroplane. By bird-derived usage, a monoplane is said to have two wings, even if there is only one connected surface. Hence a biplane has two 'sets' of wings. But, occasionally (as in 'gull-wing', etc.), the singular is used for convenience. In the last century the word 'wings' was often used technically to denote ornithoptering wings as opposed to fixed wings ('aero planes'). Cayley called a fixed wing a "sail".

WING-LOADING. The gross weight of an aeroplane divided by the wing area.

WING-WARPING. A twisting or torsion of a wing to increase or decrease its curvature and thus its angle of incidence, and effect control in roll; used first on the Wright machines. This misleading term ("wing-warping") was invented by Octave Chanute in 1903 as a kind of shorthand word for the helical twisting of the wings according to the Wrights' practice. It was first literally translated into French (1903–04) by the verb "gauchir", which did not mean a twisting of the wings, but a literal "warping" of them.

YAW. The movement of an aircraft about its vertical axis.

ZOOM. To climb briefly at an angle greater than the normal climbing angle.

Bibliography

Bibliography

NOTES

(1) Apart from a few titles, the many interesting and valuable reminiscences and biographies of pioneers have had to be omitted.

(2) The works are arranged chronologically by date of publication. Those in English, French and German should be understood as having appeared in London, Paris or Berlin unless otherwise stated.

(3) The word "airship" in early works often refers to all kinds of aircraft.

BATE, J. *The Mysteryes of Nature and Art*. 1634.

LANA TERZI, F. *Prodromo overo Saggio* (etc.). Brescia, 1670. [Chapters V and VI of this were published in translation, as *The Aerial Ship*, as No. 4 of the series *Aeronautical Classics*, 1910.]

BORELLI, J. A. *De Motu Animalium*. 2 vols. Roma, 1680–1. (Part of this was published, with the title *The Flight of Birds*, as no. 6 of the *Aeronautical Classics*, 1911.)

LAUNOY and BIENVENU. *Instruction sur la nouvelle Machine inventée par MM. Launoy . . . & Bienvenu*. 1784.

BOURGEOIS, David. *Recherches sur l'Art de voler, depuis la plus haute antiquité jusqu' à nos jours*. 1784.

GÉRARD, L.-J. *Essai sur l'Art du vol aérien*. 1784.

CAYLEY, Sir G. *Aeronautical and Miscellaneous Note-book (c. 1799–1826) of Sir George Cayley* (Edited by J. E. Hodgson). (Extra publication number 3 of the Newcomen Society.) Cambridge, 1933.

CAYLEY, Sir G. "On Aerial Navigation." Three articles in: *Nicholson's Journal of Philosophy*, vols. xxiv and xxv, 1809–10. Reprinted in full in GIBBS-SMITH (C.H.), *Sir George Cayley's Aeronautics (etc.)*. 1962 (see below).

LOUP, M. *Solution du Problème de la Locomotion aérienne*. 1853.

DEDREUX, D. *La Navigation aérienne en Chine*. 1863.

LA LANDELLE, G. J. G. DE. *Aviation, ou Navigation aérienne*. 1863.

ESTERNO, M. D'. *Du vol des Oiseaux*. 1864–65.

AMÉCOURT, PONTON D'. *Collection de Mémoires sur la Locomotion aérienne sans ballons*. 1864–1867.

NADAR (pseud. of F. Tournachon). *Le Droit au Vol*. 1865. (Translated as *The Right to Fly*, 1866.)

WENHAM, F. H. *Aërial Locomotion*, 1866. (Reprinted as no. 2 of the *Aeronautical Classics*, 1910.)

PATENT OFFICE (London). *Abridgments of Specifications relating to Aeronautics*, A.D. *1815–1866*. 1869.

WENHAM, F. H. "REPORT OF THE FIRST EXHIBITION." Appended to *Annual Report* [of the Aeronautical Society] *for 1868*. 1869.

PÉNAUD, A. "Aeroplane Automoteur: Équilibre automatique." In *L'Aéronaute*, January 1872.

MAREY, E. J. *La Machine Animale*. 1873. (Translated as *Animal Mechanism: a Treatise on Aerial Locomotion*. 1874.)

PÉNAUD, A. "*Un Brevet d'Aéroplane.*" In *L'Aéronaute*, October 1877.
DU TEMPLE, F. "L'Appareil de Locomotion Aérienne." In *L'Aéronaute*, August 1877.
LA LANDELLE, G. J. C. DE. *Dans les Airs: Histoire élémentaire de l'Aéronautique.* 1881.
MOUILLARD, L.-P. *L'Empire de l'Air: Essai d'Ornithologie appliquée à l'Aviation*, 1881. (Partially translated as *The Empire of the Air*, in the *Annual Report* of the Smithsonian Institution for 1902.)
GOUPIL, A. *La Locomotion Aërienne.* 1884.
LILIENTHAL, O. *Der Vogelflug als Grundlage der Fliegekunst.* 1889. (English translation from the second ed. of 1910, as *Bird Flight as a Basis of Aviation*, 1911.)
PILCHER, P. *Gliding*, 1890. (Reprinted as no. 5 of the *Aeronautical Classics* 1910.)
LANGLEY, S. P. *Experiments in Aerodynamics.* (Smithsonian Institution publication). Washington, D.C., 1891.
MOUILLARD, L. P. *Le vol sans battement.* 1891.
BREWER, G., and ALEXANDER, P. Y. *Aëronautics: an Abridgement of Aëronautical Specifications filed in the Patent Office, 1815–91.* 1893.
CHICAGO: International Conference on Aerial Navigation, 1893. *Proceedings.* New York, 1894.
CHANUTE, O. *Progress in Flying Machines.* (First published serially in *The American Railroad and Engineering Journal*, October 1891 to December 1893.) New York, 1894.
LILIENTHAL, O. [A number of his papers are available in English, and may be found in the three volumes of James Means' *Aeronautical Annual* (see below under 1895–1897).]
MOEDEBECK, H. W. L. *Taschenbuch zum praktischen Gebrauch für Flugtechniker und Luftschiffer.* Berlin, 1895 (2nd ed. 1904). (Translated from the 2nd ed. as *Pocket-Book of Aeronautics*, 1907.)
AERONAUTICAL ANNUAL. Edited by J. Means. 3 vols. New York, 1895–97.
LANGLEY, S. P. 1897. (See under 1911.)
LECORNU, J. *Les Cerfs Volants* (Kites). 1902.
LECORNU, J. *La Navigation Aérienne: Histoire documentaire et anecdotique.* 1903.
FULLERTON, J. D. *Report on Aerial Navigation.* Chatham, 1904.
ROOT, A. I. "Our Homes—What hath God wrought?" [his eyewitness account of the Wrights' circular flight of September 20th 1904] in *Gleanings in Bee Culture*, January 1st 1905.
BACON, GERTRUDE. *Balloons, Airships, and Flying Machines.* 1905.
ADER, C. *La première Étape de l'Aviation Militaire.* 1907.
AERO CLUB OF AMERICA. *Navigating the Air: a scientific Statement of the Progress of Aeronautical Science up to the Present Time.* New York, 1907.
LANCHESTER, F. W. *Aerodynamics.* 1907.
LANCHESTER, F. W. *Aerodonetics.* 1908.
HILDEBRANDT, A. *Airships Past and Present*, etc. (translated from *Die Luftschiffahrt*, etc., 1907). 1908.
MAXIM, Sir H. S. *Artificial and Natural Flight.* 1908.
COMMITTEE OF IMPERIAL DEFENCE. *Aerial Navigation: Report of a Sub-Committee of Imperial Defence, appointed* (in 1908] *by the Prime Minister.* 1909.
DUMAS, A. *Stud Book de l'Aviation: Ceux qui ont volé et leurs Appareils.* 1909.
RUMPLER, E. *Die Flugmaschine.* 1909.
PEYREY, F. *L'Idée aérienne: Aviation: Les Oiseaux artificiels.* 1909.
BERGET, A. *La Route de l'Air.* 1909. (Translated as *The Conquest of the Air*, 1909.)
ADER, C. *L'Aviation Militaire.* 1909. (2nd ed. 1911.)
LOUGHEED, V. *Vehicles of the Air.* 1909 [1910 given on title-page).
JANE, F. T. *All the World's Air-Ships: Aeroplanes and Dirigibles.* 1909, 1911.

JANE, F. T. *All the World's Air-Craft: Aeroplanes and Dirigibles.* 1912, 1913, 1914.
JANE, F. T. *All the World's Aircraft.* Edited by C. G. Grey [and later by others]. 1916 to date (except for 1921 when there was no issue).
FERRIS, R. *How to Fly; or the Conquest of the Air.* 1910.
FERBER, F. *L'Aviation: ses Débuts, son Développement.* 1910.
GRAND-CARTERET, J., and DELTEIL, L. *La Conquête de l'Air vue par l'Image (1495–1909).* 1910.
GRAHAME-WHITE, C., and HARPER, H. *The Aeroplane, Past, Present and Future* [includes a biographical section on early aviators]. 1911.
LANGLEY, S. P. *Langley Memoir on Mechanical Flight.* (Smithsonian Institution publication) 2 parts [the first part was written by Langley himself in 1897]. Washington, D.C., 1911.
O'GORMAN, M. *Problems relating to Aircraft.* (Institution of Automobile Engineers publication). 1911.
FRANKFURT a. M.: Exhibition, 1909. *Katalog der historischen Abteilung der ersten Internationalen Luftschiffahrts-Ausstellung* ... 1909 [including bibliog.]. Frankfurt, 1910.
LA VAULX, H. DE (Comte). *Le Triomphe de la Navigation Aérienne.* 1912.
DOLLFUS, E. H. *Petits Modèles d'Aéroplanes.* 1912.
FALKENBERG, G. VON. *Der Fallschirm* (The Parachute). 1912.
MAXIM, H., and HAMMER, W. J. *Chronology of Aviation.* New York, 1912.
DUMAS, A. *Les Accidents d'Aviation.* 1913.
WRIGHT, O. and A. [Special combined number of the *Aeronautical Journal,* July–September, 1916 on the Wright brothers.]
BARBER, H. *The Aeroplane Speaks* [including more than 240 illustrations of aircraft types, 1903–18). 1916. 7th ed. 1918.
VIVIAN, E. C., and MARSH, W. Lockwood. *A History of Aeronautics.* 1921.
BOFFITO, G. *Il Volo in Italia.* Firenze, 1921.
JONES, H. A., and RALEIGH, Sir W. *The War in the Air.* [The official history] 6 vols., with appendix, 1922–37.
WEISS, J. B. *Gliding and Soaring Flight.* 1922.
HODGSON, J. E. *The History of Aeronautics in Great Britain* (from the earliest times to the latter half of the nineteenth century). 1924.
MARSH, W. LOCKWOOD. *Aeronautical Prints and Drawings.* 1924.
LA VAULX, H. (Comte de), and TISSANDIER, P. *Joseph et Étienne de Montgolfier.* Annonay, 1926.
LAUFER, B. *The Prehistory of Aviation* (Field Museum publication). Chicago, 1928.
GAMBLE, C. F. S. *The Air Weapon: being some Account of the Growth of British Aeronautics from the Beginnings in the Year 1783 until the End of the Year 1929.* Vol. I. 1929.
GOLDSTROM, J. *A Narrative History of Aviation* [i.e. from the Wrights to 1929]. New York, 1930.
MURPHY, C. J. V. *Parachute.* New York, 1930.
DIXON, C. *Parachuting.* 1930.
MAGOUN, F. A., and HODGINS, E. *A History of Aircraft.* New York, 1931.
CIERVA, J. DE LA. *Wings of To-morrow; the Story of the Autogiro.* New York, 1931.
DAVY, M. J. B. *Henson and Stringfellow—their Work in Aeronautics* (Science Museum publication). 1931.
DOLLFUS, C., and BOUCHÉ, H. *Histoire de l'Aéronautique,* 1932. (Revised ed. 1942.)
BRETT, R. D. *The History of British Aviation, 1908–14.* 1934.
DURAND, W. F. *Aerodynamic Theory,* Vol. I (Division D): "Historical Sketch", by R. Giacomelli. Berlin, 1934.
SUPF, P. *Das Buch der deutschen Fluggeschichte.* 2 vols. Stuttgart, 1935. (2nd ed. 1956.)

GIACOMELLI, R. *Gli Scritti di Leonardo da Vinci sul Volo.* Roma, 1936.
DAVY, M. J. B. *Aeronautics: Heavier-than-Air Aircraft. Pt. III, The Propulsion of Aircraft* (Science Museum Publication). 1936.
SCHULZE, H. G., and STIASNY, W. *Flug durch Muskelkraft.* Frankfurt a. M., 1936.
RANDOLPH, Stella. *Lost Flights of Gustave Whitehead.* Washington, D.C., 1937.
GREY, C. G. *History of the Air Ministry.* 1940.
JOHNSTON, S. P. *Horizons Unlimited: a graphic History of Aviation.* New York, 1941.
BRYDEN, H. G. (ed.). *Wings: an Anthology of Flight.* 1942.
LOW, A. M. *Parachutes in Peace and War.* 1942.
DUHEM, J. *Histoire des Idées aéronautiques avant Montgolfier.* 1943.
DUHEM, J. *Musée aéronautiques avant Montgolfier: Recueil des Figures et Documents* (etc.). 1943.
MILBANK, J. *The First Century of Flight in America.* Princeton (U.S.A.), 1943.
KELLY, F. C. *The Wright Brothers.* 1944.
HEINMULLER, J. P. V. *Man's Fight to Fly: famous World-record Flights and a Chronology of Aviation.* New York, 1944.
DICKINSON, T. A. *The Aeronautical Dictionary.* New York, 1945.
SAUNDERS, H. St. G. *Per Ardua: the Rise of British Air Power, 1911–39.* 1944.
HOFF, N. J. "A Short History of the Development of Airplane Structures." In *American Scientist*, Vol. 34, Nos. 2 and 3, Spring and Summer, 1946.
LEE, A. *The German Air Force.* 1946.
NICOLSON, M. H. *Voyages to the Moon.* New York, 1948.
STORER, J. H. *The Flight of Birds* (Cranbrook Institute of Science publication). Bloomfield Hills (Mich. U.S.A.), 1948.
CHAMBE, R. *Histoire de l'Aviation,* 1948.
DAVY, M. J. B. *Interpretive History of Flight* (Science Museum publication). 2nd ed., 1948.
GREGORY, H. F. *The Helicopter.* 1948.
PUDNEY, J. *Laboratory of the Air* [The Royal Aircraft Establishment, Farnborough]. 1948.
DAVY, M. J. B. *Aeronautics: Heavier-than-Air Aircraft, Pts. I and II. Historical Survey; Catalogue of the Exhibits.* 2nd ed. (Science Museum publications). 1949.
BRITISH STANDARDS INSTITUTION. *Glossary of Aeronautical Terms.* 4th edn. 1950–52.
SCHLAIFER, R., and HERON, S. D. *Development of Aircraft Engines and Fuels* (Harvard University publication). Boston, 1950.
WRIGHT, W. and O. *Miracle at Kitty Hawk: the Letters of Wilbur and Orville Wright.* Edited by F. C. Kelly. New York, 1951.
LEY, W. *Rockets, Missiles and Space Travel.* 2nd ed. 1951.
DORMAN, G. *Fifty Years Fly-past: from Wright Brothers to Comet.* 1951.
BROKE-SMITH, P. W. L. *The History of early British Military Aeronautics.* Privately printed, 1952 (from the *Royal Engineers Journal,* 1952).
HUNSAKER, J. C. *Aeronautics at the Mid-Century.* Yale (U.S.A.), 1952.
LEE, A. *The Soviet Air Force.* New ed. 1952.
TURCK, A. *Théorie, Fabrication et Lancement des Boomerangs.* 1952.
UCCELLI, A. *I Libri del Volo di Leonardo da Vinci.* Milano, 1952.
GIBBS-SMITH, C. H. *A History of Flying.* 1953.
LINDBERGH, C. A. *The Spirit of St. Louis.* 1953.
WRIGHT, ORVILLE. *How we invented the Aeroplane.* Edited by F. C. Kelly [Orville Wright's deposition in the Montgomery trial]. New York, 1953.
WHITTLE, Sir F. *Jet.* 1953.
SHRADER, W. A. *Fifty Years of Flight: a Chronicle of the Aviation Industry in America, 1903–1953.* Cleveland, 1953.

MORRIS, L., and SMITH, K. *Ceiling Unlimited: the Story of American Aviation from Kitty Hawk to Supersonics.* New York, 1953.

RICHARDS, D., and SAUNDERS, H. ST. G. *The Royal Air Force, 1939–1945.* 3 vols. 1953–4.

STEVENS, J. H. *The Shape of the Aeroplane.* 1953.

WRIGHT, W. & O. *The Papers of Wilbur and Orville Wright.* Edited by Marvin W. McFarland. 2 vols. New York, 1953.

PRITCHARD, J. L. "The Wright Brothers and the Royal Aeronautical Society." In *Journal of the Roy. Aeron. Soc.*, December 1953.

'YEAR.' *A Pictorial History of Aviation: the complete Story of man's Conquest of the Air from his earliest Dreams to the present Jet Age.* By the editors of *Year.* Los Angeles and New York, 1953.

THETFORD, O. G., and RIDING, E. J. *Aircraft of the 1914–18 War.* New ed. Marlow, 1954.

ROLFE, D., and DAWYDOFF, A. *Airplanes of the World, from Pusher to Jet, 1490 to 1954.* New York, 1954.

KÁRMÁN, T. VON. *Aerodynamics: selected Topics in the Light of their Historical Development.* Cornell (U.S.A.), 1954.

HÉBRARD, J. A. L. *L'Aviation des Origines à nos Jours.* 1954.

KEMP, P. K. *Fleet Air Arm.* 1954.

GATLAND, K. W. *Development of the Guided Missile.* 2nd ed. 1954.

DESOUTTER, D. M. *All About Aircraft.* 1954.

GREEN, W. and CROSS, R. *The Jet Aircraft of the World.* 1955.

LIPTROT, R. N. and WOODS, J. D. *Rotorcraft.* 1955.

LENT, H. B. *The Helicopter Book.* New York, 1956.

WALLACE, G. *The Flight of Alcock and Brown.* 1955.

SMITH, G. G. *Gas Turbines and Jet Propulsion.* 6th ed. 1955.

TAYLOR, J. W. R. *A Picture History of Flight.* 1955 (2nd ed. 1960).

PEREIRA, H. B. *Aircraft Badges and Markings.* Southampton, 1955.

ROBERTSON, B. *Aircraft Camouflage and Markings, 1907–54.* Marlow, 1956.

GREEN, W., and POLLINGER, G. *The Aircraft of the World.* Revised ed. 1956.

BALLANTYNE, A. M., and PRITCHARD, J. L. "The Lives and Work of William Samuel Henson and John Stringfellow." In *Journal of the Roy. Aeron. Soc.*, June 1956.

HALLE, G. *Otto Lilienthal.* 2nd ed. Düsseldorf, 1956.

UNITED STATES AIR FORCE. *The United States Air Force Dictionary.* Edited by W. A. Heflin. Washington, D.C., 1956.

THETFORD, O. G. *Aircraft of the Royal Air Force, 1918–57.* 1957.

BRUCE, J. M. *British Aeroplanes, 1914–18.* 1957.

BECKFORD, L. *An ABC of Aeronautics.* 1957.

PRITCHARD, J. L. "The Dawn of Aerodynamics." In *Journal of the Roy. Aeron. Soc.*, March 1957.

GREEN, W., and FRICKER, J. *The Air Forces of the World.* 1958.

PRITCHARD, J. L. "Francis Herbert Wenham." In *Journal of the Roy. Aeron. Soc.*, August 1958.

WALLACE, G. *Flying Witness: Harry Harper and the Golden Age of Aviation.* 1958.

GIBBS-SMITH, C. H. "The Origins of the Aircraft Propeller." In *Quarterly Review* (*Rotol and British Messier Journal*), 1959.

STUBELIUS, S. *Studies (and further Studies) in the History of Terms for Aircraft in English:* Vol. I, *Airship, Aeroplane, Aircraft* (1958); Vol. II, *Balloon, Flying Machine, Helicopter* (1960). 2 vols. Göteborg, 1958–60.

DUHEM, J. *Histoire des Origines du Vol à Réaction.* 1959.

NAYLER, J. L. *Dictionary of Aeronautical Engineering.* 1959.

GIBBS-SMITH, C. H. "The Birth of the Aeroplane"; BROOKS, P. W. "The Development of the Aeroplane"; MENSFORTH, E. "The Future of the Aeroplane." (The three

Cantor Lectures for 1958, reprinted in the *Journal of the Roy. Soc. of Arts*, January 1959.)

GIBBS-SMITH, C. H. *The Aeroplane: an historical Survey* (Science Museum publication). 1960. (For 2nd ed., see *Aviation: an historical Survey*. 1969.)

WISSMAN, G. *Geschichte der Luftfahrt von Ikarus bis zur Gegenwart.* Berlin, 1960.

JACKSON, A. J. *British Civil Aircraft, 1919–1959.* 2 vols. 1959, 1960.

PRITCHARD, J. L. *Sir George Cayley: the Inventor of the Aeroplane.* 1960.

BROOKS, P. W. *The Modern Airliner: its Origin and Development.* 1961.

BABINGTON-SMITH, C. *Testing Time: a Study of Man and Machine in the Test-Flying Era.* 1961.

HART, I. B. *The World of Leonardo da Vinci.* 1961.

DE HAVILLAND, SIR G. *Sky Fever.* 1961.

SEIFERT, K. D. *Otto Lilienthal: Mensch und Werk.* Neuenhagen-bei-Berlin, 1961.

EMME, E. M. *Aeronautics and Astronautics; an American Chronology of Science and Technology in the Exploration of Space, 1915–1960.* Washington, D.C. (National Aeronautics and Space Administration), 1961.

THETFORD, O. *Aircraft of the Royal Air Force since 1918.* 1962.

WYKEHAM, P. *Santos-Dumont.* 1962.

HADDOW, G. W., and GROSZ, P. M. *The German Giants: the German R-Planes, 1914–1918.* 1962.

DOLLFUS, C. *Les Avions.* 1962.

THETFORD, O., and GRAY, P. *German Aircraft of the First World War.* 1962.

LEWIS, P. *British Aircraft, 1809–1914.* 1962.

GIBBS-SMITH, C. H. *Sir George Cayley's Aeronautics, 1796–1855* (Science Museum publication). 1962.

HALLE, G. *Otto Lilienthal und seine Flugzeug-Konstruktionen.* Munich (Deutsches Museum), 1962.

GIBBS-SMITH, C. H. *The Wright Brothers: a Brief Account of their Work* (Science Museum publication). 1963.

SWANBOROUGH, F. W. and BOWERS, P. M. *United States Military Aircraft since 1909.* 1963.

MEANS, J. H. *James Means and the Problem of Manflight during the Period 1882–1920.* Washington, D.C. (Smithsonian Institution), 1964.

PARKIN, J. H. *Bell and Baldwin: their Development of Aerodromes and Hydrodromes at Baddeck, Nova Scotia.* Toronto, 1964.

YOUNG, PEARL I. (ed.). *The Chanute-Wenham Correspondence, September 13, 1892 to January 23, 1908.* (Privately duplicated) Lancaster, Pa. (U.S.A.), 1964.

DOLLFUS, C., BEAUBOIS, H., and ROUGERON, C. *L'Homme, l'Air, et l'Espace: Aéronautique, Astronautique.* 1965.

LEWIS, P. *The British Fighter since 1912.* 1965 (2nd ed. 1966).

NAYLER, J. L., and OWER, E. *Aviation: its technical Development.* 1965.

WEYL, A. R. *Fokker: the Creative Years.* 1965.

NEEDHAM, J. "The Pre-History of Aeronautical Engineering." Chapter 27 (m) in *Science and Civilisation in China*, Vol. 4, Part II. Cambridge, 1965.

EMME, E. M. *A History of Space Flight.* Washington, D.C., 1965.

GIBBS-SMITH, C. H. *The Invention of the Aeroplane, 1809–1909.* 1966.

GIBBS-SMITH, C. H. *A Directory and Nomenclature of the First Aeroplanes, 1809 to 1909* (Science Museum publication). 1966.

HARVIE, E. F. *Venture the Far Horizon: the Pioneer Long-Distance Flights in New Zealand.* Christchurch (N.Z.), 1966.

KING, H. F. *Aeromarine Origins.* 1966.

RANDOLPH, S. *Before the Wrights flew: the Story of Gustave Whitehead.* New York, 1966.

SCHWIPPS, W. *Otto Lilienthal's Flugversuche.* 1966.

278

STINTON, D. *The Anatomy of the Aeroplane*. 1966.
STROUD, J. *European Transport Aircraft since 1910*. 1966.
DUVAL, G. R. *British Flying-Boats, 1909–1952*. 1966.
LEWIS, P. *The British Bomber since 1914*. 1967.
GIBBS-SMITH, C. H. *Leonardo da Vinci's Aeronautics* (Science Museum publication). 1967.
HART, C. *Kites: an historical Survey*. 1967.
PENROSE, H. J. *British Aviation: the Pioneer Years*. 1967.
WRIGHT, O. and W. *Wilbur and Orville wright: a Bibliography commemorating the Hundredth Anniversary of the Birth of Wilbur Wright*. Washington, D.C. [Library of Congress.] 1968.
GIBBS-SMITH, C. H. *Clément Ader: his Flight-Claims and his Place in History* (Science Museum publication). 1968.
MILLER, R. and SAWERS, D. *The technical development of modern aviation*. 1968.
GABLEHOUSE, C. *Helicopters and autogiros: a chronicle of rotating-wing aircraft*. 1968.
GIBBS-SMITH, C. H. *Aviation: an historical survey from its origins to the end of World War II.* (Science Museum publication). 1970.
SHAVROV, V. B. *Istoriya konstruktsiĭ samoletov v SSSR do 1938 goda*. Moscow, 1969.
PENROSE, H. *British Aviation: the Great War and Armistice*. 1969.
MASON, F. K. and WINDROW, M. C. *Air Facts and Feats*. 1970.
HART, C. *The dream of flight: aeronautics from classical times to the Renaissance*. 1972.
CHAMBE, R. *Histoire de l'Aviation*. Paris, 1972.
GIBBS-SMITH, C. H. *The rebirth of European aviation, 1902–1908*. (Science Museum publication). 1974.
WALKER, P. B. *Early aviation at Farnborough: the first aeroplanes*. 1974.
JABLONSKI, E. *Seawings: an illustrated history of flying boats*. 1974.
GIBBS-SMITH, C. H. *Early flying machines, 1799–1909*. 1975.
RENSTROM, A. G. *Wilbur and Orville Wright: a chronology*. Washington, D.C. 1975.
CHANT, C. *Aviation: an illustrated history*. 1978.
SCHWIPPS, W. *Lilienthal*. Berlin, 1979.
BURNET, C. *Three centuries to Concorde*. 1979.
COMBS, H. *Kill Devil Hill: the epic of the Wright brothers, 1899–1909*. 1980.
CROUCH, T. D. *A dream of wings: Americans and the airplane, 1875–1905*. New York, 1981.
MOLSON, K. M. *Canadian aircraft since 1909*. 1981.
SMITH, H. *Aircraft piston engines*. New York, 1981.
CASEY, L. S. *Curtiss: the Hammondsport era 1907–1915*. New York, 1981.

GENERAL BIBLIOGRAPHIES

TISSANDIER, G. *Bibliographie Aéronautique: Catalogue de Livres d'Histoire, de Science, de Voyages et de Fantaisie, traitant de la Navigation aérienne ou des Aérostats*. 1887.
FRANKFURT a.M.: Exhibition. *Katalog der historischen Abteilung* (etc. including bibliography). 1910.
PATENT OFFICE. *Subject List of Works on Aerial Navigation and Meteorology in the Library*. 1905.
WASHINGTON, D.C.: Smithsonian Institution. *Bibliography of Aeronautics*. Compiled by Paul Brockett [From the earliest times to July 1909]. Washington, D.C., 1910.
WASHINGTON, D.C.: National Advisory Committee for Aeronautics. *Bibliography of Aeronautics, 1909–1916*. Washington, D.C., 1921.
UNITED STATES: W.P.A. *Bibliography of Aeronautics*. 50 parts. New York, 1936–40.
NEW YORK: Public Library. *History of Aeronautics: a selected List of References to Material in the . . . Library*. Compiled by W. B. Gamble. New York, 1938.

LONDON: Royal Aeronautical Society. *A List of Books, Periodicals, and Pamphlets in the Library.* 1941.

WISSMANN, G. *Geschichte der Luftfahrt von Ikarus bis zur Gegenwart* [Bibliography, including Russian works, on pages 415–430]. Berlin, 1960.

STUBELIUS, S. *Studies in the History of Terms for Aircraft in English*, Vol. II [Bibliography on pages 339–356]. Göteborg, 1960.

PERIODICALS

L'Année Aéronautique (Paris)
The Aero (London)
L'Aéro (Paris)
L'Aéronaute (Paris)
Aeronautics (London)
Aeronautics (New York)
L'Aéronautique (Paris)
The Aeroplane (London)
L'Aérophile (Paris)
Air Pictorial (London)
Flight (London)
Flying (London)
Illustrierte Aeronautische Mittheilungen (Berlin)
Icare (Paris)
The Mechanics' Magazine (London)

The *Annual Reports* of the Aeronautical Society
The Aeronautical Journal (organ of the Aeronautical Society)
The Journal of the Royal Aeronautical Society

Conversion Tables etc.

METRES TO YARDS AND FEET

(taken to the nearest yard and foot for lengths over 20 metres)

metres (m.)	yards (yds.)	feet (ft.)
1	1·09	3·28
2	2·19	6·56
3	3·28	9·84
4	4·37	13·12
5	5·47	16·40
6	6·56	19·69
7	7·66	22·97
8	8·75	26·25
9	9·84	29·53
10	10·94	32·80
15	16·40	49·21
20	21·87	65·62
25	27	82
30	33	98
35	38	115
40	44	131
45	49	147
50	55	164
60	66	197
70	77	230
80	87	262
90	98	295
91	100	299
100	109	328
150	164	492
200	219	656
250	273	819
300	328	984
400	437	1311
402	440 (¼ mile)	1320
500	547	1641
600	656	1968
700	766	2298
800	875	2625
805	880 (½ mile)	2640
900	984	2952
1000 (1 km.)	1094	3282
1609	1760 (1 mile)	5280

KILOMETRES TO MILES

kilometres (km.)	miles (mi.)
1	⅝ (1093·6 yds.; 3280 ft.)
1·6	1
2	1·2
3	1·9
4	2·5
5	3·1
6	3·7
7	4·4
8	5·0
9	5·6
10	6·2
15	9·3
20	12·4
25	15·5
30	18·6
35	21·7
40	24·9
45	28·0
50	31·1
75	46·6
100	62·1
125	78·0
150	93·2

SQUARE METRES TO SQUARE FEET

(including common wing areas in early aviation)

square metres	square feet	square metres	square feet
1	10·8	22	236·8
2	21·5	24	258·3
3	32·3	25	269·0
4	43·0	26	279·9
5	53·8	30	322·9
6	64·6	35	376·7
9	96·9	40	430·6
10	107·6	48	516·7
12	129·2	50	538·2
13	139·9	52	559·7
17	183·0	55	592·0
18	193·8	60	645·8
20	215·3		

LENGTHS AND DISTANCES OF SOME FAMILIAR ITEMS AND PLACES

	km.	*m.*	*miles*	*yds.*	*ft.*
Length of cricket pitch		20·1		22	66
Length of lawn tennis court		23·8		26	78
Length of American football field		91·4		100	300
Length of International Soccer field		109·7		120	360
Length of British Soccer field		118·8		130	390
In London					
Breadth (east–west) of the Round Pond in Kensington Gardens		201.2		220	660
Length of Westminster Bridge		246·9		270	810
From Hyde Park Corner (Apsley House) to Dorchester Hotel, Park Lane		402	¼	440	1320
to (just beyond) Grosvenor House		805	½	880	2640
to Marble Arch	1·2	1207	¾	1320	3960
to Exhibition Road	1·6	1609	1	1760	5280
to (a few yards short of) Leicester Square	1·6	1609	1	1760	5280
In Edinburgh					
Length of Princes Street	1·6	1609	1	1760	5280
In Paris					
Length of the Champs-Elysées, from the Place de la Concorde to the Arc de Triomphe	2·0	2012	1¼	2200	6600
In New York					
Length of the Brooklyn Bridge		468·2	⅓	531⅔	1595
The English Channel (at its narrowest)	33·8		21		

Addenda

Addenda

Various claims to powered flight prior to December 1903

(A note by John A. Bagley, added January 1984)

A persistent theme in aeronautical history is the claim that some person or another "flew before the Wright Brothers". Many such claims prove, on investigation, to involve an unmanned model aircraft, or an unpowered glider, or a flight which can be dated to the period between December 1903 and August 1908 when the Wrights' flying prowess was fully revealed to the world.

There remain a number of cases of claimed powered flights which cannot so easily be explained, including several which were of particular concern to the late Charles Gibbs-Smith, and which he had intended to deal with in his projected second volume of this work. Of these, the most important claim was discussed at length in his book *Clement Ader—his flight-claims and his place in history* published in 1968; while the claims of Mozhaiski, Maxim and Jatho are sufficiently covered on pages 53, 61–63, and 106.

In the following sections, I have summarised the stories of some less important claimants. In doing so, I believe that I have fairly presented the substance of Charles Gibbs-Smith's research, and that he would agree with my conclusions.

It should be observed that between May 1906, when the Wrights' main patent was granted, and 1917, when the American manufacturers accepted a cross-licencing agreement to facilitate wartime production, a number of persons had a clear interest in proving the existence of "prior art" as a reason for invalidating the Wright patent. This provides an understandable reason to magnify the achievements of earlier would-be aviators. It is more difficult to excuse some claims made in recent years which seem to stem from a form of chauvinism which cannot accept that practical aviation could have been started in such an obscure place as Dayton, Ohio.

It may also be remarked that if each of the claims quoted below were accepted in full without question, the history of the development of practical aviation would not be altered at all. The events of 17 December 1903 would be of little consequence if they had happened in isolation. Their importance is that they represent an easily identified stage in the progress of the Wright Brothers from trials with a tethered kite in 1899 to demonstrations of flying in 1908 which convinced the world that the practical flying-machine had arrived at last. None of the flights discussed below had any comparable consequence.

Gilmore

Lyman Gilmore, Jr. of Nevada City, California, claimed in 1927 that he had flown a steam-powered monoplane for four miles in 1896, and versions of this story are still occasionally published. Ernest L. True carried out a careful investigation into Gilmore's history, published in the *Journal* of the American Aviation Historical Society, Summer 1967, and found no substance for any such flight. Gilmore built a number of large model gliders between about 1900 and 1907 before setting up the

Gilmore Airship Company at Grass Valley, California. He started construction of a large eight-passenger monoplane which was never completed, and a smaller two-seat machine in which he made unsuccessful attempts to fly in 1912.

Herring

A. M. Herring studied engineering in New York from 1883 to 1888, during which time he built several unsuccessful gliders. Inspired by reading of Lilienthal's activities, he built two more gliders in 1894 with which he made brief flights, and was then hired by Chanute to build and test models of h's multi-wing glider designs. From May to November 1895, Herring worked for Lar 3ley in Washington, but then returned to Chanute's employment.

It is evident from Chanute's own accounts that Herring had a significant share in the design of Chanute's most successful machine, the triplane hang-glider of August 1896 which was converted to biplane configuration in September (see p. 83). Herring was so encouraged by his successful flights (up to 109 metres) on this machine that he prepared drawings for an aircraft powered by a compressed-air engine.

As Chanute was reluctant to support this project, Herring next built a triplane hang-glider which he flew in October 1896, covering distances up to 285 metres. Then, financed by New York banker M. C. Arnot and assisted by Chanute's carpenter William Avery, Herring produced a biplane glider in August 1897 which so closely resembled the 1896 Chanute-Herring biplane that Chanute used photographs and drawings of the two craft interchangeably, to the confusion of subsequent historians. This glider was flown successfully by Herring and others on numerous occasions in September 1897.

Herring's powered aircraft—another biplane hang-glider with cruciform tail unit, similar to the 1896 design—was finally built in 1898. After unsuccessfully trying to develop a petrol engine, Herring reverted to his original scheme of a compressed-air motor, which was supplied from an air-cylinder sufficient for only 15 seconds running. The engine, mounted above the lower wing, drove two propellers on a common shaft, one ahead of and one behind the wings. On 10 and 22 October 1898, Herring was airborne for 15 and 22 metres distance, over the beach at St. Joseph, Michigan, in this machine.

These two brief hops were as close as anyone was to come to achieving powered flight before the Wrights. In later years, Herring and others claimed these "flights" as a major step towards practical aviation, and that Herring had been "robbed" of the credit due to him. But it is clear that Herring had reached a dead end[1]: his primitive form of control, by shifting body-weight alone, constrained the size of his aircraft so that they could not carry the additional weight of an adequate power-unit, even if Herring could have built or acquired one. By 1899, he had built several experimental steam engines, but admitted that the powered aircraft introduced many new problems, "particularly in the area of steering and control". Subsequently, he turned to other activities, returning to aviation in March 1909 with the short-lived Herring-Curtiss Company established to build machines designed by Curtiss.

[1] By about 1970, modern light-weight materials and engines made powered hang-gliders controlled by movement of the pilot's body alone technically feasible, but these primitive controls were soon augmented or supplanted by aerodynamic controls in a new generation of "micro-light" aircraft.

Pearse

Richard Pearse was a farmer and mechanic in a remote part of New Zealand who applied in July 1906 for a patent on a high-wing monoplane with tricycle undercarriage, driven by an engine and propeller and controlled by a combination of aerodynamic surfaces and pilot's weight-shifting. The only contemporary published references to the construction of Pearse's aircraft are local newspaper reports in November 1909 stating that it had recently flown about 25 yards.

Pearse himself, in a letter to the Dunedin *Evening Star* in May 1915, said that he began his experiments in 1904 after reading of Langley's failure; that by 1906 he had "sufficiently perfected" his monoplane to patent it; that he built only one experimental aircraft; and that he abandoned his work when it became clear that a substantial industry had been established overseas, particularly in France. In another letter published in September 1928, Pearse said that his aircraft "was uncontrollable and would spin round broadside on directly it left the ground".

Nevertheless, since 1971 an elaborate hypothesis has been constructed by a group in New Zealand to prove that Pearse flew before the Wright Brothers. On the basis of recollections gathered between 1954 and 1978 from various old inhabitants of the area, they postulate that Pearse made several flights in 1902 and 1903: notably one of about 1·2 kilometres on 31 March 1902, and another of over a kilometre exactly one year later on 31 March 1903.

Richard Pearse's own account seems so much more credible that these remarkable claims must be rejected.

Watson

A claim was made in 1953 by James Y. Watson that his brother, Preston A. Watson, had built and successfully flown a powered aircraft at Erroll, Scotland, in 1903, before the Wright Brothers. Charles Gibbs-Smith investigated this claim, and convinced James Watson that it was untenable. Preston's three identifiable machines were built between late 1908 and 1913, but there is some slight evidence that he may have built a Wright-type glider in 1903 and fitted an engine to it in 1906. Preston Watson himself, in the magazine *Flight* of 15 May 1914, stated that the Wright Brothers "were the first to fly in a practical way".

Whitehead

Gustave Weisskoff, a German mechanic who adopted the name Whitehead after migrating to the U.S.A., first comes to notice in 1897, when he built a man-powered ornithopter for the Boston Aeronautical Society. This was a biplane with cruciform tail unit, with a pair of panels mounted between the wings which were evidently intended to be flapped by the pilot. This machine almost certainly never left the ground.

The powered machine in which Whitehead claimed to have flown was built at Bridgeport, Connecticut; it was described and illustrated in *Scientific American* of 8 June 1901 and in *Illustrierte Aeronautische Mittheilungen* of October 1901. It was a monoplane with a curious boat-shaped fuselage, a horizontal tail surface, and two propellers ahead of the wing stated to be driven by a 20 h.p. two-cylinder acetylene engine. For movement on the road, the wings and tail unit were to be folded, and a separate engine of 10 h.p. drove two of the four road wheels. (The mysterious acetylene engine, described by Whitehead as "a wonder", has never been described in detail and almost certainly never existed. Contemporary photographs show Whitehead with a two-cylinder steam engine, but it is not actually installed in the aircraft.) In the *Scientific American* article, it is said that flight has not yet been attempted, but in the German magazine Whitehead states that he has made a flight lasting 1½ minutes covering 2800 feet (860 metres).

An account of this flight, full of circumstantial detail, was published in the *Bridgeport Sunday Herald* on 18 August 1901: this states that the flight was made in the middle of the night, about 2 a.m. on 14 August, from a rough field outside the town to which the aircraft was driven on its own wheels. The story was repeated (shorn of its less credible details) in the *New York Herald* of 19 August.

These reports of successful powered flight of over half a mile attracted no great attention at the time; and Whitehead's letters to the *American Inventor*, in which he claimed two flights on 17 January 1902 of 2 miles and 7½ miles over Long Island Sound, were published in the issue of April 1 and then, it seems, were totally disregarded until 1937, when a book called *Lost Flights of Gustave Whitehead* written by Stella Randolph was published. From 1963 onwards, the claims have been reiterated with increasing vehemence by a small group of Connecticut patriots, culminating in the book *History by Contract* by William J. O'Dwyer and Stella Randolph published in 1978, which charges that Whitehead's flight claims have been deliberately suppressed by a long-standing and widespread conspiracy among professional aviation historians.

The account of the flight on 14 August 1901 in the *Bridgeport Sunday Herald* reads like a work of juvenile fiction, but Whitehead's frustratingly brief statements are quite straightforward claims for a substantial achievement. They were made in reputable and widely-read journals and could certainly not have been overlooked by contemporary workers. Yet Whitehead continued to work in comparitive obscurity, building a variety of aircraft and engines with little success. The acetylene wonder-engine was discarded for the flights of January 1902: Whitehead stated that the aircraft used then was similar to his previous machine, but powered by a 40 h.p. five-cylinder engine fuelled by kerosene. Then both engines and the "successful" monoplane were abandoned, for his next aircraft was a triplane glider clearly based on Chanute's designs, to which he fitted a 12 h.p. two-cylinder kerosene engine with hot-bulb ignition. A single "flight" of 350 metres on this machine was reported in *Scientific American* of 19 September 1903. Then in December 1905 he applied for a patent, in partnership with Stanley Y. Beach, on a monoplane hang-glider quite different to any of his previous aircraft. This was built in 1906, with a four-wheeled open car underneath on which the pilot stood, and towed flights behind Beach's car were made. About the end of the year a three-cylinder 15-h.p. engine was fitted, but there are no reliable reports of flights. Then a large biplane with a 40 h.p. four-cylinder engine driving two out-rigged propellers was exhibited in unfinished state by the New York Aeronautic Society in November 1908, and failed to fly when tested in the following year; and finally Whitehead's last attempt to fly was a bizarre helicopter with sixty lifting screws in 1911–12. Such a career of retrogression from the successes of 1901 and 1902 is surely inexplicable; the simplest conclusion must be that those flights of ½ mile, 2 miles and 7½ miles were flights of fancy.

Index

Index

A-4, A-7 (Rockets), 215; Pl. XXI
A.B.20. See Bordelaire
Abbas b. Firnas 4
Abbysinian War, 204
Accelerated take-off. See Launching
Accidents and Fatalities. See Fatalities
Addison, Joseph, 17
Ader, Clément (1841–1925), 59–61, Fig. 48, Pl. VI
Aerial Experiment Association, and aircraft, 130
  June Bug, 130; Pls. XIII, XXII
  Red Wing, 130; Pl. XIII
  Silver Dart, 130
  White Wing, 130
  see also Curtiss
Aerial photography, first from aeroplanes, 141
Aerial reconnaissance, first, 161
Aerobatics, first, 166
Aero Club of Great Britain. See Royal Aero Club
Aéro-Club de France, 71, 107, 109ff, 118
  Aviation Committee formed, 107
  Chanute's lecture, 107, 108
  and the Wrights, 107 ff
  prizes offered, 113
  manifesto, 118
'Aerodrome' (aircraft), discussion of word, 257
  see also Aerial Experiment Association; Langley
Aerodromes (airfields)
  first, 101
  first in Europe, 114, 158
  European in 1910, 158
Aerodynamics
  birth of, 21–24
  influence of, 112, 178, 193
  circulation theory, 125
  growth in 1920's, 193
  growth in 1930's, 195
  see also Flight-control; Streamlining; Whirling arms; Wind tunnels; Wings; etc.
Aero-engines. See Engines (aero)
Aerofoils. See Aerodynamics; Rudders; Tail-planes; Wings; etc.
Aéronaute, L', founding of, 36, 41
Aeronautical Annual. See Means

Aeronautical Societies, first, 38
Aeronautical Society of Great Britain. See Royal Aeronautical Society
Aérophile, L'
  and Esnault-Pelterie, 114
  and the Wrights, 117
  and Lorin, 136
Aeroplanes and warfare. See Military Aviation
Aeroplanes. See also the various types, designers, manufacturers, etc.; also Gliders, Ornithopters, etc.
Aeroplanes, engines of. See Engines
Aeroplanes (powered) till 1906, (incl. designs models, full-size, etc.)
  see also Gliders
  Fixed-wing monoplanes
    Bauer, 16
    Cayley, 21ff
    Henson, 28
    Stringfellow, 29
    Loup, 31
    Julien, 31
    Carlingford, 31
    Du Temple, 34, 35
    Spencer, 35, 40
    Butler and Edwards, 38
    Telescheff, 38
    Harte, 40
    Pénaud, 43, 44
    Tatin, 45, 68
    Kibalchitch, 52
    Mozhaisky, 53
    Goupil, 53
    Hargrave, 54ff
    Ader, 59, 60, 61
    Tatin-Richet, 68
    Parsons, 70
    Ziolkowski, 70
    Boecklin, 71
    Whitehead, 71
    Pilcher, 87
    Vuia, 119
  Tandem-wing monoplanes
    Burattini, 10
    Walker, 27
    Cayley, 27
    Claudel, 27
    Danjard, 45
    Prigent, 45
    Moy, 46

Aeroplanes—*cont.*
  Tandem-wing monoplanes—*cont.*
    Kress, 46
    Graffigny, 68
    Koch, 68
    Langley, 63ff
    Steiger, 70
    Kress, 106
    Vuia, 119
  Biplanes
    Cayley, 23
    Butler and Edwards, 39
    Stringfellow (F.J.), 56
    Maxim, 62
    Hargrave, 80ff
    Wrights, 94ff
    Jatho, 106
    Ferber, 114
    Blériot, 120
    Santos-Dumont, 119, 120
    Ellehammer, 121
  Tandem-wing biplanes
    Hargrave, 80ff
    Langley, 66
  Triplanes and Multiplanes
    Cayley, 23
    Kaufmann, 35
    Stringfellow, 39
    Phillips, 68
Aeroplanes (powered—all types)
  First manned take-off (down ramp), Du Temple, 45
  Second manned take-off (down ramp), Mozhaisky, 53
  First manned take-off from level ground, Ader, 53
  Second manned take-off from level ground, Maxim, 62
  First flights (piloted, sustained and controlled), Wrights, 100ff
  First practical aeroplane, Wrights, 103; others, 140ff
Aeroplanes: as symbols of destruction, 180
Aero-Torpille. See Tatin-Paulhan
Africa, H.M.S., 165
Ailerons (and elevons). See Flight-control
Air-brakes (steering). See Flight-control
Airco, 186; Fig. 89
Aircraft carriers, 156, 165, 177
Aircraft construction. See Construction
Aircraft factories and industry. See Construction
Aircraft Transport and Travel Ltd., 187
Airfields. See Aerodromes
Airlines. See Transport (air)
Airmail flights, first, 162
Airmen and 'chauffeurs': their attitude to aviation, 58, 59, 96, 110, 126, 139

Air-mindedness, creation of
  Henson, 28, 29
  Lilienthal, 72–80
  Chanute, 82–85
  Means, 90
  Santos-Dumont, 120–123
  Blériot's Channel crossing, 144
  in 1910, 152
  Lindbergh's New York–Paris flight, 191
  see also Press
Air Ministry (British)
  ruling on metal construction, 183
  ruling on slots, 193
  and Schneider Trophy, 186
Airports. See Aerodromes
Airscrews
  first and early, 6, 9, 16, 19; Fig. 20
  da Vinci, 9
  helical, 16
  Wrights, 99, 133
  early European, 124, 133, 141
  first advanced European, 141
  metal, 194
  early variable and constant pitch, 196
  see also Helicopters; Windmills; and the individual aircraft and designers, etc.
Airscrew toys, 6; Fig. 6
Air-sea rescue, first, 162
Airship-aeroplane combination. See 'Appareil-mixte'
Airships, 24, 34, 56, 105, 152, 176, 186, 193
  Cayley predicts they will fly before aeroplanes, 24
Airspeed aircraft, 210
  Horsa, 210
Airspeed indicators, first, 158, 160
Albacore. See Fairey
Albatros, 161, 173, 174, 178
Albatros (Jules Verne), 40
Albatross. See De Havilland
Albatross (bird): copied by Le Bris, 34
Alcock, Sir John (1892–1919); and Whitten-Brown, Sir Arthur (1886–1948), 181
  Churchill on, 227
Alexander the Great, 3; Fig. 2b
Alexander II (Czar), 52
Alexander, Patrick, quoted, 121
Alexandra Palace: exhibition of models, 124
Allahabad air mail, 162
Alps, first flight over, 153
Altitude records. See at ends of sections
Amécourt, Vicomte de P. d', 36: Pl. III
America. See United States
America. See Curtiss
America (South), first flight in, 157
Amphibians: first designed, 44
  first used, 161
Anhedral. See Stability; Wings

Animal Mechanism (Marey), 48
Animals in the air, 152, 153
ANT-6, 205
Antoinette aircraft and engines. See Levavasseur
Antoinette: origin of the name, 119
Anzani engines, 124, 142
'Appareil-mixte', 54, 55
Archdeacon, Ernest (1863–1957), 61, 107ff
    creates Aviation Committee of the Aéro-
        Club, 107
    'first glider, 108; Pl. XI
    second glider, 114
    founds F.A.I., 117
    float glider, 115
    manifesto, 119
    prizes given by, 113, 128
Archytas of Tarentum, 4
Argentine: first flight in, 157
Argus engines, 169
Argyll, Duke of, 38
Aries, 19
Armen, Firman, 4
Arms, whirling. See Whirling arms
Armstrong Siddeley engines, 193
Army Aircraft Factory. See Farnborough
Armstrong-Whitworth aircraft
    Atalanta, 201
    Ensign, 202
    Argosy, 188
    Whitley, 204, 209
Arrows, 3
Artillery rockets. See Rockets
Artingstall, F. D., 27
Asia: first flight in, 157
Aspect ratio: first description, 39
Assisted take-off. See Launching
Atalanta. See Armstrong Whitworth
Atlantic flights
    first by aeroplane, 181
    Churchill on Alcock and Brown, 227
    Lindbergh on, 229
Atom bombs first dropped, 210
Atwood, H. N., 159
Aubaud, 31
Aubrun, Emil, 152
Austria, first flight in, 150
Austro-Daimler engines, 165
Autogiros (Cierva), 190
Automatic pilot, first, 166
Automatic Stabilisers. See Stability
Automobile Club. See Royal Automobile Club
Automobile-Club de France, 71
'Automobilisme', 57, 71; Pl. VII
Auvours, Camp d', location of, 133
    Wilbur Wright at, 133ff
Aviatik, 176
Aviation meetings. See Meetings
'Avion': invention of word, 60

Avion II and III. See Ader, C.
Avis, 153
Avro aircraft
    biplane (1908), 130
    triplanes (1909), 149
    biplanes (1911–14), 160, 163; Fig. 72
    cabin aeroplanes (1912), 165; Fig. 75
    type 504, 160, 167, 172, 173, 176; Fig. 78
    Lancaster, 209; Pl. XX
    see also Roe, Sir A. V.

B-2. See Curtiss
B-9. See Boeing
B-17. See Boeing
B-25. See North American
B-29. See Boeing
Ba. See Bachem
Baby Grand. See Wright, W. & O.
Baby Wright. See Wright, W. & O.
Bachem *Ba 349A Natter*, 214
Bacon, Miss G., on her first flight, 226
Bacon, Roger (1214–92), 4
Bacqueville, Marquis de, 14; Pl. I
Baden, Prince of, 16
Baden-Powell, B.F.S., Col., 91, 92, 132, 133
    man-lifting kites, 91
    on the Wrights, 132
Balbo, General Italo (1896–1940), 205
Baldwin, F. W., 130
Balloon Factory. See Farnborough
Balloon jumping, 25
Balloonomania, 17–19
Balloons, first, 17
    first used for military observation, 20
    first parachute descents from, 19
    as vehicles for the launch of aeroplanes, 31,
        91, 92
    first glider launch from, 91, 92
Balsan, Jacques, 84
Balzer, Stephen M., 64
Bangay, Dorrington, 162
Barcelona meeting, 157
Bariquand and Marre, 131
Barnier, 167
Bate, J., 10
Bat-form aircraft. See Ader, C.
Battut, Arthur, 56
B.E. See Farnborough
Bauer, Melchoir, 16; Fig. 16
Beach, S.Y., 292
Beacham, T. E., 196
Beachey, Lincoln, 159
Beardmore-Rohrbach *Inflexible*, 185
Beaufighter. See Bristol
Beaufort. See Bristol
Beaumont, A. (*pseud*). See Conneau
Béchereau, L., 164

Bell, Dr and Mrs Alexander Graham, 130
Bell aircraft, 212; Fig. 126
Bellamy, 115
Belmont Park meeting, 154, 157
Bennett, D.C.T., 197
Bennett, Gordon, prizes, 164, 194
Benning Race Track, 157
Benoist flying boat, 170
Benz, Carl, 57; Pl. V
Berblinger, Albrecht (1770–1829), 27
Berg, Mrs Hart O., 133
Bergerac, Cyrano de, 13
Berlin meeting, 157
Bernoin, 12
Berry, A., 166
Besnier, P., 12; Fig. 13
Between-wing-ailerons. See Flight-control
Beuggar, John, 56
Beverley. See Blackburn
Bf109R. See Messerschmitt
Bible. See Psalms
Bicycle (tension) wheels: invention of, 24
Bienvenu. See Launoy and Bienvenu
Biot, 45
Biplanes. See Aeroplanes
Bird flight
    da Vinci on, 8
    Borelli on, 12
    Lilienthal on, 223
    wing-warping in, 94, 95
Bird Flight as the Basis of Aviation (Lilienthal),
    74
Bird of Passage (Henri Farman II). See Voisin
Birkenhead, Lord: quoted, 229
Birmingham, U.S.S., 156
Black, Joseph, 17
Blackburn aircraft, 160
Blackpool meeting, 157
Bladud, King, 3
Blanchard, Jean Pierre (1753–1809),
    helicopter, 16
    parachutes, 19
    airscrews, 19
Blenheim. See Bristol
Blériot, Louis (1872–1936) and aircraft, 115,
    120, 122, 129, 132, 135, 142, 144, 148,
    150, 151, 152, 160, 161, 162, 165, 166,
    172
    enters aviation, 115
    those who helped to design his aeroplanes,
        122
    on the Wrights, 132
    No. II (float-glider), 115
    Nos. III and *IV*, 120; Pl. XXII
    No. V (canard), 122
    No. VI (*Libellule*), 122; Pl. XXII
    No. VII, 122, 142; Pl. XII
    No. VIII, 129; Pl. XXII

Blériot, Louis—*cont.*
    No. IX, 142
    No. X (biplane), 135, 142
    No. XI, 142, 144; Pl. XV
    No. XII, 142, 145, 146; Pl. XV
    No. XIII, 145
    Channel flight, 144
    quotes on his Channel flight, 148, 226
    on Wilbur Wright, 132
    notable flights, 150, 159, 162
    Cobham on, 144, 226
    Shackleton on, 226
    Dollfus on, 144
    at Reims meeting, 145, 146
    use of ailerons and warping, 122, 129, 142,
        147; Pl. XXII
    school at Pau, 158
Blohm und·Voss aircraft, 203
Blue Bird. See Handley Page
Body-harness control (incl. head harness)
    da Vinci, 8
    Lilienthal, 78
Boecklin, Arnold, 71
Boeing aircraft
    type 247 and *247D*, 201, 202; Fig. 108
    type 299, 205
    type 307 Stratoliner and *307B*, 203; Fig. 115
    type 314 Clipper, 203; Fig. 114
    B-9, 201
    B-17 Flying Fortress, 203, 210; Pl. XX
    B-29, B-50 Superfortress, 210, 216; Fig. 122
    Model 299, 205; Fig. 110
    Monomail, 201
    Stratocruiser, 216
Bollée, Leon, 131
Bologna meeting, 157
Bolori, 9
Bolshoi. See Sikorsky
Bombs and bombing
    first illustration, 6
    first tests, 156, 161
    first bomb-sight, 161
    in World War I, 172ff
    in World War II, 206ff
    first atom bombs dropped, 210
    see also Military Aviation
Bonnier, 167
Boomerangs, 3
Bordelaise *A.B.20*, 205
Borelli, G. A., 12
Boston meeting, 157
Boston–New York service, 187
Boulton, M. P. W., 40
Bourcart, J. J., 35; Fig. 30
Bourdon tube ornithopter. See Trouvé
Bourne, 28
Bournemouth meeting, 157
    death of C. S. Rolls at, 158

Bowman, H., 17
Bow-drill engines. See Engines
Box-kite gliders, 115; Pl. XI
Box-kite model aeroplanes, 80ff; Fig. 58
Box-kite powered aeroplanes, 80ff, 123ff; Pls. XIII, XIV
Box-kites
  invented, 80
  wrongly used term, 153, 154
  see also Kites
Brabazon of Tara, Lord (J. T. C. Moore-Brabazon), 136, 149
  first flights in Britain, 149
  takes up a pig, 153
Bravery. See Heroism
Braye, Lord, 88
Brazil, first flight in, 157
Bréant, 31
Brearey, F. W., 29, 48, 71
Breguet aircraft, 144, 154, 161, 162, 194, 197; Fig. 69; Pl. XV
  helicopter, 126
Bremen, 191
Bretonne, Restif de la. See Restif
Brewer, Griffith, 133
Bris, Jean Marie Le (1808–72), 31, 34; Pl. IV
Bristol aircraft
  'box-kite' (1910), 153
  term 'box-kite' a misnomer, 153, 154
  monoplane (1911), 160
  monoplane (1912), 164
  Bristol Fighter, 176; Pl. XVII
  type 142 (*Britain First*), 202
  Beaufighter, 209
  Beaufort, 209
  Blenheim, 202, 204, 209
  Bulldog, 185
  Bullet, 180
  monoplane racer (1922), 185; Fig. 95
  Scout, 172, 173, 176, 180
Bristol engines
  Centaurus, 216
  Cherub, 195
  Hercules, 216
  Jupiter, 194
  Mercury, 204
  Pegasus, 196, 203, 205
Britain (British Isles)
  first and early glider flights in, 23, 24
  first powered take-offs and flights in, 136, 149
  first powered flight in, 136
  first British powered pilot, 124
  first Britons to power-fly (passengers), 133
  first British resident to become pilot, 136
  first pilot's certificate given, 136
  first circular mile flown, 149
'British Army Aeroplane No. 1'. See Cody

British Empire Michelin Cup, 156
British Interplanetary Society, letter to, 197
Britons, the first to fly. See Britain
Brooks, Peter W., 194, 201
Brown, Sir Arthur Whitten. See Alcock, Sir J.
Brown, D. S., 46; Fig. 39
Browning, J., 39
Bruce, J. M., 173
Brunt, S., 17
Brussels meeting, 157
Bryan, G. H., 113
B.S. See Farnborough
Bubble cockpit covers, first, 44, 178
Bucharest, 150
Buchet engines, 125
Budapest, meeting, 157
Bulldog. See Bristol
Burattini, Tito Livio, 10
Burdin, Marios, 112
Burnelli aircraft, 191
Burton meeting, 157
Burton, R.: quoted, 221
Busk, E. T., 113, 167
Butler, Frank Hedges, 133
Butler and Edwards, 38; Fig. 33; Pl. IV
Butterfly-shaped models, 50
Buzzards: observed by Wilbur Wright
Byrd, Rear Admiral Richard E. (1888–1957), 191
Byron, Lord, quoted, 222

C-47. See Douglas
Cabin aeroplanes, first, 165
Cailletet, L. P., 119
Calcutta. See Short
Calderera, Lieut. A., 141, 144
Cambridge, R. O., 17
Camel. See Sopwith
Campania, H.M.S., 177
Campini. See Caproni etc.
Canada, first flight in, 247
Canard-type aeroplanes (early)
  Santos-Dumont, 120ff
  Blériot, 122, 159–160
  Levavasseur, 106
  Fabre, 153
  Valkyrie, 153
  Voisin amphibian, 161
Cannes meeting, 157
Canopies (lifting) on aircraft, 14, 46
Cantilever wings. See Wings
Capper, Col. J. E., 104, 116
  visit to the Wrights, 104
  on the Wrights, 104
  and Cody, 116
Caproni, 205
Caproni-Campini jet, 212; Fig. 117

Carbonic acid engines. See Engines
Cardiff meeting, 157
Carlingford, Viscount, 31
Castel, P., 50
Catalina. See Consolidated
Catapult launch, first. See Launching
Caters, Baron de, 135, 150
Cats in the air, 152
Cattaneo, 150
Caudron aircraft, 162, 174
Cavallo, Tiberius, 17
Cavalry and aeroplanes, Raleigh on, 227
Cavendish, Henry, 17
Cayley, Sir George, Bt. (1773–1857), 21–25;
    Figs. 21–24, 27; Pl. III
    list of his 'firsts', 23, 24
    added quotations, 222
    Henson on, 24
    Cayley's 'firsts', 23, 24
Cecil, Lord David: quoted, 217
Celebi, Ahmed 12
Centaurus (engine). See Bristol
Centocelle, (Rome), 141
Central Flying School, 165
Chambers, Capt. W. I., 164
Champagne industry, influence on aviation,
    121, 145
Channel flights by aeroplane (and attempts)
    first by aeroplane, 144
    second, 152
    Latham's attempts, 144
    first double, 154
    first by a woman, 166
Chanute, Octave (1832–1910), 82–85
    did not meet Wenham, 82
    his 1896 glider, 83; Fig. 60; Pl. VIII
    publishes *Progress in Flying Machines*, 82
    on Stringfellow, 29
    corresponds with Ferber, 105, 106
    did not use movable control surfaces, 83
    and the Wrights, 83, 84, 107ff
    sparks European aviation, 84, 88, 107–110
    gives vital lecture in Paris (1903), 107
    on the problem of landing, 223
    on peace and war, 223
    on the future of flying, 223
Charles, J. A. C., 17
Char Volant' (Pocock) 27
Chauffeur attitude. See Airmen and
    'chauffeurs', etc.
Chauvière propellers, 124
Chavez, Georges, 154
Cherub (engine). See Bristol
Chester, Bishop of. See Wilkins
Chicago conference, 81
Childs, John, 14
China, first flight in, 157
Chkalov, V., 205

Churchill, Sir Winston
    on the aviation proposals, 148
    as First Lord of the Admiralty, 166
    on his first flight, 227
    on Alcock and Brown, 227
Cinema-films: first taken in air, 141
Cierva Juan de la (1886–1936), and aircraft
    (Autogiros), 190; Fig. 98
Circles flown (first) 102, 128
Cirrus (engine). See De Havilland
City, first flight over a, 150
Clerget engines, 156, 174
Clipper. See Boeing
Clockwork engines. See Engines
Clydesdale, Marquess of, 205
Coachman, Cayley's 23
Coanda, H., 156, 164
Cobham, Sir Alan J. 191
    on Blériot, 144, 226
Cocking, R., 29
Cockpits (enclosed)
    first designed, 44, 70
    first used, 164, 165
Cocteau, J.: quoted, 229
Cody, Buffalo Bill, 116
Cody, Samuel Franklin (1861–1913), 107,
    116, 136ff, 149, 154, 156, 165, 169
    man-lifting kites, 107
    aileroned kite glider, 116; Pl. XXII
    powered kite, 125
    'British Army Aeroplane No. 1', 130, 136;
        Pls. XIII, XXII
    first powered flight in Britain, 136
    death of, 169
    Farnborough on, 169
Colliex, 161
Collision, first mid-air, 157
    see also Accidents, etc.
Colonial Air Transport Co., 187
Comet (1934). See De Havilland
Comet (*Komet*). See Messerschmitt
Committee of Imperial Defence. See
    Governments
Commonwealth, British, first flight in (excl.
    Britain), 247
Comparison of early flights (table of), 233ff
Competitions. See Meetings
Compressed-air engines. See Engines
Compression-ignition engines. See Engines
Concours de la Securité (Buc), 170
Concours Militaire (Reims), 161
Condor. See Focke-Wulf
Congreve, Sir William, 20
Conneau, Lieut. André (*pseud*. Beaumont),
    159
Consolidated PBY *Catalina*, 210
Constantinople, Saracen of, 4
Constellation. See Lockheed

Construction (aircraft)
  metal, 159
  monocoque, 162, 163, 171, 183
  stressed skin, 171, 183
  see also Wings
Construction (industry)
  first factories in Europe, 115
  in World War I, 179
Control (flight). See Flight-Control
Convertiplane, first design, 23
Copenhagen meeting, 157
Cordner, E. J. 34
Cornelius, William, 56
Cornu, Paul, 126; Pl. XXI
Cossus, 28
Cowper, William, 221
Cox, Sir H. Roxbee Cox. See King's Norton
    (Lord)
Crocco, G. A., 190
Cross-Channel flights. See Channel flights
Cross-Atlantic flights. See Atlantic flights
Cross-country flights, first, 135
Crowell, L. C., 50
Crystal Palace air exhibition (1868), 39, 40
Curtiss, Glenn Hammond (1878–1930), and
    aircraft, etc.
  and the Aerial Experiment Association, 130
  June Bug, 130
  Golden Flier, 143
  Reims machine, 143, 146; Pls. XIV, XXII?
  question of ailerons, 130
  standard Curtiss biplane of 1910, 156, Fig.
    70
  in 1911, 1912, 161, 164
  in 1914, 70
  take-offs and landings on ships, 156
  makes bombing tests, 156
  first seaplane, 161; Fig. 73
  second and third seaplanes (flying boats),
    164
  America flying boat, 170
Curtiss aircraft (modern)
  B-2, 185
  NC-4, 80; Fig. 87
  R3C-2, 186; Fig. 97
  Hewitt-Sperry biplane guided bomb, 177
Cycle (tension) wheel, invention of, 24
Cyrano de Bergerac. See Bergerac

D.1 (etc.). See Dunne, J. W.
D-27L. See Dewoitine
Dacians, and kite-origins, 6
Daedalus, 2, 3; Fig. 2a
Daily Mail, 144
Daimler, Gottlieb, 35, 57, 106
Dakota. See Douglas
Damian, J., 6
Dandrieux, 50; Fig. 45

Danjard, 45
Danti, G. B., 6
Dart-shaped aeroplanes, 38
Da Vinci. See Vinci
Davy, M. J. B., 62
Day, Flt.Lt. M.J., 177
Dayton-Wright R.B. monoplane, 186, 194;
    Fig. 93
DC-1 (etc.). See Douglas
De, da, etc. See also the main names
Deaths (aviation). See Accidents, etc.
De Bacqueville. See Bacqueville
De Bernoin. See Bernoin
De Caters. See Caters
Decorum and death, Raleigh, on, 228
Degen, Jacob (1761–1848), 25, 26
De Groof. See Groof
De Havilland, Sir Geoffrey (1882–19)
  first aeroplanes, 156
  joins Farnborough, 156, 157
  work on *B.E.* types, 160
  work on *B.S.1*, 163
De Havilland Aircraft
  D.H.1 and *2*, 173
  D.H.4, 176, 187, 196
  D.H.4a, 186
  D.H.9, and *9a*, 176, 187
  D.H.34, 187
  D.H.50, 191
  D.H.71, 190
  D.H.84, 201
  D.H.100, 212
  Albatross, 202; Fig. 113
  Comet (1934), 198
  Dragon-Rapide, 201
  Hercules, 188
  Mosquito, 198, 206, 209; Pl. XX
  Moth, 188, 204, 205; Pl. XVIII
  Puss Moth, 204
  Vampire, 212
De Havilland engines, 214
  Gipsy III, 194
Delagrange, Léon (1873–1910), 124, 128, 132,
    135, 136
  takes first woman passenger, 129
  death of, 158
  on the Wrights, 132
Del Prete. See Prete
Delta-wing aircraft, designs, the first
  Butler and Edwards, 39
  Telescheff, 39
Demoiselle. See Santos-Dumont
Denhaut, 164
Denmark: first flights in, 121
  see also Ellehammer, J. C. H.
Deperdussin aircraft, 153, 160, 166, 169, 170;
    Fig. 74; Pl. XVI
  Monocoque, 162, 164, 167, 171

De Pischof. See Pischof
Desforges, Canon, 16
De Telescheff. See Telescheff
Deutsch-Archdeacon prize, 113, 128
Deutsch de la Meurthe, H., 128
Deutsche Luftreederei, 186
Dewoitine *D-27*, 185
D.H. See De Havilland
Dickson, B., 157
Diesel engines. See Engines
Dieuaide, E., 50, 52
Dihedral angle. See Wings
'Dipping edge'. See Phillips, H. F.
Dirigibles. See Airships
Do. See Dornier
Doblhoff, 211
Dollfus, Charles
    on Garnerin, 19
    on Cayley, 21
    on Pénaud, 43, 44
    on Ader, 61
    on the Wrights, iii, 103, 134
    on ailerons in Europe, 139
    on Blériot, 144
Doncaster meeting, 157
Donnet-Lévèque, 164
Doolittle, James H. 186, 194
Dornier, Claude, and aircraft
    flying boats, 203
    Do X, 188; Pl. XVIII
Douglas aircraft, 191
    DC-1, DC-2, 201
    DC-3 (*C-47; Dakota*; etc.), 201, 202, 215; Pl.
        XIX
    DC-4 Skymaster, 215; Fig. 127
    DC-4E, 203, 215
    DC-6, 216
Draco standards, 6
Dragon-kites. See Kites
Dragon-Rapide. See De Havilland
Drieberg, von, 30
Driver, E. F., 162
Dublin meeting, 157
Duchesnay, 30
Dufaux brothers, 157
Dunne, John William (1875–1949), and
    aircraft, 125, 136, 149, 156, 169, 191
Du Temple. See Temple
Dutheil-Chalmers engines, 123

E.28/39. See Gloster
Eagle (engine). See Rolls-Royce
Engine-airscrew combination (for fixed-wing
    aeroplanes, incl. designs, models, etc.)
    until 1907
    Cayley, 23
    Henson, 28

Eagle (engine). See Rolls-Royce
Stringfellow, 29
Carlingford, 31
Loup, 31
Du Temple, 34, 35
Harte, 40
Pénaud, 43, 44
Tatin, 45, 46
Moy, 46
Kress, 46, 106
Mozhaiski, 53
Ader, 59ff
Maxim, 62
Langley, 63ff
Tatin-Richet, 68
Parsons, 70
Ziolkowski, 70
Steiger, 70
Hargrave, 81
Pilcher, 87
Wrights, 94ff
Jatho, 106
Levavasseur, 106
Ferber, 114
Vuia, 119
Santos-Dumont, 120ff
Ellehammer, 121, 126, 136
Edwards, E., 38
Eilmer of Malmesbury, 4
Elastic (twisted). See Engines (aero)
Electra. See Lockheed
Electric engines. See Engines
Elevators. See Flight-control
Elevons. See Flight-control
Ellehammer, Jacob Christian H. (1871–1946),
        121, 126, 136, 190
    first flight (tethered), 121; Pl. XII
Ellyson, Lieut. T., 164
Ely, Eugene, 156, 161
Empire class. See Short
Empire de l'Air (L'), 52
Empire flights, pioneering, 191
Enclosed cockpits, 44, 70
Enclosed cabins, 164, 169
Engelhardt, Capt., 157
Engines and propulsion (incl. suggestions,
        designs, etc.) early (excl. jet propulsion)
    first design, 8
    airscrew, first (on balloon), 19
        See also Airscrew
        bow-drill, 17, 24
    carbonic acid, 78, 119
    clockwork, 10, 16, 27, 34, 36
    compressed air, 45, 290
    flappers, 16, 23, 24, 27, 31, 35, 40, 45, 46,
        54, 80ff
    gas turbine, 50
        See also Jet propulsion

Engines and Propulsion—*cont.*
  gunpowder, 46
  hot air, 24, 45
  jet propulsion, see Jet Propulsion
  petrol, 64–67, 100ff, 106, 114, 119, 120
  radial, 64
  rocket, 52
  rotary, 54, 64
  rubber (stretched and twisted), 43, 45, 46,
    48, 54, 56
  steam, 27, 35, 36, 39, 40, 45, 46, 50, 53, 56,
    59–63, 68, 70, 80
  first twin engine, 60, 61, 62, 160
  first twin airscrew, 23, 28, 29, 31, 44, 60, 61,
    63ff, 100ff
Engines (non-aero)
  gas, first, 35
  hot air, first, 24
  petrol, first four stroke, 51, 57
  turbines (steam), first, 56
England. See Britain
England, Gordon, 149
English Channel. See Channel
Englishmen. See Britain
Ensign. See Armstrong-Whitworth
Éole. See Ader, C.
Esnault-Pelterie, Robert (1881–1957) and air-
    craft, 108, 109, 114, 123, 129, 136, 142
  gliders, 108; Pl. XI
  REP No. 1, 123
  REP No. 2, 129, 136; Pl. XIII
  later machines, 143
  early powered flights, 123
  wing-warping and ailerons, 108
  engines, 142
Esterno, d', 36, 37; Fig. 31
Etévé, A., 158
Etherton, P. T.: quoted, 229
Etrich, Igo, 126, 150, 153, 165
Etrich-Wels glider, 126, 153
Euler biplane, 153
Europe, aviation in
  Wrights cause revival of (1902, etc.), 105ff
  Ferber first to start (1902), 105, 106
  Wright-type gliders built (1902–05), 105–
    114
  Chanute reinforces Wright influence by
    Paris lecture (1903), 107–109
  La Vaulx on Wrights' gliding, 107
  neglect of flight-control in, 109ff
  Archdeacon and Tatin warn about Wrights'
    progress, 110
  'tricks of the trade' needed, 111
  Aviation Committee formed (1903), 107
  attitude to aviation in, 110, 111
  Ferber adds tail to Wright-type (1904), 112
  prizes offered to stimulate efforts (1904),
    112

Europe, aviation in—*cont.*
  exhibition of models (1905), 114
  Hargrave box-kite enters aviation in (1905),
    115
  news of Wrights' 1905 successes reaches,
    117
  Aérophile admits Wrights' priority, 117
  Tatin's admission and dirge, 117
European circuit race, 159
Evans, W. H. B., 169
Everest (Mount): flight over, 205
Exhibition (aeronautical), first, 39
  first Paris 'salon', 135

F.XVIII. See Fokker
F.13. See Junkers
F-51. See North American
Fa. See Focke-Achgelis
Fabre, Henri (b. 1883), 153, 161; Pl. XVI
Factories. See Construction
F.A.I. See Federation Aéronautique Inter-
    nationale
Fairey aircraft, 177
  Albacore, 212
  Firefly, 185
  Flycatcher, 185
  Fox, 185
  monoplane, 185
  Swordfish, 205, 212
Falcon engine. See Rolls-Royce
Falling leaf: gliders and (da Vinci), 9
Fansler, P. E., 170
Farman, Henri(y) (1874–1958), and aircraft,
    124ff
  in 1907, 124ff
  in 1908, 128ff, 135; Pl. XXII
  in 1909, 143ff, 151
  his nationality, 143
  flies first circle in Europe, 128; Pl. XIII
  takes first passenger in Europe, 128
  first cross country flight, 135
  Henri Farman I, 124
  Flying Fish, 129
  Henri Farman II, 129
  Henri Farman III, 143; Pls. XIV, XXII
  fitting of Gnome, 143
  1910 machine, 153
  use of ailerons, 135
  at Reims meeting, 145–147
  night flying at Hendon, 169
Farman, Maurice (1877–1964) and aircraft,
    154, 165, 166, 167
  1909–10 biplane, 154
  1911 biplane, 161
  1912 biplane (*Longhorn*), 161, 165; Fig. 76
Farman Co., 172, 196
  air service, 186

Farman, Co—*cont.*
  Goliath, 186, 187; Fig. 90
Farnborough (Balloon Factory, R.A.F.,
    R.A.E., etc.) and aircraft, 156, 162,
    172, 177, 193
  B.E.1, 160, 163
  B.E.2, 163, 165, 167, 172, 173; Pl. XVI.
    See also Fig. 80
  B.E.2a, b, and *c,* 167, 172, 173
  B.S.1, 163, 167, 174; Pl. XVI
  F.E.2A, 167
  F.E.2B, 167, 173, 174
  F.E.6, 173
  F.E.8, 173
  R.E.8, 174
  S.E.1, 162
  S.E.2, 167
  S.E.4, 174, 178
  S.E.5, and *5A,* 163, 174; Fig. 84
    '*Aerial Target*', 176
  Cody at, 107, 136ff, 149, 154, 156, 165, 169
  de Havilland at, 156, 157, 160ff
  work on aeroplanes ordered to cease, 148
  unofficial renewal of research, 157
  success in military competition, 165
  see also Capper, J. E.
  wartime developments (W.W.I.), 177
Fatalities (1800–1895)
  first death on parachute (Cocking), 29
  total of parachute deaths, 151
  Cayley on, 96
  Deaths on other heavier-than-air craft,
    Letur, 31, 151
    de Groof, 48, 151
Fatalities (1895–1909)
  first deaths on gliders, 151
    Lilienthal, 79
    Pilcher, 90
    Maloney, 92
  first death of passenger on powered aero-
    plane (Selfridge), 134
  first deaths of powered-aeroplane pilots
    Lefebvre, 146
    Ferber, 146
  total of deaths to 1909, 151
Fatalities and Accidents (1910), 157, 158
'Father of Aerial Navigation', Henson calls
    Cayley, 28
F.B.5. See Vickers
F.E. See Farnborough
Fédération Aéronautique Internationale,
    founding of, 117
Felixstowe *F.2*, 176; Pl. XVII
Ferber, Capt. Ferdinand (1862–1909) and air-
    craft, 105ff, 112, 146; Pl. XI
  influenced by the Wrights, 105
Fernandez, 151
Ferrarin, Capt. Arturo, 193

Fighters, first. See Military Aviation
Films. See Cinema-films
Finned projectiles, 8, 24
Firefly. See Fairey
Firman, Armen, 4
'Firsts'. See the individual subjects, incl. Aero-
    planes, Gliders, etc.
Fischer, 164
Fitzgerald, Prof., 88
Flanders monoplane, 162
Flappers. See Flapper propulsion
Flapper-propulsion
  Burattini, 10
  Bauer, 16
  Cayley, 23, 24, 31
  Walker, 27
  Smythies, 35
  Kaufmann, 35
  Spencer, 35, 40
  Hargrave, 54, 80ff
  Danjard, 45, 46
Flap-valve principle, 8, 16, 25, 27
Flight-control, early (including suggestions,
    designs, etc.)
  Elevator and rudder
    Cayley, 23, 24
  Steering air-brakes
    (definition, 41)
    Harte, 40
    Pénaud, 44
    Rénard, 45
    Lilienthal, 78
  Roll-control by ailerons or elevons
    Boulton, 40
    Harte, 40
    Goupil, 53
    Esnault-Pelterie, 108; Pl. XXII
    Cody, 116
    Blériot, 120
  Roll-control by wing-warping
    Lilienthal, 78
    Wrights, 94ff
  Co-ordinated three-axis control
    Wrights, 99ff
  Body-shifting
    Smythies, 35
    d'Esterno, 36
    Lilienthal, 72ff
    Hargrave, 80
    Chanute, 82ff
    Pilcher, 85ff
    Montgomery, 91, 92
    Ferber, 105
Flights, first. See Aeroplanes; also the types of
    aircraft, etc.
Float-gliders, 115
Float-planes. See Seaplanes
Florence meeting, 157

Flycatcher. See Fairey
Flyer. See Wright, W. & O.
Flying-boat, first, 164
   growth of in 1920's, 188
   see also Seaplanes
'Flying bombs'
   Lorin, 136
   in World War I, 177
   in World War II, 214
   see also Missiles (aerodynamic)
Flying control systems. See Flight-control
Flying exhibition. See Exhibitions; Meetings
Flying Fish. See Farman, II
Flying Fortress. See Boeing
Flying meetings. See Meetings
Flying records. See Records
Flying school, first (powered), 141
Focke-Achgelis helicopters, 197, 210; Pl. XXI
Focke-Wulf aircraft
   FW 61, 197
   FW 190, 209; Pl. XX
   FW 200 Condor, 198
Fokker, Anthony, H. G. (1890–1939) and air-
   craft, 162, 173, 174, 183, 187, 198
   E.1 Eindecker, 173; Fig. 83
   D.VII, 174; Pl. XVII
   triplane, 174
   Southern Cross, 191
   post-war monoplanes, 187; Fig. 96
   claim over interrupter gear, 173
   F.XVII, 197
'Fokker Scourge', 174
Folland, H. P., 178
Follic, La, 17
Fontana, Joanes, 6; Fig. 7
Ford *Stout*, 187
Forlanini, Enrico (1848–1930), 50; Pl. V
Fortress, Flying. See Boeing
Fortress, Super. See Boeing
Fourny, A., 166
Four-stroke petrol engine, introduced, 35, 51
Fowler flaps, 202
Fox, See Fairey
France
   first aero-society in, 38
   revival in, 105ff
   rivalry with U.S.A. See Europe
   slow development in. See Europe
   see also Aéro Club de France
Franklin, Benjamin, 16
French Aero Club. See Aéro Club de France
Friedrichshafen: raid on, 176
Frost, E. P., 71
Furious, H.M.S., 177
Furnas, C. W., 128
Fury. See Hawker
Fuselages (enclosed)
   first designed, 44, 70

Fuselages—*cont.*
   first used, 119–122
   first cabin aeroplanes, 165
   Monobloc Antoinette, 160
Fuselages (metal) first, 179
Fuselages (monocoque) first, 163
Fw. See Focke-Wulf
FZG-76 (V-1 flying bomb), 214

G-31, G-38. See Junkers
Gamecock. See Gloster
Gann, E. K.: quoted, 228
Garnerin, André Jacques (1769–1823) and
   family, 19, 29; Pl. II
Garnett, D.: quoted, 228
Garros, Roland (1888–1918), 163, 166, 167,
   173
Gas engines. See Engines
Gasnier, Réne, on the Wrights, 132
Gastambide, Mlle. Antoinette, 119
Gastambide, R., 119
Gastambide-Mengin aircraft. See Levavasseur
Gas turbines (jet). See Jet propulsion
Gatty, Harold, 205
Gauchot, Paul, 44
Gawries. See Glums and Gawries
Gee Bee monoplane, 198; Fig. 106
Geneva meeting, 157
Gérard, 19
Germany
   first flight in, 106, 136, 289
   first German to fly in, 150
   leads re-birth of gliding, 188
Giffard, Henri (1825–1882), 34
Gigant. See Messerschmitt
Gilmore, L., 71, 289
Gipsy. See De Havilland: engines
Gladiator. See Gloster
Glider flights
   first models, 21ff
   first man-carrying, 21ff
   first piloted, 73ff
   first piloted in Britain, 85ff
   first with wing-warping, 95ff
   first properly controllable, 98
Gliders (incl. designs, models, full-size, etc.).
   See also Flight-control
Monoplanes
   Gusmão, 14
   Meerwein, 16
   Cayley, 31
   Letur, 31
   Le Bris, 31, 34
   d'Amécourt, 36
   d'Esterno, 36
   Mouillard, 34, 38
   Pline, 38

Gliders (incl. designs, models, full-size, etc.).
　Monoplanes—*cont.*
　　Spencer, 40
　　Lilienthal, 45
　　Biot, 45
　　Montgomery, 53, 91, 92
　　Hargrave, 54
　　Sanderval, 56
　　Boecklin, 71
　　Lilienthal, 74ff
　　Hargrave, 80ff
　　Pilcher, 85ff
　　Means, 90
　Biplanes
　　Lilienthal, 78ff
　　Hargrave, 80ff
　　Chanute, 83, 84
　　Wrights, 95ff
　　Ferber, 106ff
　　Archdeacon, 107ff
　　Esnault-Pelterie, 108ff
　　Voisin-Archdeacon, 115
　　Voisin-Blériot, 115
　　Cody, 116
　Triplanes and multiplanes
　　Cayley, 23
　　Renard, 45
　　Wenham, 39
　　Linfield, 50
　　Chanute, 83, 84
　Tandem-wing
　　Brown, 46
　　Hargrave, 80
Gliders (Hang-)
　Lilienthal, 74ff
　Hargrave, 80ff
　Chanute, 82ff
　Pilcher, 85ff
Gliders, Launching of (incl. designs)
　from a balloon
　　Cayley, 32
　　Montgomery, 92, 93
　from an artificial hill
　　Lilienthal, 74
　towed by men
　　Pilcher, 87
　towed by horses
　　Pilcher, 87
　towed by an electrically operated winch
　　Chanute, 84
Gliders (modern), 187, 210
　Wright, 162
Gloster aircraft
　E.28/39, 212; Pl. XIX
　Gamecock, 185
　Gladiator, 204, 212
　Grebe, 185
　Meteor, 212

Glums and Gawries, 17; Fig. 15
Gnome engines, 143, 160, 164, 167, 169, 173, 178
Gobé, A., 163
Goddard, R. H., 40, 181, 215
Godwin, F., Bishop of Hereford, 10
Gold Bug. See Curtiss, G.
Golden Flier. See Curtiss, G.
Golden Gate (San Francisco)
Goliath. See Farman Co.
Gonsales, 10
Gordon Bennett contests, 164, 194
Gotha, 176
Göttingen: aeronautical laboratory, 178
Goué, R. de, 25
Goupil, A., 53; Pl. V
Goupy, Ambroise
　triplane, 135
　biplanes, 144; Pl. XIV
　influence on Roe, 149, 167
Governments and flying, 60, 64, 145, 148, 197
　early concern of
　　Committee of Imperial Defence, 148
　see also Military aviation; Wrights
Grace, W. G., 27
Grade, Hans (1879–1946), 150
Graffigny, 68
Graf Zeppelin. See Zeppelins
Grahame-White, Claude (1879–1959), 153, 154, 157
　quoted, 227
　his first night flight, 154
Grandseigne, R., 162
Gray, T.: quoted, 221
Great Britain, see Britain
Grebe. See Gloster
Green, Charles (1785–1870), 29
Green, F. M., 160
Grieve, Commd. K. MacKenzie, 181
Griffith, Dr. A. A., 193
Griffon. See Rolls-Royce
Groof, Vincent de (*d.* 1874), 48; Fig. 41
Guidotti, 12
Gunbus. See Vickers
Gunpowder engines. See Engines; Rockets
Guns in aeroplanes. See Military Aviation
Gusmão, Laurenço de (1686–1724), 14; Fig. 14
Gyroplanes. See Helicopters

Halberstadt, 176
Halford, F. B., 212
Halifax. See Handley Page
Halle, Gerhard, 74
Hamilton, Charles K., 156
Hamel, Gustav, 162
Hampden. See Handley Page

Handley Page, Sir Frederick and aircraft, 149,
    153, 187, 193
  Blue Bird, 149
  Halifax, 209
  Hampden, 204
  Hannibal, 198
  Heracles, 198
  H.P. 42/5, 198; Pl. XIX
  O/400, 176, 187; Pl. XVII
  V/1500, 176, 187
  W.8, 188; Fig. 92
  Yellow Peril, 160
  slotted wings, 193; Fig. 88
  claim for the *O/400*, 176
Hang-gliders. See Gliders
Hannibal. See Handley Page
Hanoveraner, 176
Hanriot, M., 160
Hargrave, Lawrence (1850–1915), 54, 80–82,
    88, 93; Figs. 57–59; Pl. VI
Harper, Harry: quoted, 227
Harte, Richard, 40; Fig. 36
Harvard meeting. See Boston meeting
Hautsch, 12
Havilland. See De Havilland
Hawk. See Pilcher
Hawker, Harry G. (1889–1921), 167, 181
Hawker aircraft
  Fury, 185; Fig. 102
  Hurricane, 204, 209; Fig. 118
  Tempest, Typhoon, 209
Head harness control. See Body harness
Height. See Altitude; Pressurisation; Records
Heinkel aircraft
  He 111, 202, 209; Pl. XX
  He 162 Salamander 'Volksjäger', 214
  He 177, 210
  He 178, 197, 212; Fig. 116
Heinkel engines, 197
Hele-Shaw, H. S., 196
Helical airscrews. See Airscrews
Helical twist. See Wing-warping
Helicopters (incl. designs, models, full-size,
    etc.) until 1906
  string-pull, 6
    medieval, 6; Fig. 1; Pl. I
  bow-drill
    Launoy and Bienvenu, 17
    Cayley, 21
  clockwork
    Lomonosov, 16
    Degen, 27
    Bourne, 28
    d'Amécourt, 36
  steam-engine
    d'Amécourt, 36
    Achenbach, 50
    Dieuaide, 50
Helicopters—*cont.*
    Forlanini, 50
    Parsons, 70
  man-powered
    Paucton, 16
    Blanchard, 16
    Mayer, 27
    Renoir, 50
  rubber
    Pénaud, 43
    Dandrieux, 50
  gunpowder
    Pomes and de Pauze, 50
  jets from rotor-tips
    Phillips, 28, 40
  internal combustion
    Melikoff, 50
  gas turbine
    Melikoff, 50
  compressed air
    Castel, 50
  uncertain
    Sarti, 27
    Aubaud, 31
    Crowell, 50
    Wootton, 50
    Ward, 50
Helicopters
  first models, xvi, 6
  first (full-size) to rise vertically with a man,
      126; Pl. XXI
  first practical, 197, 210; Pl. XXI
Heliopolis meeting, 157
Hendon meetings, 165, 169
Henke, Captain, 205
Henri Farman I and II. See Voisin
Henri Farman III. See Farman, H.
Henschel Hs 293, 215
Henson, William Samuel (1812–88), 24, 28,
    29; Pl. II
  see also Stringfellow, J.
Heracles. See Handley Page
Hérard, 56
Hercules. See De Havilland;
Hercules. See Bristol engines
Hereford, Bishop of. See Godwin
Hermes. See Handley Page
Heroism, 217, 228
Herring, Augustus Moore (1867–1926), 71,
    83–85, 290
Hewitt-Sperry biplane, 177; Pl. XXI
Hezarfen, Ahmed, 12
Hibernia, H.M.S., 165
Hill, G. T. R. and *Pterodactyls*, 169, 191, 195;
    Fig. 99
Hill-launching. See Launching
Hiroshima, 210
Hispano-Suiza engines, 174

Hitler, Adolf, 204
Hodgson, J. E., 21
Hoff, Prof. Nicholas J., 183
Holland, first flight in, 150
Hooke, R., 10, 11
Horsa. See Airspeed
Horton, H. M., 158
Hot-air balloons. See Balloons
Hot-air engines. See Engines
Howard Wright biplane, 153
H.P. See Handley Page
Hs. See Henschel
Huffman Pasture (or Prairie), 101ff
Hulls (flying boat), first stepped, 164
Humber monoplane, 153
Hurricane. See Hawker

Icarus, 2
Ilia Mouriametz. See Sikorsky, I.
Imperial Airways, 187, 197
Imperial Defence Committee, 148
India, war rockets in, 20
Indo-China, first flight in, 157
Industry, aircraft. See Construction
Inflexible. See Beardmore
Instability. See Stability
Instruments (aircraft), 167, 170, 178, 193,
    194, 203, 216
Interrupter gear for guns, 173
Issy-les-Moulineaux, 114

J.1 (etc.). See Junkers
Jacobs, J. M., 196
Jaguar engine. See Armstrong Siddeley
Janinet, 20
Jannus, A., 170
Jatho, Karl, 106; Pl. X
Jet engines. See Jet propulsion
Jet propulsion
    first proposal, 19
    first designs for jet aeroplanes, 38, 137, 156
    first rocket propulsion (of model), 6
    first rocket propulsion, 190
    work at Farnborough, 193
    early work in turboprops, 193
    first turbojet flights, 197
    Whittle's work, 193, 197
    false prophecy about, 197
    progress in World War II, 212
    first operational warplanes, 212ff
    applied to helicopters, 28, 40
    see also Rockets
Jobert, 46
Johnson, Amy. see Mollison
Johnson, Samuel, 17, 221
Jones, B. Melvill, 193

Joukowski, N. E., 193
Joy-sticks. See Flight control
Ju. See Junkers
Jullien, Pierre, 31
Jumo engine. See Junkers
June Bug. See Aerial Experimental Association
Junkers, Hugo and Junkers aircraft, 157, 171,
    179, 198
  wing system, 181
  J.1, 179; Pl. XVII
  J.2, 179
  J.4, 179; Pl. XVII
  J.7/9, 179
  J.10, 179; Fig. 85
  F.13, (J.13), 179, 187; Pl. XVIII
  G-31, 187, 198
  G-38, 198; Fig. 105
  Ju 52, 198, 215; fig. 107
  Ju 86, 202, 204
  Ju 87, 204; Fig. 111
  Ju 88, 209; Fig. 120
  Ju 90, 198
  Ju 287, 214
  K-47, 185
  W-34, 194
  Bremen monoplane, 191
Junkers engines, 194, 212
Jupiter engine. See Bristol

K, model (Wrights). See Wright, W. & O.
K-47. See Junkers
Kamikaze suicide aircraft, 214
Kapferer, Henry, 124
Kármán, T. von, 193
Kaufmann, Joseph Meyes, 35; Fig. 35
Keith, A. P., 50
Kelly, Lieut., 191
Kelvin, Lord, on aviation, 92, 224
Kent, Duchess of, 25
Kestrel engine. See Rolls-Royce
Kibaltchitch, N.I., 52
Kill Devil Hills. See Kitty Hawk
Kingsford-Smith, Sir Charles (1899–1935),
    192
Kings Norton, Lord: quoted on Whittle, 229
Kirchofer. See Steiger
Kite-carriage, 27
Kites
    early, 3, 6, 14, 16; Figs. 5, 10; Pl. I
    first use for aeroplane wing, 23
    Cayley and, 23
    Wrights and, 95
    dragon-form, Fig. 11
    carriage drawn by, 27
    as term for aeroplanes, 154
    man-lifting, 27, 34, 91, 107
    box-kites, invention of, 80

Kites—*cont.*
  box-kites used for aeroplane structures, 115
Kitty Hawk and Kill Devil Hills, the Wrights at, 97–99
  Kitty Hawk as name of aircraft, 100
K.L.M. airline, 187
Koehl, Hermann, 191
Koenig, 159
Komet. See Messerschmitt
Krebs, Arthur, 56; Pl. X
Kress, Wilhelm (1846–1913), 46, 106; Pl. X
Kutta, M. W., 193

'Lady airmen'. See Women and Flying
Lafont, B.: quoted, 228
La France (dirigible), 56
La Landelle, G. de. See Landelle
Lambert, Comte Charles de, 144, 150
Lambertye, Comte A. de, 27
Lamboley, F. X., 50
Lana de Terzi, Francesco de, 1, 13; Fig. 12
Lancaster. See Avro
Lanchester, F. W., 69, 70, 125; Fig. 65
Lanchester-Prandtl theory, 125
Landelle, G. de la, 36; Pl. III
Lane monoplane, 153
Langley, Samuel Pierpont (1834–1906)
  general description, 46, 56, 63–68
  tandem-wing origin, 46
  Aerodrome (models), 63; Figs. 49, 50; Pl. VI
  Aerodrome (full-size), 64–66; Pl. X
  Aerodrome (etymology), 257
  Wilbur Wright on, 67
  U.S. War Dept. on, 67
Lanark meeting, 157
Langley-type monoplanes. See Aeroplanes (tandem); Gliders (tandem)
Laroche, Baroness Raymonde de (1886–1919), 158
Lascelles *Ornis*, 153
Lateral control. See Flight-Control
Latham, Hubert (1883–1912), 142, 144, 151
  attempts to fly the Channel, 144
  for his *Antoinettes*, see Levavasseur
Latham monoplane, 160
Launching of aircraft (incl. suggestions, etc.)
  aeroplane, from an, 177, 197
  airship, from an
    R.23, 186
  balloon, from a
    Cayley, 31
    Montgomery, 19, 92
  cart, from a
    Le Bris, 31, 34
  catapult (various power sources)
    Langley, 63ff
    Wrights, 101, 102

Launching of aircraft—*cont.*
  Lorin, 137
  Ellyson, 164
  H.M.S. Slinger, 177
  rail (single), from a
    Wrights, 100
  rail (single) with weight and derrick
    Wrights, 101, 102
  rails (twin)
    Maxim, 62
  ramp, down a
    Henson, 28, 29
    Du Temple, 45
    Mozhaiski, 53
    Tatin-Richet, 68
    Roe, 130
  running downhill (with or without assistants)
    Lilienthal, 73ff
    Chanute, 82ff
    Pilcher, 85ff
    Wrights, 94ff
    Ferber, 105ff
    Archdeacon, 107ff
    Esnault-Pelterie, 108ff
  springboard, from a
    Lilienthal, 74
  towed (cable) by men or horses
    Pilcher, 86, 87
  towed (cable) by electrically operated drum
    Chanute, 84
  towed (cable) off water
    Voisin, 115
  towed (cable) by automobile
    Archdeacon, 114
    Roe, 130
    Whitehead, 292
  wire, down a
    Ellyson, 164
    Stringfellow, 29
    Trouvé, 46
Launoy and Bienvenu, 17; Fig. 19
La Vaulx, Count Henri de (1870–1930), 107, 117, 133
  on Chanute's 1903 lecture, 107
  founds F.A.I., 117
  on the Wrights, 133
  see also Tatin-de La Vaulx monoplane
Law, F. R., 178
Leaf, falling: gliders and, 9
Lear, King, 3
Lebaudy dirigible, 105
Leblanc, A., 158
Le Bris. See Bris, Le
Lefebvre, Eugene, 146, 151
Legagneux, Georges, 150, 158, 170
Lenoir gas engine, 35; Pl. III
Leonardo da Vinci. See Vinci

Le Prieur rockets, 177
Lesh, L. J., 130
Lesseps, de, 152
Letur, Louis Charles (*d.* 1854), 31; Pl. III
Levavasseur, Leon (1863–1922); *Antoinette* air-
      craft and engines, 112, 119, 153
      Gastambide-Mengin I, 129; Pl. XII
      Antoinette I, 129
      Antoinette III, 129
      Antoinette IV, 135, 140, 143; Pls. XV, XXII
      Antoinette V, 135, 140, 143
      Antoinette VI, 143
      Antoinette VII, 143, 144; Pl. XV
      Monobloc Antoinette (Latham), 160, 171; Fig.
      71
      Antoinette engines, 119, 122ff, 126, 129
Lewis, C. D.: quoted, 228
Libellule. See Blériot, L.
Liberty engines, 178
'Life-Pack' parachute, 178
Lifting canopies. See Canopies
Light aeroplanes
      first, 123ff
      start of the movement in 1920's, 188
      the D.H. *Moth*, 188
      progress in the 1930's, 203
Lilienthal, Gustav, 73
Lilienthal, Otto (1848–96), 35, 45, 56, 72–80,
      85–87, 223; Figs. 40, 55, 56; Pls. IV,
      VII
      Dollfus on, 73
      copies of his gliders, 83, 85ff, 105
      his description of his crash, 224
      quoted, 223, 224
Lindbergh, Col. Charles Augustus (1902–74),
      191: quoted, 229
Linfield, 50
Lion engine. See Napier
Lippisch, A., 190, 195; Fig. 103
Liz-2, 210
Lloyd-George, David: quoted, 145
Lockheed aircraft
      XC-35, 196–7
      XP-80, 214
      Constellation, 216; Fig. 128
      Electra, 202; Fig. 109
      Model 14, 202
      Vega, 185, 187, 204, 205; Fig. 100
Lôme. see Dupuy de Lôme
Lomonosov, M. V., 16
London, H.M.S., 165
Longhorn. See Farman, M.
Looping the loop, first, 166
Lorin, René, 136
Los Angeles meeting, 157
Loup, M., 31, 38; Fig. 28
Louvrié, Charles de, 38; Pl. III
L.V.G., 176

Lynx. See Armstrong Siddeley

McClean, Frank, 149, 166
McCurdy, James A. O. (1886–1961), 158
      Silver Dart, 130, 247
      first flight in Canada, 247
McKinley, President, 64
MacKenzie-Grieve, K., 181
Macchi aircraft, 186
Machine guns. See Military Aviation
Macready, J. A., 191
MacRobertson air race, 198, 205
Mail. See Airmail flights
Mallet, 126
Malmesbury, Eilmer of, 4
Maloney, D., 91, 116, 151
      see also Montgomery, J. J.
Mamet, 150
Manchester (London to) race, 154
Man-lifting kites. See Kites
Manly, Charles M., 64
      see also Langley, S. P.
Manual assisters. See Engines and Propulsion
      (flappers)
Marey, Étienne Jules (1830–1904), 48
Marriott, F., 28, 38
Martin, Glenn, and aircraft
      Model 130, 203
      NBS-1, 185
Mascots, flying, 152, 153, 166
Masefield, Peter G., 186
Maurice Farman biplanes. See Farman M.
Maxim, Sir Hiram Stevens (1840–1916), 56,
      61–63, 154, 160.
      1894 'test-rig', 61–63; Pl. VI
      on the aircraft of 1907–08, 62
      his 1910 machine, 154
Mayer, 27
Mayo, R. H., 197
Me. See Messerschmitt
Means, James, 81, 90, 91; Fig. 62
Means, Dr. James Howard, 90
Meerwein, K. F., 16; Fig. 17
Meetings (aviation), etc.
      first (Reims 1900), 145, 146
      in 1910, 157: in 1911, 161
      see also Exhibitions; Races (cross-country);
            and the individual names and locations
Melbourne race, 198
Mélikoff, 50; Pl. V
Melzi, F., 9
Mensier, General, 61
Mercedes engines, 170, 174, 178, 179
Mercury engines. See Bristol
Merlin engines. See Rolls-Royce
Messerschmitt aircraft
      Bf 109 (Me 109), 204, 205, 209; Fig. 119

Messerschmitt aircraft—*cont.*
  Me 110, 209
  Me 163 Komet, 214, 217; Fig. 125
  Me 262, 212; Fig. 124
  Me 264, 210
  Me 321 Gigant, 210
  Me 410, 209
Metal construction, 159, 183
Meteor. See Gloster
Meurisse, M., 141
Meurthe. See Deutsch de la Meurthe
Meusnier, General Jean Baptiste Marie (1754–93), 19
Meyer, Robert B., 64
Michelin prizes
Milan meeting, 157
Milemete, Walter de, 6
Military aviation (incl. Naval)
  first aerial observation, 161, 240
  Napoleonic fantasy, 20
  first bombing raid (balloons), 241
  first bombing raid (aeroplanes), 176
  the Blériot 'scare', 144
  opposition to, 148
  British production stopped (1909), 148
  first bombing tests, 156, 161
  first ship landings and take-offs, 156
  intransigence of the military authorities, 158
  'Concours militaire' (1911), 160, 161
  Britain revives (1911), 161
  Zeppelins and aeroplanes in 1911, 161
  first meetings, 161
  first live bombing tests, 161
  first guns in aeroplanes, 161
  first bomb-sight, 161
  first use of aeroplanes in war, 161
  prototype 'scouts', 163, 167
  grows in Europe (1912), 165
  Royal Flying Corps founded, 165
  first British competition, 165
  first British take-offs from ship, 165
  aircraft review at Hendon, 165
  ban on monoplanes, 165
  the *B.E.2c*, 167
  first aeroplane designed to fight, 167
  World War I, 172–180
  interrupter gear, 173
  early radio-controlled aerial bombs, 177
  parachutes in World War I, 178
  breeds new type of man, 228
  as symbols of destruction, 180
  influence of 'Billy' Mitchell, 185
  preparations for war, 204
  modern long-range bomber, 205
  World War II, 206–217
  first operational jets, 211, 212
  flying and rocket bombs, etc., 212, 214

Military aviation—*cont.*
  rocket aeroplanes, 214
  quotations on, 221–229
  Chanute's prophecy on, 223
  Orville Wright on, 227
  see also Parachutes; Rockets
Miller, W., 30
Minos, King, 2
Miolan, 20
Missiles. See Rockets, etc.
Mitchell. See North American
Mitchell, Brig. Gen. William E. (1879–1936), 185
Mitchell, R. J., 186, 198
  see also Supermarine *Spitfire*
Moisant, John B., 152
Mollison, Amy Johnson, 204
Mollison, Capt. James A., 204
Monaco meetings
  1912, 164
  1913, 169
Mona Lisa, 166
Monobloc Antoinette. See Levavasseur
'Monocoque Deperdussin'. See Deperdussin
Monocoque and stressed skin construction
  definitions, 163, 171
  early, 162
  lack of progress in Britain, 183
  modern concept of, 183
  influence of Rohrback, 183
Monomail. See Boeing
Monoplanes (before 1906). See Aeroplanes
Monoplanes (from 1906 onwards)
  first tractor, 122
  firmly established, 142ff
  first cabin, 165
  eclipse of, 166ff
  ban on, 165
  modern ascendency of, 181ff
  see also Tandem-wing aeroplanes
Monosoupape engines, 173, 174
Montgolfier, Jacques Étienne (1745–99), and Joseph Michel (1740–1810), 17, 19; Fig. 18
Montgomery, John Joseph (1858–1911), 53, 91, 92, 116, 163; Pl. XII
Moon travel fiction, 17, 40, 181
Moore-Brabazon. See Brabazon
Morane and Morane-Saulnier aircraft, 160, 166, 167, 173; Fig. 82
Moreau, Captain von, 205
Morris, R., 17
Mosquito. See De Havilland
Moth. See De Havilland
Motor-cars. See 'Automobilisme'
Moulinets à noix, and Moulinets à vent, 6
Motors. See Engines
Mouillard, Louis Pierre (1834–97), 34, 38, 52

Mount Everest, 205
Mountains, first flight over, 153, 205
Movable control surfaces. See Flight-Control
Moving pictures. See Cinema-films
Moy, Thomas, 46; Fig. 43
Mozhaiski, Alexander Feodorovitch (1825–1890), 53; Fig. 46
Mueller, Johann. See Regiomontanus
Multiplanes (in general)
    first suggested and used, 21–24
    see also Biplanes; Triplanes
Multiplanes (more than three)
    Wenham, 39
    Renard, 45
    Phillips, 68
    Hargrave, 80–82
    Chanute, 83
    Sellers, 137
Munich meeting, 157
Murrell, M. H., 50
Musical Kites. See Kites
Mustang. See North American
Myths and legends, 1–3

Nadar (Félix Tournachon) (1820–1910), 36
Nagasaki, 210
Nakajima 'Liz-2', 210
Napier engines, 185, 186, 194
Natter. See Bachem
Naval aviation. See Military aviation
NBS. See Martin
Neale monoplane, 153
Nesterov, Lieut., 166
Netherlands, first flight in, 150
Newcomb, Simon, 225
Newspapers. See Press
Nice meeting, 157
Nicholson monoplane, 153
Nieuport, Édouard (1875–1911) and his aircraft,
    153, 160, 161, 163, 166, 167, 173, 174
Night flights, first, 152, 154, 169
N1M. See Northrop
North American aircraft
    B-25 Mitchell, 209
    P-51 Mustang, 209; Pl. XX
Northcliffe, Lord. See Daily Mail
North Pole, flight to, 191
Northrop aircraft
    N1M, 195
Nye, James, 34

Oars, aerial. See Flapper propulsion
Oberursel engine, 178
Observation (aerial). See Military aviation
Oehmichen, Etienne, 190

O'Dwyer, W.J., 292
O'Gorman, M., 165
Ohain, H. von, 197
Oil technology, 51
Oka II, 214
Oleo-undercarriages. See Undercarriages
Oliver of Malmesbury, 4
Olivier, 54
Olympia (London), 157
Opel, Fritz von, 190; Fig. 101
Ornis aeroplane, 153
Ornithopters (since 1750), including designs, models, full-size, etc.
  man-powered
    Besnier, 12
    Desforges, 16
    Meerwein, 16
    Blanchard, 16
    Renaux, 19
    Gérard, 19
    Aries, 19
    Goué, 25
    Degen, 25
    Berblinger, 27
    Lambertye, 27
    Miller, 30
    Aubaud, 31
    Bréant, 31
    Bourcart, 35
    Struvé and Telescheff, 35
    Lilienthal, 35
    Cornelius, 56
    de Groof, 48
    Dandrieux, 48
    Hérard, 56
  clockwork-powered
    Hooke, 10
  rubber-powered
    Tatin, 45, 48
    Jobert, 48
    Villeneuve, 48
    Pénaud, 48
    Brearey, 48
    Pichancourt, 56
  steam-powered
    Artingstall, 27
    de Louvrié, 48
    Smythies, 56
    Frost, 71
  gunpowder-powered
    Trouvé, 46
  internal combustion powered
    de Louvrie, 48
  carbonic acid gas
    Lilienthal, 75ff
  uncertain power-sources
    Swedenborg, 14
    Duchesnay, 30

Ornithopters—*cont.*
  von Drieberg, 30
  Seguin, 30
  Boulton, 40
  Prigent, 45
  Quimby, 50
  Keith, 50
  Lamboley, 50
  Murrell, 50
  Wheeler, 50
  Wellner, 70
Otto, N. A., 35, 51

P-47. See Republic
P-51. See North American
Paltock, R., 17
Parachutes
  general description of invention, and early, 9
  da Vinci, 9
  Veranzio, 9
  first human drop from the air, 19; Pl. II
  Cayley, 29
  first drop from an aeroplane, 166
  first free-type, 178
  for lowering models, 36
  in World War I, 178
'Paris, Miss' (a cat), 152
Paris, first flight over, 150
Parke, Lieut., 165
Parrots, Wilbur Wright on, 226
Parsons, Sir Charles A., 56, 70
Passarola. See Gusmão
Passenger-carrying, first, 112, 128
Paucton, A. J. P., 16
Paulhan, Louis, 143, 154
  see also Tatin-Paulhan
Pauze, de la, 50
PBY. See Consolidated
Pearse, Richard William, 71, 291
Pegasus balloon, 130
Pegasus engines. See Bristol
Pégoud, Adolphe (1889–1915), 166
Peltier, Mme. Thèrese, 129
Pénaud, Alphonse (1850–80), 43, 44, 48
  Planophone, 44; Figs. 38, 44; Pl. V
Pendulum stabilisers. See Stability
Pennsylvania (U.S.S.), 156
Pequet, 162
Pescara, Marquis de I., 190
Petrograd. See St. Petersburg
Petroleum technology, 51
Petrol engines. See Engines
Pettigrew, J. Bell, 48
Peugeot engines, 114
Peyret, 173
Peyrey, François, 128, 132

Pfalz aeroplanes, 174, 178
Phillips, Horatio, F (1845–1924), 53, 54, 68, 124; Figs. 47, 51; Pl. VI
  makes first hop-flights in Britain, 124
Phillips, W. H., 28, 40
Photography, first (from aeroplanes), 141
  first air-to-ground cinema films, 141
  of Lilienthal's glides, 73
  first from a kite, 56
  first rapid sequence, 48
Piazza, Capt., 161
Pichancourt, 56
Pigeon, wooden (Archytas), 4
Pig, flying, 152, 153
Pilcher, Percy Sinclair (1866–99), 81, 85–90
  quoted, 224; Fig. 61; Pl. VIII
Pilot-operated control systems. See Flight-control
Pilot position, prone. See Prone pilot position
Pilots, attitude of mind of. See Airmen and Chauffeurs
  in war, 217, 228
Piraud, Pompeien, 56
Pischof, Alfred de, 124; Pl. XII
Pixton, C. H., 170
Planophore. See Pénaud, A.
Platz, Reinhold, 183
Pline, Joseph, 38
Pocock, George, 27
Pocock, Martha, 27
Poles, flights over the, 191
Polytechnic Institution (London), founded by Cayley, 24
Pomés, 50
Ponche and Primard *Tubavion,* 164
Ponton d'Amécourt, Vicomte de. See Amécourt
Porte, J. C., 170, 176
Porte *'Baby',* 177
Portugal, first flight in, 150
Post, Wiley, 205
Powered flights, first, 100–104
'Power-kites', 154
Power-Plants. See Engines
Prandtl, Ludwig (1875–1953), 112, 125, 178, 193
Pratt and Whitney engines, 215
  Wasp, 201
  Twin-Wasp, 196
'Pratt truss', 95; Fig. 60
Press (the), and aviation, 28, 29, 73, 94, 144
Pressurisation of aircraft, 196, 216
Prete, C. P. Del, 193
Prévost, M., 167, 169
Prier, P., 159
Prieur (Le) rockets, 177
Prigent, 45
Primard, 164
Pritchard, J. L., Capt., 21, 29, 62

Pritchard, J.L.,—*cont.*
  and Stringfellow, 29
  on Maxim, 62
Projectiles (finned), 8, 24
Prone pilot position
  da Vinci, 8, 9
  Meewein, 16
  Wenham, 39
  Wrights, 95ff
Propellers. See Airscrews
Prophecies, 221ff
Prophecies (false)
  Kelvin, 92
  British Under-Secretary for Air, 197
Propulsion. See Engines and Propulsion
Proteus engines. See Bristol
Psalms: quoted, 1
Pterodactyl. See Hill, G.T.R.
'Ptérophore', 16
Pulitzer trophy, 186
Pulse-duct engines. See Jet propulsion
Pup. See Sopwith
Puss Moth. See De Havilland

Quimby, Miss Harriet, 163, 166
Quimby, W. F., 50

R, Model. See Wright, Wilbur and Orville
R-3. See Verville-Sperry
R3C. See Curtiss
R-4, R-4B, R-5. See Sikorsky
R.23 (dirigible), 186
R.34 (dirigible;, 250
Races
  in 1909, 145, 146
  in 1910, 157, 158
  in 1911, 159
  Schneider trophy, 169, 170, 186, 198
  see also Meetings
Radial engines. See Engines
Radio and aircraft, 158, 162
  radio-controlled aerial bombs, first, 177
  see also Instruments
R.A.F. engine, 178
Raiche, Dr. Bessica, 163
Raleigh, Sir Walter: quoted, 104, 225, 226,
    227, 278
  on the Wrights, 104, 225
  on the spirit of the R.F.C., 228
Ram-jets. See Jet propulsion
Randolph, S., 292
Rapide (*Dragon*). See De Havilland
Raynham, F. P., 162
R.E. See Farnborough
R.E. (types). See Farnborough
Reaction propulsion. See Jet propulsion;
    Rockets

Read, Albert Cushing (1887–19), 181
Rebenstein, George, 30
Reconnaissance, aerial. See Military aviation
Records (aviation). See at ends of Sections,
    from 1909
Red Wing. See Aerial Experiment Association
Refuelling in flight, 194, 197
Regent Street Polytechnic, 24
Regiomontanus (Johann Müller), 6
Reims (meetings)
    1909, 145, 146
    1910, 157
    'Conours Militaire' (1911), 161
Reissner, Hans, 164
Reliant. See Stinson
Renard, Charles 45, 56
Renard and Krebs dirigible, 56
Renault engines, 165
Renaux, A. J., 19
REP aeroplanes and engines. See Esnault-
    Pelterie, R.
Resnier de Goué. See Goué
Restif de la Bretonne, 17
Retractable undercarriages. See Under-
    carriages
R.F.C. See Royal Flying Corps
Rheims Meetings. See Reims
Rhóne (Le) engines, 178
Richet, Charles, 68
Ridge, T., 162
Robins, B., 21
Robinson, Hugh Armstrong, 162
Rocket propulsion. See Rockets
Rockets and missiles
  principles of rocket propulsion, 266
  invention of, and early, rockets, 6, 20; Pl. II
  birth of modern rocketry, 180
  Goddard's publication (1919), 180, 215
  first liquid fuel, 181
  early aeroplanes propelled by, 6, 190
  Lorin missiles, 136
  radio-controlled aerial bombs, 177
  first rocket-propelled aeroplanes, 6; Fig. 7
  V-1 Flying Bombs, 214
  V-2 rocket bombs, 215, 217
  rocket-propelled aeroplanes, 214; Fig.
    125
  see also Jet propulsion
Rodgers, Calbraith P., 159
Roe, Sir Alliott Verdon (1877–1958), 124,
    130, 149, 160, 167
  influenced by Goupy, 149
  first hop-flights, 130
  triplanes, 149; Pl. XVI
  see also Avro aircraft
Roe, G. Verdon-. See Verdon-Roe
Rohrbach, A., 171, 183, 201
Roland, Scout, 178

Rolls, Hon. Charles Stewart (1877–1910), 133,
    142, 149, 154, 158
  death of, 158
Rolls-Royce engines, 186, 209, 216
  Eagle, 178
  Falcon, 176
  Griffon, 216
  Kestrel, 194
  Merlin, 196, 210, 216
Romas, Jacques de, 14
Rotary engines. See Engines
Rouen meeting, 157
Roumania. See Rumania
Royal Aero Club, 71
Royal Aeronautical Society, 38, 80
  exhibition at Crystal Palace, 39, 40
Royal Aircraft Establishment. See Farnborough
Royal Aircraft Factory. See Farnborough
Royal Automobile Club, 71
Royal Flying Corps
  founded, 165
  Raleigh on its spirit, 228
Royal Society, 10
Rubber-tyred wheels. See Undercarriages
Rubber (twisted) engines. See Engines
Ruchonnet, 162, 164
Rudders. See Flight-control
Ruinart Champagne firm, 121, 152
Rumania, first flight in, 150
Rumpler aeroplanes, 153, 173
Russia, first flight in, 150
Ryan aircraft
  Spirit of St. Louis, 191; Pl. XVIII

S.5; *S.6*; *S.6B*. See Supermarine
S.38. See Short
S-42; *S-51*. See Sikorsky
Sagan, F. (quoted), 58
Saint André, T. de, 19
St Petersburg meeting, 157
Salamander. See Heinkel
Samson, C. R., 165
Sander, F. W., 190
Sanderval, de, 56
Santos-Dumont, Alberto (1873–1932), 105,
    120–123, 136, 143; Fig. 66; Pls. X, XII,
    XXII
  first flights in Europe, 120
  first light aeroplanes, 122, 123, 136, 143
Saracen of Constantinople, 4
Sarti, V., 27
Saulnier. See Morane-Saulnier
Savoia aircraft, 191, 205
Scarff ring, 174
Schkrouff, Van den. See Van den Schkrouff
Schlaifer, R., 198
Schneider, 173

Schneider Trophy, 169, 170, 186, 198
  won outright by Britain, 198; Fig. 104
Schott, Gaspar, 13
Scientific American prize, 130
Scott, Miss Blanche, 163
Scott, Lieut. Riley, 161
Scout, first, 163
Scylla. See Short
S.E. aeroplanes. See Farnborough
Seaplanes
  first design, 44
  first, 153
  first practical, 161
  first meeting, 164
  second meeting, 169
  first flying boat flies, 164
  come into their own (1912), 164
  development in the 1920's, 188
  development in the 1930's, 203
  in World War II, 210
  see also Amphibians
Seguin, Louis and Laurent, 143
Seguin, Marc, 31
Sellers, Matthew Bacon, 137, 194
Selfridge, Lieut. Thomas E., 130, 134
Sesquiplane (Coanda). See Coanda
Sewell, E. R., 90
Shackleton, Lieut.: quoted on Blériot, 226
Shaw, H. S. Hele-. See Hele-Shaw
Shaw, Hudson, 81
Sheldon, J., 19
Ship-to-shore kites, 34
Ships, first take-offs and landings. See
    Launching
Shock-absorbers (undercarriage). See Under-
    carriages
Short aircraft, 142, 149, 153, 165
  Short-built Wrights, 142, 149
  Short-built Wright-type glider; Pl. XXII
  'Short No. 2', 149
  S.38, 165
  'Tandem twin', 161
  'Triple twin', 160
  'Modified S. 38, 165
  float-planes, 166, 176
  Calcutta, 188
  Empire, 203; Pl. XIX
  Mercury, 197
  Scylla, 201
  Singapore, 188
  Silver Streak, 183; Fig. 94
  Stirling, 209
  Sunderland, 203, 209; Fig. 123
  Swallow, 183
Short-Mayo, 197
'Side-curtains'. See Wings
Sigrist, F., 167
Sikorsky, Igor Ivan (1889–19   )

Sikorsky, Igor Ivan—*cont.*
  and da Vinci, 211
  Bolshoi, 169, 170; Fig. 79
  Ilia Mouriametz, 170
  VS-300, 211; Pl. XXI
  XR-4, 211
  R-4B, 211
  R-5 (S-51), 211
  S-42, 203
Silver Dart. See Aerial Experimental Association
Silver Streak. See Short
Skid (tail): first designed, 44
Skid-undercarriages. See Wrights, etc.
Slotted wings, 193
Ski-jump ramp. See Launching
Skirts (women's), aviation hazards of, 133
Skymaster. See Douglas
Smeaton, J., 21
Smith-, Sir C. Kingsford. See Kingsford-Smith
Smith, Ross, 191
Smithsonian Institution, 63
  written to by the Wrights, 101
Smoke, used in wind tunnels, 48
Smoke-jack, 9
Smythies, John K., 56
Société Aérostatique (etc.), 38
Societies, aeronautical, first, 36, 38
  see also the individual names
Société d'Encouragement, etc., 36
Solid of least resistance (Cayley's), 24
Sommer, R., and aircraft, 153, 162
Sopwith, T. O. M., and aircraft, 157
  Camel, 174, 177, 186
  Pup, 174, 177; Pl. XVII
  Tabloid, 163, 167, 170, 172, 173, 174; Fig. 77
  '1½-strutter', 174
South America, first flight in, 157
Southern Cross. See Fokker
South Pole, flight to, 191
Space fiction, early, 17, 40
  see also Rockets, etc.
S.P.A.D., 174
Spain
  first flight in, 157
  civil war, 204
Spatted undercarriage, first, 160
'Spearhead' helicopter, 50
Specifications. See the makers, etc.
Speeds, note on, 137, 172
Speeds (records). See Records
Spencer, Charles, 35, 40
Sperry, Lawrence (1892–1923), 166, 170, 177, 193; Pl. XXI
Sperry (Verville-) Racer, 194
Spinning, first cases of, 162
Spirit of St. Louis. See Ryan
Spit, roasting (airscrew operated), 9

Spitfire. See Supermarine
Split flaps, 196
Spoilers (steering). See Steering Air-brakes
Spotting (for artillery), first, 165
Staaken aircraft, 176
Stability
  Cayley, 21ff
  Pénaud, 44
  Renard, 45
  Brown, 46
  Langley, 63ff
  Lilienthal, 75ff
  Hargrave, 80ff
  Pilcher, 85ff
  Chanute, 82–84
  Wrights' concept of inherent instability, 96ff
  Ferber, 112, 114
  box-kite, 80
  box-kite incorporated in aircraft, 115
  European concept of inherent, 111, 112, 115, 126, 127
  Farnborough B.E. *2C*, 167
  pendulum and other stabilisers, 45, 121
  gyroscopic stabilisers, 170
  see also Aerodynamics; Automatic Pilot; Flight-control; Wings; Wing-warping
Staggered biplane, first. See Wings
Stamer, F., 190
Steam engines. See Engines
'Steamer, Aerial'. See Henson, W.S.
Steam turbine, invention of the, 56
Steel construction. See Metal construction
Steering air-brakes, 40, 41, 52, 82
Steering spoilers. See Steering air-brakes
Stepped flying-boat hull, first, 164
Steiger-Kirchofer, Carl, 70; Figs. 52, 53
Stevens, Leo, 177
Stinson *Reliant*, 204; Fig. 112
Stirling. See Short
Stirling Castle, 8
Stout, William B., 187
Stratocruiser. See Boeing
Stratoliner. See Boeing
Streamlining
  da Vinci, 9
  Cayley, 23, 24
  later, 160, 164, 193
Stressed-skin construction, 171, 183
Stringfellow, F. J., 56
Stringfellow, John (1799–1883), 28, 29, 39, 40; Pls. II, IV
  triplane model, 39, 40
  see also Henson, W. S.
Struvé, 35
'Stuka'. See Junkers
Suicide aircraft. See Kamikaze
Sunderland. See Short

Superchargers, early, 178
Superfortress. See Boeing
Supermarine aircraft
  S.5, 186
  S.6, S.6B, 186, 194, 198; Fig. 104
  Spitfire, 204, 209; Pl. XIX
Superposed wings. See Biplanes; Multiplanes;
  Triplanes; Wings
Super Sportster, (Gee Bee), 198
Swallow. See Short
Sweden, first flight in, 150
Swedenborg, E., 14
Swept wings. See Wings
Swift, J., 17
Switzerland, first flight in, 157
Swordfish. See Fairey

Tabloid. See Sopwith
Tabluteau, Maurice, 159
Tailless aeroplanes. See the individual types
Tailor of Ulm, 27
Tail skid: first designed, 44
'Tandem twin', 161
Tandem-wing aircraft. See Aeroplanes;
  Gliders
Tarentum, Archytas of, 4
Tatin, Victor (1843–1913), 45, 48, 68, 110,
  117; Pl. V
  on copying the Americans, 110
  admits defeat by Wrights, 117
Tatin–La Vaulx monoplane, 126
Tatin-Paulhan aeroplane, 160
Tatin-Richet model, 68
Taube. See Etrich; Rumpler
Taylor, R., 23
Taylor aircraft, 204
TB-3, TB-7, 197, 210
Telescheff Nicholas de, 35, 38; Fig. 34
Tempest. See Hawker
Temple, Du Félix (1823–1890), 29, 34, 45;
  Figs. 29, 42
Tennyson, Lord: quoted, 1, 222
Tension wheel, 24
Terzi. See Lana de
Tethered aeroplane models, 45, 46, 68, 121
Thibaut de Saint André, 19
Thomas, 157
Thompson Trophy, 198
Tiger Moth. See De Havilland
Times, The
  on the Wrights, 132
Tipoo Sahib. See Tipu Sultan
Tipu Sultan, 20
Tissandier, Paul, 134, 142
'Torpille (Aero-)', 160
Tournachon, F. See Nadar
Tower-jumpers, 4; Fig. 3

Towler, H.F., 176
Town, first flight over a, 150
Tractor (caterpillar) invented by Cayley, 24
Tractor biplanes. See Biplanes
Transatlantic flights. See Atlantic crossings
Transport (air)
  first passenger flights, 128
  Zeppelin service, 152, 193
  first airlines, 170, 186
  first modern airliners, 201ff
  influence of the Lockheed *Vega*, 185
  spread of in the 1920's, 186–188
  rise of the basic types of aircraft, 187, 198,
    201ff
  first successful large British machine, 198
  growth of, 1919–29 (figures), 188
  flying boats, 203
  growth of in the 1930's, 205
  birth of the modern airliner, 201
  the Douglas *DC-1* to *DC-3*, 201, 202
  the Douglas *DC-4*, 202
  the four-engined era starts, 202
  development of medium size, 201ff
  transport development left to U.S.A., 206
  development in U.S.A. (1939–45), 215, 216
Tricycle undercarriage. See Undercarriages
Triplanes
  first model, 39
  first full-size, 39
  first full-size (powered), 126
  see also Goupy; Multiplanes; Roe, Sir A. V.
'Triple Twin', 160
Triptolemus, 2
Trouvé, G., 14, 46; Fig. 37
True, E.L., 289
Tubavion. See Ponche
Turbine (gas). See Jet propulsion
Turbine (steam), invention of, 56
Turbojets/Turboprops. See Jet propulsion
Turkey, first flight in, 150
Turning spoilers. See Steering air-brakes
'Twin', Tandem and Triple, 160, 161
Twin-airscrew aeroplanes, first, 23, 28, 29, 31
Twin-engine aeroplanes, first, 60, 61
Twin-Wasp. See Pratt and Whitney
Typhoon. See Hawker

Ulm, Tailor of. See Berblinger
Ulm, Capt. Charles T. P., 193
Undercarriages; first designs
  first oleo, 160
  first pneumatic tyred, 119
  retractable (first designs), 8, 44
    (first used), 137, 160
    (first practical), 186, 194
    (growth of), 196
  first shock absorbers, 44

Undercarriages; first designs—*cont.*
  three-wheel, 28, 197
  Wrights, 154
  see also Launching; also the individual
    inventors
'Undulator', 48

V-1 (flying bomb), 214; Pl. XXI
V-2 (rocket), 215; Pl. XXI
V/1500. See Handley Page
Valier, M., 190
Valkryrie aeroplanes, 153; Fig. 67
Vallet, 19
Vampire. See De Havilland
Van den Schkrouff, 150
Vaulx, de La. See La Vaulx
Védrines, Jules, 159, 164, 166
Vega. See Lockheed
Veranzio, Fausto, 9; Fig. 9
Vergeltungswaffen, 214, 215
Verne, Jules, 40, 181, 222
Vertical Stabilisers. See Stability
Verville-Sperry Racer (R-3), 194
Vickers and Vickers-Armstrong aircraft
  monoplane, 160
  F.B.5 Gunbus, 167, 173; Fig. 81
  Vimy, 181, 187; Pl. XVIII
  Vimy Commercial, 187
  Wellesley, 205
  Wellington, 204, 209; Fig. 121
Vickers Supermarine. See Supermarine
Villeneuve, H. de, 36, 48
Vimy. See Vickers
Vinci, Leonardo da (1452–1519), 8, 9, 166,
  211; Fig. 8; Pl. I
  Mona Lisa, 166
Vindex, H.M.S., 176
Viper. See Bachem
Vivinus engines, 143
Voisin Charles (1882–1912), and Gabriel
  (1880– 19), and their aircraft, 81,
  115, 123, 124, 143, 154, 161; Pl. XIV
  Charles joins Ferber, 108
  float gliders (1905), 81, 115
  Voisin-Delagrange, 124
  Voisin-Kapferer, 124
  Voisin-Farman I, 124; Pl. XIII
  Brabazon and, 136, 149
  see also Reims meeting
Voisin-Archdeacon float glider, 115; Pl. XI
Voisin-Blériot float glider, 115
Voisin-Delagrange biplane, 124; Pl. XII
Vol des Oiseaux (Esterno), 36
'Volksjäger' (*He 162*). See Heinkel
Von—. See the main names
VS-300. See Sikorsky
Vuia, Trajan (1872–1950), 119, 122; Pl. XI

W.8. See Handley Page
W-34. See Junkers
Waco *CG-4*A, 210
Wagner, H. A., 183
Walker, Dr. P. B., 171
Walker, T., 27
Walter engines, 214
Ward, J. B., 50
Warchalowski brothers, 158
Warfare (aerial). See Military Aviation
Warping. See Wing-warping
Warp-rudder linkage. See Flight-control full
  lateral control
Warships. See Military Aviation; Ships
Wasp. See Pratt and Whitney
Watchspring engines. See Engines (clockwork)
Watson, Preston, A., 71, 291
Weiss, José, 149
Weisskopf. See Whitehead
Wellesley. See Vickers
Wellington. See Vickers
Wellner, Professor, 70
Wels, F., 126
Wells, H. G., on Blériot, 148
Wenham, Francis Herbert (1824–1908), 39,
  82; Fig. 32
Wenham, Jane, 221
Westland aircraft, 205
Westland-Sikorsky. See Sikorsky
Wheeler, I. M. 50
Wheels, cycle-type tension
  Cayley invents, 24
Whirling arms (for aerodynamic research)
  Robins, 21
  Smeaton, 21
  Cayley, 21
  Maxim, 61
  Langley, 63
  Ferber, 106
White, C. Grahame-. See Grahame-White
Whitehead, (Weisskopf), Gustave, 71, 291
White Wing. See Aerial Experimental Assoc.
Whitley. See Armstrong-Whitworth
Whitten-Brown, Sir A. See Alcock, Sir J., 180
Whittle, Sir F., and engines, 193, 212
  Lord Kings Norton on, 229
Wiencziers aircraft, 160, 194
Wilkins, John, 10
Willkie, 92
Willughby, Francis, 12
Windmills, 3; Fig. 4
  see also Airscrew toys
Windmill toys, 8
Wind-tunnels,
  first used, 39
  smoke used in, 48
Wings (general)
  aerodynamics of (early). See Cayley,

Wings (general)—*cont.*
    Wenham, etc.
  ailerons. See Flight-control
  anhedral (Wrights), 97
  box-kite, 115ff
  cambered, 24, 39, 53, 54
  cantilever, 159
  delta, first design, 38
  dihedral first suggested, 23, 24
  double surfaced, first designed, 28
  elliptical, 120
  flap-valve. See Flap-valve principle
  'flying wings', 157, 195
  kites as, 23
  metal, early, 64, 179
  modern configuration, first, 23, 24
  'side curtains', 115ff
  slotted, 193
  staggered, 144
  superposed, 23, 24
  swept (see also 'delta' above), 125
  tandem, 27, 46
  undulating, 48
  wing-warping. See Flight-control
  see also Aerodynamics; Ailerons; Biplanes;
      Multiplanes; Triplanes; Wing-warping;
      etc.
Wing-warping
  technique of, 94, 95
  illustration of, Fig. 63
  early, 78, 94ff
  Wrights', 94ff
  later use, 123, 143
  see also Ailerons; Steering air-brakes
Wireless. See Radio
Wise, J., 29
Witches and flying, 221
Women and flying
  first pilot, 158
  first to fly in an aeroplane, 129
  first U.S. pilot, 163
  skirts a hazard, 133
Wood construction
  avoidance in warplanes, 183
  revival in *Mosquito*, 206
Wootton, J., 50
Worcester, Marquis of, 12
World Wars I and II. See Military Aviation
Worsley, Miss K. See Kent, Duchess of
Wright (Howard) biplane, 153
Wright, Orville (1871–1948) and Wilbur
    (1867–1912)
  general description, 94–104, 131–133
  Lilienthal's influence, 94
  observing buzzards, 94
  first idea of warping, 94, 95; Fig. 64
  the word 'warp', 97
  first contact with Chanute, 95

Wright Brothers—*cont.*
  debts to Chanute, 95
  their first aircraft (with warping), 95; Fig.
    63; Pl. XXII
  their three gliders, 96–99; Pls. VIII, IX
  Wilbur's Chicago lectures, 98
  invention of the warp-rudder linkage, 99
  problem of engine and airscrews, 99
  powered *Flyer I* (1903), 100; Pl. IX
  world's first powered flights, 101, 289
  their telegram, 225
  their account, 225
  distance through the air, 101
  Flyer II (1904), 101, 102
  first assisted take-off, 102
  first circle flown, 102
  first eyewitness account, 102
  first 5 minute flight, 102
  Flyer III (1905), 102–104; Pl. IX
  first flight of half an hour, 103
  offer of *Flyers* to U.S. and British govts.,
    103, 104
  visit from Col. Capper, 104
  Capper's opinion of Wrights, 104
  they precipitate European revival, 105ff
  powerful influence on Europe, 107ff
  Chanute lectures on them in Paris (1903),
    107, 108
  news of 1905 season reaches France, 117,
    118
  their basic patent published in France, 117,
    118
  warming-up flights in U.S.A. (1908), 131
  make first passenger flights, 131
  Wilbur comes to Europe (1908), 131
  Wilbur's flights in Europe (1908), 131–134
  revolutionises European aviation, 132; Pl.
    XIII
  the myth about Wright engines not being
    effective for flight, 131
  Press on Wilbur, 132
  takes first British passengers, 133
  takes first women as passengers, 133
  hazard of women's skirts overcome, 133
  makes first hour flight, 134
  first 2 hour flight, 134
  Orville flies in public in the U.S.A., 134
  Selfridge killed, 134
  Wrights in 1909, 141, 142; Pl. XIV
  take up first cinematographer, 141
  first to use dual control, 141
  in 1910, 154; Fig. 68
  influence waning, 154
  Wilbur dies (1912), 166
  Orville is joint inventor of split flap, 196
  Wilbur on parrots, 226
  Wilbur on learning to fly, 224

Quotations on the Wrights by
    Baden-Powell, 132
    Besancon, 117
    Blériot, 132
    Capper, 104
    Chanute, 98, 110
    Delagrange, 132
    Dollfus, iii, 103, 134
    Ferber, 112
    Figaro, 132
    Gasnier, 132
    La Vaulx, 107, 133
    Peyrey, 132
    Raleigh, 225
    Tatin, 110, 117
    Times, The (London), 132
    Wright (Bishop), 166, 227
    Zens, 132
Wright-type gliders. See Archdeacon; Esnault-
    Pelterie; Ferber; Short; etc.; also
    Gliders

XC-35. See Lockheed

XFY-1. SS Convair
*XP-59*A. See Bell
XP-80. See Lockheed
XR-4. See Sikorsky

YB-17. See Boeing
Yellow Peril. See Handley Page

Zahn, A. F., 53
Zanonia plant, 125
Zens, Paul, on the Wrights, 132
Zeppelin, Count Ferdinand von (1838–1917),
    105, 152, 170, 193
Zeppelins, 152, 176, 177, 193
    passenger-carrying, 152
    Graf Zeppelin, 193
    Hindenburg, 252
Zeppelin, Staaken aircraft, 176; Figs. 86, 91
Ziolkowski, K. E., 71; Fig. 54
Zipfel, Armand, 150
Zodiac aircraft, 153